Making Music with SONAR™ Home Studio™

Craig Anderton

Course Technology PTR
A part of Cengage Learning

COURSE TECHNOLOGY
CENGAGE Learning™

Australia • Brazil • Japan • Korea • Mexico • Singapore • Spain • United Kingdom • United States

COURSE TECHNOLOGY
CENGAGE Learning™

Making Music with SONAR™ Home Studio™

Craig Anderton

Publisher and General Manager,
Course Technology PTR:
Stacy L. Hiquet

Associate Director of Marketing:
Sarah Panella

Manager of Editorial Services:
Heather Talbot

Marketing Manager: Mark Hughes

Acquisitions Editor: Orren Merton

Project Editor/Copy Editor:
Cathleen D. Small

Interior Layout Tech: MPS Limited,
A Macmillan Company

Cover Designer: Mike Tanamachi

Indexer: BIM Indexing Services

Proofreader: Karen Gill

For product information and technology assistance, contact us at
Cengage Learning Customer & Sales Support, 1-800-354-9706

For permission to use material from this text or product,
submit all requests online at **cengage.com/permissions**

Further permissions questions can be emailed to
permissionrequest@cengage.com

SONAR and Home Studio are trademarks of Cakewalk, Inc. All other trademarks are the property of their respective owners.

All images © Cengage Learning unless otherwise noted.

Library of Congress Control Number: 2009924522

ISBN-13: 978-1-59863-973-5

ISBN-10: 1-59863-973-0

Course Technology, a part of Cengage Learning
20 Channel Center Street
Boston, MA 02210
USA

Cengage Learning is a leading provider of customized learning solutions with office locations around the globe, including Singapore, the United Kingdom, Australia, Mexico, Brazil, and Japan. Locate your local office at: **international.cengage.com/region**

Cengage Learning products are represented in Canada by Nelson Education, Ltd.

For your lifelong learning solutions, visit **courseptr.com**

Visit our corporate website at **cengage.com**

Printed in the United States of America
1 2 3 4 5 6 7 12 11 10

*This book is dedicated to my father, David Anderton,
who introduced me to the joy of music, the
appreciation of technology, and the technique
of writing.*

Acknowledgments

I'd like to thank the following people, who were instrumental in making this book happen.

Mitch Gallagher (editorial director at Sweetwater), a great friend and valued associate, who said, "You oughta write a book for these guys."

Steve Thomas of Cakewalk, who said, "You oughta write a book on SONAR Home Studio 7 for these guys."

Orren Merton of Course Technology PTR, who said, "You oughta write a book for us guys."

Cathleen Small, the "above and beyond the call of duty" editor for this book, whose razor-sharp skills helped shepherd this book through the production process. Usually editors make authors look good but never get the credit, so let's make an exception: Cathleen, please take a virtual bow!

About the Author

Craig Anderton is currently editor-in-chief of www.harmonycentral.com and executive editor of *EQ* magazine. He has played on, produced, or engineered more than 20 major label releases and written more than 20 books, as well as given seminars on technology and the arts in 38 states, 10 countries, and three languages. He maintains an active musical career; in addition to playing with German underground legend Dr. Walker, he's also one-half of the "power duo" EV2 with Brian Hardgroove of Public Enemy.

Contents

Chapter 3
Clip Editing in Track View

Chapter 4
Snapping and Grids

Chapter 5
Editing with the Process Menu

Chapter 6
MIDI Basics   63

Chapter 7
Piano Roll View MIDI Editing   77

Chapter 8
MIDI Drum Grid Editing   93

Chapter 9
Other MIDI Editing Options 105

Chapter 10
The Step Sequencer 115

Chapter 11
MIDI Plug-Ins 125

Chapter 12
Backing Up Data with System Exclusive Messages   137

Chapter 13
Software Synthesizers   143

Chapter 17
Using Signal Processors and Busses
241

Chapter 18
SONAR Home Studio's Plug-Ins
255

Chapter 19
Automation in SONAR Home Studio

Chapter 20
Control Surfaces

Chapter 21
ACT: The Key to Hands-On Control

Chapter 22
Groove Clips
319

Chapter 23
Recording Guitar with SONAR Home Studio
341

Chapter 24
Songwriting with SONAR Home Studio   357

Chapter 25
Creating Beats   365

Chapter 26
Recording Bass with SONAR Home Studio   375

Chapter 27
Creating Loop-Based Music with SONAR Home Studio   383

Chapter 28
Combining Audio and Video with SONAR Home Studio   389

Index   399

Introduction

When I started recording, it was simply not possible to obtain the fidelity and flexibility of today's music software at any price. Now, for less than a thousand dollars (including the computer!), you can have a studio in your bedroom that rivals the capabilities of million-dollar studios of not that long ago. But while computers have changed the way we make music, it's crucial to remember that they're just tools—ultimately, the kind of music you make with a computer depends far more on *you* than on the computer you use.

I've used Cakewalk SONAR in a professional capacity since it was first introduced, and I know the program inside and out. As a result, I was a bit taken aback when I tried SONAR Home Studio 7 XL for the first time, and I realized it really wasn't all that limited compared to its big brother. But because the program comes with a printed manual and extensive online help, I wanted to take a bit of a different approach with this book and drill down deeper into the program to reveal tidbits you might not find out about otherwise. I also wanted to stress how to use SONAR Home Studio 7 in the actual process of *making* music, not just talk about particular features. Hopefully I've succeeded, and this book will provide you with many "Cool! I never realized that!" moments. Some of the contents may be a bit intimidating at first, but the more you play with SONAR Home Studio 7, the more everything will fall into place.

So now that you have the program and this book, what's the next step? Making music, of course. But let me give you a bit of advice: Be true to yourself and use music to express something that's uniquely you. I've heard people make music that's extremely competent but offers nothing I can't get from other artists. You are unique, and you have your own contribution to make. Listen for what your inner voice wants to express to the world and then express it.

Remember this: No one cares what mic preamp you used, what software, or what computer; no one cares whether your song was recorded in two hours or two years. *All that matters is the emotional impact of the music itself.*

Okay, that's enough of an introduction...if you're reading this, then I'm keeping you from making music. So boot up your computer, start playing, and above all, have fun!

1 SONAR Home Studio Overview and Navigation

Let's "zoom out," and get an overview of the main elements that make up SONAR Home Studio; we'll start with the Track view, so follow along by referring to the numbers in Figure 1.1. Later in this chapter, we'll cover how to navigate within SONAR Home Studio.

Track View

A SONAR Home Studio project contains *tracks,* each of which can provide one element of a project—for example, guitar, voice, drums, sound effects, and the like. Note that SONAR Home Studio has different *views* that are optimized for different tasks. Figure 1.1 shows the Track view, which is ideal for working with a project when recording and editing and is always visible.

Track Types

There are two types of tracks. Audio tracks (1) contain digitized audio from acoustic or electric sound sources. These are recorded through your computer's audio interface, converted into digital data (similar to the kind found on a CD), and stored on your computer's hard drive. That stored data can then play back through SONAR Home Studio, exit through your computer's audio interface, and feed speakers or headphones. Audio tracks display waveforms that indicate audio levels.

MIDI tracks (2) contain data representing a performance, typically one played on a keyboard—which notes are played, when they're played, the dynamics, and the like. A controller that generates MIDI data (keyboard, drum triggers, and so on) plugs into your computer's MIDI interface, which captures the performance data and, like audio, stores this data to hard disk. This can then play back through software instruments loaded into SONAR Home Studio, which produce audio that exits through your computer's audio interface, or it can exit the MIDI interface's MIDI Out and trigger sounds in external devices, such as MIDI-compatible hardware synthesizers.

Busses

The audio output from tracks feeds into busses (3). The main bus will be the stereo master bus that carries the signals from all your tracks to the output, but there are other types of busses,

Figure 1.1 The numbers refer to elements described in the accompanying text.

which you'll meet in Chapter 17, "Using Signal Processors and Busses." Note that you don't see any audio recorded in a bus, because the audio plays back in real time—it's not recorded in the bus.

Transport

The Transport buttons (4) provide functions for navigating through a project: Play, Stop, Record, Return to Zero (in other words, go back to the beginning of the project), Fast Forward, and Rewind. The "dashboard" readout to the right of these buttons shows the tempo and the location of the project's *Now time* (in other words, the current measure or time where playback or recording will start). There are also several buttons to the right for functions such as creating a looped section of the project that plays over and over.

Toolbars

The main Control Bar (5) has seven buttons for often-used functions, such as adding tracks or importing/exporting audio and choosing different views (Track view, Console view, Loop Explorer view, and Piano Roll view for MIDI data editing). Individual windows can also have toolbars.

Splitter Bars

These are horizontal lines (6) that separate different sections of the Track view; to change their position, you click and drag up or down. (The cursor changes to a double cursor.)

For example, the topmost splitter bar is in the full "up" position. If you click on it and drag it down, you'll reveal a video track, as described in Chapter 28, "Combining Audio and Video with SONAR Home Studio." (You can also show the video track in Track view by clicking on the button to the immediate left of the Now time or by typing L.) The middle splitter bar shows either more tracks or more busses, depending on whether you drag it down or up, respectively. The lower splitter bar is showing the very top of the Loop Explorer—drag it up to show more of the Loop Explorer and less of the various tracks and busses. (Incidentally, you can show/hide the Loop Explorer with the Loop Explorer View button in the main toolbar—so you can adjust the Loop Explorer to show as much or as little as you want with the splitter bar, but then show it or hide it by using the toolbar button.)

Zoom

The + and – buttons zoom in and out, respectively; these are available for both the horizontal and vertical scroll bars. Repeatedly clicking on these buttons increases or decreases the zoom level. But, also note there are mini-slider controls in between these two buttons. Click and drag on these to zoom in or out continuously.

In Track view, the toolbar at the top of the track list has a Zoom tool (magnifying glass). Click on this, and when you draw a marquee around one or more tracks, the area will expand to fill the available window space.

Help

The Big Help button (8) is where you click to learn more about SONAR Home Studio. You can also type F1 for context-sensitive help, based on whichever window has the focus.

Individual Track Options

Each track can be minimized, or different sections can be maximized. The key to maximizing sections is the small circle with the arrow (see Figure 1.2).

The Bass track at the top of Figure 1.2 is minimized. What you see is the track icon and the "essential" track buttons: Mute, Solo, Record, Echo Input (lets you monitor the input signal for the track through any plug-in effects), Track Freeze, and Automation Write. All of these

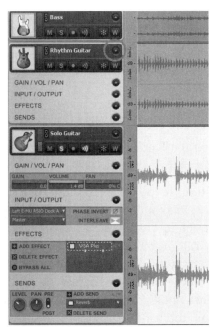

Figure 1.2 Tracks can be minimized to show a minimal number of parameters, or maximized to show additional parameter fields, by clicking on the circled button.

parameters are described later in the book; the point is that these important options are put in a centralized place, which you can see even when the track is minimized.

The next track down, Rhythm Guitar, has been expanded to show additional groups of parameters by clicking on the drop-down button (circled). You can show one or more parameter groups by clicking on their individual drop-down buttons. If these functions don't make sense, no worries—most are described later in the book, or you can click on the Big Help button.

The next track down, Solo Guitar, has all parameter fields maximized. The Gain/Vol/Pan field lets you adjust—this is probably no big surprise!—Gain, Volume, and Pan parameters for the track. (Gain is the level coming into the track, Volume is the level coming out of it—in other words, the amount of signal that typically gets sent to the master bus—and Pan sets the position in the stereo field.)

The next field down (Input/Output) lets you select the track input and track output. Also note that you can invert the phase and edit the interleave (a fancy word for changing between stereo and mono).

The subsequent field, Effects, is the equivalent of a software rack where you can insert and remove effects, as well as bypass them.

The lowest field, Sends, is where you manage feeds to different busses. Chapter 17 describes sends in more detail.

Console View

Console view emulates the look of a traditional hardware mixing console. For those who've worked with consoles, it provides a familiar mixing environment (see Figure 1.3). Those whose introduction to recording involved computers may be more comfortable with the Console view or Track view; it's a matter of personal preference.

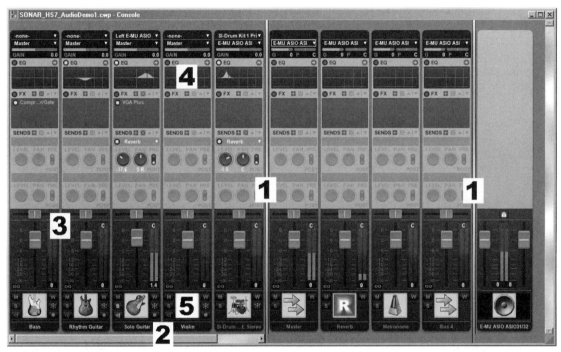

Figure 1.3   The Console view resembles a traditional mixing console. It can be onscreen simultaneously with the Track view.

The biggest difference compared to Track view is that you can't see the audio and MIDI data. As a result, Console view is most commonly used when recording and editing is done, and it's time to mix.

Console View Layout

There are two vertical splitter bars (1) that separate the groups of individual tracks, busses, and master output. Clicking and dragging the left splitter bar left or right changes the visual balance between the tracks and busses, while the right splitter bar changes the balance of the busses and master output. If there are more tracks or busses than can be shown in the allotted space, you'll see a scroll bar (2) so you can choose which tracks or busses you want to see.

Track Strip (Channel) Controls

Each channel has the same basic parameters as the maximized channel in Track view, but there are some differences.

The Input and Output fields are visible at the top, along with the Gain Trim control. However, the Level and Pan controls (3) are located toward the bottom of the mixer instead of being grouped with the Gain control.

The biggest difference compared to Track view is that you can see a graph of the built-in channel EQ response curve (4), as well as enable/bypass EQ and (by clicking on the small, right-facing arrow) reveal the EQ parameters for making edits to the EQ settings.

Below the EQ is an FX bin for adding virtual signal processors, and below that, a sends section similar to the one in Track view. If there are more than two sends, you can click on the down arrow next to the send name, and a drop-down menu will show all available sends. Choose the one you want to see/edit.

Toward the lower part of the channel, there are the "essential" buttons (5) you can see in the minimized Track view version (Mute, Solo, Record, Echo Input, Freeze, and Automation Write).

Other Views

From the main Track view, you can use toolbar buttons to access the Loop Explorer view (Chapter 22, "Groove Clips") and MIDI Piano Roll view (Chapter 7, "Piano Roll View MIDI Editing"). What's more, there's a Status Bar strip along the bottom of the program (see Figure 1.4).

Figure 1.4   The Status Bar provides a variety of useful information about SONAR Home Studio's status.

Going from left to right, you'll find:

- The current location of the Now time in measures, beats, and ticks.

- A readout that shows whether certain QWERTY keyboard keys are latched. (For example, if Number Lock is on, you'll see N; Scroll Lock = S, Caps Lock = C, and Pause/Break = P.)

- Audio Engine Running. (This field is blank if it's stopped.)

- Mute, Solo, and Record Arm indicators. If M is on, then at least one track is muted; if S is on, at least one track is soloed; if R is on, then at least one track is record-enabled. These aren't just read only—for example, if you click on S, it will un-solo *all* tracks that are soloed.

- Sample rate and bit resolution.

- Free disk space on the drive that holds SONAR Home Studio's WAV data directory.

- CPU activity.

- Hard disk activity.

For the latter two, if you want a more detailed, technical explanation about what the CPU and Disk meters are measuring, check the Help file. (Look for "Status Bar" in the index.)

Additional views are available from the Views menu, such as the Synth Rack, Meter/Key, Video, and so on. One of the most overlooked is the Tempo view, as described in Chapter 6, "MIDI Basics."

Navigation

An important element of any program like SONAR Home Studio is getting to where you want to go in the song as quickly as possible. The process of getting around a song is called *navigation.*

The Time Ruler and Now Time

The Now time is a key concept in SONAR Home Studio: It's a line that indicates a particular time or measure within a project, as measured by the Time Ruler just above the Track view. You can place the Now time anywhere you want simply by clicking in the Clips pane or on the Time Ruler.

During playback or recording, the Now time moves in time with the music; if, for example, four measures have elapsed, the Now time will be at the beginning of Measure 5 and will continue to move to the right as more measures elapse.

The Time Ruler can show time in Measures:Beats:Ticks (ticks are subdivisions of a quarter note), Hours:Minutes:Seconds:Frames (frames are subdivisions of a second), Samples, or Milliseconds. You choose the Time Ruler calibration by right-clicking on the Time Ruler and choosing Time Ruler Format and then selecting the desired option (see Figure 1.5). In most cases, you'll choose Measures:Beats:Ticks, or M:B:T.

If playback or recording is stopped, the Now time places a marker with a green triangle to indicate where playback or recording will begin if initiated. However, you have some leeway over where the Now time ends up when you stop playback or recording.

Customizing Where the Now Time Stops

There are two general options for choosing where the Now time locates when you stop playback, as selected in the Options > Global > General tab. If you check On Stop, Rewind to Now Marker (see Figure 1.6), when playback or recording stops, the Now marker will return to where it was before playback began. This is the probably the best option to use if you're overdubbing parts over the same section of a tune.

If you uncheck On Stop, Rewind to Now Marker, when the transport stops, the Now time will stay at its stopped position. If you click on Play, the Now time will now continue playback from

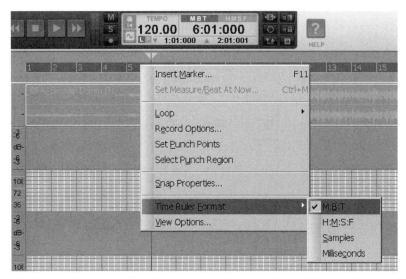

Figure 1.5   You can see where you are in a project referenced to musical time (measures and beats), absolute time (hours:minutes:seconds), samples, or milliseconds.

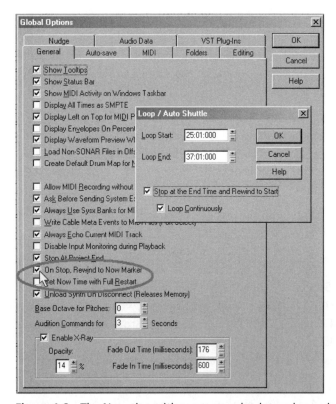

Figure 1.6   The Now time either can snap back to where playback started or can stay where it was when the transport stopped. However, the Loop/Auto Shuttle settings also influence the Now time position.

where it left off. This is the option I tend to use while composing, where I'll block out sections of a tune without being too concerned about the part itself—my goal is simply to get parts down before the inspiration goes away.

While we're discussing the Global Options menu, there's one other item that involves the Now time—although practically, this has relevance only if you're synchronizing SONAR Home Studio with other devices. If you check Set Now Time with Full Restart, then whenever you change the Now time, the transport will stop before restarting playback to ensure more reliable synchronization.

There is one other factor regarding where the Now time ends up, but this matters only if you've looped a portion of the project and looping is enabled. Select Transport > Loop and Auto Shuttle; with Stop at the End Time and Rewind to Start checked, when the Now time reaches the loop end, the transport will stop automatically, and the Now time will rewind to the loop start and stay there. Unchecking this turns off looping. If you'd prefer to have looping run continuously, check the Loop Continuously box. (With Loop Continuously checked, closing the Loop/Auto Shuttle dialog box creates a loop as indicated by the Loop Start and Loop End fields.)

And what happens if you click on Stop before the Now time hits the loop end? That depends on whether On Stop, Rewind to Now Marker is checked under Global > Options. If checked, the Now time will snap back to the beginning of the loop, or if unchecked, it will remain at the stop point.

Finally, note that if you click Play while the transport is playing, the transport will pause and then resume if you click Play again.

Navigating with Markers

The main purpose of markers is to simplify navigation around a piece of music, as you can jump to a particular marker without having to set the Now time or use the transport controls. For example, you could jump instantly to the first verse or chorus. It's important to strike a balance between having too many markers, which can be confusing, and too few, which makes it difficult to go exactly where you want. Markers can also identify sections of a song or lock to SMPTE time so they always indicate a certain position in time, even if the song tempo changes.

The general process is to add markers where desired and then use various tools to jump to them. Note that you can move or copy a marker, and if Snap to Grid is selected, the marker will snap to the selected grid value.

Markers are visible in the Time Ruler at the top of the Track, Staff, and Piano Roll views.

Adding Markers in Real Time

There are four main ways to insert markers while your tune is playing. The marker will be indicated by an orange "flag," and with one exception, it will go where the Now time position was when you gave the command to insert the marker. Here are your options.

- Press F11.

- Choose Insert > Marker.

- Right-click on the Timeline and select Insert Marker.

- Ctrl-click on the space just above the Time Ruler, where the markers hang out. With this method, though, the marker will land on the nearest rhythmic value to where you clicked, based on the Snap to Grid value.

When adding a marker in real time, the marker gets a default name with a letter and number. For example, the first marker will be A1, the next A2, and so on. If you stop the transport, the next marker you place will be B1, then B2, and so on. Every time you stop the transport and create a marker, the letter increments. (If you go past Z, then it starts over again with A.) If you want the marker to have a distinctive name, you will need to do this as described later.

The Markers View

There's a special view for markers; to call it up, choose Views > Markers. The Markers view compiles a list of all the markers you've created and allows for managing markers (see Figure 1.7).

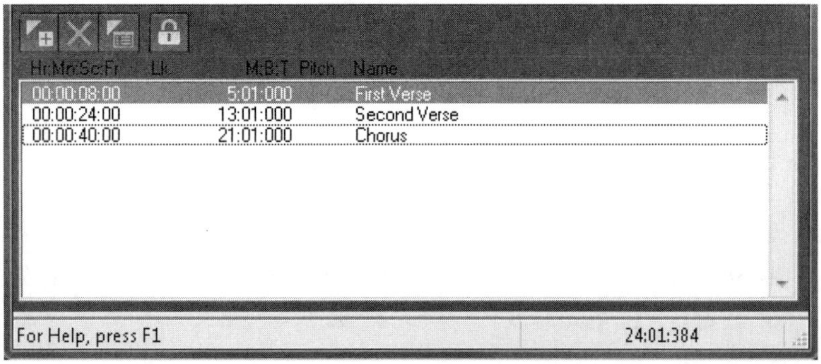

H:Mn:Sc:Fr	Lk	M:B:T	Pitch	Name
00:00:08:00		5:01:000		First Verse
00:00:24:00		13:01:000		Second Verse
00:00:40:00		21:01:000		Chorus

For Help, press F1   24:01:384

Figure 1.7 There are four options for marker management, as selected by the four buttons toward the Markers view's upper left.

- **Insert Marker.** This provides yet another way to add a marker and works whether the transport is running or stopped; just click on the button to deposit a marker at the current Now time. Although you won't be able to see the Timeline as a reference, you can refer to the transport's position readout or place markers as you listen to a project.

- **Delete Marker.** Click on the marker to select it and then click on the X button or type D. You can Ctrl-click to select noncontiguous markers; click on one marker and then Shift-click on another to select all markers in between, and including, the selected markers; or type Ctrl +A to select all markers. This selection process also works if you want to lock markers, as described shortly.

- **Change Marker Properties.** Click on a marker and then click on the third button from the left to bring up the Marker Properties dialog box. Shortcuts: Double-click on a marker or, after selecting a marker, type C.

- **Lock a Marker or Group of Markers.** Click on the Lock icon to lock markers to specific SMPTE times (see the upcoming "What Is SMPTE Time?" sidebar) in the song. This is used mostly for marking where sound effects occur. For example, suppose you have a marker at Measure 5, Beat 1 that indicates a door slam. If the tempo is 120 BPM, this marker places the door slam sound effect at a time of 0 hours, 8 seconds, 0 frames. Now suppose you change the tempo to 140 BPM. If the marker isn't locked, it remains at Measure 5, Beat 1, but in terms of time, it's now at 0 hours, 6 seconds, 26 frames—not where the door slams. If the marker is locked, it stays at the original 0 hours, 8 seconds, 0 frames. Note that you can also lock a marker within its Properties dialog box, as described next.

What Is SMPTE Time? SMPTE stands for *Society of Motion Picture and Television Engineers*, a professional organization involved with film and video. Both film and video show a certain number of static frames per second, but the consecutive frames occur rapidly and give the illusion of motion. For example, film has 24 frames per second. So in addition to hours, minutes, and seconds, SMPTE specifies a certain number of frames. The time format is HH:MM:SS:FF, where HH=hours, MM=minutes, SS=seconds, and FF=frames. SMPTE time code is very useful for placing sound effects, as sounds can be associated with particular SMPTE times.

Editing Markers While in the Track View

You can also manage markers from the Track view, although your options are slightly more limited.

Right-click on the marker to bring up the Marker Properties dialog box. You can specify the following properties in this dialog box:

- **Name.** Rename by typing a name in the Name field (see Figure 1.8).

- **Lock to SMPTE time.**

- **Marker time (placement, in Beats:Measures:Ticks).** To change this, type a new value in the Time field or use the field's +/− buttons or spinner button.

Figure 1.8 A marker is being named First Verse.

- **Groove-Clip Pitch.** This causes the marker to define transposition, which is information used by Groove Clips. For example, if a song's project pitch is C, and a marker changes that to D, all Groove Clips will transpose up a full step. For more information, see Chapter 22 on Groove Clips.

You can also copy, move, and delete markers from the Track view.

- **Move.** Click on the marker and drag. It will snap to the grid.

- **Copy.** Either click-Ctrl or Ctrl-click (you can click either before or after hitting Ctrl) on a marker and drag. When you release the mouse, the Properties dialog box will appear.

- **Delete.** Click on the marker and hold. While holding down the mouse button, hit the QWERTY keyboard's Delete key.

Adding Markers While the Transport Is Stopped
You can use any of the methods for adding markers while the transport is running to add a marker while the transport is stopped. If you add a marker while stopped, the Marker Properties dialog box will appear after adding the marker.

Navigating with Markers
So now the markers are placed…it's time for navigation! You can jump around markers in several ways, and all of these are functional while the tune is playing.

- Use the menu commands: Go > Previous Marker or Go > Next Marker.

- Use SONAR Home Studio's key equivalents: Previous Marker = Ctrl+Shift+Page Up, Next Marker = Ctrl+Shift+Page Down.

- Use the Key Bindings function (under the Options menu) to assign what I think are more logical equivalents: Previous Marker = Shift+F11, Next Marker = Shift+F12.

- Click on a marker listing in the Markers view.

- Hit F5 twice. A Markers window will show up with not just the markers you placed, but default markers for beginning, end, punch in, punch out, loop start, loop end, and so on. To jump to one of these markers, double-click on the desired marker and then click on OK (or hit the Enter or Return key) when the Go box appears.

Using Markers for Range Selection

In addition to navigation, markers serve one other purpose: Clicking between any two markers in the strip just above the Time Ruler causes them to define a time range. You can set this range to a loop by right-clicking between the two markers that define the loop and selecting Loop > Set Loop Points from the context menu.

Key Bindings

SONAR Home Studio has extensive QWERTY keyboard shortcut options, but you can also use a MIDI keyboard's keys to trigger shortcuts. (And the two are not mutually exclusive.) This is particularly useful if you want to use something like a mini-keyboard as a control center for SONAR Home Studio and control functions such as the transport or marker navigation remotely. (Remote control is also a good use for old drum machines if the pads output MIDI notes.)

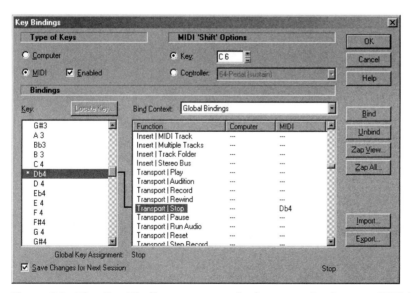

Figure 1.9 The Key Bindings menu works for computer keys or MIDI keyboard notes. Here, Db4 is bound to the Transport Stop function. Note that you have to check the Enabled box for the MIDI key triggers to have an effect.

Setting up MIDI control keys is pretty easy. Choose Options > Key Bindings and click on the MIDI button (see Figure 1.9).

SONAR Home Studio lets you designate a single keyboard note as a Shift key, so that you can play the keyboard normally, but holding down the Shift key and then hitting another note triggers a particular function. (I use the highest note as the Shift key, because I seldom hit it in normal playing.) To set the Shift key, highlight the Key field and play the desired note. (You can also use a controller, but I find using a key easier.)

Now "bind" a note to a specific function. Hit the key you want to use for the trigger, and the key will be highlighted in the leftmost window. Scroll down the list in the right window to the desired function. Click on the function and then click on Bind (or press Alt+B). This creates a line from the key name to the function.

After you create a binding, a dot shows up to the right of the key name. Click on any of these dotted keys, and you'll see the function to which it is bound. Unbind a key by highlighting the key name and clicking on Unbind, or use Zap View to disconnect all bindings in the current view or Zap All to disconnect all bindings. Note that you can enable/disable all MIDI bindings with the Enabled check box, which you'll want to do if you're playing a part that requires the use of the designated Shift key. (Otherwise, SONAR Home Studio will just ignore that key if you play it.)

Incidentally, here are the key bindings that work for me: C = Rewind, C# = Stop, D = Previous Marker, D# = Play, E = Next Marker, F = Record, F# = Undo, G = Record Automation.

Note that you can use the same basic procedure for setting up QWERTY key bindings.

2 Recording Audio and MIDI

ecording either MIDI or audio is a simple process in SONAR Home Studio. This chapter assumes you've connected an audio interface properly and know how to identify its inputs and outputs. If not, refer to the manual that came with SONAR Home Studio, which has lots of general information about digital audio, computers, and working with projects. Note that a new, blank project opens with no tracks or busses; after clicking on a new project, consider loading the Normal template file, which loads a pair of audio tracks and MIDI instrument tracks, to get started as easily as possible.

Setting Up the Metronome

For any type of recording, if you don't have some kind of rhythmic reference, such as a steady drum part, you'll probably use the metronome to provide a rhythmic reference. To set this up, go to Options > Project and click on the Metronome tab. This presents all adjustable metronome parameters (see Figure 2.1)

In the General section, you can choose to have the metronome sound during playback, recording, or both, as well as set a count-in specified in either measures or beats. A count-in of one measure gives the familiar "1-2-3-4" countdown (although, of course, SONAR Home Studio uses clicks or sounds, not speech). This is also where you choose between using SONAR Home Studio's internal audio metronome or sending MIDI notes to an external MIDI-compatible instrument.

For the internal metronome, you can choose any of several sounds for the downbeat and other beats and set their levels and their routing. (They usually go to the master bus.) Using the internal metronome is the simplest way to go, but if you want to drive an outboard instrument (such as drum sounds from a drum machine), you can do that, too. Select Use MIDI Note, and in the MIDI Note section, specify the interface port, MIDI channel, note duration, and the note/velocity for the downbeat (first beat), along with a separate note/velocity setting for the other beats.

Recording Audio

Now that the metronome's squared away, let's record some sounds.

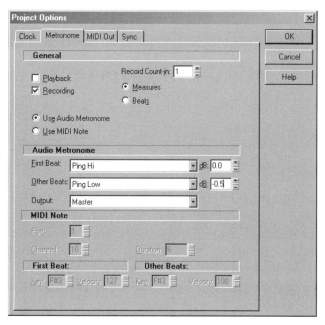

Figure 2.1   All metronome parameters are controlled from a single dialog box.

1.   If you loaded the Normal template, there are already two MIDI tracks into which you can record audio. Otherwise, to insert an audio track, choose Insert > Audio Track, or right-click on a blank space in the Track view channel strip and select Insert Audio Track, or click on the + button in the Control Bar (main toolbar).

2.   Click on the Show/Hide Controls button to unfold the track controls and then click on the Input/Output button to reveal the input/output options (see Figure 2.2). Ctrl-clicking on the selected track's Show/Hide controls exposes all modules and controls.

Figure 2.2   Open up two of an audio track's Show/Hide controls so you can specify the audio interface input through which you will record your instrument or mic.

3. Click on the Input drop-down arrow, and you'll see a list of all available audio inputs
    that SONAR Home Studio recognizes. These can be physical (from a hardware audio
    interface) or virtual (from something like a software synthesizer output). Choose the
    audio interface input through which you want to record (see Figure 2.3). In this
    example, the mic input from an E-MU interface is being selected.

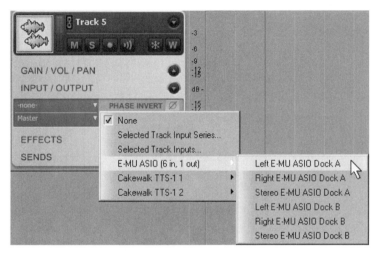

Figure 2.3 Select the desired audio interface input. The output typically goes to SONAR Home Studio's
Master output.

4. Click on the Record Enable button. The track background in the Clips pane will turn
    light red to indicate recording is enabled. Then observe the meter. (In Figure 2.4, the
    Record Enable button and the meter are circled for clarity.) Adjust the audio interface
    input or source output from your mic or instrument so that the meter lights green at
    consistently high levels, but rarely (if ever) lights red. If the top red LEDs stay lit, that
    means the input level exceeded what the interface can handle. Reduce the audio
    interface input level or source output level and then click on the LEDs to reset them.

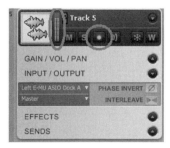

Figure 2.4 The meter toward the left should seldom go into the red zone, and if the top red LEDs stay
lit, the incoming levels need to be reduced.

5.   Click on the transport's Record button (see Figure 2.5). The Now time will start moving, and the track will show what's being recorded as you record it. The top and bottom of the waveform should not touch the upper or lower track border; if this happens, reduce the incoming level.

Figure 2.5   Audio is being recorded into a SONAR Home Studio track.

6.   When you're finished recording, click on the transport Stop button—your audio track is recorded.

Recording MIDI

Recording MIDI isn't all that different from recording audio, except that you're recording data instead of waveforms. You'll need to have some kind of MIDI controller (keyboard, drum pads, and so on) that generates MIDI data in order to record this data.

1.   Choose Insert > MIDI Track or right-click on a blank space in the Track view channel strip and select Insert MIDI Track. (You can also click the + sign in the main Control Bar and select MIDI Track.)

2.   Click on the Show/Hide Controls button to unfold the track controls and then click on the Input/Output button to reveal the input/output options and the Quantize/Key/Time button (see Figure 2.6). The last one might not be necessary; you'll see why in Step 6.

3.   Click on the Input down arrow and choose the MIDI interface input to which your MIDI controller (keyboard, guitar, drum pads, and so on) connects. In Figure 2.7, a Line 6 KB37 keyboard is being selected, and the input is set to Omni so that it will record any data coming in on any MIDI channel.

Figure 2.6 For MIDI recording, you'll want to choose the MIDI input and output and possibly quantize the incoming MIDI data.

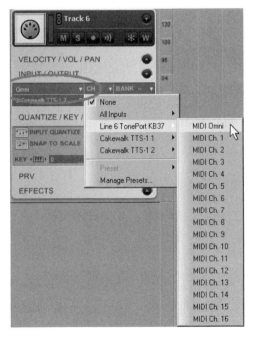

Figure 2.7 Select the desired MIDI interface input.

4. Click on the Output down arrow and choose where to send the track's MIDI data (for example, a soft synth, external hardware connected to an interface's MIDI port, and so on). Usually this sends what's at the input through to the output. In Figure 2.8, the MIDI input is being routed through to a second instance of the Cakewalk TTS-1 soft synth.

Figure 2.8 Select the desired MIDI data destination, such as a soft synth.

5. Play a few notes on your controller. The MIDI track should register that input is being received, and you should hear some notes from the instrument you specified in the Output field. Note that it doesn't matter if the MIDI track's velocity meter goes to the highest level; unlike audio, instead of indicating that distortion has occurred, it simply indicates that your controller is producing the highest-level MIDI velocity values.

6. If you want, you can quantize incoming MIDI notes to a rhythmic grid. Click on the Input Quantize button and then set a quantization value from the drop-down menu. Figure 2.9 shows eighth notes being selected.

    However, note Quantize Settings, the additional option at the bottom of the drop-down menu in Figure 2.9. Here you can choose options that relax the tightness of quantization somewhat, such as changing the Strength or Swing values (see Figure 2.10). For more information on quantization, see Chapter 5, "Editing with the Process Menu."

    Quantizing while recording can save time if you're recording fairly simple parts, but don't forget that SONAR Home Studio includes a MIDI plug-in (see Chapter 11, "MIDI Plug-Ins") that does quantization in real time. This makes it easy to try out different quantization options and decide which one works best.

7. Click on the MIDI track's Record Enable button (the track background in the Clips pane will turn light red to indicate recording is enabled) and then click on the

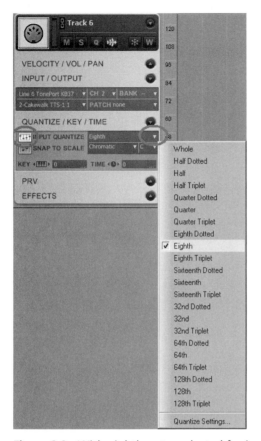

Figure 2.9   With eighth notes selected for input quantize, all incoming MIDI notes will be quantized to the nearest eighth note.

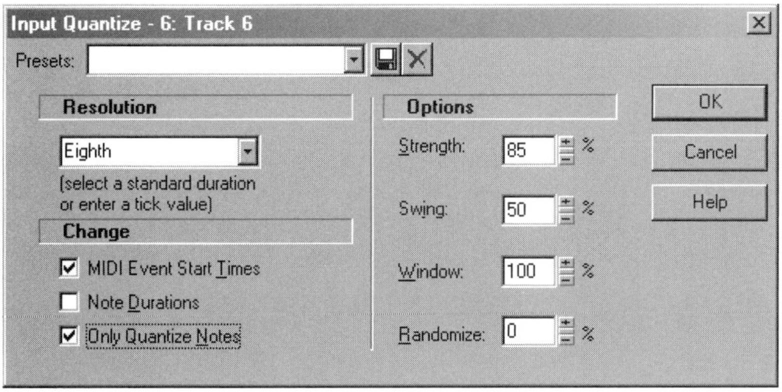

Figure 2.10   You can customize the quantize settings to produce a less robotic effect.

transport's Record button. The Now time will start moving, and the track will show a clip being drawn (but not the notes themselves; they're drawn after you click the transport Stop button to stop recording).

8. When you're finished recording, click on the transport Stop button, and your MIDI track will be recorded.

3 Clip Editing in Track View

I n Track view, MIDI and audio data appear as *clips*. A clip can be anything from a single note, to a short phrase, to a track that lasts the duration of a song. You can also split long clips into shorter clips or join short clips together to make a longer clip. All in all, clips are a very flexible way to build an arrangement. For example, if you have a bass clip that works perfectly for the first verse, you can copy it for the second verse and then edit the clip slightly to add a few variations.

SONAR Home Studio treats MIDI and audio clips as interchangeably as possible, so you can think of both types of clips similarly—however, note that MIDI clips won't play back from within audio tracks, and audio clips won't play back from within MIDI tracks. The main difference is that audio clips show a waveform inside the clip boundaries, while MIDI clips show what looks like little blobs that represent MIDI notes (see Figure 3.1).

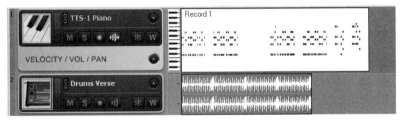

Figure 3.1 The upper track shows a MIDI clip; you can see the individual MIDI notes. The lower track shows an audio clip, which displays the audio waveform.

As background, audio clips "point" to audio material recorded on your hard drive. As a result, editing a clip is nondestructive—the data pointed to by the clip remains, regardless of what you do to the clip. This is why you can, for example, trim an audio clip, yet if you import the audio to which the clip points into the project, it will be unedited.

Note that clips can have envelopes that modify level, panning, and so on. Clip envelopes are covered in Chapter 19, "Automation in SONAR Home Studio."

Context Menu Clip Editing Options

There are many ways to edit clips, including options in the Track view Toolbox, right-clicking on a clip and calling up a context menu (see Figure 3.2), or using the Edit menu.

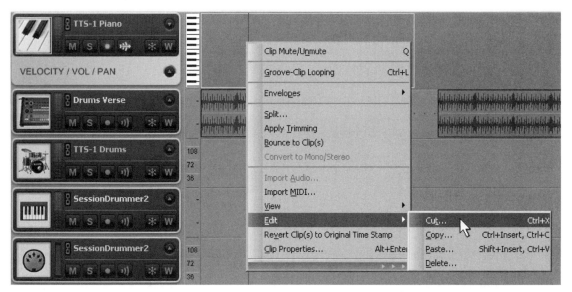

Figure 3.2   Right-click on a clip to bring up a context menu with multiple editing options; this example shows the Edit submenu selected.

The following are general methods of editing a clip; note that some are accessible in more than one way. For example, if you select a clip and want to cut it, you can select Edit in the main menu bar and choose Cut, or right-click on the clip and select Edit > Cut (or you can just click on the clip and hit the Delete key).

Also note that there are several ways to select a clip, or portion of a clip. For example, you can just click on a clip with the standard Select tool to select the entire clip. To select a portion of a clip with the standard Select tool, either Alt-drag inside the clip, or click-drag across the desired range in the timeline (this applies only to selected clips, of course). Furthermore, there's a Free Select tool in the Track view Toolbox whose button has what looks like an I-beam symbol. With this tool, clicking within the top or bottom third of a clip selects the entire clip, but positioning the tool in the center of the clip and click-dragging selects a portion of the clip.

Trim clip. A clip may extend longer than it needs to or start before there are actual notes. Trimming lets you eliminate extraneous notes or empty space at the beginning or end of a clip. (This kind of editing is also called *slip editing* because you're "slipping" the clip's end or beginning.) To trim the beginning, hover the cursor over the beginning of the clip until the left side of the clip changes to a bracket. Click and drag right to trim the beginning. Similarly, you can trim the end by hovering the cursor over the end of the clip until the clip's right side changes to a bracket. Click and drag left to trim the end.

Make trim permanent. When trimming via the aforementioned method, the data remains, so if you "untrim," the data will reappear. However, you can make changes to the clip (not the underlying data) caused by trimming permanent. Right-click in the clip and then select Apply Trimming.

Cut clip. Right-click on the clip and choose Edit > Cut. A dialog box will open that specifies what you're going to cut. You can delete any of the following that lie within the clip's duration: events in track, clip automation, track/bus automation, tempo changes, meter/key changes, and markers.

Another dialog box option is Delete Hole, which means that material to the right of the clip on the same track moves left to fill up the hole created by cutting the clip. (You can also specify whether the clip to the right gets shifted by whole measures.) For example, suppose a clip occupies Measures 1 and 2, and another clip in the same track occupies Measures 7 and 8. If you cut the clip in Measures 1 and 2 and don't specify Delete Hole, the clip in Measures 7 and 8 will stay put. But if you specify Delete Hole, cutting the clip in Measures 1 and 2 leaves a two-measure "hole." Thus, the clip in Measures 7 and 8 moves two measures to the left to fill up the hole, so the clip now shifts to being in Measures 5 and 6.

Note that cutting data places that data in the computer's clipboard memory, so you can paste it later if desired.

Copy clip. Right-click on the clip and choose Edit > Copy. As with cutting, a dialog box will open that specifies what you're going to copy that lies within the clip's duration. The clip being copied doesn't change, but the data you copied goes onto the clipboard for later pasting. Note that the clipboard is only one level deep; for example, if you copy a clip and later copy another clip, the second clip's data will overwrite the first clip's data.

Paste clip. If there's clip data on the clipboard, right-click in the track where you want to paste the data and choose Edit > Paste. A dialog box will open with options on how to paste the clip data (see Figure 3.3).

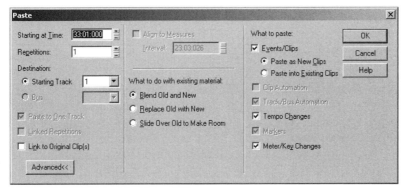

Figure 3.3   The Paste dialog box provides many ways to paste the data on the clipboard.

Most of the options are self-explanatory.

- If you right-clicked in a particular track at a particular measure, that data will be filled in for the Starting at Time and Destination Starting Track fields.

- The Repetitions value will paste the data multiple times if desired. (This is useful if, for example, you have a one-measure drum loop you want to paste four times so it becomes a four-measure loop.)

- If you check Link to Original Clip(s), edits made to the original clip (for example, removing notes) will also be made to the pasted/repeated data.

- The Advanced button toggles between the full dialog box and an abbreviated version that will nonetheless cover your editing needs most of the time.

- The What to Do with Existing Material section has three useful options. Blend Old and New means that if there's already data where you want to paste the clip, the new data will not replace the old data. Thus, if you paste an audio clip over another audio clip, they'll both play back simultaneously. Replace Old with New causes any old data to be replaced if the new clip overlaps with it. Slide Over Old to Make Room means that any old data won't be replaced if the new clip overlaps with it, but instead, it will slide to the right to "get out of the way" of the new data. For example, suppose there's a two-measure clip on the clipboard, and there's already a clip covering Measures 5–8. If you paste the clipboard contents at Measure 5, the data will occupy Measures 5 and 6, and the clip that previously occupied Measures 5–8 will start at the end of Measure 6.

- What to Paste is sort of the mirror image of the dialog box that appeared asking you what you wanted to copy. For example, suppose you copied a clip where a tempo change occurred in the middle of the clip. When you paste the clip, you might want to retain the tempo change, in which case you would check Tempo Changes, but if you paste the clip again, you might not want to repaste the tempo change, in which case you'd uncheck the Tempo Changes box.

- The other options (such as Align to Measures and Paste to One Track) are less commonly used; check the Help menu for information.

Delete clip. Right-click on the clip and choose Edit > Delete. Or, simply click on a clip to select it and then press the Delete key. This is similar to cutting, except it doesn't place data on the clipboard. This is very handy if you want to copy and paste a clip, but before pasting, you want to delete other clips. By using Delete, the original copied data remains on the clipboard.

Split clip. Right-click in the clip where you want to split it and then select Split. A dialog box will appear with split options (see Figure 3.4), and where you right-clicked will already be entered into the Split at Time field. Click on OK, and you'll have a single split where you right-clicked.

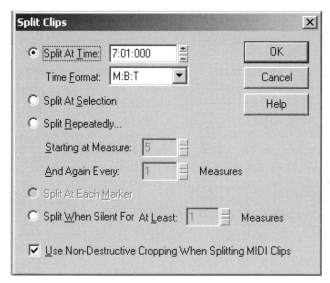

Figure 3.4 The Split Clips dialog box controls how splits occur within a clip.

An even simpler option is to click in the clip where you want the split and type S. Here's what the other options mean.

- If you want a split on each side of a selection within a clip (selected by click-dragging in the Timeline where you want the selection or by Alt-dragging within the clip), right-click in the clip, choose Split (this brings up the Split Clips dialog box), and select Split at Selection in the Split Clips dialog box.

- Split Repeatedly lets you specify where the first split should be and the interval for subsequent splits. For example, suppose you have a four-measure drum loop you want to rearrange by cutting it up into four one-measure loops. With Split Repeatedly selected, indicate the measure where you want splits to begin and the interval of the splits. If your four-measure drum loop started at Measure 9, you'd split it into four parts by entering 10 for the Starting at Measure value and entering one measure for the And Again Every value.

- If there are markers within the range of the clip, selecting Split at Each Marker creates a split at each marker (which is probably not too surprising…).

- Split When Silent for at Least *X* Measures splits a MIDI clip (but *not* an audio clip) at the boundaries of silences if those silences are equal to or longer than the number of measures you specified.

- Another MIDI-specific choice is Use Non-Destructive Cropping When Splitting MIDI Clips, and I highly recommend checking this. When it's checked, if you split in the middle of a MIDI note, the original MIDI note length is maintained, but the note stops sounding at the split. However, if you slip-edit the clip to extend the original boundary, the remaining part of the note will be revealed.

Clip Mute/Unmute. This toggles between muting and unmuting the clip.

Groove Clip Looping. A Groove Clip can be MIDI or audio; once a clip is converted to a Groove Clip, you can click on a boundary and drag left or right to "roll out" the loop for additional iterations. For more information on Groove Clips, see Chapter 22. As with mute/unmute, this is a toggle.

Convert to Mono or Convert to Stereo. This applies to audio clips only. If a clip is mono, the option will say Convert to Stereo. Select this, and the clip will change to stereo, with the same audio in each channel. If a clip is stereo, the option will say Convert to Mono. Select this, and the audio in each channel will be mixed into a single mono channel.

Finally, also note that there are many editing tools available in the Track view Toolbox. From left to right, these are: Select (with drop-down options for what is to be selected), Free Edit tool, Zoom tool, Snap to Grid tool (with access to the Snap Options via the down arrow), and Split tool (Scissors).

Combining (Bouncing) Audio or MIDI Clips within a Track

This is the opposite of splitting. If you have lots of little pieces of clips scattered around in a track, you might want to bounce them together into a single clip, or at least bounce some clips to a single clip.

To do this, select the clips you want to combine (they should all be in the same track) and then choose Edit > Bounce to Clip(s). Any space between clips will be represented as silence in the new clip, which will start where the first clip to be combined started and will end when the last clip to be combined ends (see Figure 3.5).

Figure 3.5 The upper track shows three clips prior to being bounced, while the lower track shows the results of bouncing.

- If you combine Groove Clips, their grooviness will not be retained—the bounced clip will be a non–Groove Clip.

- You can select clips in multiple tracks, but any bounces will still be within individual tracks. For example, if you select three clips in Track 1 and four clips in Track 2, the three clips will bounce together in Track 1, and the four clips will bounce together in Track 2.

Combining (Bouncing) Audio or MIDI Clips to a Separate Track

Bouncing replaces the original track data with the bounced data. However, it's also possible to bounce the clips to a separate track (thus preserving the original track data) using the Bounce to Track(s) function (see Figure 3.6). This can also mix data from separate tracks.

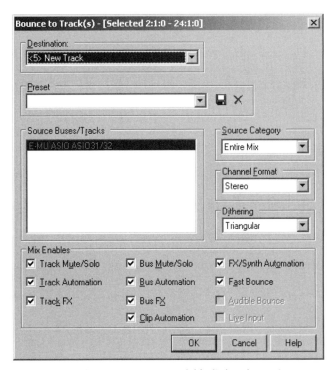

Figure 3.6   The Bounce to Track(s) dialog box gives numerous options for how you want the bounce to occur.

This procedure is different from bouncing to clips because it mixes down *everything* within a selected region. Therefore, in addition to selecting what you want to bounce, it's a good idea to mute any tracks you don't want to bounce. (Also note that if you want to include a virtual instrument track as part of the bounce, its corresponding MIDI track must also be selected.)

Once you've chosen which tracks you want to bounce and muted the ones that shouldn't be part of the bounce, choose Edit > Bounce to Track(s). When the dialog box appears, specify the destination track in the Destination field. The dialog box defaults to a new track one number higher than your highest existing track. (In other words, if your project has eight tracks, the new track will be Track 9.) However, you can also specify an existing audio track, in which case the bounced data will overwrite what's in that track.

As for the other parameters in the dialog box, most of the time you'll want to just leave the defaults as is. But if you want to bounce without automation, effects, or whatever, you can disable those elements from the bounce.

One parameter that sometimes confuses people is Fast Bounce. If this option is checked, the bouncing occurs faster than real time. (In other words, it takes much less than 30 seconds to bounce a 30-second piece of music.) This is what you'll choose most of the time. However, if you're using processors outside of SONAR Home Studio, such as going through an external hardware effects unit or using digital effects that connect through FireWire (such as TC Electronic's PowerCore or SSL's Duende), their effects are computed and applied in real time. In this case, you need to disable Fast Bounce.

If you're still confused, there's a simple solution: Try Fast Bounce first, and if the bounced track sounds garbled or has audio dropouts, disable Fast Bounce.

One other problem that trips people up is that if you have the source as Entire Mix, then the level of the track will be the same as the level appearing at the master out. If the master's level is low, the bounced track will be low. Conversely, if the master's level is high enough to be distorted, the bounced track will be distorted as well.

Quick Clip Edits

In addition to the editing options described earlier, there are many ways to move clips around quickly.

Move a clip within a track. Click on the clip and drag left or right to change its position. If Snap to Grid is selected, the clip boundaries will move at the rhythmic interval specified in Snap to Grid.

Move a clip to a different track. Click on the clip and drag up or down into the desired track.

- If you hold Shift while dragging, the clip will be constrained to the same start time.

- If you drag the clip into a blank space in the Track view, a track will be created to accommodate it.

- You can drag an audio clip into a MIDI track or a MIDI clip into an audio track, and they will be visible, but they won't play back.

Copy a clip to another location in the same track or a different track. Click on the clip, and while holding the Ctrl key, drag the clip to where you want another version of the clip. This can also be copied to another track, and if you hold down Shift+Ctrl, the clip will be constrained to the same start time.

Delete a clip. Click on the clip and press Delete.

Copy a clip. Click on the clip and press Ctrl+C. This will still bring up the Copy dialog box. Or, click-drag the clip while holding down the Ctrl key.

Cut a clip. Click on the clip and press Ctrl+X. This will still bring up the Cut dialog box.

Paste a clip. Assuming there's clip data on the clipboard, click in the track where you want to paste the clip, select the track (for example, by clicking on the track icon), and then press Ctrl+V.

Clip Properties

This lets you edit various clip aspects, from color to stretching characteristics. There are differences between clip properties for audio and MIDI clips, but the General tab is the same for both, so we'll start with that.

General Tab

The General tab is where you can see and edit clip characteristics (see Figure 3.7).

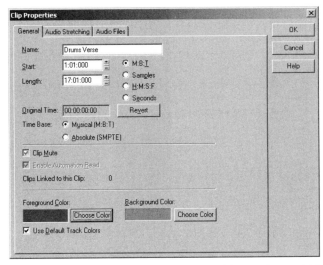

Figure 3.7 The General tab is identical for audio and MIDI clips.

The Name field lets you enter or change a clip's name. The Start and Length fields show the clip's current start time and length, and depending on which radio button to the right of these fields is selected, they display the values in Measures:Beats:Ticks, Samples, Hours:Minutes:Seconds:Frames, or Seconds.

The Original Time field shows either a clip's time stamp if present (for example, Broadcast WAV File format) or the time at which the clip was originally imported into a project. If you move the clip, clicking on Revert returns the clip to its original start time.

The Time Base parameter affects what happens to a clip's position when you change tempo. For example, suppose a clip starts at Measure 33, Beat 1, 0 ticks (M:B:T = 33:1:0) and that in this particular project, that's equivalent to a start point of 58 seconds, 19 frames (H:M:S:F = 00:00:58:19). With Musical selected, no matter what you do to the tempo, this clip will always start at M:B:T = 33:1:0, but its position based on H:M:S:F will change. With Absolute selected, this clip will always start at H:M:S:F = 00:00:58:19, but its position based on M:B:T will change. One use for this is audio-for-video, where you want a sound effect to happen at a certain time. If that sound effect is a clip whose time base is Absolute, then even if you decide you need to speed up or slow down the music, the sound effect will always trigger at the same place in the video.

Clip Mute simply parallels the Clip Mute/Unmute option in the context menu, while Clips Linked to This Clip is a read-only parameter that shows whether any clips are linked.

Finally, you can choose colors for both the background and foreground (in other words, the waveform for audio tracks or the note data for MIDI tracks) or choose to use the default track colors if you want to revert to the original coloring. Even though SONAR Home Studio lets you load track icons to parse track contents quickly, some people prefer coloring particular track groups. (For example, all drums are red, all vocals are blue, and so on.)

Audio Stretching Tab

Like the General tab, this is very similar for both MIDI and audio clips (see Figure 3.8).

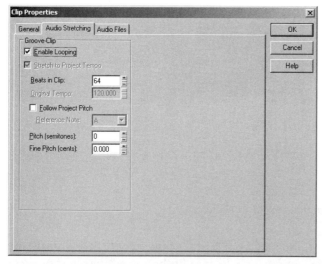

Figure 3.8   The Audio Stretching tab looks the same for audio and MIDI clips, but the Original Tempo and Fine Pitch parameters apply only to audio clips. (They're grayed out for MIDI clips.)

If Enable Looping is checked, you can click on a MIDI or audio clip boundary and drag to "roll out" the clip for multiple iterations. If it's not checked, then clicking and dragging on a boundary does slip editing, and all other parameters for MIDI clips are grayed out. With audio clips, disabling Enable Looping enables the Stretch to Project Tempo option. (This makes sense; if the clip is a loop, it already conforms to the project tempo, so there's no need to stretch it.) If looping is enabled, the Beats in Clip field will be active. However, this figure is based on an educated guess, so you can edit the value in case SONAR Home Studio guesses incorrectly. (This is rare, but it can happen.)

With audio clips, if Stretch to Project Tempo is enabled, you'll see a display of the clip's original tempo. Change this to the current project tempo, and the clip will shrink or expand (within reason) to match the project tempo. This is also very helpful if you want a quick reality check of the original tempo to determine whether it's too far out of range to stretch. (You wouldn't want to use a drum-and-bass loop recorded at 160 BPM with a hip-hop project that hovers around 85 BPM—that's asking a lot of the stretch algorithms.) With MIDI clips, Stretch to Project Tempo isn't relevant, because MIDI notes inherently stretch to match the project tempo. However, if looping is enabled, you will get a readout of how many beats are in the clip (in the Beats in Clip field); as with audio loops, you can edit this if needed.

With either Enable Looping or Stretch to Project Tempo checked, you'll have the option to check Follow Project Pitch. Following pitch requires that you select a reference note (the key in which the loop was recorded); SONAR Home Studio then uses this data to decide how much transposition to apply to match the project key or any pitch markers in the Time Ruler that indicate key changes. However, you can add additional transposition manually by editing the Pitch (Semitones) parameter, and with audio clips you can also edit the pitch in cents (Fine Pitch parameter). The latter is great if you're using a loop that was recorded slightly out of tune.

Audio Files Tab
This tab exists only for audio clips (see Figure 3.9).

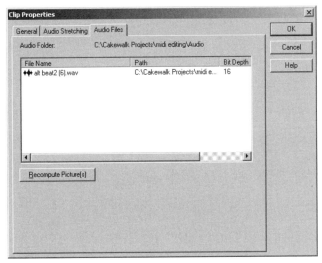

Figure 3.9 The Audio Files tab is mostly about information regarding the clip.

This tab is the simplest of all Clip Properties tabs. It displays the location of the project's audio folder toward the top, then below that, the file name, the path to the folder containing the file (usually the project audio folder, unless you haven't chosen to save audio with the project, and the file is located elsewhere in your computer), and the file bit depth. The one thing you can adjust is asking SONAR Home Studio to recompute the picture of the waveform in the audio file. Usually this won't be necessary, but if you do a lot of processing, the waveform picture may not be accurate. Clicking on Recompute Picture(s) redraws the waveform for the selected file(s).

4 Snapping and Grids

Music has a lot to do with timing and rhythm, and SONAR Home Studio includes a function called *snapping* that can make recording and arranging much easier. Snapping essentially aligns clips, notes, and other events to rhythmic values, but it also applies to setting the Now time, making a time selection in the Time Ruler, dragging and dropping clips to particular locations, slip editing, drawing controller curves, and selecting partial clips.

For example, if you want to create a two-measure time selection, instead of zooming in and laboriously placing the cursor as close as possible to a measure boundary, you can simply enable Snap and set it for one measure. As you drag across the Timeline to select the two measures, the cursor will "snap" to the beginning of the first measure and the end of the second measure, as if the Now time was magnetized to these boundaries.

Although snapping may seem like a simple concept, in practice, if you don't set it up correctly, you can end up with some perplexing problems. So, I've devoted this chapter to describing how snapping works.

Showing Vertical Grid Rules

In Track view, SONAR Home Studio has a grid that you can show or hide, with grid lines that align to bars. To show grid lines, right-click in the Track view Timeline and select View Options (see Figure 4.1).

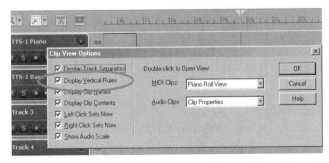

Figure 4.1 Check Display Vertical Rules to show the grid lines.

Check Display Vertical Rules, and you'll see vertical grid lines in the Clips pane at every measure. However, although these are only the grid lines you can see, SONAR Home Studio's grid resolution extends down to thirty-second-note triplets.

Defining a Grid

The Snap to Grid dialog box lets you specify the grid resolution, but it also provides many other options. Note that you can have different snap values in different views, so if you're doing wholesale moving of clips in the Track view, you can set Snap to a measure, but if you're entering notes or controllers in the Piano Roll view, you might want to snap them to sixteenth or thirty-second notes.

The Snap to Grid dialog is the same for all views where it's relevant, including PRV mode in Track view. Let's look at the various options (see Figure 4.2).

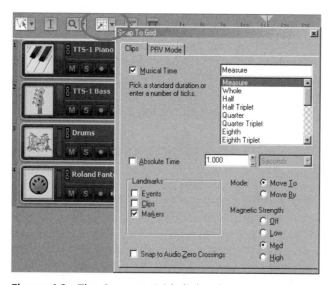

Figure 4.2 The Snap to Grid dialog box, accessed by a drop-down menu, is where you control all aspects of snapping anything to SONAR Home Studio's timing grid.

First, you have to choose what you want to snap to: Musical Time, such as a particular rhythmic value, or Absolute Time (for example, snapping to a certain number of samples, frames, or seconds). More than likely, you'll use Musical Time for most projects. However, you can also have both active and snap to a particular rhythmic value or Absolute Time value.

You can also choose to snap to particular "landmarks," specifically events, clips, or markers. For example, with Events, you can align the start of a clip with a particular MIDI note event (or audio event) in another clip. Given the large number of MIDI and audio events in a given project, this may get unwieldy to use, but it can come in handy.

Choosing Clips as the landmark lets you snap a clip to the end of another clip within the same track, but not to start and end points for clips in other tracks. With Markers selected, you can snap clip starts to markers, which is often very convenient when arranging a song.

The Mode parameter determines whether a clip (or note, for that matter) moves to the snap interval or by the snap interval. For example, suppose the mode is Move To, the snap interval is one measure, and a clip starts at Measure 1. If you move it to the right, the clip start will snap to the start of Measure 2, Measure 3, Measure 4, and so on. But suppose the mode is set to Move By and the clip is offset from a measure boundary, starting at Measure 1, 26 ticks. If you move it to the right, it will move by one measure exactly, so it will snap to Measure 2, 26 ticks; Measure 3, 26 ticks; Measure 4, 26 ticks; and so on.

Magnetic Strength determines how strong the snapping action is. I always leave this on High, because if I want snapping, it might as well be an industrial-strength snap. Having a Magnetic Strength of zero is the same as disabling snapping (by clicking on the Snap to Grid button to the left of the down arrow), so I never could figure out why you'd want to choose this option.

Like Move To and Move By, Snap to Audio Zero Crossings trips up a lot of people. I saw a magazine review of SONAR once that said the program was deficient because if you put the cursor on top of an audio clip in a certain place, it would often jump slightly to the left or right. Obviously, Snap to Audio Zero Crossings was on, so the cursor would move to the next available place where the audio passed through 0. This is a useful option when trimming an audio clip, because if you trim the clip to a place where there's some level, you'll hear a click when the cursor transitions from no audio to audio. However, if the transition happens at a zero crossing, there's a smooth transition from no audio to audio, minimizing the chance of getting a click.

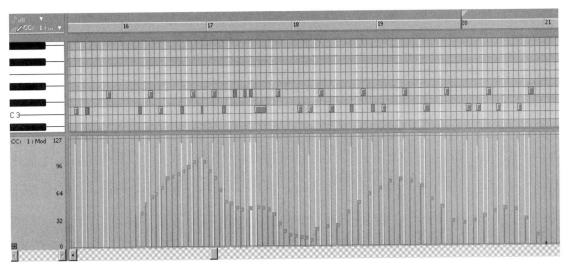

Figure 4.3 The left part of the controller curve was drawn with Snap set to sixteenth notes, while the right part was drawn with Snap set to eighth notes.

The snap options for MIDI PRV inline editing (Chapter 7, "Piano Roll View MIDI Editing") are the same, except there's no option to Snap to Zero Crossings because PRV inline editing pertains only to MIDI clips, not audio clips.

Snapping Controllers

For a practical application of snapping other than notes or clips, consider controllers. Often you don't need to clutter the MIDI stream with controllers happening on every tick, so you can enable snapping for when you draw controllers (see Figure 4.3).

Snapping Rules When Snap to Grid Is Turned Off

If the Snap to Grid option is turned off, certain ground rules still apply. The Now line will snap to individual samples, and if Snap to Audio Zero Crossings is checked, the Now line will still snap to zero crossings. This makes sense, because even if you don't want to snap to particular rhythmic values, you will probably want to snap to zero crossings if, for example, you're looking for a splice point within an audio clip. However, if you want the finest Now line resolution, uncheck Snap to Audio Zero Crossings—even if Snap to Grid is disabled.

5 Editing with the Process Menu

The Process menu offers several ways to edit selected audio or MIDI events.

Audio-Only Process Menu Functions

With audio events, the Process menu functions affect any selected clips. We'll cover the audio-related DSP options first; these are all chosen by selecting Process > Audio first and then selecting the desired option from the Audio side menu. We'll then cover applying audio effects and fades.

Gain

Calling this a "gain" function is a bit modest, because it does a lot more than just set gain. You can weight a stereo file more toward the left or right, convert stereo to mono, swap channels, reverse polarity of one channel in a stereo pair, balance channel levels in a stereo file where one side is at a lower value than the other, and more.

It does this by letting you specify what percentage of the original left and right channels will end up in "new" left and right channels after applying the gain function. For example, normally the new left channel would consist entirely of the left channel signal, and the new right channel would consist entirely of the right channel signal. But you're not limited to this; probably the best way to explain how to use this feature is with some examples.

Suppose you have a rhythm guitar part recorded in stereo, and you want it to spread not from left to right, but from center to right. SONAR's Pan control acts like a balance control with a stereo signal, so if you try to pan the signal more toward the right, the left channel gets softer while the right channel stays at its full level. We want both guitar channels to be equally loud, but what would be the left channel should come from the center instead of the left. This is easy to do with the Gain function; refer to Figure 5.1.

1. Choose Process > Audio > Gain.

2. Because we want the left channel centered, put half of it into the left channel (in New Left Channel, set From Left to 50%) and half in the right channel (in New Right Channel, also set From Left to 50%).

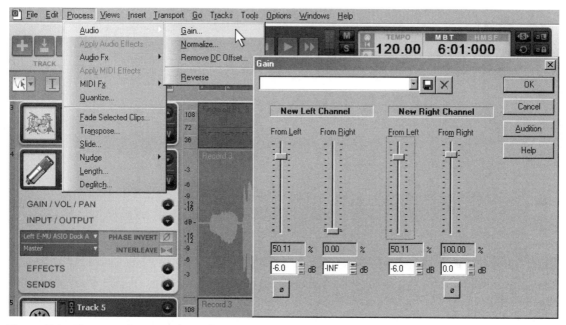

Figure 5.1 These settings use the Gain process to weight the stereo image from center to right rather than left to right.

3. For the right channel, leave From Right in the New Right Channel at 100% and at 0% in New Left Channel.

The signal is now weighted as desired.

Gain also makes it easy to swap channels. In New Left Channel, set From Left to 0% and From Right to 100%, while in New Right Channel, set From Left to 100% and From Right to 0%.

Polarity changes are more flexible with the Gain option as well. On a channel strip, you can flip the polarity (phase) for the entire track, but with Gain, you can flip polarity for the individual channels independently.

Normalize

This function raises the level of the digital audio so that the highest peak in a selected region reaches a specified percentage of the maximum possible dynamic range. Typically, signals are normalized to 100% of maximum gain, but this isn't always the case; you can normalize to any predictable level where you want peaks to hit no higher than a particular value (see Figure 5.2).

Remove DC Offset

DC offset is a phenomenon where an audio signal's 0 reference isn't really 0 but is offset by a certain voltage. There is a variety of ways this can happen, with the most common being a DC

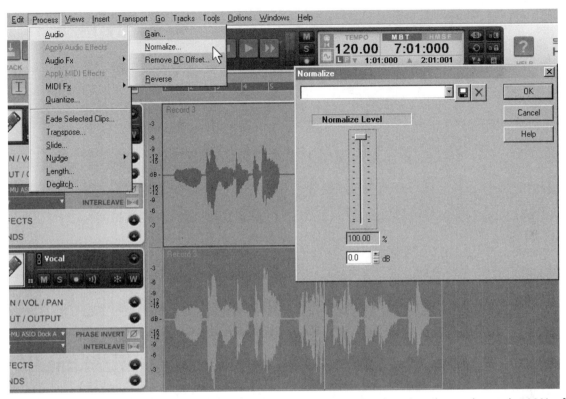

Figure 5.2   The lower audio track has been selected and normalized so that the peaks reach 100% of the maximum available headroom. The upper audio track is the same signal, but prior to normalization; note how its overall level is much lower.

voltage getting into the audio interface somehow (for example, aging coupling capacitor or small errors in high-gain preamplifier stages). This doesn't affect the audio per se, but it can reduce headroom, because one half of the waveform won't have as much headroom due to this offset. It can also throw off compressors and other processors that need to sense input levels accurately (see Figure 5.3).

Although you can see DC offset in extreme cases, it's also possible to check for smaller amounts (see Figure 5.4). With Remove DC Offset selected, click on Audition (the transport must be stopped), and the Analyze section will show the level of any offset. If it's significant, click on OK to remove (or at least minimize) any offset.

Incidentally, you might as well check Compute DC Offset from First 5 Seconds Only, because that should be enough, especially if there's some air at the beginning of the clip. This needs to be unchecked only if there's something like a digitally generated fade-in (for example, using SONAR Home Studio's Fade function) that could throw off the accuracy of any readings.

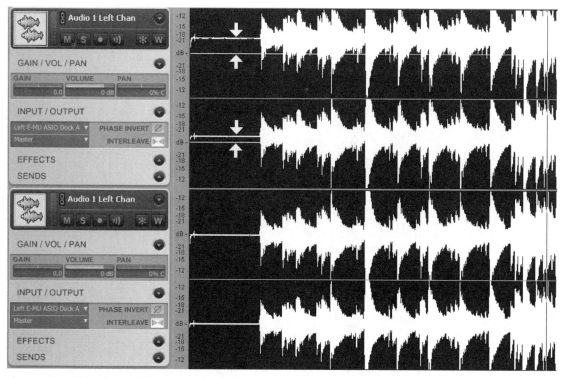

Figure 5.3   This shows the same waveform duplicated in two tracks. In the upper track, the arrows point to the offset between the signal's 0 point and the true 0 point (the centerline). In the lower track, the DC offset has been removed.

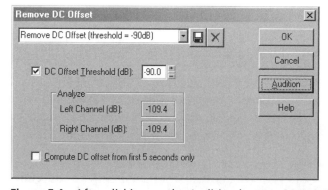

Figure 5.4   After clicking on the Audition button, SONAR Home Studio has measured a selected track's DC offset at –109.4 dB, which is so low as to be negligible. The DC Offset Threshold has been set to –90 dB, because anything below that isn't really worth worrying about.

Reverse

This has no adjustable parameters; just choose Process > Audio > Reverse to flip any selected clips so that the clip plays from end to beginning rather than beginning to end (see Figure 5.5). The Reverse function is ideal for imitating those backwards-tape effects from the "Psychedelic Sixties" or, for that matter, for creating backwards "Satanic" messages to irritate people with too much time on their hands.

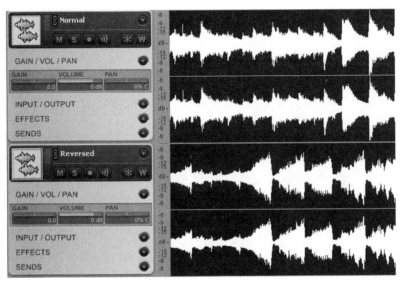

Figure 5.5 The upper track shows a typical waveform; note that the notes decay from high amplitude to low amplitude. The lower track is a reversed version, so notes attack from a low amplitude to a high amplitude.

Fade Selected Clips

This option is located seven entries down in the Process menu, in the same area as the MIDI processing options, not with the other audio processes; this is to accommodate a shortcut, as described later. Access this function by choosing Process > Fade Selected Clips.

Adding Simple Fades

The usual way to add a fade with SONAR is to drag the upper corner of a clip inward; dragging inward from the beginning creates a fade-in, and dragging inward from the end creates a fade-out. Furthermore, you can choose a linear, slow, or fast fade by right-clicking on the fade's envelope and selecting the desired curve.

The Fade Selected Clips Process menu option offers a more detailed way to create fades; here's how it works (see Figure 5.6).

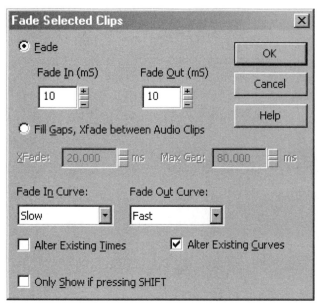

Figure 5.6 This function lets you specify fades and crossfades with extreme precision.

1. Begin by selecting the clips you want to process.

2. To add fades, click on Fade and enter a fade-in and a fade-out time. For example, if you want to add a very short fade to audio clips to make sure they start and end at zero volume and therefore avoid any clicks due to transitioning abruptly from no audio to audio (or vice versa), specify a fade time between 7 and 10 ms for the fade-in and fade-out.

3. Choose a fade-in curve and a fade-out curve. For the "de-clicking" application, you want a slow fade-in so that the signal rises slowly from zero to maximum amplitude and a fast fade-out so the signal falls rapidly from maximum amplitude to zero.

4. If fades already exist in the clip(s), check Alter Existing Times and Alter Existing Curves. This way, whatever you've specified will override whatever curves already exist. If there aren't any existing fades you don't need to check these, but I leave them checked anyway because if I'm adding a fade, I probably don't care whether any fades already existed.

5. Click on OK, and the fades are finished.

Cross-Fading Selected Clips

Fade Selected Clips can also handle crossfades between clips that have a gap between them, albeit in a limited way.

- The gap between them must be 200 ms or less.

- The amount of the crossfade must be 100 ms or less.

- Crossfades are created by extending the beginning of the clip that's later in the Timeline so that it overlaps the end of the clip that's earlier in the Timeline, and then SONAR Home Studio applies a crossfade to the overlap.

Here's how to cross-fade selected clips.

1. Select the clips to be cross-faded on each side of the gap.

2. Click on Fill Gaps, Xfade between Audio Clips instead of clicking on Fade.

3. Enter the crossfade time and the maximum gap time to be cross-faded.

4. Choose the fade-in and fade-out curves, as well as whether you want to alter existing times or curves (as we did before with fades).

5. Click on OK to complete the operation (see Figure 5.7).

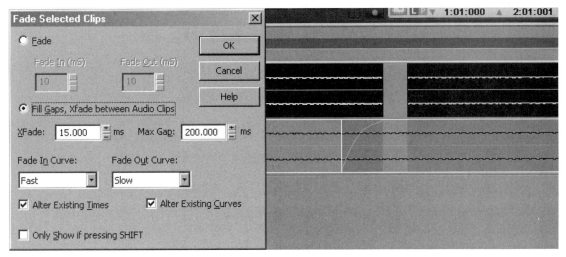

Figure 5.7   The upper track shows two clips prior to cross-fading with the Fade Selected Clips process, while the lower track shows the results of cross-fading the tracks using the parameters shown in the dialog box.

Fade Shortcut

If you check Only Show if Pressing SHIFT, then simply choosing Process > Fade Selected Clips will apply the operation to whatever clips are selected; you don't have to go through the dialog box or click on OK. If you want to see the dialog box, hold down the Shift key as you choose Process > Fade Selected.

Conventional Crossfades

Although this is not a part of the Process > Audio set of functions, as we're discussing fades this seems like an appropriate place to cover the topic of doing standard crossfades, especially because it's not all that obvious from looking at the interface.

SONAR Home Studio will automatically cross-fade two clips that overlap if you press the X key prior to overlapping one clip on another. The default crossfade is linear, but you can alter the curves by right-clicking on the crossfade curve and choosing a different curve from the pop-up menu (see Figure 5.8). If the Drag and Drop Options dialog box appears, check Blend Old with New and click on OK.

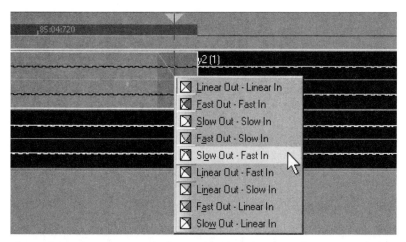

Figure 5.8 The upper track shows two clips that have been cross-faded. Right-clicking on the crossfade curve brings up a pop-up menu where you can choose one of nine crossfade curves.

Apply Audio Effects

Apply Audio Effects lets you permanently modify the files in the selected track with the associated effect(s); this option will be available if the selected audio track has at least one effect inserted in the FX bin. This is unlike using a plug-in, which modifies the file in real time while leaving the original file unchanged.

There are several reasons why you might want to modify the file permanently.

- You want to save CPU power. After applying the effect(s), you can then delete them from the FX bin.

- The effect is an essential part of the file. For example, you may have recorded a sound that lacks treble, so you use EQ to boost the treble to compensate. You don't want to use the original sound at all, so it makes sense to apply the effect.

- You're collaborating with someone who doesn't have the plug-in effect you're using or perhaps doesn't even have SONAR Home Studio. You can apply the effect to the file and then export it for sending to your collaborator.

- If you back up the WAV file, you will back up the fully processed sound—if you bring the file into another project, you won't need the plug-in.

Choose Process > Apply Audio Effects, and a dialog box will appear (see Figure 5.9).

Figure 5.9 The Apply Audio Effects dialog box gives you the option to delete the effect after applying it and apply the effect in faster than real time.

You can delete the effect(s) from the FX bin after applying the effect, which prevents any chance of having the track processed twice—once because the effect was applied to the file, and again from the effect(s) still being in the FX bin.

The Fast Bounce option means that SONAR Home Studio doesn't have to play the track in real time as it applies the effect; the applying process happens faster than real time. However, there are two main situations in which this should not be used.

- If the effect isn't part of SONAR Home Studio but is an external effect that connects to your computer via FireWire (TC PowerCore, SSL Duende, and so on), effects have to be applied in real time. This is also true for most effects based around hardware cards (for example, the effects reside in DSP chips on a PCIe card that inserts into your computer).

■ If you want to hear what's being bounced, then the operation must be in real time. If you uncheck Fast Bounce, you then have the option to check Audible Bounce so you can hear the bounce as it progresses.

Audio FX

This is a variation on the process of applying audio FX, but it lets you call up an effect and apply it to any selected audio clips in any track. Note that this effect is not in the FX bin but is called up as needed to process the selected clips. Furthermore, if the transport is stopped, you have the option to audition how the effect will affect a portion of the clip before you commit to applying it.

As to why this would be useful, suppose you have a rhythm guitar track going through much of a song, and at one point, a lead guitar comes in for a few measures on a different track. However, the two guitars interfere with each other because they're in the same frequency range. You could bring down the rhythm guitar's level, but that might be too drastic. Instead, you can split the rhythm guitar clip where the lead part enters and ends and apply a slight midrange cut to the rhythm guitar using an EQ effect so that it doesn't interfere with the lead. If the transition between the straight and processed rhythm guitar is too abrupt, you can cross-fade so that the transition happens smoothly.

To process a selected clip or clips, choose Process > Audio FX and then choose the effect you want to apply. Its user interface will appear (see Figure 5.10).

Figure 5.10   The Audio FX function lets you select an effect and apply it to multiple clips without inserting the effect into the FX bin. In this screenshot, two vocal clips are selected, and the High Frequency Exciter processor will affect both of them. Note that the clips can be anywhere in the project; they don't have to be adjacent to each other, as they are here.

Click on the Audition button with the transport stopped, and you'll hear the effect processing the clip. The section being auditioned defaults to playing the clip's first three seconds. If multiple clips are selected, the first three seconds of the clip with the leftmost (earliest) start point will be auditioned; if any part of any other selected clips on any tracks overlaps in terms of time with that section, it'll be part of the audition as well. You can change the default audition time by selecting Options > Global; toward the bottom of the General tab, choose the desired number of seconds in the Auditioning Commands for [ ] Seconds field.

For example, suppose Clip A starts at the beginning of the song, Clip B starts one second into the song, both clips are selected, and both clips are 10 seconds long. If you click on Audition, you'll hear the first three seconds of Clip A along with the second of silence before Clip B starts and then the subsequent two seconds of Clip B.

Process Menu Functions for Audio or MIDI

The following Process menu functions affect audio or MIDI, depending on which type of clip is selected. Similarly to audio events, the Process Menu MIDI functions affect any selected clips or selected portions of clips. It doesn't matter whether these are selected in the Piano Roll, Drum Grid, Event List, or Staff view—or even if you've selected a clip (or several clips) of MIDI events—invoking a MIDI editing process from the Process menu will affect any selected events, regardless of how they're selected.

As you might expect, there are some differences in the way audio and MIDI are processed.

About Quantization

Quantization moves the start of audio clips or MIDI events so that they fall exactly at a specified rhythm. For example, suppose you're triggering a closed hi-hat note via MIDI every sixteenth note, but some hits are a little early and some are a little late. Quantizing to sixteenth notes will move the hits so that they fall exactly on the nearest sixteenth note (see Figure 5.11).

Similarly, you could cut up an audio snare track to isolate each snare hit into its own clip and then quantize the clips (see Figure 5.12).

Quantization is a significant part of recording, as it can tighten up timing automatically. However, before we get into quantization from a technical standpoint, it's important to think about some of the musical ramifications.

While turning rhythms into perfect rhythms might seem like a good idea, musicians often play "around" the beat and don't always play with metronomic precision. One of rock's best drummers, Led Zeppelin's John Bonham, tended to hit the kick precisely on the beat but hit the snare just a little bit late, which gave the drums more "space." If someone had quantized John Bonham's snare so it hit exactly on the beat, he would have sounded like a boring drum machine, not the great drummer he was.

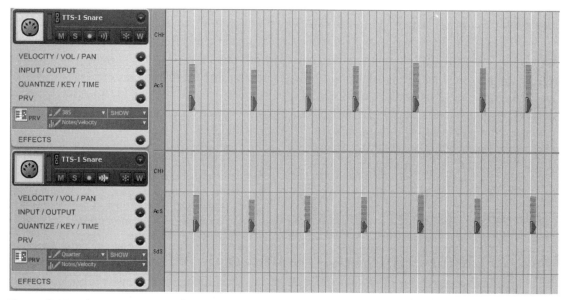

Figure 5.11   The MIDI notes in the upper track are quite a bit off the correct rhythm. These same notes are quantized to the nearest sixteenth note in the lower track.

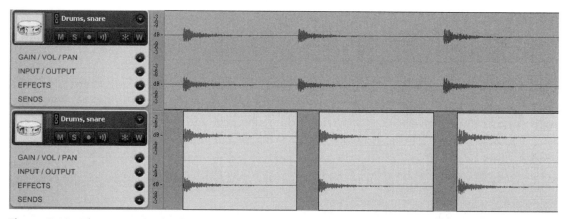

Figure 5.12   The snares in the lower track are isolated clips from the upper track, which were then quantized to eighth notes.

On the other hand, groups such as Kraftwerk (who pretty much invented electro music) aim for a really tight, machine-like rhythm. For them, having drums hit precisely on the beat is part of what the music is all about.

The point of all this is that quantization is an option, not a necessity. Don't automatically quantize something if it doesn't sound like there's anything wrong with the rhythm; quantize if there's a problem with the rhythm or if quantization is essential to the musical genre—otherwise, leave well enough alone. But also, note that SONAR Home Studio has ways to make quantization less rigid (and of course, we'll cover these methods), and as a result, sometimes you can get the best of both worlds: a tight rhythm that nonetheless retains a human feel.

To hear the results of quantization, SONAR Home Studio's Quantize dialog box incorporates a convenient Audition button. This lets you hear the results of your quantization settings before you click on OK.

It's also worth noting that the Quantize menu defaults to quantizing note durations (not just note starts) to the nearest rhythmic value and also quantizes only notes, lyrics, and audio—not controllers and other data. This may not be what you want, and if it isn't, you'll be happy to know that you can save quantization presets.

Quantize

Select the clip(s) you want to quantize and then choose Process > Quantize. The Quantize dialog box will appear (see Figure 5.13). Let's look at the various options.

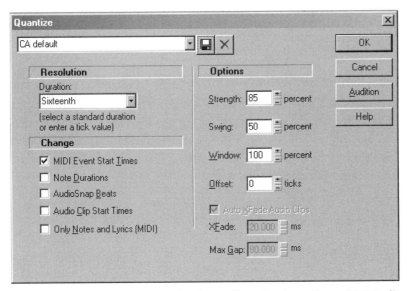

Figure 5.13 The Quantize dialog box affects both audio and MIDI clips, but some functions apply to only one or the other.

Resolution

Resolution is the most fundamental quantize parameter and sets the resolution of the rhythmic grid to which events will be quantized; the range is from whole notes to thirty-second dotted note values. Generally, you want to use the lowest resolution for a given part. For example, if a snare part hits on eighth notes, there's no point in using sixteenth-note resolution because the snare might shift to the nearest sixteenth note instead of the nearest eighth note; unless the sixteenth note falls on an eighth note, the snare will be off. On the other hand, if the snare hits on eighth notes but there's also a sixteenth-note roll, then you'll need to use sixteenth-note resolution.

Change

This section chooses what the quantize operation will affect. These options are pretty self-explanatory, with a few exceptions.

- There's no point in checking AudioSnap Beats because that functionality is not present in SONAR Home Studio.

- You can select audio and MIDI clips and then quantize the start times of both simultaneously by checking MIDI Event Start Times and Audio Clip Start Times.

- If MIDI Event Start Times is checked, all MIDI events (including controllers, program changes, and so on) will be quantized. If you only want to quantize notes, in addition to checking MIDI Event Start Times also check Only Notes and Lyrics.

- Checking Note Durations quantizes MIDI note durations to the quantize resolution value. This can be done in conjunction with quantizing MIDI start times, or it can be done independently.

Options

Strength is my favorite quantize option because it moves notes a certain percentage closer to the beat. Thus, if your playing is basically okay but isn't quite as tight as you'd like, this option tightens it up without getting metronomic. The Strength parameter in the Quantize dialog sets how much closer the notes move each time you apply quantization. (I usually set this to 50%.) When quantizing, I usually just invoke quantizing once to move the notes 50% closer to the rhythmic grid, and if that doesn't sound tight enough, I apply it again to move the notes another 50% closer. (Twice is usually enough.) The result is a track that sounds rhythmically correct but retains most of a performance's feel. If I don't want to take the time to do successive quantizations, I use a preset with 85% strength, which works well most of the time.

For example, if a note is 12 ticks ahead of the beat, quantizing with 100% strength will move it right on the beat. Quantizing it with 50% strength moves it halfway toward the beat, or six ticks ahead. Quantizing with 66% strength would move it two-thirds closer to the beat, so it would end up four ticks ahead of the beat.

The Swing function affects the timing of pairs of equal-value notes. Each note normally defaults to taking up 50% of the total duration of both notes; adding swing lengthens the first note of the pair, and to keep the total duration of both notes the same, shortens the second note of the pair. This imparts the kind of feel found in shuffles, some jazz tunes, and a lot of hip-hop.

With the Window option, notes that are farther away from the quantize grid than the percentage specified here will not be moved. For example, if you set Window to 100% and quarter-note resolution, the "window" extends 50% later than the quarter note and 50% earlier (100% total). Thus, all notes are quantized. If you specify 50%, then the window extends 25% later than the quarter note and 25% earlier. I usually just leave this at 100%.

Offset slides quantized events forward or backward by a certain number of ticks. For example, you could quantize a hi-hat part to sixteenth notes but add an offset of –20 ticks to move the notes slightly ahead of the beat. (Negative values offset the events earlier in time, while positive values offset events later in time.) See the section on the Slide function for more information on how to use this from a musical standpoint.

Auto XFade Audio Clips will be available only if Audio Clip Start Times is checked, and it automatically adds a crossfade if quantizing an audio clip causes it to overlap with another clip. However, the crossfade won't be applied if the gap between the two clips in the unquantized state exceeds the number of milliseconds entered for the Maximum Gap parameter, whose maximum value can't exceed 200 ms. Also, if the XFade time is greater than the area that overlaps, the crossfade will not be applied.

Transpose

Choosing Process > Transpose chooses the Transpose dialog box, which allows transposing MIDI clips up or down a maximum of 127 semitones by changing MIDI note numbers and/ or audio up or down a maximum of 12 semitones (one octave) via audio pitch-shifting techniques. With audio, although the dialog box lets you enter values higher than 12 semitones (which may be necessary if you're transposing both audio and MIDI data simultaneously), the amount "wraps around"—in other words, if you select +13 semitones, the audio clip is transposed up +1 semitone. MIDI has no such restrictions, but there are a few other rules regarding transposition (see Figure 5.14).

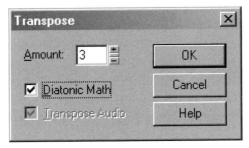

Figure 5.14 The Transpose dialog box specifies the amount of transposition in semitones but also allows transposing MIDI clips according to diatonic math.

■ If only MIDI clips are selected, there's a check box for Diatonic Math. Checking this constrains transposed notes to fit within the original key signature. For example, if you transpose a MIDI part in the key of C major by +1 semitone, the E will only transpose a half-step up to F, because F# is not part of the C major scale.

- If only audio clips are selected, check Transpose Audio, or the audio clips won't transpose.

- If both MIDI and audio clips are selected, check Transpose Audio but note that you won't have the option to transpose MIDI notes diatonically.

Slide

Choose Process > Slide to open the Slide dialog box (see Figure 5.15), which lets you slide audio or MIDI clips earlier or later on the Timeline.

Figure 5.15   The Slide function gives a great deal of control over shifting events forward or backward in time.

How Slide Can "Humanize" MIDI and Audio Sequences

Before describing how to use Slide, let's explain why you'd want to use it. Timing is everything, and that's especially true with music; yet as previously noted with quantization, mathematically perfect timing is most certainly not everything; otherwise, drum machines would have replaced drummers a long time ago. When working with MIDI, musicians and engineers often forget about the importance of timing changes and quantize everything. This can suck the life out of a piece of music—good drummers enhance music by subtly speeding up or slowing down to change a tune's "feel" and leading or lagging specific beats to push a tune or make it lay back a bit more in the groove.

Often, these time changes ahead of or behind the beat are very small; even a few milliseconds can make a difference. This may be surprising, as sound itself moves at about 1 foot per second, so a 6-ms change theoretically affects a track about as much as moving 6 feet farther away from the drummer. Yet once you start experimenting with timing shifts, it becomes obvious that even very small timing differences can change a tune's groove when you hear these changes in comparison to a relatively steady beat. For example, jazz drummers tend to hit a ride cymbal's bell a bit ahead of the beat to "push" a song. Rock drummers sometimes hit the snare behind the beat for a big sound. Of course, the sound isn't really bigger; but our brain interprets slight delays as indicating a big space, because in a big space, sound travels a while through the air before it reaches us, thus delaying the sound somewhat.

Applying Slide

The Slide dialog box lets you shift the MIDI or audio clip by measures, ticks, seconds, or frames. A negative number shifts the clip left (earlier); otherwise, the clip shifts to the right (later). You can shift only events by checking Events in Tracks, only Markers by checking Markers, or both by checking both boxes. If a marker indicates a specific place in the clip you're shifting, make sure you check both boxes.

Specific Timing Tricks

Here are some musical ways to use Slide.

- Keep the kick drum on the beat as a reference and use track shifting to change the timing of the snare, toms, and percussion by a few milliseconds to alter the feel.

- For techno, dance, and acid jazz tunes, try moving any double-time percussion parts (shaker, tambourine, and so on) a little bit ahead of the beat to give a faster feel.

- Sometimes it pays to shift individual notes rather than an entire track. With tom fills, delay each subsequent note of the fill a bit more (for example, the first note of the fill is on the beat, the second note approximately 2 ms after the beat, the third note 4 to 5 ms after the beat, the fourth note 6 to 8 ms after the beat, and so on until the last note ends up about 20 ms behind the beat). This can make a tom fill sound gigantic.

- If two percussion sounds often hit on the same beat in a rhythm pattern, try sliding one part ahead or behind the beat by a small amount (a few ms) to keep the parts from interfering with each other.

- Track shifting does not apply only to drum parts. Suppose there are two fairly staccato harmony lines in a tune. If you advance one by 5 ms and delay the other by 5 ms, the two parts will become more separate and distinct instead of sounding like one combined part. If the parts are panned opposite in the stereo field, the field will appear even wider.

- Hitting a crash cymbal a bit ahead of the beat makes it really stand out. Moving it behind the beat (later) meshes it more with the track.

Nudge

By choosing Process > Nudge, you can select an audio or MIDI clip (or of course, Ctrl-click to select multiple clips) and "nudge" it forward or backward in time by any one of three specified amounts. There are also nudge up and down options, which transpose notes up or down one semitone at a time and/or clips up or down one track at a time.

This may not seem too terribly useful, because there are plenty of ways to move clips around—from clicking and dragging to using the Slide feature we just covered. But once you start using Nudge, you'll likely find it very convenient.

One Nudge application is adding the same "feel"-type effects you'd add with Slide, but with less mouse-clicking. In addition, setting up a sixteenth-note Nudge is useful when experimenting with percussion parts, because changing a clip's offset can give an entirely different feel. Nudge is also essential for trimming out delays, as described in Chapter 23, "Recording Guitar with SONAR Home Studio."

Setting Nudge Presets

Three of the Nudge options are editable under Options > Global (or by choosing Process > Nudge > Settings); see Figure 5.16.

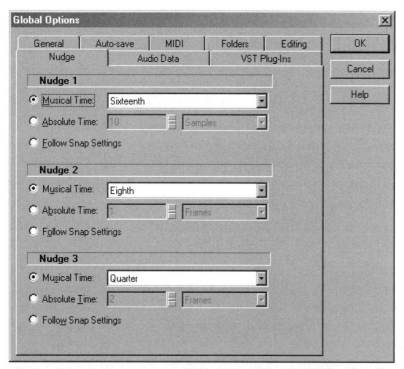

Figure 5.16 This dialog box is where you set up the Nudge presets. The three are set to sixteenth-, eighth-, and quarter-note Nudge amounts.

For each Nudge option you can specify a time increment as musical time (rhythmic note values) or as absolute time (seconds, milliseconds, frames, samples, and ticks), or you can have the nudged clip (or notes within Piano Roll view) follow Snap settings. One cool feature is that Nudge remembers the last selected value for both musical time and absolute time, so whenever you select either one, it will default to whatever you used last.

Using Nudge

Select Process > Nudge and then choose which of the three Nudge options you want to use and whether you want to nudge left or right or up or down (see Figure 5.17).

Figure 5.17   You can choose the Nudge amount from a menu, but keyboard equivalents are a lot faster.

Power users will prefer the keyboard shortcuts, which are based on the numeric keypad and logically laid out. You can see the shortcuts spelled out next to the Nudge choices in Figure 5.17.

Length

Length can stretch or shrink an audio or MIDI clip or selected MIDI notes. With MIDI clips, changing the length can shorten or lengthen the individual notes within the clip or the total length of the clip itself. With audio, SONAR Home Studio uses sophisticated signal processing to stretch or shrink the audio itself.

Select Process > Length to call up the Length dialog box (see Figure 5.18).

MIDI Clip Length Processes

■   To change only the length of MIDI notes, check Duration, leave the other boxes unchecked, and choose the desired percentage of change.

Figure 5.18 The Length function works on audio and MIDI clips. In this screenshot, the upper two clips are identical to the lower two clips, except that the length of the lower clips has been shrunk by 50%.

- To change a MIDI clip's total length but leave the individual notes the same duration, check Start Time, leave the other boxes unchecked, and choose the percentage of change for the clip length.

- To change a MIDI clip's total length and change the individual notes correspondingly (for example, shortening a clip by 20% also shortens its notes by 20%), check Start Times and Durations (without checking Stretch Audio) and then specify the desired percentage of change.

You can apply these to selected parts of MIDI clips (for example, by Alt-dragging over the area you want to select in the Timeline), not just the entire clip. However, if you shorten the selection's length, the length of the selection will be shorter, but the rest of the clip won't "close up" to fill in the space (see Figure 5.19).

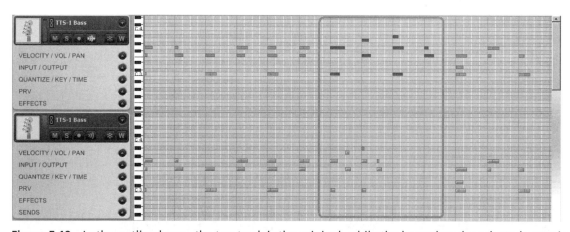

Figure 5.19 In the outlined area, the top track is the original, while the lower has the selected notes in the upper track shrunk by 50%. Note how this leaves an empty space where notes used to be.

If you lengthen a selection instead of shrink it, the selection will expand out to the right of the selection and overlap any existing notes.

Audio Clip Length Processes

With audio clips, you can change only the clip duration but not the audio by cutting off or extending the end; however, because this doesn't affect the pitch or duration of audio within the clip, it's easier just to slip edit the length by dragging the right edge inward or outward. (For the record, you do this with the Length command by checking Start Time and nothing else and then specifying the percentage by which you want to shorten or extend the length.)

More commonly, you'll want the audio to shrink or expand with the clip length. To do this, check Durations and Stretch Audio, but don't check Start Times. Specify the desired percentage, and the audio will change to match the new clip length. However, note that bigger changes degrade the audio quality more than smaller changes.

MIDI-Only Process Menu Functions

As with audio events, the Process Menu MIDI functions affect any selected clips or selected portions of clips.

Apply MIDI Effects

If the selected MIDI track has at least one MIDI effect inserted in the FX bin, this option will be available and will let you permanently modify the files in the selected track with the associated effect(s). This is unlike using a plug-in, which modifies the file in real time while leaving the original file unchanged.

Choose Process > Apply MIDI Effects, and a dialog box will appear (see Figure 5.20).

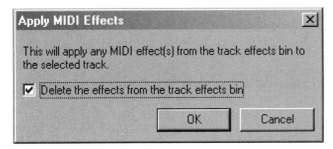

Figure 5.20 The Apply MIDI Effects dialog box gives you the option to delete the effect from the effects bin after it's been applied to the selected clip or part of a clip.

As with applying audio effects, you can delete the effect(s) from the FX bin after applying the effect so the track isn't processed again after processing has already been applied to the clip.

MIDI FX

This is like applying MIDI FX, but you can call up a MIDI effect and apply it to any selected audio clips in any track. As with processing audio with the Process menu, the MIDI FX is not in the FX bin but is called up as needed to process the selected clips. Also as with the audio equivalent, there's an Audition button so you can hear a bit of what the effect does before committing to applying it.

To process a selected clip or clips, select Process > MIDI FX and then choose the effect you want to apply. (For more information on what various MIDI effects do, see Chapter 11, "MIDI Plug-Ins.") Click on the Audition button, and if the transport is stopped, you'll hear the effect processing the clip. The section being audited will be approximately the first three seconds of the clip, unless the default audition time was changed. (Edit this time on the General tab under Options > Global.) If multiple clips are selected, auditioning follows the same protocol as for audio effects—the first three seconds (or whatever default audition time is in effect) of the clip with the leftmost start point will be auditioned.

Deglitch

This might as well be called "the MIDI Guitarist's Friend," but it has other uses as well. When you choose Process > Deglitch, a dialog box will appear that lets you remove notes meeting particular characteristics from selected MIDI clips or portions of MIDI clips (see Figure 5.21). Here are characteristics you can edit; checking multiple boxes means that a note needs to meet all the specified characteristics.

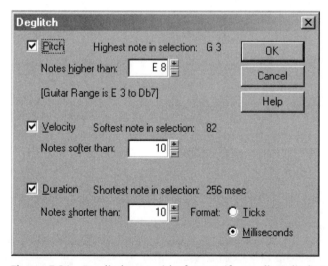

Figure 5.21   Deglitch gets rid of most, if not all, "glitchy" notes with a few mouse clicks.

Pitch. The dialog box shows the pitch of the highest note in the selected MIDI notes. You can choose to remove any notes higher than this pitch or any other pitch you specify.

Velocity. Sometimes you'll brush against a keyboard key or a MIDI guitar fret and generate a very low-velocity note. If you remove all notes with a velocity lower than 10, you'll almost certainly be removing notes you didn't intend to play. Sometimes you'll need to increase this value to get rid of all unintended notes.

Duration. These unintended notes may also be of extremely short duration—so short you wouldn't notice them on a Piano Roll view unless it was really zoomed in—but these short-duration notes can sometimes create havoc by cutting off the start of a note you intended to play. Here you can specify a minimum duration in ticks or milliseconds for notes to be removed.

As a practical example of how to use this, if you're a MIDI guitarist, you would typically check Velocity (with a velocity value around 10 to 20) and Duration (with a time value of 10 to 20 ms). Thus, any notes with a velocity lower than the minimum amount, with a duration shorter than the minimum time, would be deleted.

6 MIDI Basics

Unleashed on the world back in 1983, amid choruses of "it's just a passing fancy," MIDI (*Musical Instrument Digital Interface*) recording—based on recording and playing back data instead of audio—looked as if it was on the wane in the '90s, as hard disk audio recording became the main focus of recording. But with the advent of plug-in virtual instruments, MIDI has gained new life as the protocol used to trigger software synthesizers.

As a result, we're in the unusual position of having MIDI be something new and different to people who weren't even alive when it was born. So before getting into SONAR Home Studio–specific aspects of editing MIDI and creating satisfying MIDI performances, this chapter investigates some of the most important highlights of this protocol and how it relates to today's recording world.

But first of all, don't let the term "Musical Instrument Digital Interface" throw you; just remember that the key word is "interface." MIDI's main purpose is to allow musical machines to communicate musical data to each other, such as which note is being played, how hard you hit the key playing that note, which footswitch is being pressed, and so on. Stripped to its basics, you can think of MIDI as a catch-all name for the process of sending control messages from one device (such as a footswitch, keyboard, sequencer, and so on) to another device (for example, a synthesizer). This can happen over a physical cable or within a computer.

How MIDI Recording Works

MIDI is a special-purpose computer language devoted to music. This language expresses various aspects of a musical performance, such as the notes that are played, their dynamics, and more.

For example, suppose you have a physical keyboard synthesizer that supports MIDI. The first thing it has to do is hook into a MIDI interface that communicates with your computer; otherwise, SONAR Home Studio won't see the MIDI data. There are two main types of interface. One includes physical MIDI In and Out connectors that hook up to hardware MIDI devices, such as keyboards and drum machines. For example, you would send a keyboard's MIDI output that sends MIDI data through a physical cable that patches to an interface's MIDI In, which receives that data (see Figure 6.1).

Figure 6.1 Tapco's LINK.midi 4x4 is a typical dedicated MIDI interface for computers, with four MIDI inputs and four MIDI outputs. If you patch a keyboard's MIDI Out to the interface's MIDI In, the keyboard data can travel through the interface to your computer.

In addition to MIDI In and Out connectors, you'll sometimes see a MIDI Thru connector as well. This retransmits the incoming data at the MIDI In, which you can then feed to another MIDI-compatible device. So, for example, a master keyboard can feed one sound generator, and the sound generator's MIDI Thru can feed another sound generator's MIDI In. This allows the keyboard to control two sound generators.

Some devices dispense with physical connectors and hook into your computer via USB (or more rarely, FireWire). MIDI data is sent and received over the USB line, so you don't need a special MIDI interface as long as your computer has a spare USB port. For example, Line 6's KB37 (see Figure 6.2) is a combination keyboard/audio interface with a USB port. MIDI data from the keyboard travels over USB into the computer.

Figure 6.2 Line 6, Cakewalk, and many other companies make MIDI controllers that connect directly to your computer via USB, thus eliminating the need for traditional five-pin MIDI connectors.

The kind of MIDI data a keyboard produces relates to what you play on the keyboard. If you play a C#4 note, then a piece of data will exit the MIDI Out that says the computer equivalent of, "A C#4 has just been played." When you release the note, another piece of data will say "C#4 has just been released." If you hit the note really hard or really softly, another piece of data will indicate those dynamics.

You can record this string of data into SONAR Home Studio. If you play this data back into your keyboard synthesizer, it will reproduce the performance exactly as you performed it. This is very much like a modern version of the player piano, except instead of punching holes into paper, you're "punching" data into a SONAR Home Studio track.

The MIDI protocol is about far more than just notes, though. As described later, there are also commands that relate to timing, synchronization, changing sounds, altering effects parameters, and more.

Advantages of Recording MIDI Data Instead of Audio

If you have a synthesizer, why not just record its audio into SONAR Home Studio? You certainly can, but there are several advantages to recording MIDI data.

The primary advantage is editability. You can change a MIDI note's pitch, dynamics, start time—almost any aspect of the note. This makes it very easy to correct mistakes; if you hit a couple wrong notes, just change the pitch. It's very difficult to do something like change one note inside a chord when dealing with audio, but with MIDI, it's easy. What's more, with SONAR Home Studio you can do this graphically by just, say, grabbing a note and extending its length or moving it up or down on a grid to change pitch. However, if you want to geek out and edit with a great deal of precision, you can get a numeric list of all data associated with a note and type in new values. The next chapter is about MIDI editing, so I won't dwell on the different editing options here.

Another advantage is being able to change an instrument's sound, because all you need to do to change the sound is send the MIDI data to a different instrument. And when you're writing a song, MIDI-driven tracks handle pitch transposition and tempo changes far better than digital audio can, because you're just changing the data being fed to notes—not the timbral quality of the notes themselves. (Granted, DSP-based pitch stretching is getting pretty clean, to the point where with small changes, you might not even notice any difference. But MIDI is still better.)

As a result, using MIDI instruments is great when you're writing a song and it begins to take shape. You can experiment with different keys and tempos without having to re-record or stretch anything—just invoke the pitch transposition and tempo change options if needed. After the song has settled down, you can then replace the MIDI scratch tracks with digital audio tracks from piano, guitar, and so on. Then again, with virtual instruments sounding so good these days, maybe all you'll really need to do is tweak the MIDI instrument tracks a bit.

The MIDI Language

MIDI groups information in multi-byte "sentences" or "messages" of one or more "words." There are two types of MIDI words:

- Status words (which identify a particular function, such as note on, note off, pitch wheel change, and so on)

- Data words (which give data on the function identified by the status word, such as *which* note is on and *how much* the pitch wheel has changed)

We don't really need to investigate this further; many readers will likely be familiar with MIDI, and beginners can check out any of several references on MIDI. Besides, you can use MIDI without knowing the nuts and bolts—just like you can drive a car without knowing how fuel injection works.

However, we do need to cover one more crucial concept before proceeding: MIDI channels and MIDI modes. MIDI can send and receive data over 16 different virtual channels; each channel can carry unique data and drive its own polyphonic MIDI instrument. In the case of SONAR Home Studio sending data to a physical keyboard over MIDI, you might wonder how MIDI can transmit 16 different channels over a single MIDI cable—after all, to send 16 different audio signals somewhere, you would need 16 different audio cables.

But remember that MIDI transmits *information,* not audio. Also, it sends this data serially—in other words, each individual piece of information is sent consecutively. If we tag each piece of data with a channel identification number (ID), then we can program a particular MIDI instrument to look only for data that has a particular channel ID.

A good analogy would be sorting mail by ZIP code. Imagine a conveyor belt where each piece of mail goes past a mail sorter, one piece of mail at a time. As each letter goes by, it's scanned for its ZIP code, and letters are sorted into individual piles according to their ZIP codes. MIDI works similarly. Each instrument monitors the MIDI data stream (analogous to the mail going past on the conveyor belt), and when an instrument detects data with the same channel ID number as the channel for which the instrument is programmed, it acts on that information. For example, if a note-on message is sent over Channel 1, only those synthesizers tuned to Channel 1 will receive this note-on command; devices tuned to other channels will ignore the data. This situation is also analogous to a television, which selects a particular channel for viewing out of the many signals coming down the antenna or cable line.

One of the great aspects of SONAR Home Studio is that it can load virtual software instruments that react the same way as a physical instrument. As with physical instruments, you can assign these to particular channels and have particular SONAR Home Studio tracks send data to specific instruments. What's more, some instruments—such as the TTS-1—can receive information relating to more than one channel, known as *multi-timbral* operation. For example, the TTS-1 might have a piano sound loaded in Channel 1, a bass sound in Channel 2, a brass section in Channel 3, and so on. This allows a signal instrument to produce a variety of sounds.

Virtual instruments have evolved so much that some musicians don't even buy physical synthesizers anymore; they just get a keyboard controller that produces MIDI data but no sounds, and they use that to trigger virtual instruments.

In addition to channel data, there are two main MIDI *modes* that determine how devices respond to channelized data.

- Omni mode accepts data coming in over *any* channel. In other words, regardless of the channel ID, an instrument or track in Omni mode will attempt to act on *any* incoming data. This is handy if your MIDI keyboard transmits over a specific channel and you want it to trigger a synth, but you can't remember the channel it's transmitting on. Rather than dig into the synth assignments, you can just set the synth to Omni mode, and it will react to whatever the keyboard is transmitting.

- A receiver in poly mode will be set to one of the 16 MIDI channels and receive only messages intended for that channel. Thus, two MIDI receivers set to receive different channels could be monitoring the same data stream but could be controlled independently of each other. For example, with the TTS-1, Channel 10 might be assigned to drums and Channel 1 to piano. If a SONAR Home Studio track outputs on Channel 1, its data will trigger piano sounds. But if you change the output to Channel 10, its data will trigger drum sounds.

MIDI Ports

When MIDI was invented, hardware synthesizers were expensive and relatively large, so 16 channels seemed like a reasonable number—those who could afford 16 synthesizers, let alone actually use them, were in a distinct minority. However, it became clear this wasn't enough when multi-timbral synths were introduced, because they could accept data over all 16 channels.

As a result, interfaces were introduced with several MIDI ports, each of which could carry 16 channels. For example, an interface with four ports could deliver data on $4 \times 16 = 64$ MIDI channels. This became increasingly important as MIDI was expanded to do more than just play synthesizers, such as trigger lighting, change signal processor sounds, and even set off pyrotechnics (really!).

Program Changes

So far we've talked primarily about MIDI note messages, but there are many other types of MIDI data. For example, program changes allow you to change an instrument sound (and sometimes multi-effects presets, too) on the fly, even in the middle of a phrase if necessary. This, of course, assumes the target device responds to program changes. When the MIDI spec was drawn up, provisions were made for 128 MIDI program change messages. This is why many signal processors offer 128 programs. As usual, people wanted more—so now an addition to the MIDI spec, bank select messages, can select up to 16,384 banks of 128 programs, for a grand total of more than 2,000,000 programs. (That should hold you for a while.)

For example, suppose you're adding percussion to a song, and you want tambourine in one section and shaker in another. Instead of inserting two instruments on two tracks, you can just insert one and use program changes to determine when the instrument plays back a tambourine sound and when it plays back a shaker sound.

MIDI Controllers: The Key to Greater Expressiveness

Changing from one program to another is a good start, but sometimes you'd like to vary a particular parameter within an individual program (delay feedback, filter frequency, distortion drive, and so on). A wah-wah sound is a good example of changing a particular parameter (filter frequency) in real time, and thankfully, the powers behind MIDI recognized early on that just playing notes was b-o-r-i-n-g—and thus controller messages became part of the MIDI specification. Think about what happens when you play an acoustic instrument: There's incredible complexity to the sound—whether it's a vibrating string or a blown reed—that changes over time according to performance gestures. Hitting a string or a drum head harder doesn't just make it louder, but it often increases brightness and alters pitch slightly.

The idea of *continuous controllers* came about because synthesizers have pedals, knobs, levers, and other physical "controllers" that alter some aspect of a synth's sound over a continuous range of values. (This is why they're called *continuous controllers,* as opposed to a controller such as an on-off switch, which only selects between two possible values; see Figure 6.3.) Non-keyboard musicians can use other controllers, such as foot pedals or data entered into a sequencer, to alter some aspect of a signal processor's sound.

Figure 6.3   Roland's Fantom-G synthesizer has (among other controllers) eight sliders and, above them, four knobs. While these can alter synthesizer parameters, they also generate MIDI continuous controller messages you can record into SONAR Home Studio and apply to anything you'd like. For example, you might want a slider to control the volume of a virtual synthesizer.

Unlike a program change, which is a single event, continuous controllers generate a series of events, such as a volume fade-in (each event raises the volume a bit more than the previous event) or a change in some other parameter (for example, increasing chorus depth or altering the wah-wah filter frequency).

Like program changes, continuous controller messages are transmitted over a MIDI output and received by a MIDI input. The transmitter usually digitizes the physical controller motion into 128 discrete values (0–127). As one example, consider a foot pedal that generates continuous controller messages. Pulling the pedal all the way back typically generates a value of 0. Pushing down on the pedal increases the value until at midpoint, the pedal generates a value of 64. Continuing to push on the pedal until it's all the way down generates a value of 127 (see Figure 6.4).

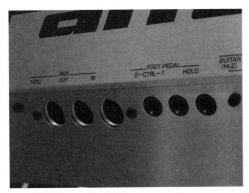

Figure 6.4   The rear of the Fantom-G not only includes MIDI connectors (on the left), but also jacks for two control pedals and a hold footswitch.

Note that continuous controller transmitters only send messages reflecting a change; for example, leaving a pedal in one position doesn't transmit any messages until you change the pedal's physical position.

Continuous Controller Numbers

MIDI "tags" each continuous controller message with an ID from 0 to 127. Don't confuse this with channel IDs; each channel can support up to 128 controllers, so something like a Controller 7 message appearing over Channel 2 is independent from a Controller 7 message appearing over Channel 3. Therefore, a signal processor with 100 different parameters could have each assigned to a unique controller number (1 for reverb first reflection time, 2 for reverb high-frequency decay, 3 for reverb low-frequency decay, and so on).

When controlling a parameter via continuous controllers, the basic idea is to assign a particular parameter (echo mix, filter cutoff, envelope attack, and so on) to a particular continuous controller number. Then all you need is to record continuous controller messages in the track driving the target parameter.

At the receiving end, the parameter being controlled changes in response to incoming message values. For example, if you're controlling filter cutoff and it receives a value of 0, the cutoff frequency is at minimum. When it receives a value of 64, the cutoff might be halfway up, and upon receiving a value of 127, the cutoff might be up all the way. The reason for saying "might be" is that some signal processors let you scale and/or invert the values, as explained later, in the "How Parameters Handle Controller Value Changes" section.

Here are some other examples. If a device's level parameter is assigned to Controller 7, and a foot pedal can generate Controller 7, hook the pedal's MIDI Out to the device's MIDI In, and your pedal will control level (provided that both are set to the same channel, of course). If you assign the chorus depth parameter to Controller 12 and then set the pedal to generate Controller 12 data, the pedal will vary chorus depth.

In many cases, you can assign several parameters to the *same* controller number so that, for example, a single pedal motion could increase the level *and* reverberation time *and* raise the filter cutoff frequency.

Other Control Message Options

In addition to responding to continuous controllers, some synths and effects respond to other MIDI control messages. None of these has a controller number, because each is deemed important enough to be its own distinct class of message.

- **Pitch bend.** Most synthesizers have some type of modulation wheel or lever that allows for bending note pitch (like bending a string; see Figure 6.5).

Figure 6.5   The Fantom-G has a combined pitch bend level and modulation trigger, shown here toward the bottom of the picture. There are also two general-purpose switches—for example, hitting one might add in another sound.

- **Velocity.** This indicates the dynamics of playing a keyboard by measuring how long it takes for a key to go from full up to full down. The assumption is that the longer it takes for a key to go down, the more softly it's being played.

- **Pressure (also called aftertouch).** After a keyboard key is down, pressing on the key produces an additional pressure message. A common application is to use this to introduce vibrato to a sound that's being sustained or to change a sound's tone (for example, to make it brighter).

How Parameters Handle Controller Value Changes

There are several ways that differing virtual instruments and processors decide how continuous controllers will take over from a preprogrammed setting. One approach is to add to (or subtract from) the programmed setting; usually scaling and inversion parameters will be available.

Scaling determines how far the parameter can vary from the programmed setting in response to a given amount of controller change. Inversion sets whether increasing controller values will increase (+ scaling) or decrease (– scaling) the parameter value. Often these are combined into one number, such as +50 (which represents 50-percent scaling of full value in a positive direction), –37 (37-percent scaling of full value in a negative direction), and so on.

Figure 6.6 shows an example of an input control signal scaled to +100, +50, and –100. Each one covers a different range of the available parameter values. Greater controller amplitudes increase or decrease the programmed parameter value, depending on whether the polarity is positive (+) or inverted (–).

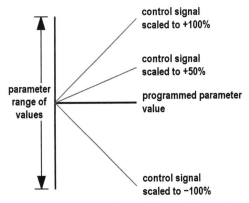

Figure 6.6   Controller scaling and inversion affect the degree to which the receiver responds to continuous controller messages.

If you encounter a situation in which the continuous controller messages don't change a parameter very much, check the programmed value of the parameter being controlled. If its value is close to minimum or maximum, there may not be enough headroom for the controller to make much difference, especially with scaling close to 100 percent.

Another design approach is to simply have the parameter follow the incoming controller value. An incoming controller value of 0 would set the parameter to its minimum value, and an incoming controller value of 127 would set the parameter to its maximum.

Yet another method will not let parameters respond to continuous controllers until the controller passes through the preprogrammed value, at which point the parameter follows the controller messages. This is helpful when switching between programs where a controller is programmed to control different parameters. The parameter will stay as originally programmed until you start using the pedal and go past the existing setting.

Summary: Assigning Continuous Controllers in a Nutshell

To recap, here's how to assign controllers. We'll use a keyboard's mod wheel as an example of a typical transmitter, but the same concepts apply to controller data in a SONAR Home Studio sequencer track or even something like a foot pedal.

1. Set the mod wheel to the same MIDI channel (1–16) as the target parameter you want to control.

2. Assign the parameter you want to control to the desired controller number. The mod wheel controller number is fixed as Controller 1, so you'd set the parameter to respond to Controller 1.

3. If we weren't using the mod wheel, but some other nonstandardized hardware controller, you'd need to program the hardware controller to the controller number that matches what you programmed in the previous step.

4. Adjust the controller amplitude (how much the sound is affected when you move the controller) and scaling (whether increasing the controller's position increases or decreases the parameter value).

MIDI and Tempo

One of the advantages of MIDI recording is that it's easy to change tempo. Standard digital audio tracks cannot easily follow tempo changes, because that requires stretching the audio on-the-fly so that it speeds up and slows down in tandem with the tempo changes. However, Groove Clips and MIDI tracks can follow pretty much any tempo changes you throw at them, with MIDI data being particularly adaptable to tempo changes.

Musicians generally set a project's tempo to the desired beat and then just let it sit there. But that's not the way real music works; even though pop music doesn't change tempo as much as classical pieces, real drummers insert subtle tempo changes, inserted over several measures or just in selected parts of individual measures, to build anticipation and change moods.

SONAR Home Studio lets you draw in tempo changes. Select View > Tempo, and you'll find familiar tools: a pencil for drawing in the changes, the ability to snap changes, zoom, etc. (Figure 6.7). You'll likely want to zoom way in on the vertical axis so you can do subtle tempo changes.

Because tempo track changes can have a powerful effect on a song, I sometimes set up a rhythm track using MIDI and tweak the tempo as desired. I can then record digital audio parts, like vocal and guitar, over that because the tempo changes are already in place, so the audio tracks go on top of those tempo changes—just like recording vocals over a drummer who speeds up and slows down. If that's not possible, I'll break audio files into multiple Groove Clips so they can follow the tempo changes.

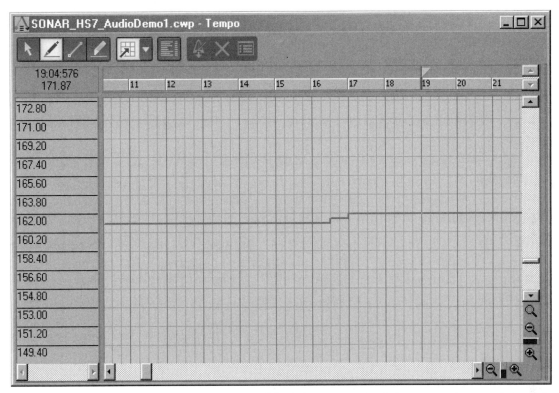

Figure 6.7   The Tempo view makes it easy to add subtle, or not-so-subtle, tempo changes that can help "humanize" your project. Here, the tempo is increasing slightly as it transitions from Measure 16 to Measure 17.

Here are some examples of tempo track tweaks.

- To boost a song's energy level, increase the tempo slightly (by 0.5 to 1 beats per minute). This is the timing equivalent of modulating pitch upward by a semitone; both increase excitement. Decreasing tempo has the reverse effect. Tempo shifts are useful when transitioning between song sections (verse to chorus, chorus to instrumental, etc.) as well as within a particular section (such as upping the tempo for the last two measures of a solo).

- Change tempo a little bit *before* the first beat of the measure you want to change. For example, if you're going from verse to chorus, increase the tempo halfway through the measure prior to the chorus, as shown in Figure 6.7. This creates a smoother lead-in than having the tempo change coincide with a measure change.

- For really dramatic effects, ritard the tempo over the course of a measure (for example, one BPM or less lower on each beat) and then return to the original tempo. Having a drumroll during the ritard creates a particularly effective transition.

MIDI inside the Computer

You may have heard complaints about MIDI being slow or having timing delays. But this is an issue only when the computer is driving *outboard* MIDI gear through a MIDI interface, because MIDI is a serial protocol where a new piece of data gets transmitted every millisecond or so. Furthermore, the instrument or sound generator takes some time to react to this data. When a computer sends MIDI to an external sound module, the data has to exit through a port, be scanned by the keyboard, be interpreted, and be turned into a sound.

With virtual instruments, MIDI data flies around inside the computer, and timing is extremely tight. With outboard gear, sending lots of controller data can choke the data stream; with native MIDI devices, it takes *a lot* to bog down a fast processor. Bottom line: If you need tight timing, virtual MIDI instruments are pretty close to perfect.

However, even today's computers have limits, and playing back lots of notes simultaneously puts a lot of demands on your CPU. Therefore, you still want to avoid stressing your computer unnecessarily. If you do start running out of CPU power, you can always freeze tracks, as described in Chapter 14, "Track Freezing."

Another way to conserve power is to avoid recording unneeded data. In SONAR Home Studio, choose Options > Global and select the MIDI tab (see Figure 6.8).

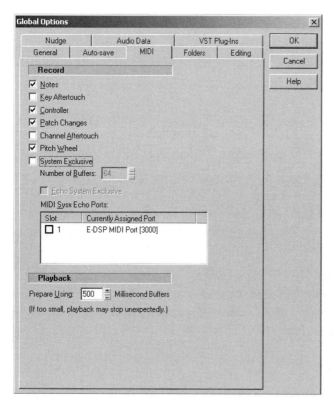

Figure 6.8 In SONAR Home Studio, you can choose the type of data you want to record.

The most resource-hungry data is key aftertouch, which generates a controller whose value depends on how hard you press a key; each key produces its own data. Channel aftertouch is similar, but the value reflects the highest value of any key that's held down, not each key, so it requires much less data. If you're using a master keyboard with aftertouch to trigger a soft synth sound that responds to aftertouch, by all means record the aftertouch data. Otherwise, filter it out, because it takes up a lot of MIDI bandwidth. You can always erase the data later if you don't need it.

It's usually a good idea to uncheck System Exclusive, because this can also represent a lot of data. However, there are some cases in which System Exclusive is used to change a sound during playback, and also, System Exclusive can save patch data (as described in Chapter 12, "Backing Up Data with System Exclusive Messages"). In these cases, you want it to be enabled (checked).

7 Piano Roll View MIDI Editing

As mentioned in Chapter 6 on MIDI basics, one big advantage of MIDI recording compared to audio is the way in which you can edit data with exceptional flexibility. Not surprisingly, SONAR Home Studio has plenty of capabilities to exploit MIDI editing.

There are several ways to edit MIDI data; as with audio clips, one MIDI editing option is on a clip level. In this case, in Track view, MIDI data appears like an audio clip, except that instead of having a waveform showing digital audio, there's a clip showing MIDI data (see Figure 7.1).

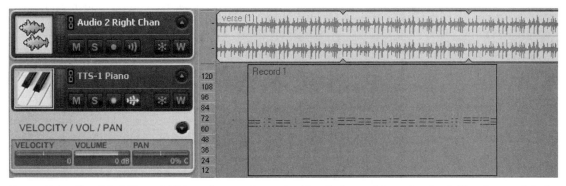

Figure 7.1 The TTS-1 Piano MIDI track contains a clip. The little markings that look like dots and dashes are MIDI notes.

Track view editing is ideal for moving around large amounts of data—copying a clip, trimming it, and the like. Chapter 3 described general editing options for audio and MIDI clips. However, you often want more detailed editing than what you can do with clips, and the Piano Roll view is a very common way to edit MIDI data quickly, accurately, and efficiently. The next chapter covers other MIDI editing options, including the Drum Grid, Event List editing, and Staff view.

Piano Roll View Basics

The Piano Roll view (see Figure 7.2) excels for fairly detailed editing and features an easy-to-use graphic interface. The name Piano Roll view comes from the fact that notes are shown on a grid, with the vertical axis representing pitch and the horizontal axis showing the Timeline. Each note

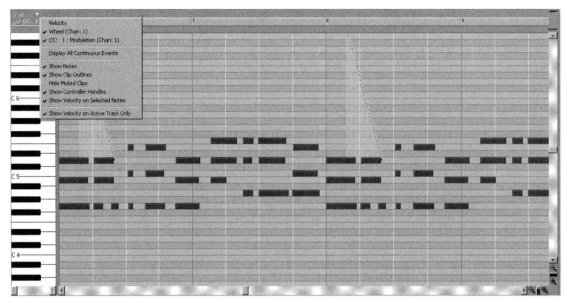

Figure 7.2 The basic Piano Roll view shows notes, with the pitch referenced to a keyboard on the left. The notes are the rectangular blocks; the lighter lines indicate controller data. In the upper-left corner, a drop-down menu lets you choose several view options.

appears as a rectangle, very much like the way notes looked in player piano rolls when they were punched into the paper roll itself.

Note that you can edit MIDI drum parts using the Piano Roll editor, but the specialized drum editing grid (Chapter 8, "MIDI Drum Grid Editing") is optimized for editing drums.

To call up the Piano Roll view, either:

- Click on the rightmost View toolbar button.

- Right-click on a MIDI clip and then select View > Piano Roll.

- Double-click on a MIDI clip.

- Select a MIDI clip and then press Alt+5.

Choosing the Track You Want to See

One of the advantages of working with the standard Piano Roll view is that you can see multiple MIDI tracks simultaneously and choose a specific one on which you want to work. Examples of where you might want to see multiple tracks are keyboard parts where the right- and left-hand parts are in separate tracks, drum tracks where different drums and percussion are on separate tracks, and doubled parts where you want to create some variations in one track compared to another.

To work with multiple tracks, select the tracks you want to see in the Piano Roll view. With the Piano Roll view open, type T (for "Pick Tracks") or click on the Pick Tracks toolbar button (the one with the double arrows). In the Pick Tracks dialog box that appears, Ctrl-click on the tracks you want to see or Shift-click to select multiple contiguous tracks (see Figure 7.3).

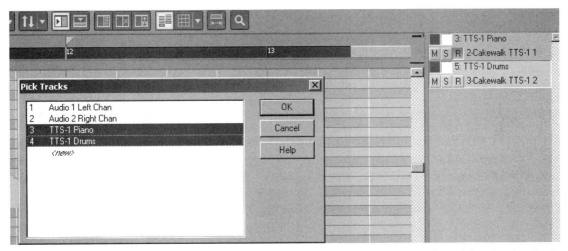

Figure 7.3   In this screen shot, the TTS-1 Piano and TTS-1 Drums tracks are selected for viewing in the Piano Roll view and will appear after you click on OK. Note the Pick Tracks toolbar button with the two arrows, which is directly above the word "Pick" in the Pick Tracks window.

If you don't see a list of the tracks toward the right of the Piano Roll view window, make sure that the Show/Hide Track Pane button is on. This button is to the immediate right of the Pick Tracks button. There's also a splitter bar to the left of the Track pane, which you can drag to determine the Track pane size.

To highlight a track so it becomes the "active" track (as indicated by its notes being brighter than the other tracks) and therefore can be edited, click on its Enable/Disable Track Editing button in the Track pane (see Figure 7.4). When it's white, the track can be edited. When it's gray, you can't edit it. You can enable multiple tracks if you want to work on several tracks at the same time and edit the active track(s) at will—enter notes, erase, and so on.

Also note that each track in the Track pane has Mute, Solo, and Record buttons. Sometimes it's handy to be able to access these functions from within the Piano Roll view rather than having to jump over to the Track or Console view.

One useful trick is that you can switch all tracks in the Track pane to the next higher or lower number using the drop-down menu to the immediate right of the Pick Tracks button. For example, if the Track pane shows Tracks 5, 8, 9, and 13, selecting Show Previous Track(s) will cause the Track pane to show Tracks 4, 7, 8, and 12; selecting Show Next Track(s) will cause the Track pane to show Tracks 6, 9, 10, and 14.

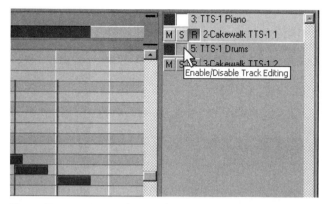

Figure 7.4 You can choose the track(s) you want to edit in the Track pane. Tracks that are enabled for editing are brighter; tracks you can't edit are grayed, but the data is still visible.

If the notes on two tracks overlap, the track with the highest position in the Track pane (normally the lowest-numbered track) displays its notes on top of any other notes that take up the same space. However, you can move any track in the Track pane to any position (including the highest position) by simply clicking on the track name and dragging it up or down.

Also note that you can show/hide track data by clicking on the track's Color button (the leftmost square associated with a track). If the color is visible, you'll see the notes; click on it to turn it white, which hides the notes. If some tracks are hidden and some are visible, you can use the Invert button (or type V) to reverse these. For example, if Tracks 2 and 6 are hidden, while 3 and 10 are visible, type V, and Tracks 2 and 6 will become visible, while Tracks 3 and 10 become hidden.

Choosing the Track Data You Want to See

The drop-down menu in the Piano Roll view's upper left (see Figure 7.5) can show and hide various types of data, which is important because a dense MIDI track can get pretty cluttered. Checking an option shows the particular data type and unchecking hides it. Here are your options.

- **Velocity.** When checked, each note has a line at its attack whose height indicates the relative velocity; higher lines show higher velocities. While in this view, pointing the Draw (Pencil) tool at the *top middle* of the note causes eight horizontal lines to appear (see Figure 7.6). Their presence means the Draw tool is in Velocity Editing mode. Click while the lines are visible and then drag up or down to change the velocity amount.

- A small tooltip shows the note name, note number, duration, velocity, and number of notes being affected. As you drag, the tooltip changes to show the current velocity, its difference in value compared to the original value (in Figure 7.6, it's –17), and how many notes are being affected.

- **Show Velocity on Selected Notes.** This option is invaluable when you have a chord, and you want to change velocity on several notes simultaneously. When checked, if you change the

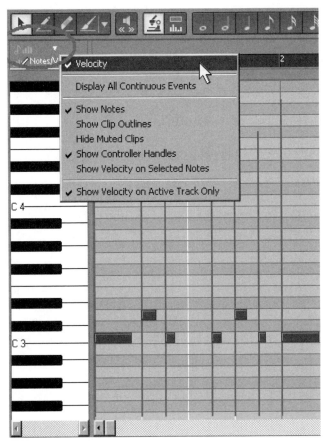

Figure 7.5 The drop-down menu (circled) lets you choose the data you want to see. Note the lines at the head of each note; the height of the line indicates velocity.

velocity on one note, it will change the velocities on all other selected notes by the same amount.

- **Wheel and CC Options.** If there is pitch wheel or MIDI continuous controller data in the track, it will be listed directly below velocity. Checking or unchecking a data type shows/hides this data. However, note that later on in this chapter, we'll discuss a different way of editing controller data using controller "lanes."

- **Show Notes.** If you want to edit controller data, you may find it easier to uncheck Show Notes. However, if the controller relates to modulating individual notes, you'll probably want to show them for reference.

- **Show Clip Outlines.** This puts a very light screen in the background of data that belongs to a particular clip.

Figure 7.6 Use the Draw tool to edit velocity in the Piano Roll view, assuming velocity "tails" are visible (as selected in the upper-left drop-down menu).

- **Hide Muted Clips.** This doesn't eliminate a graphic representation of the data, but it "ghosts" it so that it's light gray.

- **Show Controller Handles.** When this is checked, each piece of controller data has a small square at its top to simplify editing. You can click on an individual handle to modify the value of a single piece of data, or you can use the Select tool to select multiple pieces of controller data. You can drag selected data left or right to change its position or up or down to change the controller value.

- **Show Velocity on Active Track Only.** If you're looking at multiple tracks, seeing velocity lines for all tracks can be pretty confusing. This option blocks the velocity lines for all tracks except the active track.

When displaying multiple controllers, the window can get extremely cluttered. So, when you click on data for one of the controllers for editing, it gets sent to the front compared to the other controllers, which are shaded lighter and put in the background. This makes it easy to adjust one controller while still seeing it in context with other controllers. However, even then, you can have too many controllers for comfortable viewing—which is why being able to hide particular controllers is very helpful, as is being able to edit controller data in lanes, as described later.

Adding Note and Controller Data

You're not limited to just viewing or editing data in the Piano Roll view; you can also add notes or controllers. The key to this is the second drop-down menu in the upper left of the Piano Roll view (see Figure 7.7). Here, you can select the type of data you want to add, or if the type of data isn't already present, you can specify a new value type.

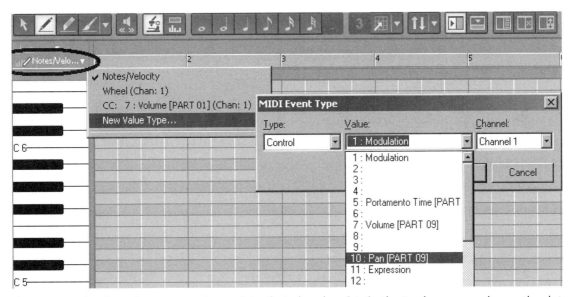

Figure 7.7 The drop-down menu shows data that already exists in the track; you can choose the data you want to add. For example, if you choose Notes, the Draw tool will add notes. In this shot, pan data is about to be added to the track, so Pan is being selected as a New Value Type.

If you want to add data that's not listed, you can add it by selecting New Value Type. The MIDI Event Type window will appear, where you can select a value type, value, and channel.

There are two main ways to enter notes.

To enter *individual* notes, select the Draw tool and click where you want a note. Its duration will be the Note value selected in the Note Rhythm toolbar above the Piano Roll view (see Figure 7.8).

SONAR Home Studio also includes a note-drawing option called the Pattern Brush. This calls up preset drum and percussion patterns where you simply drag the Brush across the Piano Roll view grid to enter a complete note pattern.

To enter a pattern of notes, such as a kick or snare pattern, click on the Pattern Brush tool (see Figure 7.9). The drop-down menu to the right of this tool lets you choose the desired pattern. We'll discuss this more in the next chapter on editing using the Drum Grid.

To enter controller data, select the type of data you want to add as described previously and then select the Draw tool. You have three main options.

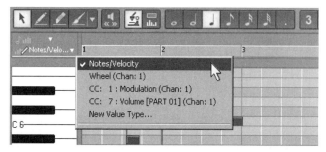

Figure 7.8 The drop-down menu is being used to select notes as the data to be added. Look above the cursor arrow: The eighth-note button is enabled, so any notes you enter will be eighth notes. The 3 button in the upper-right corner, when enabled, creates a triplet value for the selected rhythm.

- Click the Draw tool where you want to enter individual pieces of data.

- To draw freehand data, hold the Ctrl key and then click and drag to draw a curve.

- To draw a straight line, hold the Ctrl and Shift keys and then click and drag to draw a line.

Regardless of which method you use, the points you draw will snap to the selected Snap to Grid value. If Snap to Grid is not selected, then you pretty much have no limit on how many points you can have in a curve. However, all this data can clog the MIDI data stream, so consider using no more resolution than is necessary.

Also note that controller values represent a *change* in value. If you click and drag horizontally, you'll only see one piece of controller data; because you're dragging horizontally, the value doesn't change until you move the cursor off the horizontal axis.

Editing Note Parameters

There are several ways to change note parameters.

The Select Tool

Use the Select tool (click on the Select toolbar button, which looks like an arrow, or type S to select) to move a note in any direction, thus changing pitch or start time. Click on the note and then drag as desired.

The Draw Tool

The Draw tool (click on the toolbar button that looks like a pencil or type D to select it) is a multipurpose tool whose function depends on where it sits on the note. Here are the various options.

- **Pointing at the top middle of the note.** Click and then drag up or down to change the note velocity, as described earlier.

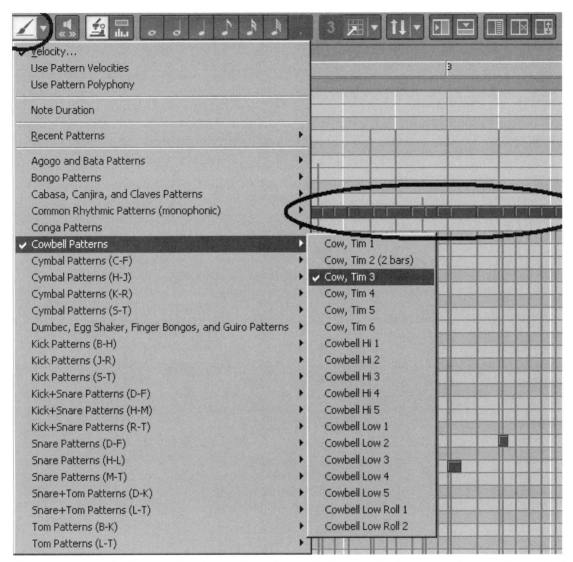

Figure 7.9   A cowbell pattern has been selected, and the Pattern Brush (upper-left corner) is enabled. The circled series of notes toward the mid-upper right of the screenshot were drawn using this pattern.

- **Pointing at the note start.** The cursor changes to a left/right arrow. Click and then drag left or right to change the note start time.

- **Pointing at the note end.** The cursor changes to a left/right arrow. Click and then drag left or right to change the note duration time.

- **Pointing at the bottom edge of the note.** The cursor changes to an up/down arrow. Click and then drag up or down to change the note pitch. The note's start time and duration will not change.

The Erase Tool

The erase tool can erase single notes or multiple notes.

- **To erase one note.** Choose the Erase tool (click on the toolbar button that looks like an eraser or type E) and then click on the note you want to delete.

- **To erase multiple notes.** The Erase tool can work like a blackboard eraser—click, hold down the mouse button, and then drag over any notes you want to erase. Or, you can use the Select tool to select multiple notes and then hit the Delete key.

Microscope Mode

When you're zoomed out beyond a certain point, it becomes difficult to make fine adjustments on notes. Fortunately, there's Microscope mode (see Figure 7.10).

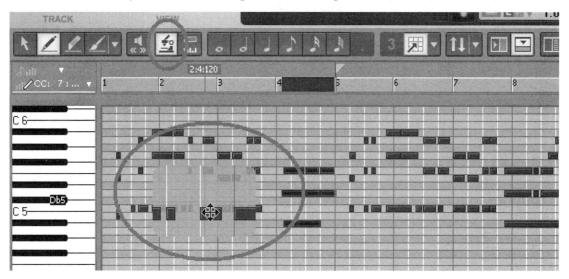

Figure 7.10 The Microscope Mode button (circled, toward the top) magnifies the area immediately under the Select, Draw, or Erase tool. The large circled area shows the magnified area.

Microscope mode magnifies the area under the selected tool to make it easier to see detail on individual notes. All the note editing parameters mentioned in this section still apply—for example, place the Select tool on a note to move it.

Note that once you've zoomed in far enough, Microscope mode has no effect.

Detailed Note Editing

If you right-click on a note with the Select, Draw, or Eraser tool and hold down the mouse button, a tooltip appears that shows the note name, note number, start time, duration, and velocity. When you release the mouse button, a Note Properties window appears that allows precise editing of time, pitch, velocity, duration, and MIDI channel (see Figure 7.11).

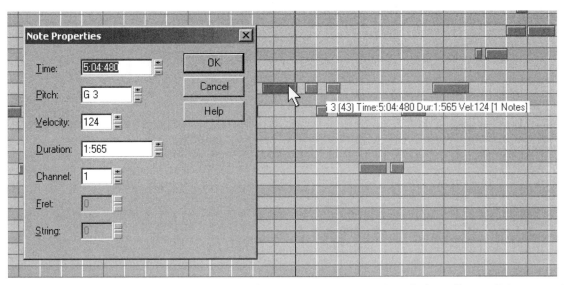

Figure 7.11   For exceptionally precise note editing, the Note Properties window allows editing several parameters numerically. This screenshot also shows the tooltip that appears when you right-click and hold down the mouse button.

Controller Lanes

The Piano Roll view offers the option to edit controllers in separate lanes. This can be very helpful when you're using lots of controllers and showing them on the Piano Roll itself gets too cluttered.

For example, the upper part of Figure 7.12 shows controller data for only two controllers along with the notes and velocity tails; that's a lot to take in. The lower part shows the same data, but with the controller and velocity data broken out into separate lanes toward the lower part of the window.

Accessing Controller Lanes and Editing Lane Data

Here's how to edit velocity and controller data.

1. Click on the Use Controller Pane button (refer back to Figure 7.12). Or, with the Piano Roll view active, type C to toggle the Controller pane on or off.

2. The default Velocity lane will appear. To edit velocity values, do the following:
   - Drag the Draw tool across the velocity line at the new value.
   - To conform velocity values to a freehand curve, click in the lane with the Draw tool and drag to create the desired curve shape.
   - To conform velocity values to a line, Ctrl-Shift-drag with the Draw tool across the velocities you want to adjust; while continuing to hold down the mouse, drag up or down to change the angle of the line if desired.

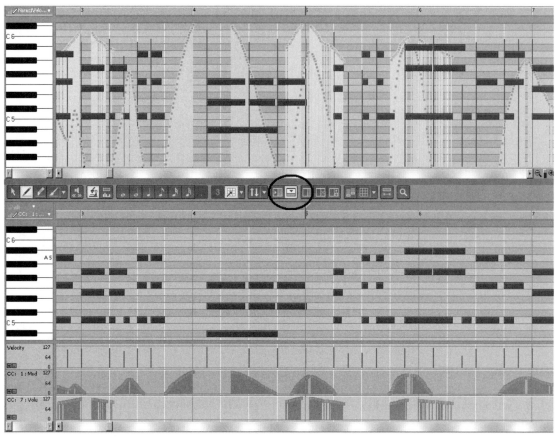

Figure 7.12 The upper view shows controller data superimposed on notes, while the lower view shows controller (and velocity) data broken out into separate lanes. The button for showing controller lanes is circled for clarity.

3. To show a controller lane, click on the + symbol toward the velocity lane's lower left. You can open up additional controller lanes by clicking on a lane's + symbol; the new lane will open up under the lane where you clicked on the +. If you click on the + and a second velocity lane appears, that means there is no more controller data to display.

4. To hide a controller lane, click on its associated – sign (to the right of the + sign).

5. To edit controller data in a lane, do the following:

   ■ For individual pieces of controller data, click on the data's handle with the Select or Draw tool and drag up or down.

   ■ To edit multiple pieces of controller data, use the Select tool to drag a rectangle around the data you want to edit. Place the cursor over one of the selected handles and then drag left or right and/or up and down to move the entire group of data.

- To erase data, select the Erase tool and drag over the controller data you want to delete.

- To conform controller values to a freehand curve, Ctrl-click in the lane with the Draw tool and then drag to create the desired curve shape.

- To conform controller values to a line, use the Draw tool to Ctrl-Shift-drag across the velocities you want to adjust; while continuing to hold down the mouse, drag up or down to change the angle of the line if desired.

PRV Mode: Inline Piano Roll View

It's not necessary to call up a separate Piano Roll view, because you can see a Piano Roll view within a MIDI track when Track view is selected. In Track view, open up the PRV section and click on the PRV button. The track will now show a Piano Roll view (see Figure 7.13). Cool, eh?

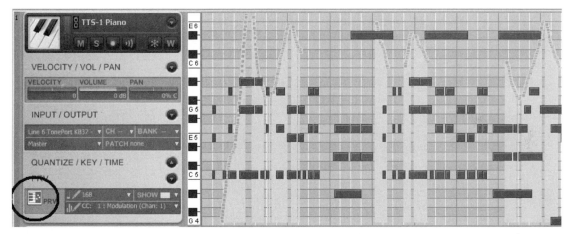

Figure 7.13 It's possible to show a Piano Roll view within a MIDI track while in Track view—simply select PRV mode.

This view works very similarly to the standard Piano Roll view, but let's cover the most important differences.

- **Zooming.** For horizontal zooming, use the Zoom In/Out Horizontal buttons. For vertical zooming, you can use the Zoom In/Out Vertical buttons, but this affects all tracks. If you want to zoom vertically on only the MIDI track, hover the cursor over the keyboard notes toward the left of the inline Piano Roll view; the cursor changes into a small keyboard with up and down arrows. Click within the keyboard notes and then drag up to zoom in or drag down to zoom out. Also note that opening up additional track header options (for example, Input/Output) increases the track height, which does the equivalent of zooming in.

- **Tools.** The default tool in this mode is the Draw tool. To access the Select tool, hold down the Alt button, and the Draw tool will work as a Select tool. To erase one note, click on it with the Draw or Select tool and, while holding down the mouse button, hit the Delete key. To erase multiple notes, use the Select tool to select multiple notes and then hit the Delete key.

- **Microscope mode.** This happens automatically once you've zoomed out by a certain amount.

- **Entering notes.** As with the standard Piano Roll view, use the Draw tool. Note that there is a field with a drop-down menu where you can choose the default duration (see Figure 7.14).

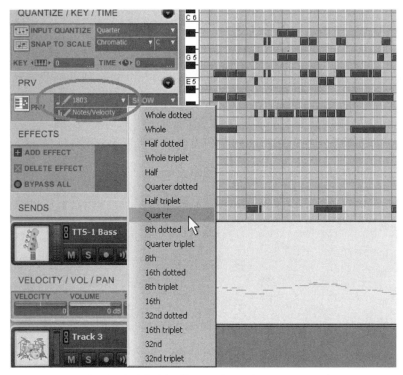

Figure 7.14   The circled field offers a drop-down menu where you can choose the default MIDI note duration value when inserting notes.

- **Showing different data types.** This works like the standard Piano Roll view. Click on the Show field and select what you want to show from the drop-down menu.

- **Inserting different data types.** The lower field (see Figure 7.15) shows which data will be inserted with the Draw tool. Clicking on the field reveals a drop-down menu where you can choose the type of data to be inserted or choose a new data type for insertion.

PRV Tool Configuration

The Piano Roll view tools (Draw, Select, and Erase) have defaults that make a lot of sense and will probably work for 95% of SONAR Home Studio users. However, there's always that other

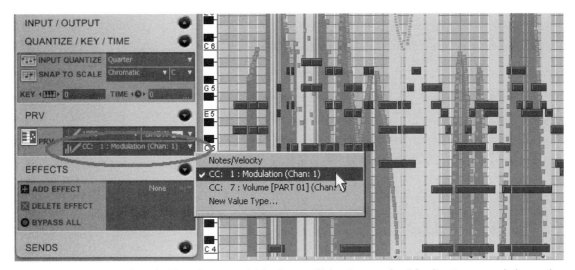

Figure 7.15 The circled field indicates which data will be inserted with the Draw tool, but when clicked, it opens a drop-down menu where you can choose whatever type of data you want to insert.

5% who want to customize everything exactly to their liking, and for those people, SONAR Home Studio offers several ways to configure the Piano Roll view tools.

For example, if the Select tool is currently selected, holding down the Alt key turns it into the Draw tool, and vice versa. However, maybe you'd prefer to use a different modifier key, like Alt-Shift. You can make these kinds of changes with the PRV Tool Configuration options.

To configure the PRV Tool, go to Options > PRV Tool Configuration; this opens the dialog box in Figure 7.16.

Basically, to assign a particular action to a Piano Roll too, you need to specify:

- **Piano Roll tool.** This would be either Select, Draw, or Erase, which are called PRV Tool 1, PRV Tool 2, and PRV Tool 3, respectively.

- **Mouse button.** This can be the left, right, or middle (if present) mouse button.

- **Keyboard modifier keys.** This specifies a particular combination of the Ctrl, Shift, and/or Alt key.

- **Mouse location (context).** Where you click within a note affects which function happens—for example, clicking on a note's right edge with the draw tool and dragging to the left shortens the note, while clicking in the middle of the note and dragging up or down transposes it.

- **Mouse action.** For example, whether the mouse button is up or down, and whether the mouse is moving (e.g., dragging).

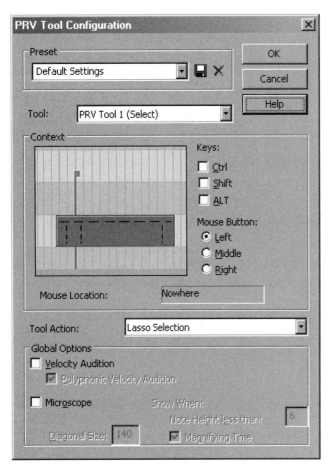

Figure 7.16 You can create different key and mouse button combinations for various tool actions when editing in the Piano Roll view.

So you could say that if a particular mouse button is up while the PRV Tool 1 is selected, you're holding down a particular keyboard key, and you click on a particular part of a note, a particular action will happen.

This is an advanced technique; as noted earlier, the defaults (which were obviously carefully thought out) will work for most people. If you want to get deeper into this topic, call up the Help menu from the PRV Tool Configuration dialog box, and you'll find out how to modify the Piano Roll view tool in more ways than you ever thought possible.

8 MIDI Drum Grid Editing

Although the Piano Roll is probably the most common way to edit MIDI performances, SONAR Home Studio offers several other options, one of which might be more convenient for particular tasks. We'll go over those options next, starting with the Drum Grid—an efficient view for creating any kind of drum part, looped or not, and an ideal environment for using SONAR's Pattern Brush tool for painting patterns of individual drums or even entire parts.

Drum Grid Basics

Newcomers to SONAR Home Studio often wonder how you call up the Drum Grid, because it's not represented in the View menu. Instead, you call up a track's Piano Roll view. There is no separate "drum grid view" per se. Rather, it's the top pane in the Piano Roll view, and you can drag down the splitter bar that's just above the Piano Roll to reveal it. As with the Piano Roll view, there's another pane below the Piano Roll for viewing a controller strip, which you can show/hide by typing C (or clicking on the User Controller Pane button in the toolbar above the Piano Roll view). The controller strip works the same way as the Piano Roll, and so does showing particular notes and controllers, as well as entering note or controller data.

However, if you have a MIDI track that's driving drums, and you have assigned a drum map to that track, SONAR Home Studio is smart enough to realize you probably want to edit using the Drum Grid. So, when you call up the Piano Roll view, it won't show the traditional piano roll, but instead will open to the Drum Grid pane.

Because the Drum Grid is so closely tied to the Piano Roll, most of what we discussed in the previous chapter—the toolbar, the ability to show/hide/pick different tracks, and the like—applies here as well. However, there are a few major differences, particularly with regard to how notes are displayed.

If you're not familiar with the concept of a drum map, it simply correlates drum sounds to MIDI notes. For example, if MIDI Note #56 triggers a cowbell, rather than having to remember which note number triggers which sound, you can simply create a drum map where you enter "cowbell" along with the note number. When you call up the Drum Grid pane, you'll see the drum name next to the note number.

Unlike the Piano Roll view, where you would normally see a key representing a note, you see data about the drum played by that note (see Figure 8.1).

Figure 8.1 Where you'd normally see a key in the Piano Roll view, the Drum Grid shows a drum name and data about each drum. Note the controller strip below the main pane, which is currently showing velocity; "velocity tails" (the small horizontal lines) associated with the drum notes are also visible.

Each line shows the drum name, In note (the MIDI note value represented on the grid), Out note (the note to which the In note is mapped—this defaults to the same note but can be changed), Mute button, and Solo button. Being able to solo and mute individual drum notes is something you can't do with a standard Piano Roll view; you would have to do this at the drum module itself.

The reason for separate In and Out notes becomes clear if you created a drum part for something like a General MIDI drum machine but then decided to play back through a different set of sounds that aren't GM compatible. You can simply map, say, the original snare note to a different note that drives the new snare sound.

Drum Map Manager Basics

Although convenient, these In and Out notes, drum names, and so on don't magically appear out of nowhere. They come from templates in the Drum Map Manager (DMM for short).

SONAR Home Studio provides a ton of templates for drum modules for a variety of manufacturers, so you may be able to use these as is (or get by with only minor tweaking). This map specifies the parameter values you see in the Drum Grid and provides control over other drum note characteristics—channels, output ports, and so on. As a result of this flexibility, a single drum map can trigger a variety of notes over a variety of channels, as well as drive both internal soft synths and external drum machines connected to a MIDI hardware port. If none of the included templates does the job, you can create your own from scratch—although you probably won't need to.

The drum map is truly a mapper. It accepts incoming notes (In notes) from the track, remaps them (thus creating Out notes), and then sends them to an output. Because the drum map is providing an output signal to a track, it's not surprising that you select a drum map in a MIDI track's Output field.

For example, suppose you inserted the Cakewalk TTS-1 soft synth and are using one of its drum kits. Where the Track view's MIDI Out field would normally show Cakewalk TTS-1, you would instead select a drum map (see Figure 8.2). You needn't worry about channel, bank, or patch assignments—the drum map handles all those chores.

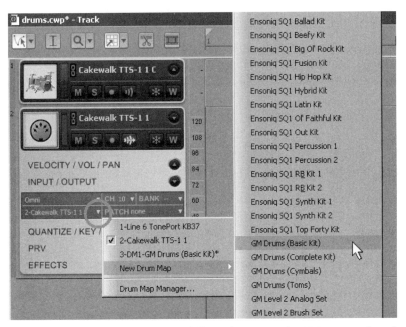

Figure 8.2 The TTS-1 drum kits follow the General MIDI protocol, so here we're calling up a General MIDI drum map to drive the TTS-1 drum kit in Channel 10.

You'll note that there are a lot of drum maps, and it can take time to scroll through all of them. Fortunately, there's a shortcut. After the New Drum Map list appears, type the first letter of what you're looking for—for example, if you want the map for a Novation DrumStation, type

N, and you'll be at the top of the list of all drum maps beginning with N. From there, it's easier to scroll down and find the Novation DrumStation.

Once you've selected the drum map, if you put the focus on the MIDI track and play a few notes on your keyboard or drum controller, you probably won't hear anything. That's because the Drum Manager defaults to sending its outs to the MIDI device specified under Options > MIDI Devices, which will likely be a physical MIDI port. Although this works if you're using a hardware drum machine connected to the physical MIDI Out, with a soft synth, you'll need to change the output assignment so it feeds the synth. This is easy to do with the DMM.

Working with the DMM

To edit DMM parameters, click on the down arrow in the track's MIDI Output field and select Drum Map Manager (see Figure 8.3).

Figure 8.3   After you've selected a drum map, you may need to edit it. Calling up the Drum Map Manager provides the needed editing tools.

The DMM appears in its own window. You'll see lines with a variety of fields for each drum sound: In Note, Out Note, Name, Channel, Output Port, Velocity Offset, and Velocity Scaling (see Figure 8.4).

Note that in the picture of the DMM, the outputs are feeding a Line 6 TonePort KB37, because that's specified as the output device under MIDI Devices. However, we want to direct MIDI to the TTS-1, so our first order of business is to change the drum map outputs.

You can change outputs one at a time by clicking on the arrow in the Out Port field and selecting the desired output from the pop-up menu, but that's tedious. A shortcut for changing output

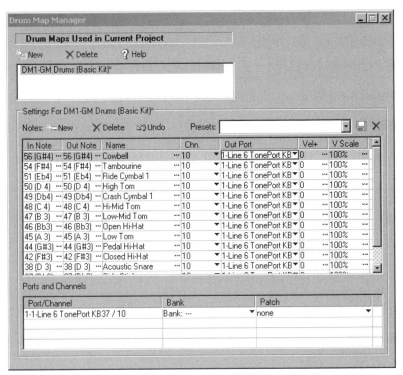

Figure 8.4   The Drum Map Manager window is where you can edit (and create) drum maps.

or MIDI channel is to hold down the Ctrl and Shift keys as you select the desired output or channel, because this assigns all notes to your selection (see Figure 8.5).

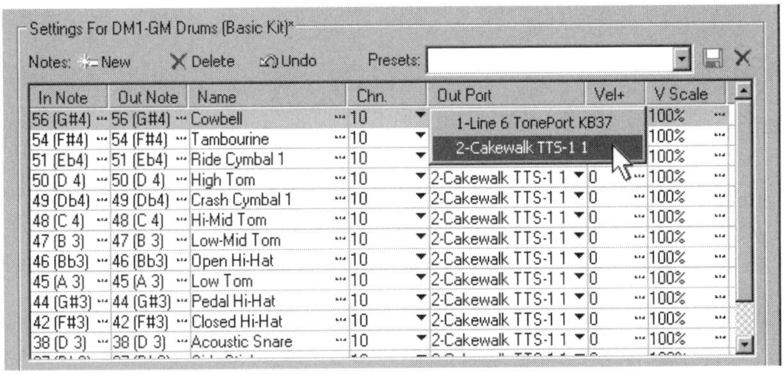

Figure 8.5   By holding Ctrl and Shift while selecting Cakewalk TTS-1 for the first output, all outputs are assigned simultaneously to the Cakewalk TTS-1.

You can edit other parameters by double-clicking in the appropriate data field and typing in the desired value or by using the +/– buttons or the spinner bar for numericals. (Note that you cannot click and drag on the parameter to change values).

The In Note and Out Note fields represent the before and after mappings. The Name field is, of course, the drum name, and Channel is the MIDI channel to which a drum is assigned. Velocity Offset (Vel+) can be positive or negative. This is very handy to even out differences between different modules. For example, you might replace a snare drum with one that's more dynamically responsive, so the new snare sounds weaker. Kick up the velocity offset to compensate.

Velocity Scaling (V Scale) is a terrific feature. Numbers below 100% compress the velocity curve. Like a "real" compressor, this reduces the difference between minimum and maximum velocities, and also like a real compressor, you'll need to add some makeup gain. For example, suppose a drum part's velocities cover the full MIDI velocity range from 1 to 127. Next, you compress it by 50%. The velocities now range from 1 to 64. To bring the peaks back up to 127, use the velocity offset to add 63. Now the velocity range goes from 64 to 127 because you've added 63 to each value—you've essentially compressed the drum velocities by 2:1.

Numbers above 100% add expansion. This is useful, too, because with high expansion values, all the mid-to-high velocities are scaled up, and the lower velocities disappear. It's almost like a noise gate effect, where medium and high velocities come through at maximum, and everything else falls by the wayside.

There are two other important DMM functions. You can save edited maps by entering a name in the Presets field and then clicking on the floppy disk (Save) button. You can also choose a preset from this field and click on the Delete (X) button if you want to delete a map permanently.

However, you can also remove the map from the MIDI Output field without deleting the map itself. In the upper left, under Drum Maps Used in Current Project, highlight the map you want to remove and then click on the associated Delete button. (It's also possible to create new maps from here by clicking on the New button.) Also note that the DMM "centralizes" all drum maps used in all tracks; you can call up any map at the Drum Map Manager window itself by using the Presets field.

Another cool DMM trick is that you can rearrange the lines. Click anywhere in a line and drag up or down. For example, you can group all the toms together or all the hi-hat parts. You can also delete lines; just click on the line you want to delete (Shift- or Ctrl-click to select multiple lines) and then click on the Delete button just above the parameter listing, between the New and Undo options. (Yes, it is confusing to have three Delete buttons in the DMM that all use the X symbol. Just remember the top one deletes maps from your project, the one on the right deletes maps from disk, and the one on the left deletes any highlighted line or lines).

It's good practice to delete any notes that aren't being used, because this gives an easy-to-handle, compact list when you move over to the Drum Grid pane. You don't have to save this as a custom map; any changes to the map will be stored as part of the project.

Creating Drum Maps from Scratch

If you're not using a setup covered by one of the Drum Map Manager's presets, it can be tedious to create a new map—unfortunately, there's currently no way to import drum names into the DMM. However, it's unlikely that you'll use all the drums in a given kit, which can save some time.

One option is to call up a blank map and click on the Notes – New button for each drum you want to add. But I find it easier to call up the Pass Thru map. This creates a list of all notes, expressed as MIDI note numbers and pitches. I then enter info for the drums that will be used. Eventually, after I'm sure I won't be adding any more drums, I delete the notes that don't have associated drums.

The Drum Grid: Going Deeper

Although you can show a controller strip in the Drum Grid, for editing a drum's velocity it's not always useful because multiple drums often hit on the same beat, making it difficult to work with an individual tail. (On the other hand, using the controller strip makes it easy to set velocity for multiple drums at once, such as making the downbeat hit really hard. Just drag the Draw tool across the velocity value you want all the tails to have.)

Fortunately, as with the standard Piano Roll view, you can choose to show or hide velocity tails for notes, whose height indicates velocity. (Type V to toggle between show and hide the tails.) If you point at one of these tails with the Draw tool, the cursor adds a series of lines that shows it's in Velocity Edit mode. Click on the tail and drag up to increase velocity or down to decrease velocity. Another Piano Roll feature is the ability to right-click on a note and bring up a Note Properties box, which lets you edit individual note parameters with extreme precision.

Zooming in vertically will show more resolution on the velocity tails. The controller strip is also invaluable with drum modules that allow using continuous controllers to affect sound parameter values.

Another display option, Show Durations (see Figure 8.6), lets you see notes either as individual hits or as the actual length. You can toggle between these two options by typing O or by

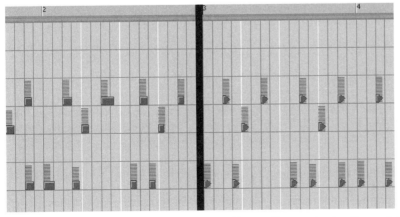

Figure 8.6 The Show Durations button affects all notes in the Drum Grid, so this shot uses a collage— the drums on the left show durations, and the ones on the right don't.

clicking on the Show Durations button (two buttons to the right from the Show Velocity Tails button).

I generally switch over to viewing duration at some point and then shorten notes as appropriate. Most drum triggers are one-shots; you don't need to sustain a note to keep hearing the drum. Otherwise, I'll display the smaller hits, which clean up the display.

You can also edit the map from within the Drum Grid. Double-click on one of the lines with a drum sound, and a Map Properties window will appear (see Figure 8.7). Here you can edit the name, In and Out notes, velocity settings, and so on—just like the DMM. In fact, you can also click on the Map Properties Map Mgr. button and call up the full DMM.

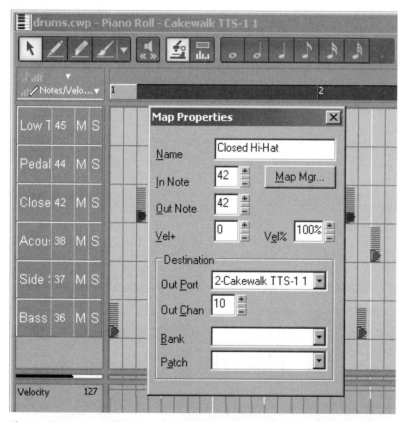

Figure 8.7   It's possible to edit DMM parameters for individual drums without actually opening the full Drum Map Manager.

Painting Drum Notes in the Drum Grid

We touched on "painting" rhythms in the previous chapter, but this feature really comes into its own when you're doing drum parts. Click on the Paint Brush button's down arrow, and you'll find a library of rhythmic patterns.

Once you've selected a pattern, there are three setup options. I strongly suggest checking Use Pattern Velocities to preserve any dynamics built into the pattern. The alternative is to click on Velocity (the default) and select a specific velocity value, which means all notes will be painted at that velocity. Note Duration must be unchecked to select Pattern Velocities.

A pattern can consist of a single drum or multiple drums playing on multiple pitches. For simple patterns (for example, a single clave part), leave Use Pattern Polyphony unchecked; however, when playing back multiple drums, make sure Use Pattern Polyphony is checked. If it isn't, the notes will all be "collapsed" to the same note. For this reason, it's probably best to create polyphonic patterns that adhere to a standard drum map, such as General MIDI. Otherwise, you never quite know what will play back when you paint in the pattern...although I suppose that could also lead to some happy accidents.

Selecting Note Duration deselects any pattern you might have chosen and uses the current note duration setting in the Piano Roll toolbar as the interval between notes.

Painting a pattern is easy. Pick a pattern from the Library, click on the Drum Grid where you want the pattern to start, and then drag for however long you want the pattern to last.

Creating Your Own Brush Patterns

Here's how to create a simple pattern.

1. Call up a blank project and enter the pattern you want in the Piano Roll or Drum Grid view.

2. At the start of the pattern, enter a marker (press F11 at the desired Now time where you want the marker) and name it with the pattern name, such as HH Closed Off-Beat.

3. At the end of the pattern, insert another marker named End (see Figure 8.8).

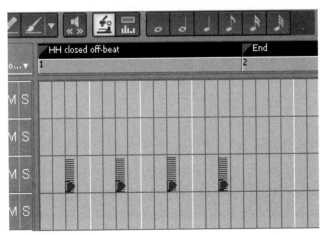

Figure 8.8 Note the markers that indicate the start and end of the pattern.

4. Choose Save As, and for Save As Type, choose MIDI Format 1.

5. Name the file. This will be the name that identifies the pattern, so choose carefully.

6. Navigate to the folder holding the brush patterns. You can find the folder path by choosing Options > Global > Folders tab and then seeing which path leads to Patterns (typically C:\Documents and Settings\Administrator\Application Data\Cakewalk\ SONAR Home Studio 7\Pattern Brush Patterns).

7. Save the file. If you're using a drum map, you'll be told that the drum map can't be stored in a Standard MIDI File—but that doesn't matter, as we only want to save the note pattern, and we don't need anything else. So, click on Yes.

8. Close SONAR Home Studio 7 and then reopen it to see your pattern as a new brush option.

You can also create multiple patterns under the same category (for example, four or five different hi-hat or tambourine patterns). The process is a bit more involved than creating a single pattern; you create a string of multiple patterns in a single MIDI track, separated by markers (see Figure 8.9).

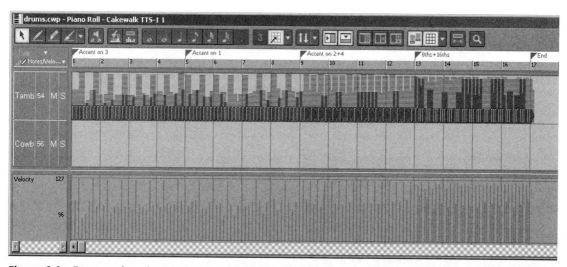

Figure 8.9 Four tambourine patterns, separated by markers, have been created. Once this is saved as a Standard MIDI File into the Pattern Brush Patterns folder, you'll be able to paint the patterns into the Piano Roll or Drum Grid view.

Suppose you want to have a library of tambourine patterns. You create the first pattern, and as with single patterns, you drop in a marker to indicate the pattern start. Then you create the second pattern at the end of the first one and indicate its start with a marker as well. You can keep creating patterns and adding markers at the start of each pattern until you have all the patterns you want.

The next step is to save the string of patterns as a .MID file, such as Tambourines.mid. As with single files, the file name will identify the pattern type; so the next time you open SONAR Home Studio, there will be an entry called Tambourines in the Pattern Brush drop-down menu, with side entries for the various patterns. Their names will be the same as the markers that identify their starts.

The main use I've found for the brush patterns is when you need some place-marker patterns fast, such as a kick or shaker part—it's possible to create pretty decent drum parts in minutes. Once you have your song fleshed out, then you can edit these or replace them with something created in a more deliberate fashion.

And that covers most of what you need to know about drum maps and grids. Once you become familiar with how the Drum Grid and Drum Map Manager work, I doubt you'll go back to using the Piano Roll view for entering and editing drum parts.

9 Other MIDI Editing Options

The remaining MIDI editing options are more specialized than the Piano Roll or Drum Grid options, but they definitely have their uses. This chapter covers the Event List view, Staff view, and Lyrics view.

Event List View Basics

You call up the Event List view as you would other views—either choose Views > Event List (or press Alt+4) or right-click on a MIDI clip and choose Views > Event List. When the Event List appears, you'll see what initially appears to be something that would look more at home in an accounting program (see Figure 9.1).

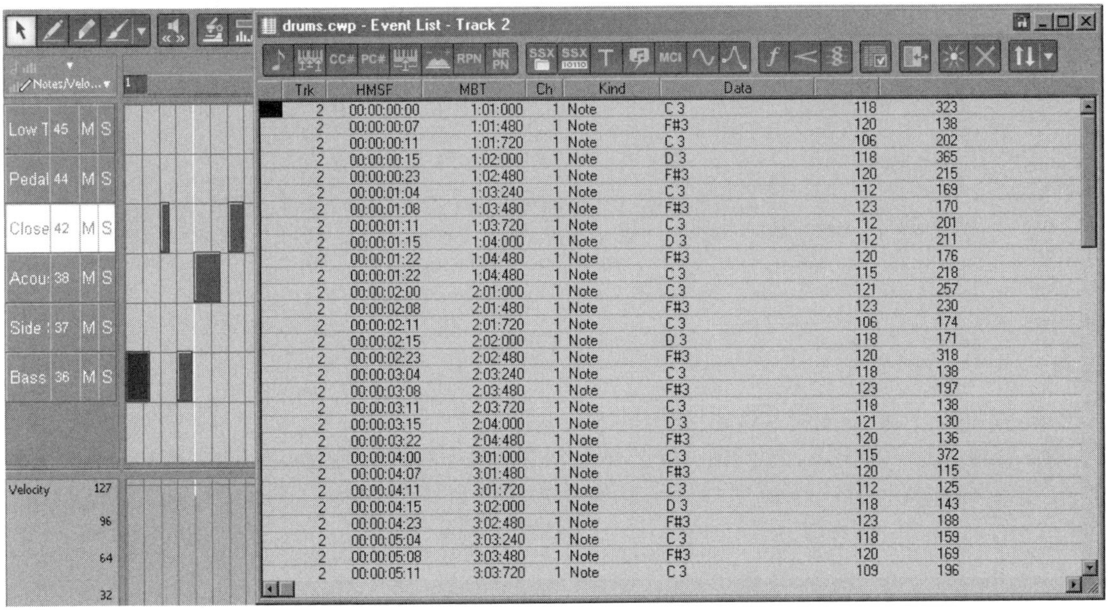

Figure 9.1 The Event List view shows details about every event in a MIDI track, from notes to controllers. In the background, you can also see the events in the Drum Grid view.

Each line contains MIDI event data. Going from left to right, these are:

- **Trk.** The project track number to which the events belong.

- **HMSF.** Where the event starts in hours:minutes:seconds:frames.

- **MBT.** Where the event starts in measures:beats:ticks.

- **Ch.** The MIDI channel number associated with the event. Note that this can be overridden in the Track view MIDI output assignment.

- **Kind.** The type of event. Double-clicking in this field brings up a list of all possible events (see Figure 9.2).

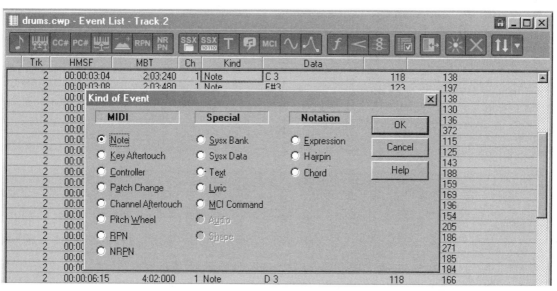

Figure 9.2 You can change any event to any other event by double-clicking on the event and choosing a new type. This is important when inserting a new event, so you can choose the type of event being added.

- **Data.** This varies, depending on the type of event. Figuring out what the data means can get a little confusing; the data columns don't have labels because an Event List usually shows multiple types of data. In Figure 9.2, I'm showing notes, so the data consists of the note name, velocity, and duration. With a controller, Data shows the controller number and then the value.

With some fields, double-clicking brings up a dialog box that indicates what the data field represents. For example, with patch changes, the first data field is the Bank Select method, and the second is the patch being chosen. Double-clicking on either of these data fields brings up a dialog box where you can enter the Bank Select method and patch.

Showing/Hiding Events

Because the Event List view shows everything, the display can get overwhelming if you have, for example, lots of controller data, and you want to edit only notes. There are two ways to deal with this.

In the Event List window toolbar, the 18 buttons toward the left show/hide the various data types. For example, clicking on the CC# button hides all controller events. You can also manage all views simultaneously from a single window; just click on the Event Manager button to the immediate right of the 18 data type buttons (or type V). This brings up a dialog box similar to the one in Figure 9.2; checking an event type displays it, and unchecking hides it. This happens while the dialog box is showing, which is convenient—you don't have to close the box to see the results of your changes.

Other Event List Toolbar Buttons

Continuing along to the right after the Event Manager, the next button chooses whether to show events outside the slip edit boundary for the clip or only in the selected clip.

The Insert Event button inserts an event (no surprises there!). Clicking on any field in any event and then clicking on Insert Event inserts a new event with the same parameter values as the event you selected. For example, if you click on a note's name, a note will be inserted that's identical to the one on which you clicked. If you want a different event type, double-click on the Kind field and choose the desired type.

To delete an event, click on any field in the event and then click on the next toolbar button to the right—Delete Event. The remaining two toolbar buttons are track picker buttons, as described previously in Chapter 7.

Identifying Notes Easily

To the left of the Trk field is a field where you can click to select notes. Doing so selects the same notes in the other views, but this also works in reverse—selecting notes in other views shows selections in the Event List view (see Figure 9.3). This makes it easy to select notes for editing in the Event List.

Staff View Basics

Similar to other views, either choose Views > Staff (or press Alt+7) or right-click on a MIDI clip and choose Views > Staff. SONAR Home Studio 7 converts the MIDI data into standard notation and then displays it (see Figure 9.4).

Editing notes is similar to other views we've already discussed—use the Draw tool to add notes (or click on an existing note to play it back), use the Erase tool to delete notes, snap notes to a grid, zoom in and out, and so on. So, we'll cover only those features unique to the Staff view. For additional information, the help is very informative—when the Staff view has focus, press F1 to show help.

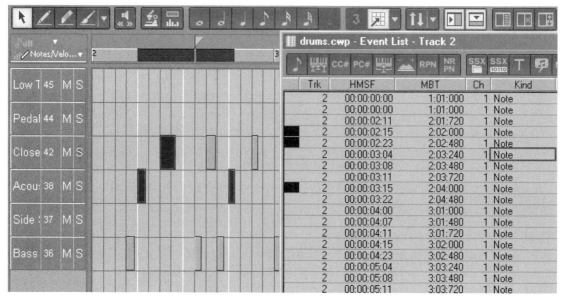

Figure 9.3 In this image, notes selected in the Drum Grid view are selected in the Event List, as shown by the black bars to the left of the Trk field.

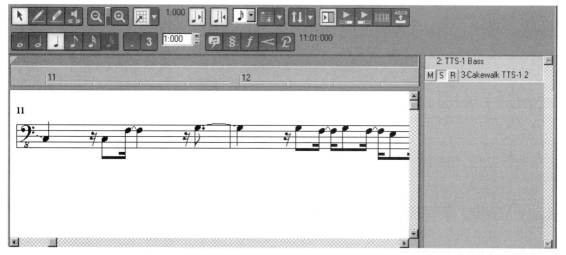

Figure 9.4 A bass line displayed in Staff view. This isn't just read-only; you can also edit in this view.

Staff View Upper Toolbar

The seven leftmost buttons reprise other functions we've discussed in previous MIDI views. The two buttons to the right of these, Fill Durations and Trim Durations, visually round up or round down note durations, respectively, if they end a little bit before or extend a little bit past the start of the next note. This is to make the display more readable and is not something you'd use when entering notes.

The next button to the right, Display Resolution, sets the minimum duration that will be displayed. Notes below that minimum duration will be displayed as notes having the minimum duration.

Clicking on the Staff View Layout button brings up a dialog box for adjusting the staff properties (which clef, whether there's a split between clefs, and so on; see Figure 9.5).

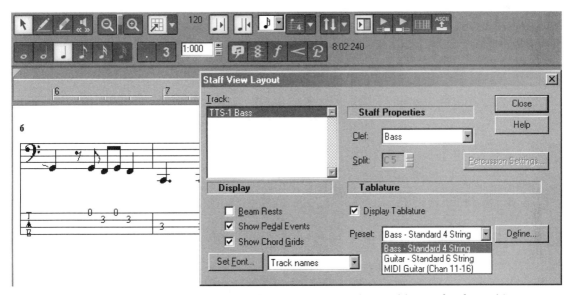

Figure 9.5 In addition to changing the staff layout, you can show tablature for fretted instruments. Note how below the notation, toward the left, there's tablature for the bass part; in the dialog box, Display Tablature is checked, using the Bass – Standard 4 String preset.

Of the five rightmost buttons, the next two to the right show the Track Picker and Show/Hide Track Pane, which we've covered before. The next two, Play Previous and Play Next, let you step through the Staff view note by note, playing these notes as you go along. The second button from the right calls up Fret view (more on this later), and the rightmost button exports tablature to a standard ASCII text file.

Staff View Lower Toolbar

The buttons to the left in the lower toolbar specify the note duration that the Draw tool will enter, along with dotted and triplet options. The numeric field shows the current note duration in ticks; you can edit this if needed.

The five buttons to the right turn the Draw tool into a tool for entering (from left to right) lyrics, chords, dynamic expressions, crescendos/decrescendos, and pedal markings.

Staff View Tablature

Tablature provides a more user-friendly form of notation for stringed-instrument players. Instead of showing notes on a staff, tablature shows strings and where notes would be fretted on those strings (see Figure 9.6). This works really well in conjunction with Fret view, which you can select by clicking on the Fret View button in the upper toolbar or by typing V.

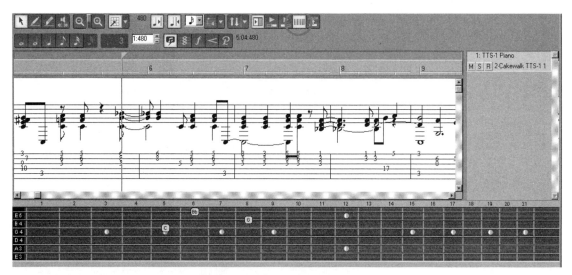

Figure 9.6 Note the two lines of staff. The upper line shows conventional notation, while the lower line shows the same notation expressed as tablature. The Fret view, selected by clicking on the circled button, is toward the bottom. The Now time is over three notes, which show up in the appropriate frets on the Fret view.

Setting Up Tablature

When you call up the Staff View Layout box, you have the opportunity to click on the Define button and edit various tablature settings (see Figure 9.7).

Tablature Settings has a preset box at the top for choosing among 4-string bass, 6-string guitar, and MIDI guitar. That's all most people will need, but clicking on the Tablature tab brings up more options. The Method value can be floating, where notes are assigned to frets based on optimizing to the instrument's open position, or fixed, where you can specify a range on the neck where the notes should be assigned, if possible. (The range is defined by a span of frets and the lowest fret to be part of the range.) A third option, MIDI Channel, assigns notes to strings based on MIDI channel, which is relevant when using MIDI guitar that assigns different strings to different channels. For all of these, you can also specify the number of frets in the guitar neck.

There are several presets for string tunings and alternate tunings, and you can choose the number of strings, from 1 to 8. (Ukulele and 7-string guitar players can rejoice.)

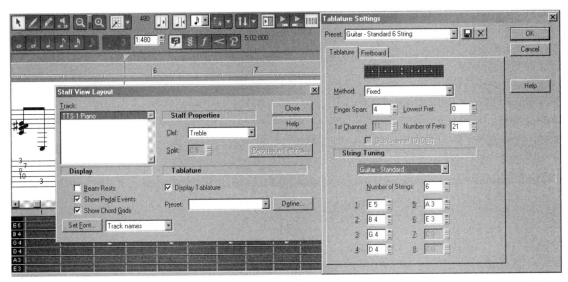

Figure 9.7 Clicking on the Define button while in the Staff View Layout box brings up the Tablature Settings dialog box, which has many options for specifying the type of virtual guitar you're using.

The Fretboard tab is all about eye candy: You can choose from three "virtual woods" in two different levels of resolution, but you can also have the low string on the top or bottom of the neck graphic.

QuickTab versus Regenerate Tab

In the Staff view upper toolbar, the drop-down menu to the right of the Staff View Layout button chooses between QuickTab and Regenerate Tab. If tab isn't already showing, select QuickTab, and SONAR Home Studio will generate tablature.

Generating tab from a part other than MIDI guitar can be hit or miss, because the voicing on, say, a piano is very different from guitar. Nonetheless, SONAR Home Studio will do its best to create tab that can be played by actual human beings, and it succeeds much of the time. If not, you can select notes that you want to "re-tab" in the Staff view and then select Regenerate Tab from the Staff View Layout drop-down menu. This brings up a dialog box that's a subset of the Tablature Settings dialog box, where you can specify the method of generating tab (floating, fixed, or MIDI channel), finger span, and lowest fret.

"MIDI Guitar" for Starving Musicians

Compared to keyboards, one of the great aspects of guitar is the wide-open chord voicings that use a mix of open and fretted strings. If you're a guitar player who dabbles at keyboards, odds are you can play the basic majors, minors, and so forth. But what about those wonderful jazz voicings that you're only comfortable with when playing guitar? And what if you're a keyboard player who knows a little guitar but has a hard time fingering some of the more challenging guitar chord shapes?

MIDI guitar is a possible solution, although it's out of reach financially for many guitar players. Fortunately, SONAR Home Studio's Fret view provides a great workaround for getting guitar voicings into a keyboard world. You can enter notes on a guitar fretboard and then have them play back in a project.

Start by loading a suitable patch, guitar or otherwise, from a soft synth (or external tone module). Decide which MIDI track will contain the notes, make it the active track, and then choose View > Staff and click on the Fret View button.

Click on the measure indicator above the staff where you want to enter the chord. Select the Draw tool and then click on the desired notes on the fingerboard or on an open string (in other words, below the first fret). Like a real guitar, you're allowed one note per string. As you enter each note, it will show up as notation on the staff along with notes on the guitar neck (see Figure 9.8).

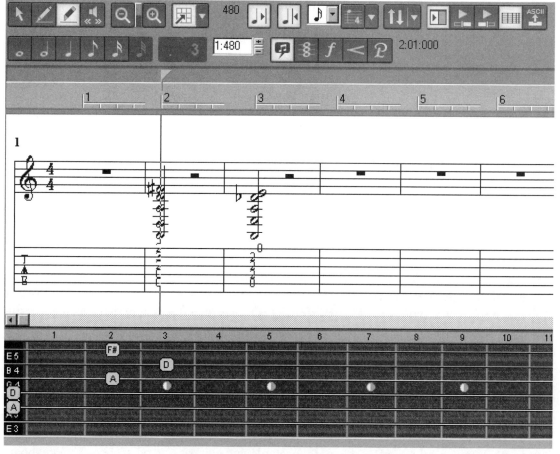

Figure 9.8 Enter notes on the guitar neck while in Staff view, and they also show up as notation and will play back like any other notes—but if desired, you can also open up the part in the Piano Roll view for additional editing.

As with any other kind of notation screen entry, you can cut, copy, paste, and so on individual notes or groups of notes.

If you start playback, notes will light in red on the staff (and blue on the neck) as they sound. Otherwise, notes are black. You can play the next note/chord or previous note/chord by clicking on the Play Next or Play Previous button.

For the most realistic guitar effect, you'll want to "strum" the notes, but this requires some manual editing. Open the Piano Roll view so you can edit the chord notes to create a strum effect. To do this, spread the note attacks so that the lowest note starts a bit ahead of the beat, the highest note starts a bit behind the beat, and the other note attacks follow an even gradient between the highest and lowest notes. You can also try moving the whole chord, including offsets, so that the highest note hits right on the beat. This provides a different kind of phrasing; guitarists use both, depending on the feel of the song.

Entering Lyrics in Staff View

Although there is a separate Lyrics view, it's basically like a text editor and is useful mostly for having a version of lyrics vocalists can see as they sing. However, note that you can also enter the lyrics in a project's File Info window (choose File > Info)—there's a huge "notepad" area toward the lower part of this window.

The most appropriate use of lyrics is in Staff view, because you can see which words go with which notes. You enter lyrics in Staff view, below the staff, as follows (see Figure 9.9).

1. Click on the Draw tool and then click on the Lyrics button.

2. Place the cursor under the first note to have an associated lyric. When it's in a valid place to enter a lyric, it will turn into a Pencil icon.

3. Click with the Pencil, and an insertion box will appear.

4. Enter the lyric (word or syllable) associated with that note. To move on to the next note and enter another word, hit the spacebar or the Tab key and then enter the next lyric in the insertion box. To move on to the next note and enter another syllable, type a hyphen and then enter the next lyric. To skip notes, hit spaces or tabs until the insertion box is under the next note where you want to add a lyric.

5. If you need to backspace to correct an error, press Shift+Tab to return to the previous note.

6. When you're finished entering lyrics, hit the Return key.

Editing lyrics is simple. Use the Draw tool to click on the lyric you want to change and then retype the lyric in the insertion box. When you're finished, hit Return.

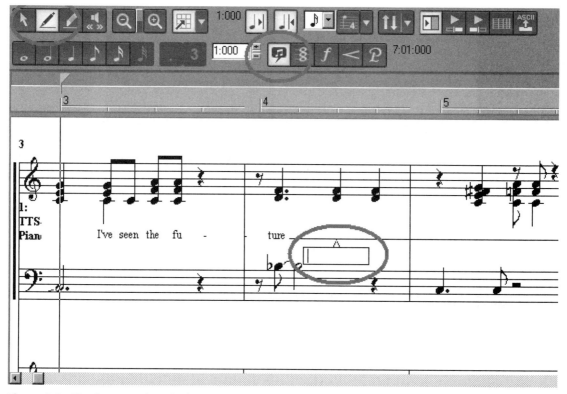

Figure 9.9   The Draw tool, Lyrics button, and insertion box where text will be entered are all circled for clarity. Note how the two syllables in "future" are split over two notes because they're separated with a hyphen.

10 The Step Sequencer

Available only in SONAR Home Studio 7 XL, the Step Sequencer's origins lie in the days of analog synthesis. Typically having 8 to 16 steps, these control modules *stepped* through a *sequence* of control voltages that went to a control voltage output. For example, if you patched this voltage output to an oscillator's control voltage input, you could create short melodies.

These steps usually generated a trigger as well as a voltage, suitable for triggering an envelope or other modulation source. This type of sequencer was later applied to drum machines, where with devices like Roland's TR-808 (or Reason's ReDrum, for that matter), you had 16 steps, and each step could contain one or more triggers for triggering drum sound events at that particular step. For example, with a 16-step sequencer, if you programmed a trigger to occur on the first, fifth, ninth, and thirteenth steps and sent this to the kick drum, you'd have a "four on the floor" kick drum beat.

But step sequencing isn't limited to drums; one of the most famous applications was the step sequencer in the Roland TB-303 Bassline, which was the foundation for a lot of "acid" dance music. The repetitive, cyclic nature of step sequencer–generated patterns lent itself well to this musical style.

About SONAR Home Studio's Step Sequencer

Along with the Piano Roll, Event List, and Staff views, SONAR Home Studio's Step Sequencer (Figure 10.1) represents a particular way to view, create, and edit MIDI clips. There are several significant differences other than the interface (for example, the Step Sequencer inherently creates a MIDI Groove Clip, and all notes must be quantized to a grid), but the concept is the same. You can have as many Step Sequence clips running as you want, on multiple tracks or the same track.

Like other step sequencers, this one consists of a matrix, with horizontal rows representing a particular note and vertical columns representing a particular beat or subdivision thereof. You click at the junction of a row and column when you want to trigger a particular note event (or drum hit) at a particular time. Because step sequencers are often used with drums, it's not surprising that this one integrates with SONAR Home Studio's drum map feature: You can select a

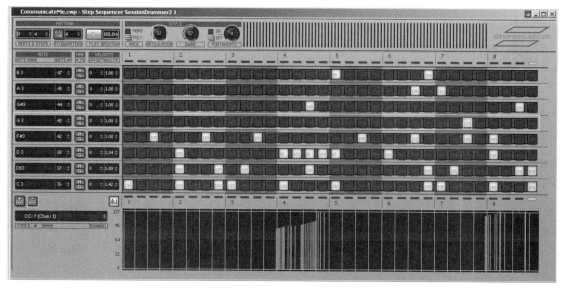

Figure 10.1 The Step Sequencer is driving SONAR Home Studio's Studio Instruments Drum Kit. Note the controller strip along the bottom of the Step Sequencer window.

drum map for the Step Sequencer by choosing one from the associated MIDI channel's output field. (Hint: SONAR Home Studio has, at last count, 5,344,785 drum maps. Or maybe it just seems that way! To find a drum map quickly, while the list of drum maps is open, type a letter to scoot to a particular company. For example, type Y, and you'll jump to the part of the list with drum maps for Yamaha gear.)

Because of the drum map tie-in, each row can send to a different MIDI channel or even MIDI port, if desired. You can either make these assignments in the Drum Map Manager itself or, as a shortcut, double-click on a note name in a Step Sequencer row, and it will bring up a Properties box where you can make a variety of changes, including remapping of notes (see Figure 10.2). If no drum map is assigned, double-clicking on a note name will bring up the Drum Map Manager, where you can open a drum map or create a new one.

The Step Sequencer has a seemingly unlimited number of rows—I gave up after inserting 130 of them, which covers the available range of MIDI notes and then some. (Note that you can assign events in multiple rows to the same MIDI note, which may seem useless—but you can get some cool flanging effects with sounds like snare hits.)

You can mute and solo individual rows with the M and S buttons, respectively, and if you right-click on the right side of a row, you have the option to insert or delete a row, shift all notes in the row left or right, or clear all triggers in all rows. Furthermore, you can drag an entire row up or down to change its position by clicking and dragging on the row's background (for example, the strip between the Mute/Solo buttons and the Row Note Name or Row Velocity Offset field) and

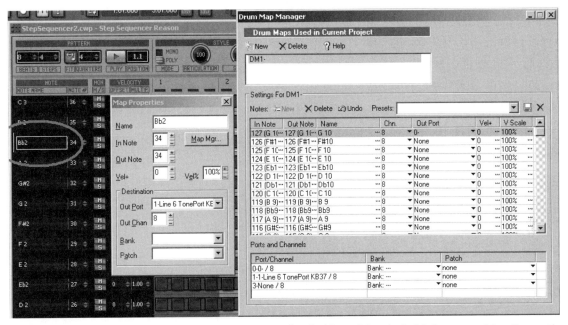

Figure 10.2 Double-clicking on a row's note name (circled in red for clarity) brings up a Map Properties dialog box, where you can make a variety of changes. If you want to modify the drum map more extensively, clicking on Map Mgr opens up the Drum Map Manager window.

then, if desired, reassign the note it plays. This can be handy if you change drum sound generators and find that notes that triggered, say, hi-hat for one drum set don't trigger hi-hat in a different set.

The step sequence can be up to 64 beats long, with up to 16 steps per beat. So not only can you have step sequences, but they can be pretty long and feature rapid-fire note sequences. This, to me, is the most important Step Sequencer feature; you're not limited to, say, four beats of sixteenth notes.

The Step Sequencer also includes a controller strip along the bottom where you can do the same kind of controller editing as in Piano Roll view, which is a very useful addition.

The final feature is Fit to Quarter Note, where you can take a clip and force it to fit into a specific number of quarter notes. This is kind of like time-stretching, as the notes get stretched to fit into a larger number of quarter notes or shrunk to fit into a smaller number. For example, if you have an eight-beat, 4/4 sequence, and you make it fit 16 quarter notes, the sequence plays back at half time.

Adjusting Velocity

When you drop a note in place, it defaults to a velocity value of 100. If you double-click on it, you can type in a new value (or use + and – buttons or a "spinner" to change the value), but I find it most convenient to just use the mouse's scroll wheel. Holding Shift while using the wheel provides a "fine-tuning" function.

You can also affect all notes in a row with a per-row velocity offset or multiply all velocities in a row by a constant (see Figure 10.3). You can't, however, display velocity tails as you can in the Piano Roll view.

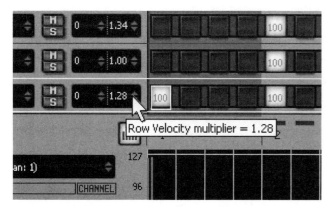

Figure 10.3 You can multiply an entire row by a specific ratio or offset it by a specific amount (the parameter to the immediate right of the Mute/Solo buttons).

Additional Controls

There are controls for Articulation, Portamento, Swing, and Mode. Here's what they do:

- Articulation sets a gate time for notes that holds the note on for a certain amount of time. The default is 100%, which holds for the full value of the note; smaller settings give a more staccato effect with melodic lines. This has little effect with drums.

- Portamento is used for melodic lines as opposed to drums and slides the pitch between notes rather than jumping from one note to the next. It has an associated Portamento time control that sets the rate of the glide and an on-off switch; of course, the instrument you're controlling needs to support portamento for this to matter.

- Swing changes the "spacing" between beats. With a 50% value, the beats are evenly spaced, as normal. Decreasing Swing shortens the time between the first and second beats, while lengthening the time between the second and third beats to compensate, so that the total length remains the same. Increasing Swing does the reverse.

- The Mode switch chooses between Poly (allows you to enter several notes in the same column) and Mono (allows only one note per column, which typically makes sense for bass lines).

Step Sequencer Groove Clip versus Notes

As you work with the Step Sequencer, it creates a MIDI Groove Clip on the selected MIDI track. However, if the track is in PRV mode, you won't see the Clip—only the notes within the Clip. To see the notes as a Step Sequencer Groove Clip, exit PRV mode (Figure 10.4). Note that Step Sequencer Groove Clips have a distinctive "steps" icon in the clip's upper left.

Figure 10.4   Click on the PRV button to toggle in and out of PRV mode. In this screen shot PRV is disabled, so the Step Sequencer MIDI data appears as a Step Sequencer Groove Clip.

Because the Step Sequencer creates a Groove Clip, you can "roll out" the clip for as many repeats as you want, as with any standard Groove Clip.

Unlinking Step Sequencer Clips

Suppose you roll out a Clip for four repeats, but you want to make a few small changes on the last repeat. All repeats are linked to the same Step Sequencer pattern, even ones that are copied or split. However, you can unlink a Step Sequencer Clip by right-clicking on the Clip you want to unlink and choosing Unlink Step Sequencer Clips. This command may be one of the "hidden" ones, so if you don't see it, hold your mouse over the arrows that appear at the bottom of the context menu, and the additional options will appear (see Figure 10.5).

Piano Roll Editing with the Step Sequencer

If you right-click on the Step Sequencer–generated Groove Clip and choose View > Piano Roll, you'll see the Step Sequencer notes in the Piano Roll. However, these notes still "belong" to the Step Sequencer; you cannot edit them. What you can do is create, delete, and otherwise edit non–Step Sequencer notes in the Piano Roll view. These create "mini-clips" on top of the Step Sequencer Clip in the Track view.

If you want to bail out of the Step Sequencer and convert its notes into a standard MIDI Clip, select the Step Sequencer Clip (and any other Clips you might have created "on top" of it by

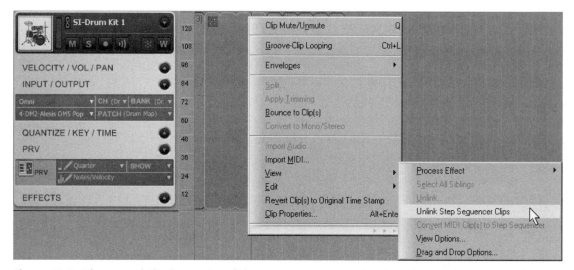

Figure 10.5 The second Clip in a series of three Step Sequencer Clips is about to be unlinked. Note that this menu is accessed by holding the mouse over the lower blue band of the main context menu.

already editing in the Piano Roll view), and go to Edit > Bounce to Clip(s). The result will be a standard MIDI Clip.

But note that this is a bidirectional process: You can also convert a MIDI Clip to a Step Sequencer Clip. Right-click on the MIDI Clip and select Convert MIDI Clip(s) to Step Sequencer. (If you don't see this command, don't forget to hover the mouse along the bottom of the window to see additional, less-used commands.) Note that there are two limitations:

- The Step Sequencer can't place notes that don't fall on the beat—for example, notes that lead or lag slightly. As a result, upon converting, you'll be asked to specify a quantize resolution.

- Any controller data contained in the MIDI Clip will be lost during the conversion process.

Considerations for Melodic Parts

If you want longer or shorter notes than a simple trigger for use with melodic lines, such as bass parts, tie notes together into longer notes by Ctrl-clicking in the space between them or just clicking and hitting Enter. The series of notes will play as one note, using the first note's velocity.

Musical Applications

So why bother with step sequencing, when you can do much of the same thing in the Piano Roll view? It's primarily a matter of personal preference, but it's also a matter of speed. With the Piano Roll, you need to place the note with more care than you do with a step sequencer. There are also no zooming issues, because the Step Sequencer buttons always stay the same size.

Another useful feature is that a step sequencer tends to promote experimentation. It's so easy to erase and place notes that you can get into just "painting" notes and then judging whether the results are any good. Being able to mute and solo individual drum sounds, as well as shift a row of hits left or right and copy/cut/paste rows, makes it easy to try out various "what if" rhythmic scenarios with different sounds.

Finally, a step sequencer seems to put you in a certain "mood," for lack of a better term. The bass parts I come up with using a step sequencer are very different from the ones I would play on a keyboard, and I suspect most people would have a similar experience.

(Incidentally, the 7.0.1 update fixed some Step Sequencer quirks. If you're still on SONAR Home Studio 7, make sure you download the patch.)

Step-By-Step: Step Sequencing a Drum Part

1.   Insert the Studio Drums by going to Insert > Soft Synths > Studio Instruments > SI-Drum Kit.

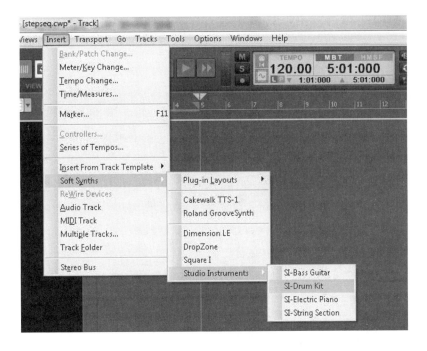

2.   On the Insert Soft Synth Options screen, click on MIDI Source, Synth Track Folder, and First Synth Audio Output. Also click on Synth Property Page if you want to see the drum interface when you insert the instrument. Then click on OK.

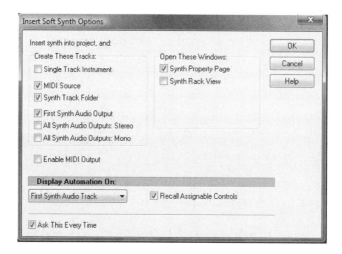

3.   Select the MIDI track, open it, and then open the PRV section. Turn off PRV if it's on. (The PRV icon will change from white to gray.)

4.   Go to Views > Step Sequencer. The Step Sequencer will appear.

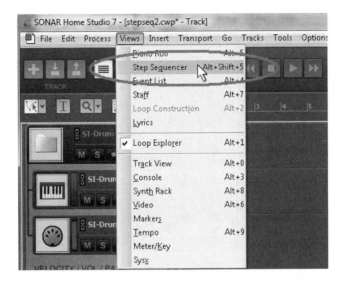

5.   Open the track's Input/Output section and the Output field. Go to New Drum Map > Studio Instruments Drums. (Remember that after selecting New Drum Map, you can type S to take you to the maps starting with S.)

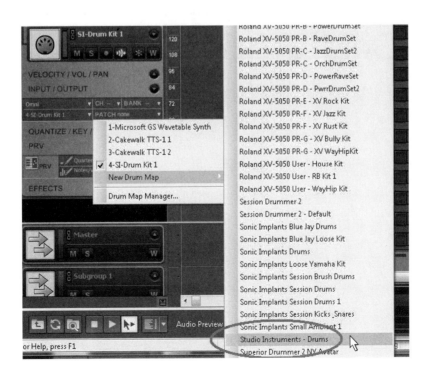

6. The Step Sequencer now will show the drum names for the various rows. Click the Step Sequencer's Play button and then click on the various steps to program beats.

7. Have fun and experiment with the various controls—changing velocities, adding more beats, and so on.

11 MIDI Plug-Ins

There's a lot of excitement about audio plug-ins (such as signal processors and virtual instruments), but MIDI plug-ins—which provide effects for MIDI tracks—also deserve some attention. Granted, it may not be quite as sexy to massage MIDI data as it is to warp audio beyond all recognition or play a dead-on accurate emulation of some impossible-to-find vintage synth, but MIDI plug-ins definitely have their uses.

MIDI plug-ins work very much like the audio kind: They can process a track or input signal in real time or be applied destructively to anything from individual clips to complete tracks. There are two ways to insert a MIDI plug-in in a MIDI track.

- In the Track view, unfold the track's Effects section. Click on Add Effect and then choose MIDI > Cakewalk FX and select the desired effect (see Figure 11.1).

Figure 11.1 The MIDI Event Filter plug-in is being selected for a bass MIDI track.

- In Console view, click on the + button just above the rectangular FX bin (and to the right of the FX button), choose MIDI Plugins > Cakewalk FX, and then select the desired effect.

125

With this method of insertion, the plug-ins work nondestructively, in real time. To apply the effect and make it permanent, choose Process > Apply MIDI Effects. This will apply the effect to all selected notes in the MIDI track.

You can also apply MIDI effects in three ways.

- With a MIDI clip in Track view, right-click on the clip, select Process Effect (it may be necessary to click on the arrows at the bottom of the menu to show this) > MIDI Effects > Cakewalk FX, and then choose the desired effect. Make your adjustments and then click on OK to apply the effect to the clip.

- When in PRV mode (inline MIDI editing) in Track view, use the PRV Select tool to select the notes you want to process. Right-click anywhere within the MIDI track and choose MIDI Plugins > Cakewalk FX, then select the desired effect. Enter any edits and then click on OK to apply the effect.

- Whether in PRV mode or viewing clips in Track view, select the notes you want to process, then choose Process > MIDI Fx > Cakewalk FX and choose an appropriate effect. Make your adjustments and then click on OK to apply the effect.

With these three options, note that you can click on the Audition button to hear a portion of the processed sound before you commit to applying the effect. If the Piano Roll view is open, SONAR Home Studio will redraw the data to show the effect of adding the plug-in. (For example, if you're using the Echo Delay plug-in, you'll see the additional echoed notes.) These changes are also visible in the Clips pane.

When you click on Stop, the clip stops playing, and the data reverts to how it looked before. Click on Cancel, and the selected data remains unchanged, or click on OK to apply the effect to the data permanently.

Applying MIDI effects is crucial if you save your file as a Standard MIDI File (SMF), because the MIDI effects are not part of the SMF spec. When you apply the effects to a track, upon saving the file, the track's data reflects the results of any processing.

SONAR Home Studio's Roster of Plug-Ins

SONAR includes several MIDI plug-ins. Fortunately, the Help menus are well written and descriptive, so I won't take up space repeating them; just click on the MIDI plug-in and press F1 to bring up the Help menu. I'll start with brief descriptions and then present useful applications for these plug-ins.

Arpeggiator

If you're a fan of arpeggiation—adding a cascade of additional, harmonically related notes to the notes you're playing—you'll love this Arpeggiator. Not only can you specify the number of repeats, but you can add swing, have the Arpeggiator analyze the chord you're playing and arpeggiate based on that data, set the note range over which notes will be arpeggiated, and much more (see Figure 11.2).

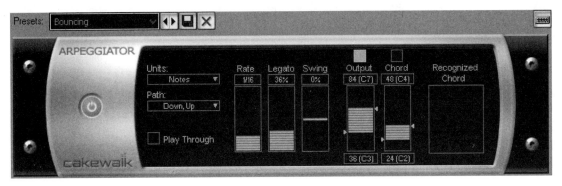

Figure 11.2 The Arpeggiator MIDI effect is not only versatile, but it can provide arpeggiations if your keyboard controller doesn't have an arpeggiator feature.

Chord Analyzer

This looks at MIDI input or track data every 1 to 128 MIDI ticks (you set the sampling rate), displays the notes being played on a virtual keyboard, shows the notes on a staff, and tells you what chord it recognizes. If the chord is ambiguous (for example, the voicing is the same for an F major chord or A minor+5, second inversion), the Analyzer will display all voicings it recognizes. This plug won't make a profound difference in the course of Western civilization, but it's a very useful learning tool.

Echo Delay

This is like an echo unit for MIDI data. You can specify delay in ticks, milliseconds, or rhythmic value (or tap tempo), the number of echoes, velocity decay rate from one echo to the next, whether echoes are transposed (chromatically or diatonically, up or down, and the interval), and—something you won't find on standard plug-ins—swing value. Cut this baby loose on 55% swing, and you'll be impressed (see Figure 11.3).

You can also enter a pitch value, where successive echoes change pitch—in other words, if you specify pitch as –1, each echo will be one semitone lower in pitch than the previous echo. Echo Delay makes it particularly easy to play those staccato, "dugga-dugga-dugga" synth parts that serve as rhythmic underpinnings to many dance tracks. The only downside is that long, languid echoes eat up synth voices.

MIDI Event Filter

For advanced MIDI users, the Edit > Select > By Filter option can apply editing only to specific types and/or values of events. As this is a pretty sophisticated feature, if you're interested in

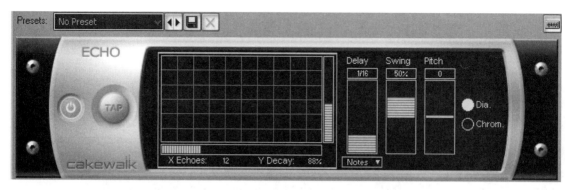

Figure 11.3 Swing adds interesting rhythmic effects to echoes and can be a negative or a positive amount. It's possible to set a decay percentage above 100%, in which case each successive echo becomes louder.

checking it out, click on the window's Help button. Besides, there's an easier way to do many of the same functions with the MIDI Event Filter plug-in.

One reason this is a quicker way to achieve some types of filtering is because you can easily create presets regarding which data to remove (for example, channel aftertouch or key after-touch), as well as specific value ranges (such as all key aftertouch events with values under 10 or all notes with durations under five ticks). I find the way to get the most out of this plug-in is to create presets that take care of common editing situations, such as removing unintended after-touch data. It's also useful for creating keyboard splits, as described later in this chapter.

Quantize

Sure, SONAR Home Studio already has a Quantize function, but remember, the plug-in works in real time. I find this indispensable for doing quick quantization on, say, a drum part while laying down tracks—the part remains unaltered, so I can take off the plug-in later and do any permanent quantizing with a bit more finesse. This plug-in has what you'd expect from a quantization plug-in: resolution, strength, swing, window, offset, randomization, and so on (see Figure 11.4).

Transpose

This flexible plug-in has capabilities that far exceed just going through the usual Process > Transpose route. It will transpose by intervals or diatonically, but it can also transpose from one key to another and change scales in the process (as well as show which notes are mapped to which target notes). It's also possible to create a custom transposition map (which can serve as a drum mapper if you're not into using SONAR Home Studio's drum grid pane) and constrain notes to a particular scale if they fall outside the accepted roster of notes for a given scale (see Figure 11.5).

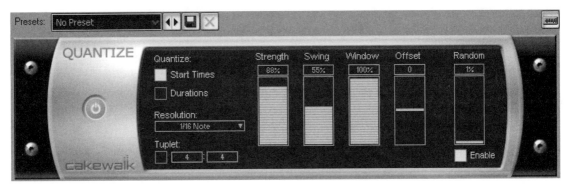

Figure 11.4 The Quantize plug-in not only works in real time, but it offers strength, swing, and randomization options.

Figure 11.5 Here, material recorded in the key of C, based on the Ionian scale, is about to be transposed to the key of A and changed to a Spanish Phrygian scale. The note map toward the right shows the original notes and the target notes to which they are mapped.

Velocity

This plug-in can set all velocities to a constant, add or subtract a constant, scale to a certain percentage of the current value, randomize, and limit range. (That is, velocities lower than a certain limit are brought up to that value, while velocities higher than another limit are reduced to that value.) This function is well suited to "compressing" the amplitude of MIDI data.

Using Plug-Ins to Auto-Correct MIDI Tricks

If you use Microsoft Word and enable auto-correct, Word can fix your typing mistakes as they happen. In other words, if you type "ahppen," Word knows you meant to type "happen" and will fix it as you type—you don't have to go in later and fix it. Most of the time, Word understands what you want, and its ability to correct your errors in a preemptive manner can save quite a bit of time.

So what does this have to do with SONAR Home Studio? If you're playing MIDI parts, you can use the MIDI plug-ins to implement several real-time auto-correction options that can make sure what you play falls within a certain velocity range, is constrained to a particular scale, or hits a particular rhythm. Far from "robotizing" your music, you can choose the extent to which you want auto-correction to influence your playing. For example, although SONAR Home Studio has an auto-input quantize feature so incoming notes hit *exactly* on the specified rhythmic value, you can also ask the program to be a little bit looser about the procedure or add some swing to your playing.

If you learn how these tricks work, sometimes you'll be able to play MIDI parts without having to do *any* editing afterward…especially with drum and percussion parts. If you think this saves hassles, you're right! So, following are the auto-correction tricks I like to use when playing MIDI parts into SONAR Home Studio.

For Those Who Play Only in C

Or D, for that matter, if you prefer minor keys…let's face it, some wannabe keyboard players are better at playing in particular keys than others. So if the song is in G# but you want to play in C, SONAR Home Studio has just the ticket: The Transpose MIDI plug-in. Here's how to use it.

1. As described earlier, when we discussed how to insert MIDI plug-ins, insert the Transpose MIDI plug-in.

2. Under Transpose Method, choose Interval.

3. Use the Offset slider to select the desired amount of transposition. For example, if you want to play in the key of C and have the notes come out in the key of G#, set Offset to +8 to transpose up or –4 to transpose down (see Figure 11.6).

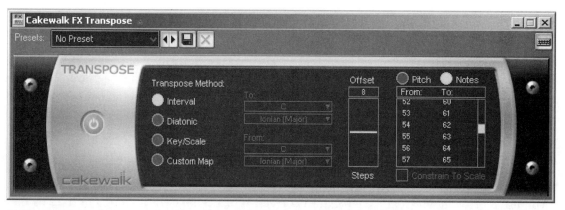

Figure 11.6 In this example, the Transpose MIDI effect is transposing all notes up by eight steps (semitones).

4. To verify the amount of transposition, click on the plug-in's Notes button, and the right To column will display the result of playing the note listed in the left From column.

Although you'll hear the transposed part, the notes that actually get recorded in a track are the notes you played, not the transposed versions. So, you'll need to leave Transpose enabled to maintain the transposition during playback. To alter the track permanently to the target key, select the track (or clip, if that's all you want to change) and choose Process > Apply MIDI Effects. SONAR will give you the option to delete the MIDI effect automatically after processing, so that it doesn't transpose the newly transposed notes by mistake.

For Those Who Can't Play in C, Period

If you have a hard time playing accurately in *any* key, SONAR Home Studio can help with that, too. Again, the solution is the Transpose MIDI plug-in.

1. With the Transpose MIDI plug-in inserted, under Transpose Method, choose Key/Scale.

2. In the From field, choose the key in which you're playing. I recommend selecting Chromatic as the scale. This means that *any* incoming note will be constrained to the scale you specify in the next step.

3. In the To field, choose the key in which you're playing, and directly below that, the scale to which you want to constrain the note.

4. Leave Offset at 0 and click on the Constrain to Scale button.

Although it's always a good idea to try to play in the correct scale, if you play a "wrong" note, it will be constrained to the nearest "correct" note. However, as in the earlier example, SONAR records what you play, so you need to apply the MIDI effect if you want any changes to be permanent. On the other hand, you can also experiment with choosing different To scales and listening to what they sound like.

And If You Can't Play in Key, in a Scale, or to a Rhythm...

Maybe you should consider a different line of work! Meanwhile, SONAR Home Studio can apply quantization in real time to incoming notes as you play. Enable the Input Quantize field (under Quantize/Key/Time) in a MIDI track and specify the input quantization value (for example, sixteenth notes).

When you apply input quantization, the notes are placed as specified. But what if you don't like the rigid, lock-step aspect of quantization and would like SONAR to tighten up your playing just a little bit? At the bottom of the Input Quantize Resolution menu, you'll find an option for Quantize Settings (see Figure 11.7).

Here you can choose whether you also want to quantize controller events (you probably do; make sure Only Quantize Notes is unchecked), and you'll also find parameters for Strength, Swing, and Window. You'll likely want Window set to 100% so that all notes are affected. Setting it to a lesser value "pulls" the window closer to the quantization value, meaning that

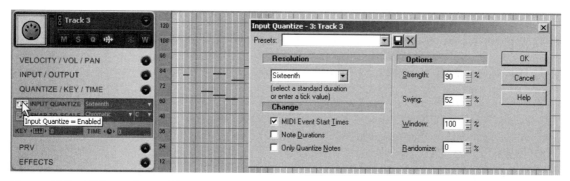

Figure 11.7 Click on the enable box for input quantization and then select the desired quantization value from the drop-down menu to the right. If you select Quantize Settings from this menu, you can alter how the quantization affects the incoming MIDI data—including such features as adding swing or randomization.

notes outside the window's range won't be quantized. (I never did quite understand this parameter; I'd prefer to have notes close to a specified rhythmic value be left alone, while quantizing those that are farther away.)

Note that there's also a Randomize box, but I leave that unchecked—if I wanted a random performance, I'd feed the drummer a couple of beers!

Velocity Fixes

Many times with drum parts, you want to restrict your velocity values to specific ranges—as if you were using a compressor. This is easy to do with the Velocity MIDI plug-in, which works in real time: Even though the part that gets recorded is what you play, you hear the processed part as you play.

For example, suppose you want to add dynamics to a dance tune kick drum part. During the soft hits, you don't want the kick to be *too* soft, but while it's easy to just whack a key to get maximum velocity, it might be a little harder to have a refined enough touch so that your lowest velocity hits never go below, say, a velocity of 86. Fortunately, there's a MIDI effect that can tweak your velocity to solve these types of problems, as well as other ones.

To get started, insert the Velocity plug-in into the FX bin for the desired MIDI track. From here, you can do several useful things.

- **Limit the range of incoming notes.** Click on the Limit button and set an upper limit, a lower limit, or both (see Figure 11.8). Setting an upper limit can be handy when playing percussion parts if you want to keep really prominent hits to a minimum.

- **Set all incoming notes to a constant value.** Click on the Set To button and specify a particular velocity value. This is invaluable for those "four on floor" kick parts where you want every kick to hit at the maximum possible level.

Figure 11.8 In this screen shot, the Velocity MIDI plug-in is limiting incoming velocities between a maximum of 127 and a minimum of 90. As a result, any note with a velocity of 90 or below plays at 90.

- **Velocity "sensitizer" or "de-sensitizer."** The Change option adds or subtracts a constant amount to the incoming velocity value. Click on the Change button and then set a value with the slider. This is sort of like changing the sensitivity curve on a MIDI keyboard; use positive values to make the keyboard more sensitive (for example, setting the value to 20 will add 20 to all incoming MIDI notes) or set negative values to make the keyboard less sensitive.

- **Velocity "compressor."** This plug-in increases low velocity values while restricting peaks to the maximum available MIDI value—pretty much the equivalent of a MIDI velocity value compressor. Just click on Scale and select a value above 100%. (Higher values give more "compression.") For example, with a value of 150%, a velocity of 20 becomes 30, a velocity of 40 becomes 60, a velocity of 64 becomes 96, and all velocities over 85 hit the maximum value of 128.

- **Velocity randomizer.** I'm not a huge fan of randomizing, but a little bit can sometimes be effective with percussion parts, such as tambourine and congas. Once Randomize is checked, the Amount slider determines the maximum amount the input value can be offset, while the Tendency slider sets the tendency of the offset to be lower (negative values) or higher (positive values).

Proofreading Your Sequence

This application is unlike most of the previous ones, because it's designed to act more like a spell-checker that fixes problems after the fact.

No matter how good a keyboard player you are, odds are you'll hit some wrong notes that you don't even hear—maybe you brushed your finger against a key while changing from one chord to another, thus producing a low-velocity, short-duration note. And if you play MIDI guitar, odds are you'll know exactly what I'm talking about—little "ghost" notes are a fact of life. But there's an easy way to get rid of them.

Insert the MIDI Event Filter into a MIDI track's FX bin and click the Notes button. Set the lower Velocity slider limit to around 20 and the lower Duration value to around 100.

(A thirty-second note has a duration of 120 ticks at the usual 960 ticks per quarter note resolution.) Then select the track and choose Process > Apply MIDI Effects. All those funky little useless notes will disappear (see Figure 11.9).

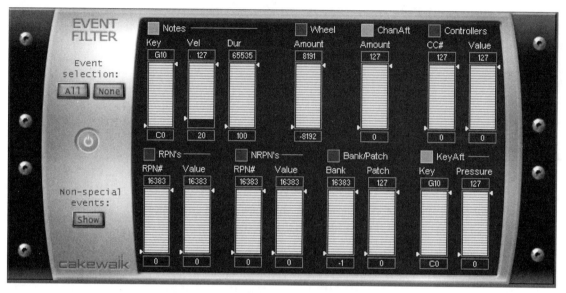

Figure 11.9   The Event Filter has been programmed to remove all notes with a Velocity under 20 and/or a Duration of under 100, as well as all channel aftertouch and key aftertouch events.

While you're at it, if your part didn't use any aftertouch, you might as well check Chan Aft and Key Aft (if you're lucky enough to have a keyboard with polyphonic aftertouch!), because that will remove any aftertouch that might have been recorded accidentally by hitting a key too hard.

Saving Often-Used Settings as Presets

If you use a particular MIDI plug-in setting a lot, you can save it as you would any audio plug-in effect. Just type a preset name in the Preset field and then click on the floppy disk icon to save it.

Creating Keyboard Splits

Although we've mostly covered fixing problems, because we're talking about MIDI effects, here's a useful trick for doing splits using the MIDI Event Filter.

Suppose you want a piano sound in the upper part of the keyboard (C4 and above) and a bass sound in the lower part (B3 and below). Here's how to do it (see Figure 11.10).

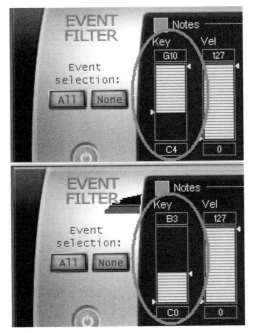

Figure 11.10 In this example, the upper Event Filter is sending notes C4–G10 to the piano track, while the lower Event Filter is sending notes C0–B3 to the bass track.

1. Insert the two requisite soft synths.

2. Turn Input Echo On for the two MIDI tracks driving the soft synths.

3. Insert a MIDI Event Filter in each track.

4. With each MIDI Event Filter, click on the Notes button.

5. Adjust the Key parameter for each MIDI filter to send the desired note range to the desired destination.

SONAR Home Studio's MIDI effects may be a little overlooked, but check them out—you'll be glad you did.

12 Backing Up Data with System Exclusive Messages

If you have hardware MIDI-compatible gear, such as drum machines, signal processors, or synthesizers, you can use SONAR Home Studio to back up their data. You probably don't think too much about saving data, because today's gear is pretty reliable, but anything from a bad memory backup battery to a parts failure can cause a piece of hardware to lose all its data. If you use only factory presets, this probably isn't an issue because you can always get them back, but if you create your own presets, it can be heartbreaking to lose all that work.

What System Exclusive Is and How It Works

The parameters in a hardware instrument or effects box are all just numbers being crunched by a computer, and a program is simply a collection of parameter numbers. So, everything that needs to be saved is basically computer data.

The MIDI specification includes a way for manufacturers to send equipment-specific data in a format that only equipment trained to recognize that data will accept. This type of data is called *system exclusive* (as opposed to data that's common to a wide variety of gear) and is called *SysEx* for short (or, in the case of SONAR Home Studio, Sysx). Furthermore, this SysEx data can be sent and received via MIDI.

Although SysEx data is used in many ways, one of the most common applications is to translate patch or program parameters into SysEx. If you send this data over the MIDI Out connector, and the data enters the MIDI In of a device or program (such as SONAR Home Studio) that stores SysEx, your program data will be saved.

What's really cool about saving SysEx with SONAR Home Studio is that it can store this data and play it back into your gear. So, you don't need to save patches in your synth, use memory cards, or employ any other messy techniques: Just back up your data as part of a project.

SONAR Home Studio has sophisticated SysEx capture/editing/playback options, but let's keep it simple and just cover how to save SysEx within a project and reload the SysEx into target instruments when you start that project.

1. Patch a MIDI cable between the source device output and the MIDI input of the interface that connects to SONAR Home Studio (as selected in Options > MIDI Devices).

2. Choose Options > Global, select the MIDI tab, and make sure System Exclusive is checked (see Figure 12.1).

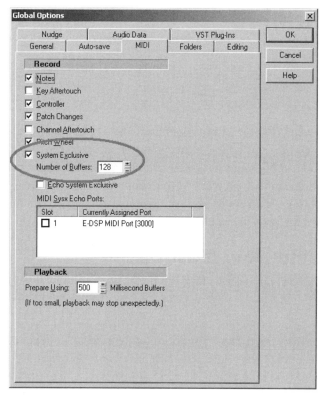

Figure 12.1 If the System Exclusive box isn't checked as a global option, you can't record SysEx data into SONAR Home Studio.

3. Choose View > Sysx. This displays a view of 8,192 banks of SysEx. A bank could be something like a complete synth setup, a particular program, a mixer preset, and so on.

4. As shown in Figure 12.2, click on the orange arrow (Receive Bank). This opens a menu with a plethora of supported synths. If your device happens to be on this list, select it and click on OK. From this point on, the process is pretty much automatic.

5. If your device is not on the list, select You Start Dump on Instrument and click on OK (also shown in Figure 12.2).

6. A screen will appear that shows SysEx reception status. It should read 0 Bytes Received, followed by the available space for SysEx storage.

7. Initiate the dump on the source instrument. You may need to dig in the manual to find which button to push to send the bulk data dump.

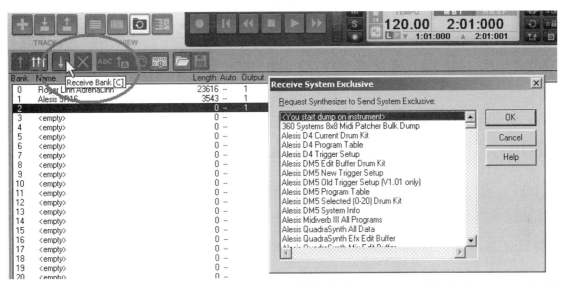

Figure 12.2   Check the list of supported instruments. If the device containing the SysEx you want isn't in the list, click on You Start Dump on Instrument.

8.   SONAR Home Studio's counter will increment as SONAR receives the data. When the counter stops, the SysEx has been received; click on Done (see Figure 12.3).

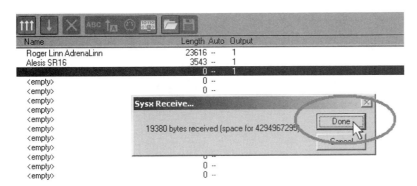

Figure 12.3   Once the counter stops incrementing, all data has been received. Click on Done.

9.   The toolbar at the top of the Sysx view window is now functional, because some actual SysEx has been stored. Click on the ABC icon to name the bank (always a good idea!).

If you now save the project, the SysEx data will be part of it. You can do three things with the stored SysEx bank:

- Save it to disk as a SysEx file. (Click on the floppy disk icon, navigate to where you want to save, and then save.)

- Send the bank to a target device. (Click on the black arrow at the left.)

- Send the bank automatically when you open the project. (See the next few steps.)

Here's how to do automatic bank sends:

1. In the Sysx view, highlight the bank you want to send automatically.

2. Click on the Auto Send Bank button (the one to the right of the ABC button). This places a check mark in the Auto column for the selected bank (see Figure 12.4).

Figure 12.4 The SysEx from Roger Linn's AdrenaLinn guitar processor has been selected for auto send, so the data will be sent via the interface MIDI Out every time the project opens.

3. Save the project file so it contains this additional information.

4. The next time you open the project, a screen will appear while loading and will remind you that the file contains SysEx data that is supposed to be sent automatically to your MIDI gear. To send it, click OK; otherwise, click on Cancel.

You can disable this screen so it doesn't appear by unchecking Ask This Question Every Time. I leave it checked, though—sometimes you don't want to overwrite works in progress, and it helps to be reminded that you're about to blast new data into RAM.

Overall, it's extremely convenient to store all the presets for your outboard gear in the same file as your main data. If you haven't taken advantage of this feature, get into the habit of doing so.

Sending SysEx from within a Track

What I've described so far is a non-real-time process—SysEx is sent automatically at the beginning of a project or manually at any point. However, if the System Exclusive option is checked under Options > Global > MIDI, SONAR Home Studio can record SysEx data into a MIDI track in real time and play it back in real time. Unfortunately, the message length limit for real-time SysEx is 255 bytes—enough to send a control setting or the like, but certainly not enough for even a modestly sized MIDI synthesizer preset.

However, if you have SysEx banks stored in the Sysx view, you can "embed" triggers for the SysEx banks in a track and have them play back at any time. Messages can be as short as a single preset or as long as an entire bulk dump.

To play back a SysEx bank from within a track, place the Now time where you want SONAR Home Studio to send the data and then open up the MIDI track's Event List view by choosing View > Event List (or pressing Alt+4). Next, press the computer keyboard's Insert key to insert an event into the Event List at the Now time position.

Double-click in the event's Kind field. When the Kind of Event window appears, under Special check Sysx Bank and then click on OK.

In the Event List entry's Data field, enter the number of the SysEx bank that should play back at this particular Now time (see Figure 12.5). When the project plays back and the Now time hits the position you specified, the SysEx data will be triggered and will play back.

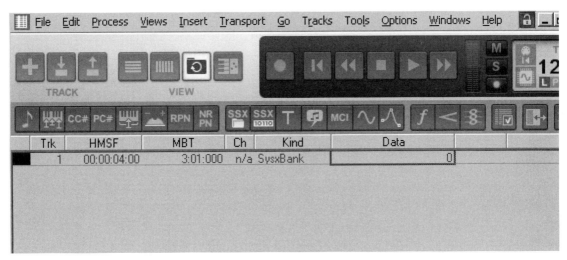

Figure 12.5   In the Event List view, the inserted event triggers playback of a SysEx bank.

Sending a big bulk dump will take a while, and some instruments may choke when receiving a large dump. If all you need to do is change a patch, you're probably better off saving individual patches as SysEx banks and triggering them. Also note that because SONAR Home Studio is playing in the background, make sure you trigger the SysEx early enough so that the dump process is complete before the data is needed.

Wouldn't it be easier just to insert program changes instead? Yes, except that this assumes you have the same presets loaded into your instrument that were loaded when you inserted the program change command. If you edit and tweak programs a lot, that may not be the case. By sending SysEx, you're sending the actual program data itself, not just something that calls up a particular memory slot.

13 Software Synthesizers

It used to be that synthesizers were costly, and sometimes temperamental, hardware devices. But all that changed when Steinberg introduced Virtual Studio Technology (VST), which allowed people to create synthesizers as software applications and insert them directly into hosts such as SONAR Home Studio. These applications are called *soft synths* or *virtual instruments*, and they are a type of *plug-in*—because they plug into a program such as SONAR Home Studio the way hardware synthesizers used to plug into mixers and recorders with patch cords. The big difference is that today's patch cords are virtual ones.

VST is a specification that lays out a set of rules so that software engineers can develop software synthesizers that can work with any programs that follow the VST spec. However, VST is not the only protocol, and SONAR Home Studio accepts instruments that follow either of two protocols: VST or DXi (a variation on Microsoft's DirectX plug-in specification). These are by far the most common protocols for Windows; VST is also common on the Mac, but you can't use a Mac VST instrument with a Windows program, or vice versa. You cannot use AU instruments with SONAR Home Studio, because these are only for Mac programs, nor can you use RTAS, which work only with Digidesign products.

SONAR Home Studio includes several soft synths, and they are part of what make SONAR Home Studio such a value—they provide the types of sounds you would expect from hardware synthesizers costing (at least) hundreds of dollars. As a result, we'll go into these in quite a bit of detail. The following synths are included with the program; the first four are VST, and the last two are DXi.

- **Dimension LE.** This is a playback-only "junior" version of Cakewalk's Dimension Pro synth, although the LE version still offers a host of editing features and includes an extensive library of sounds, including Garritan Pocket Orchestra. Dimension LE is available only in SONAR Home Studio 7 XL.

- **DropZone.** This provides an easy way to play back samples and REX files. REX files are designed to follow tempo changes, much like Groove Clips, but they use a somewhat different approach that is optimized for percussive sounds.

- **Square I.** This re-creates the analog synth sounds of yesteryear, typified by classic instruments such as Bob Moog's Minimoog.

- **Studio Instruments.** This is a suite of four instruments: Bass Guitar, Drum Kit, Electric Piano, and String Section. The Drum Kit is available in both versions of SONAR Home Studio 7, but the full suite of instruments is available only in the XL version. They not only provide great instrument sounds, but also include patterns you can practice with or even use "as is" in your music. They're also ideal for creating backing tracks.

- **TTS-1.** This is a general-purpose instrument that can deliver up to 16 different instrument sounds simultaneously, each driven by a different MIDI channel. It's very useful as a "sketchpad" for blocking out arrangements because you can do it all in one instrument, and it's very efficient in terms of power drain from the CPU. Of course, if you want to replace, say, a bass track created in the TTS-1 with the Studio Instruments Bass Guitar, no problem—just insert the Studio Instruments Bass Guitar and assign the MIDI track output that used to play back through the TTS-1 to the Studio Instruments Bass Guitar.

- **Roland Groove Synth.** This is more of a special-purpose synth for rap, dance, hip-hop, and other rhythmic forms of music, but it is usable in many other contexts as well. It's also very easy to use.

As your needs and budget permit, you can purchase additional VST and DXi soft synths from Cakewalk and other vendors. Once they are installed on your computer, SONAR Home Studio will recognize them, and you'll be able to use them in your projects.

Soft Synth Tradeoffs

Soft synths are great, but there are some limitations. They require a lot of computational power, and therefore they put a fair amount of strain on your CPU. As a result, you might not be able to run as many soft synths as you'd like. One solution is a more powerful computer, but there are also less expensive workarounds.

- **Use less polyphony.** The more notes that sound at once, the more power the synth requires. Sometimes you'll have notes decaying in the background that you can't even hear, but they're taking up power nonetheless. Many instruments (including the TTS-1) let you put a "governor" on the number of notes it will play. For example, with bass, you'll seldom have more than one or two notes sounding at a time, so you can limit the number of bass notes to one or two.

- **Use track freeze.** This function temporarily converts a soft synth track to an audio track and disconnects the soft synth from the CPU. Audio tracks require far less power than soft synth tracks, with the tradeoff being that you can't edit synth parameters if the track is frozen. However, you can always "thaw" the track, make your edits, and then re-freeze. For more on freezing, see Chapter 14, "Track Freezing."

About Latency

When you play a note, it takes a finite amount of time for the computer to process that note, perform its computational magic with the soft synth, and output a sound. This computer-caused delay is called *latency*. The greater the latency, the less satisfying the playing experience. Worst case, you might even hear a note as an echo instead of it occurring when you hit a key.

Using ASIO drivers with your audio interface cuts down dramatically on latency, because this protocol (again, designed by Steinberg) was created specifically for high-performance audio. Other Windows drivers, such as MME and DirectX, are more oriented toward games and other less critical audio applications where a few milliseconds of delay don't really matter. So, always make sure you're using an interface that has ASIO drivers and always select ASIO in your audio options, as described in Chapter 23, "Recording Guitar with SONAR Home Studio."

A fast computer will not only let you run more soft synths, but it also will cut down on latency. Power is good! But it's also not cheap, so here are some other ways to reduce latency if you have more musical talent than disposable income. Remember that with audio interfaces, you can adjust the amount of latency—so you can set it as low as possible when you're recording a keyboard part and not much else is going on, but when you're mixing and several soft synths are playing back, you can increase the latency somewhat without noticeable problems.

Here are some other ways to help reduce CPU power, and thus let you reduce latency.

- Record soft synth parts early in the recording process, when there are few other virtual instruments or effects. The fewer demands being placed on your CPU, the lower you can set the latency.

- For "guide" tracks, use audio tracks (recorded instruments or loops), because they require less CPU power than virtual instruments.

- Some instruments have low-resolution options available—a holdover from the days of slower CPUs. Enable low resolution when recording so you can reduce the latency; then on mixdown, switch to high resolution and increase the latency to compensate.

- Don't use CPU-hungry effects. (Convolution reverb is the main culprit.) Add these during mixdown.

- A "workstation" (or multi-timbral sampler) plug-in loaded with instruments will usually require less CPU power than an equivalent number of individual instruments.

- Don't have other programs running, even in the background, when recording. They all demand at least a little bit of RAM, CPU power, or both.

Inserting Soft Synths

There are several ways to insert soft synths, as you'll find out during this chapter. But at some point, all of them involve the Insert Soft Synth Options dialog box. Let's run through the options (see Figure 13.1).

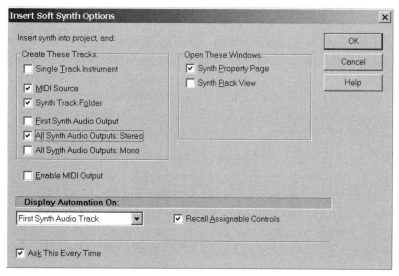

Figure 13.1 This is the dialog box that appears when you want to insert a soft synth, unless you've unchecked Ask This Every Time. I recommend leaving this option checked, though; this figure shows the options I normally choose.

Create These Tracks Options

This section of the dialog box contains the following options:

- **Single Instrument Track.** Originally, SONAR Home Studio required separate MIDI and audio tracks for software instruments. The Single Instrument Track option combines both MIDI and audio soft synth functions into a single, streamlined track. There are some limitations: For example, you can add audio effects to process the audio output, but you can't add MIDI effects to process the MIDI input. However, if you want the simplest way to add a soft synth, this is it. Note: If you export or bounce a Simple Instrument Track, the MIDI data will feed the instrument during the bounce and generate the audio—as if the track was frozen.

- **MIDI Source.** Checking this option creates a MIDI track whose output is preset to the soft synth you selected. You can always add a MIDI track later to drive a soft synth (in fact, you will need to if the synth is multi-timbral and can play different instruments on different channels), but there's seldom any reason *not* to check this box, unless you're using the Single Instrument Track option.

■ **Synth Track Folder.** I recommend checking this, because it puts the MIDI source track and any audio output tracks into a folder. That way, no matter how many outputs or MIDI tracks you use, you can collapse the folder when you're not working with that synth and tidy up your workspace.

■ **First Synth Audio Output.** Some synths offer multiple outputs, so different instruments can feed different tracks in SONAR Home Studio and therefore can be processed differently within the program. Others have only a stereo mixed output. This option and the next three determine how many outputs are created for the synth. First Synth Audio Output inserts one track for a stereo mixed signal. If a synth does not have multiple outputs, regardless of which of these three options you choose, the result will be the same as if you chose First Synth Audio Output.

■ **All Synth Audio Outputs: Stereo.** All available synth outputs end up as stereo tracks. Note that some instruments allow you to limit the number of outputs, which constrains the total number of tracks. For example, if a synth offers up to eight outputs but is limited to four outputs, then you need only four tracks. I recommend choosing this option because you can always delete tracks, but once a soft synth is inserted, you can't add more tracks.

■ **All Synth Audio Outputs: Mono.** This is the same as the above option, but it produces mono tracks. With many synths, including stereo effects on outputs, stereo is usually (but not always) the better way to go.

■ **Enable MIDI Output.** This is relevant only if the instrument can output MIDI that ends up on its MIDI track. Few instruments do this; one of the exceptions is Steinberg's Groove Agent, which is a "virtual drummer" program. If you create a pattern you like, you can send it to a MIDI track and use it with other drum instruments—but only if Enable MIDI Output is checked. Leave this unchecked unless you know your instrument has this capability.

Open These Windows Options

This section of the dialog box contains the following options:

■ **Synth Property Page.** This opens the instrument's GUI upon inserting the instrument. I recommend you select it.

■ **Synth Rack View.** This opens the Synth Rack when you insert the instrument.

Other Options

Other options in the dialog box include:

■ **Display Automation On.** Using this drop-down menu, you can choose a track to display automation. This doesn't have to be an instrument track; it can be any track. This option isn't available for the Single Track Instrument because the automation by default goes into the single track.

- **Recall Assignable Controls.** If you've created controls in the Synth Rack that affect instrument parameters, these can be recalled whenever you insert the instrument. There's more on this in the upcoming Synth Rack View section.

- **Ask This Every Time.** I leave this checked because I don't always want an instrument inserted in the same way. If you do want this, you can uncheck the option, but then you won't see the Insert Soft Synths Options dialog box when you insert the synth. The only way to get this back is via the Synth Rack, described next.

The Synth Rack View

The Synth Rack view presents a "greatest hits" version of what's happening with the various soft synths you've inserted, so you can do much in terms of instrument manipulation without having to open the GUIs for your various instruments.

It does this by centralizing crucial controllers as well as allowing easy access to automation options, freezing and unfreezing, preset selection, and more (see Figure 13.2). The window can be resized (within reason), so it doesn't have to take up too much space. If you have a dual-monitor setup, though, one common layout strategy is to put the Track view or Console in one monitor and instrument and plug-in GUIs in the other. The Synth Rack is ideal for putting in the second monitor

Figure 13.2 The Synth Rack view provides a consolidated overview of the soft synths you have installed and lets you bring out crucial controls so you can adjust them without having to open up the synth's user interface.

because it provides access to all your instruments in an abbreviated form, but when you want to open the Properties page for a selected synth and do more detailed editing, that's easy enough to do.

Let's start with a general overview of the Synth Rack. Note that it's very easy to jump to the synth's GUI while in the Synth Rack: Double-click on any empty space in the Rack or on the synth icon to open an instrument's GUI.

The Synth Rack Toolbar

From left to right, here's what the buttons on the Synth Rack toolbar do (see Figure 13.3).

Figure 13.3   The Synth Rack toolbar (circled) has five buttons for various functions.

- **Insert Soft Synths and ReWire Devices.** This duplicates the Insert > Soft Synths and Insert > ReWire Devices menu commands found in the main program. It's included for convenience to make the Synth Rack view as useful as possible.

- **Delete.** Use this to remove whichever synth is currently selected in the Synth Rack.

- **Properties.** This calls up the GUI (properties) for the currently selected synth.

- **Insert Soft Synth Options.** This opens the same dialog box as when you insert a soft synth. The advantage of having it in the Synth Rack is that if you want to set up several synths with the same options, you can set up the options here and uncheck the Ask This Every Time option. Then, when you insert a synth, it will be inserted with the options you chose, and you will bypass the Insert Soft Synth Options dialog box.

- **Freeze.** This affects the selected soft synth in the Synth Rack and duplicates the Freeze button found in the Track view and to the upper right of each instrument in the Synth Rack. If the selected synth is not frozen, clicking on the button freezes it. If the selected synth is frozen, clicking on this unfreezes it.

Rack Controls

Each synth has its own Rack (see Figure 13.4). Again, we'll go from left to right.

Figure 13.4   Each instrument in the Synth Rack has its own set of controls. If controls aren't visible, then the corresponding function isn't available in the soft synth.

- **Power button.** Toggle this to change the synth's status. When it's orange, the synth connects to the CPU and is active. When it's gray, the synth is disconnected from the CPU, thus saving CPU power.

- **Synth icon.** You can load a synth icon for each instrument in the Rack. I'm not sure how valuable that is, because the synth name shows in the title bar, which you can't hide anyway. But it does make for some nice eye candy! Right-click on the icon and you can choose to load an icon, reset an icon to the default, or set the current icon as the synth default. The latter option is great: Load the icon you want associated with a synth, set it as the default, and when you load the synth, its icon loads with it...but only in the Synth Rack. In the Track view, you'll still need to load the icon manually.

  Incidentally, I find the icons included with SONAR Home Studio somewhat hard to read, and some non-Cakewalk instruments I use aren't included. So, I made some of my own icons that involved zooming in further on the instrument, so that any features are more easily identified, and I also try to include part of the name.

  Any 96×96 pixel .bmp file will work as a track icon (see Figure 13.5). Most of the time, I create slightly larger icons and reduce them in an image editing program.

Figure 13.5   The upper instance of Dimension LE uses the stock icon, while the lower one uses a custom icon designed to be somewhat more readable.

- **Plug-in name.** Double-click in this field to rename the plug-in. This is helpful if you have several instances of the same synth, which would normally read something like Cakewalk TTS-1 1, Cakewalk TTS-1 2, and so on. You could change these to Cakewalk TTS-1 Drums, Cakewalk TTS-1 Bass, and so on.

  At this point the GUI splits into upper and lower rows of buttons, so we'll do the upper row first and then the lower one. The eight buttons (four with some instruments) located toward the right pretty much duplicate functions found elsewhere, but of course, the whole point is that they're conveniently located in the Synth Rack.

- **Choosing programs.** To the right of the instrument title, there's a box with a drop-down menu for preset selection. However, this can be confusing, because presets show up with some synths but not others. The following might be tough if you're not a techie, but if you work your way through it, you'll find out what works and what doesn't.

If a VSTi plug-in allows loading/saving .fxb files from within its own GUI interface or has presets coded directly into its DLL file (the actual instrument plug-in file that SONAR Home Studio recognizes as a plug-in), then these *.fxb presets show up in the Synth Rack preset list. If you have multiple .fxb banks, the most recently opened one populates the preset list. Also, some instruments are programmed so that SONAR Home Studio recognizes their proprietary presets, and presets show up for some (but not all) DXi synths.

Confused yet? Well, let's make it simple. The bottom line is if the presets appear, great! But if they don't, here's a workaround (see Figure 13.6) for populating the list.

Figure 13.6 If a synth's programs don't show up in the Synth Rack preset selector, type the name of the preset into the black Presets field on the instrument itself (this shows Cakewalk's Rapture) and then click on the Save button (floppy disk icon). The preset will then appear in the Synth Rack's preset selector.

1. Call up a preset from a synth whose presets don't show up in the Presets drop-down menu.

2. Type the preset name into the black Presets field in an instrument's upper-left corner.

3. Click on the Save floppy disk icon. (For younger readers, a floppy disk was a storage medium used by ancient civilizations; its legacy lives on to indicate a "save" function, but it is otherwise pretty much forgotten.)

The preset will now be saved in a format that allows it to show up in the Synth Rack's program browser in the future.

At first I thought this was a major limitation (who wants to retype all those program names?), and in some ways it is, but I've also actually found a benefit, because this approach lets you treat the Synth Rack preset selector as a list of "favorites." Whenever I find a preset I think I'll want to use in the future, I save it as described here. That way, only my favorite presets show up in the list for instruments whose presets normally don't show up. (Of course, I can always access the other presets via the instrument's user interface or custom browser.)

- **Mute.** Click to mute the synth's output. However, note that the synth still connects to the CPU and draws power. Because of this, unmuting turns on the synth sound with no pauses or delays.

- **Solo.** The audio output consists solely of the selected synth.

- **Freeze.** This option renders the synth audio to a hard disk track, thus saving CPU power. However, synth parameters cannot be edited in the frozen state. For more information, see Chapter 14 on Freezing.

- **Thaw.** This option unfreezes the synth to allow for editing.

And now, here's what's in the lower row. Note: If a soft synth (for example, the TTS-1) doesn't allow for VST host automation (in other words, you don't see Read/Write buttons for it in the Synth Rack), you can't treat any of its parameters as assignable controls. The Assign and Show/Hide control buttons won't even appear.

- **Automation Assignment drop-down menu.** You can put the automation data for a soft synth on any track. (I usually put it on the track containing the audio output.)

- **Automation Read.** This causes the instrument to read any automation data in the track.

- **Automation Write.** This allows writing automation in a track.

- **Assign Controls and Show/Hide Controls.** See the following "Controller Assignments" section for more information.

Controller Assignments

This is one of my favorite aspects of the Synth Rack because it lets you mirror various synth controls at the Synth Rack itself, thus letting you bring the most tweakable and important synth parameters to a common location. You can edit the instrument sounds or create automation moves by changing the control positions, or you can bind the controls to a hardware controller.

There are two buttons involved with real-time control: Show Controls (the button toward the right that says Show) and the button to its left, Assign Controls (with the graphic of a control and the + sign). You can assign instrument controls to the Synth Rack in two different ways (see Figure 13.7).

Figure 13.7 Ten important controls from the Dimension LE soft synth have been assigned to the Dimension LE section of the Synth Rack. They are visible because the Show button (toward the upper right) is on.

One method works very similarly to the ACT controller assignment method (as described in Chapter 21, "ACT: The Key to Hands-On Control"). To assign controls using this method:

1. Click on the Show button to enable it.

2. Click on the Assign Controls button for an instrument in the Rack. The instrument GUI will appear.

3. Move the parameters you want to assign as controls. Note that although the dialog box mentions parameters being "touched," you can't just click on a parameter; you actually need to alter it from the existing setting. Also note that the order in which you move the controls is important, because the controls will be assigned from left to right along the bottom of the instrument's Rack, in the order in which you moved them.

4. After you've moved the controls you want to add, click on the Assign Controls button again. A dialog box will open that says "X parameters [where X is the number of parameters you moved] were touched during Learn. Are you sure you want to assign these controls?"

5. Click on Yes, and the parameters will appear as controls along the bottom of the Rack. (If they don't, make sure the Show button is enabled.)

The other method is more labor intensive, but some may prefer it.

1. Click on the Show button to enable it.

2. Right-click on the Assign Controls button. A pop-up menu will appear with all the parameters that are available for assigning as controls.

3. Select a control, and it will be added to the first empty control slot.

4. Continue assigning controls until you've added all the controls you want.

With either method, as you move the controls in the Synth Rack, the corresponding controls will move on the instrument's GUI.

Another interesting point is that if you assign particular controls for a synth, you can choose to have SONAR Home Studio remember them (even in a different project or if you've closed and reopened SONAR Home Studio). To do this, when you see the Insert Soft Synth Options dialog box when installing a soft synth, check Recall Assignable Controls.

Controller Assignment Right-Click Control Options

You can do a lot more than just move a Synth Rack control to vary an instrument parameter. If you right-click on a knob, you'll see a bunch of options.

Group Options

The upper four options relate to Groups. Soft synth controls can be made part of a Group, which means that one control motion (either an onscreen control or one from a hardware remote controller) can change multiple synth parameters simultaneously. All of the following options assume you've already right-clicked on the control.

- **Add a control to a Group.** Click on Group and then select a Group (see Figure 13.8). Each Group has a name and a distinctive color. Upon selecting the Group, the grouped control acquires a small yellow outline, and a square with the Group color appears in the upper-left corner of this outline. The outline follows whichever control you select to show it's active, but the colored square always remains so you can see at a glance that a particular control belongs to a particular Group.

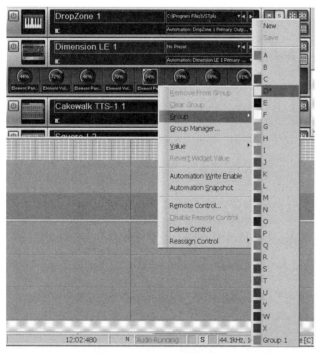

Figure 13.8 Right-clicking on a control and selecting Group makes that control part of a Group. If 24 Groups isn't enough, you can create more with the New option.

- **Create a new Group.** Click on Group and then select New. A dialog box will appear, where you can name the Group and choose a Group color (see Figure 13.9). After doing so, click on OK.

- **Remove from Group.** To remove a control from a Group, select Remove from Group.

- **Clear Group.** If you right-click on any control in a Group and select Clear Group, that Group no longer exists, and all controls are "released" from the Group.

Figure 13.9   After you click on New, a dialog box appears that lets you name a Group and give it a distinctive color.

The Group Manager

The Group Manager defines how controls vary when they're changed. In other words, grouped controls don't necessarily move in lock-step; you can set things up so that one grouped control covers a wider range than a different grouped control or moves in a reverse direction—for example, moving a single pan control might pan one sound more to the left while another pans more to the right. Following are explanations of the Group Manager options (see Figure 13.10).

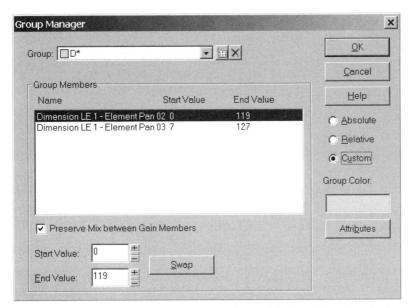

Figure 13.10   The Group Manager provides sophisticated options for how the controls in a Group relate to each other.

- **Group drop-down menu.** Although the Group Manager opens up to the Group associated with the control on which you right-clicked, you can use the drop-down menu to select any Group. Note that an asterisk (*) next to a Group indicates that it contains grouped controls.

- **Create Group.** The button to the right of the drop-down menu allows you to create a new Group.

- **Delete Group.** The X button to the right of the Create Group button deletes the current Group.

- **Group members.** This section is read-only unless Custom is selected, and it shows the parameters included in a particular Group.

- **Absolute radio button.** When this option is selected, any difference between synth parameter settings that exists when you choose to group them remains as you move the associated onscreen or hardware control. For example, if Parameter 1 is set to 1.000 and Parameter 2 to 0.500 when grouped, and you turn the control associated with Parameter 1 to change its value to 0.500, Parameter 2 will be at 0.000 to maintain the same absolute difference between the two controls.

- **Relative radio button.** The two parameters track ratiometrically. With the previous example, if you change the value of Parameter 1 to 0.500 (half the original value), then Parameter 2 (which is grouped) will also go to half the original value, or 0.250.

As one example of how you'd use this, when controlling the level of two different synth oscillators, you'd probably want to use ratiometric control. That way, the volume relationship between the two oscillators would remain the same, and turning one down all the way would cause the other to turn down all the way as well, regardless of their initial settings. But if you're lowering the LFO rate, for example, you'd probably want the rates to change linearly, by the same absolute amount. That way, if one LFO's speed was offset by 2 Hz compared to a second LFO, that absolute 2-Hz difference would be retained as you changed the LFO speeds.

- **Custom radio button.** This allows you to set separate start and end values for individual controls and to do so in two different ways. One option is to enter start and end values in the appropriate fields in the Group Manager dialog box. The other option involves right-clicking on the control—this will be covered shortly. The Start Value, End Value, and Swap options are active only with Custom selected.

However, note that certain "rules" apply to grouping when you choose specific start and end values. For example, if you've set Control 1 to cover a range from 80–90, and Control 2 covers a range of 0–127, and you rotate Control 2 over its full range, Control 1 will go from 80–90. If you move Control 1 over its full range, it will cover that range, but Control 2 will remain at 0 until Control 1 hits 80, go to 127 as Control 1 goes to 90, and remain at 127 as Control 1 goes higher than 90.

Also note that if the end value is lower than the start value, you can reverse the "sense" of a control. A good use for this is lowering the level somewhat when raising the resonance or doing crossfading effects (for example, morphing between two different sounds).

- **Preserve Mix between Gain Members.** Check this option to maintain the gain differential in dB when controls are moved. Unchecking this maintains only the visual difference between controls.

- **Swap.** If you highlight a parameter in the Group Members field and click on Swap, the start value becomes the end value, and vice versa.

Value Options

When you right-click on a control, the section below the Group options on the context menu includes Value options. This lets you set start and end values in the Group Manager based on actual control settings (see Figure 13.11). Set the control to the desired start or end position, right-click on the control, and choose Value > Set Start = Current or Value > Set End = Current, respectively. These values will be entered in the Group Manager.

Figure 13.11   You can set the minimum and maximum settings for an automated control using the Value options.

If you set a control value, right-click on the grouped control, and select Value > Set Snap-To = Current, it means that whenever you Ctrl-double-click on the control, it will snap to the value you selected prior to setting the Snap To value.

Regarding why you would want a Snap To setting, if you're doing automation by moving controls in real time, and you want to be able to jump instantly to a particular value, moving a knob manually may overshoot or undershoot the value. By using Snap To, you can hit that value precisely.

Automation Options

These are available when you right-click on a control.

- **Automation Write Enable.** This allows the selected control to write automation data. It differs from the Write button on the Synth Rack because the Write button enables *all* of an instrument's parameters for automation. With some synths, this can be a lot—Dimension

LE has 862 automatable parameters! If you're not going to use them, enabling all these can slow down performance, so in that case it makes sense to automate only the control(s) whose automation you want to write.

- You can check the status of automation writing by looking at the Synth Rack's Write button:

    1. **Red.** All parameters are enabled for automation.

    2. **Gray.** No parameters are enabled for automation.

    3. **Light blue-gray.** Selected parameters are enabled for automation.

- **Automation Snapshot.** Refer to Chapter 19, "Automation in SONAR Home Studio," for more information about snapshot automation.

Other Control Options

Other control options include:

- **Remote Control.** To assign (what Cakewalk calls *bind*) one of these controls to an external hardware controller, right-click on the control and choose Remote Control to bring up the Remote Control Assignment dialog box. You can specify a controller, but it's a lot easier to wiggle the hardware controller of your choice, click on the Learn function, and then click on OK. As soon as you do, the hardware controller will be registered as the bound control.

    Remote control and limiting the range of grouped controls make a good combination, particularly when you want a hardware controller to cover a limited range of a parameter—typically for finer control. For example, you can group the limited-range synth control you want to vary with a "dummy" synth control (that is, a control that doesn't affect the sound) set to vary over its full range and then bind the hardware control to the dummy control. For example, suppose you want fine hardware control from something like a foot pedal over filter cutoff, where the foot pedal should cover just a one-octave range of the cutoff frequency. You'd set the range of the filter cutoff control to one octave by setting start and end values as described previously and then group it with another synth control that covers its full range (for example, the attack parameter of an unused parameter, such as a pitch envelope or whatever). Bind the foot pedal hardware control to the pitch envelope attack parameter; when the attack is at minimum, the filter will be at the lower range of the specified octave. With the attack at maximum, the filter will be one octave higher.

- **Disable Remote Control.** Once a Synth Rack control has been assigned to a remote control, you can de-assign it with this option. If Disable Remote Control is grayed out, then the control has no remote assignment.

- **Delete Control.** Don't find a control useful anymore? Right-click on it and then select this option to delete it.

- **Reassign Control.** If you want to reassign a control to a different parameter, right-click on the control and select Reassign Control. This brings up a list of available parameters (which can be pretty lengthy with some instruments).

Step-By-Step: Creating a Single Track Instrument

1. Choose Insert > Soft Synths and then click on the soft synth you want to open.

2. Check the Single Track Instrument box. If you want the synth GUI to open when you insert the instrument, also check Synth Property Page. Then click on OK. Leave all other boxes unchecked except for Ask This Every Time.

3. The track will appear, with the default name being the instrument you inserted. Unfold the track to reveal all available parameters (see Figure 13.12). Single Track Instruments default to PRV (inline MIDI editing) enabled.

Figure 13.12   MIDI parameters are outlined; other parameters, including Mute and Solo, are audio parameters.

4. Unfold the Input/Output section. Use the Input drop-down menu (at the upper left of this section) to select the MIDI input (for example, MIDI port connected to a keyboard controller).

5.   Use the Output To drop-down menu to select the audio output (for example, master bus).

6.   Because the MIDI and audio tracks have been condensed into one, some features of individual tracks are not available. For example, volume and pan affect audio, not MIDI. Also, the FX bin accepts only audio effects, not MIDI effects.

7.   Because the Simple Instrument Track outputs audio, you can add sends and do read/write automation as you would with standard audio tracks. To add a send, unfold the Sends section and then click on Add Send and choose New Stereo Bus or Insert Send Assistant.

SONAR Home Studio's Instruments

Now let's look at the individual instruments included with SONAR Home Studio. But first, let's look at a few "global" options that apply to various (but not all) instruments.

Soft Synth Shortcuts

With many Cakewalk synths, including DropZone and Dimension LE, there are fields with numerical parameters (see Figure 13.13). Here are ways to change these values. All involve first clicking on the numerical field.

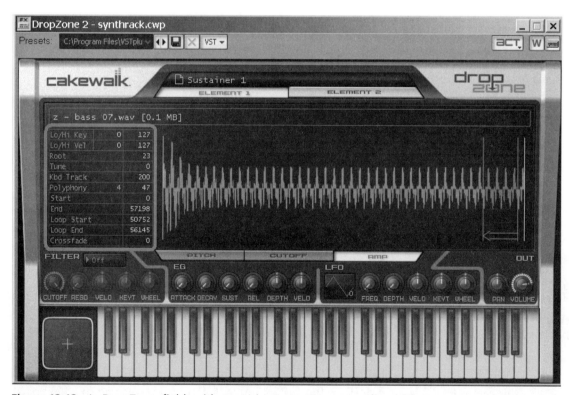

Figure 13.13   In DropZone, fields with numeric parameters are outlined. There are several shortcuts for changing these values.

- **Click and drag.** This changes coarse values.

- **Shift-click and drag.** This fine-tunes values in small increments.

- **Ctrl-click and drag.** This changes values in large increments. This is very helpful with fields that can have large values.

- **Mouse wheel.** Rotate to change values 10 units at a time.

- **Ctrl-mouse wheel.** Rotate to change values in larger increments.

Finding Synth Patches

One of SONAR Home Studio's lesser-known features is the ability to browse synth patches for soft synths loaded into the program and do searches based on certain strings of words and/or numbers. Here's how.

To browse patches, right-click on a blank space in the MIDI track header associated with the soft synth you want to browse and choose Track Properties. This shows the input, output, channel, and other characteristics of the track, including the selected bank and patch (see Figure 13.14). If more than one bank is available, you can use the bank's drop-down menu to select a new bank for browsing, and once within the bank, you can browse patches using the Patch drop-down menu.

If you don't have a specific patch in mind, but you want to see all patches whose name includes, for example, the word bass, piano, or whatever, you're covered there, too. Click on the Search icon (folder with a magnifying glass) to the right of the Bank and Patch fields to call up the Patch Browser window. For example, if you type **brass**, you'll see a list of all patches, in all banks, that include the word brass. Click on the desired patch, and it will load into your synth. Nice!

This is a useful feature, but it also underscores the importance of proper patch naming. Galactic Swirl may sound evocative, but you're better off sticking in at least one key word, such as Galactic Swirl Pad. Or if you develop patches for use with specific projects or artists, you should include some sort of consistent identification so that you can easily find the patches used with those projects (for example, MicheleB_Strings).

TTS-1 General MIDI Synthesizer

The TTS-1 is a General MIDI synth that doesn't use a lot of CPU power, but it's quite capable, especially once you know how to take full advantage of it.

What's General MIDI? The General MIDI specification assigns particular sounds to 128 different programs. For example, Program 1 is Grand Piano. If you write a MIDI-based piece of music and you want to make sure the person playing it back hears it as you intended, choose programs that conform to the General MIDI specification and make sure the piece plays back through a General MIDI–compatible synthesizer, such as the TTS-1.

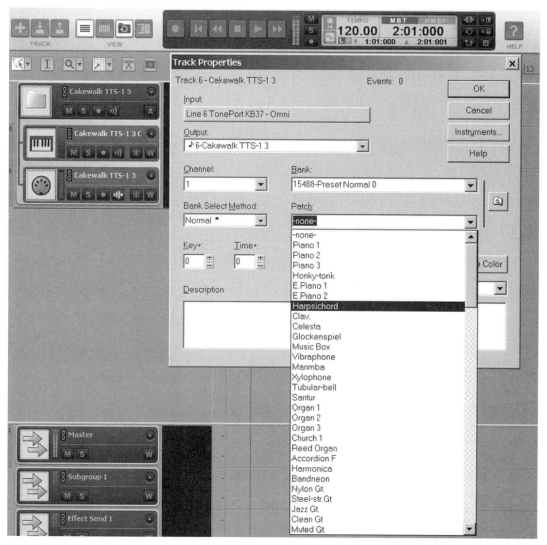

Figure 13.14 Need to find a patch? With some SONAR Home Studio instruments, it's an easy, searchable process.

Note that General MIDI does not resolve all incompatibilities, because the piano in one General MIDI instrument might sound different than the piano sound in a different instrument. Still, the sounds will be relatively close. A further enhancement to the General MIDI specification, General MIDI or GM2, specifies additional sounds.

The TTS-1 is 16-part multi-timbral and is both General MIDI and GM2 compatible. Each part is "hardwired" to MIDI channels so that Channels 1 through 16 are mapped to TTS-1 Parts 1 through 16 (see Figure 13.15).

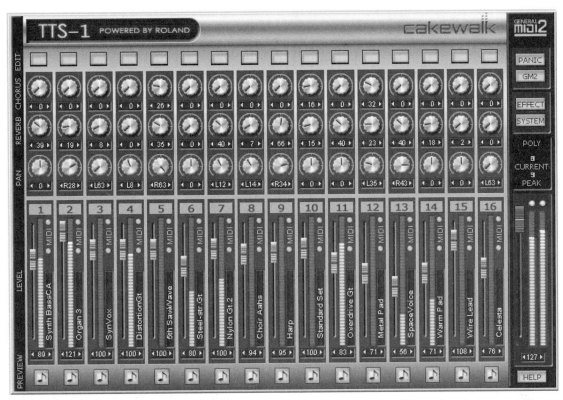

Figure 13.15 The visuals are that of a 16-channel mixer, but it's really an interface for up to 16 instruments. Additional windows allow for fairly extensive editing.

The parts are arranged visually as 16 channels of a virtual mixer, complete with Level fader, Pan control, two effects sends, and a master output section. Additional pop-up windows allow digging deeper than the mixer's surface.

Using the TTS-1 Multiple Outputs

Let's start our tour with the four individual outs, which allow sending TTS-1 sounds to individual tracks in SONAR Home Studio. This is handy if, for example, you have a string sound in one TTS-1 channel and a drum part in another. Suppose you want reverb on the strings but not on the drums and EQ on the drums but not the strings. By sending each sound to its own track in SONAR Home Studio, each can have its own processing.

To take advantage of the multiple outputs, when you insert the TTS-1 into SONAR Home Studio, check All Synth Audio Outputs (Stereo) instead of First Synth Audio Output when the Insert Soft Synth Options window appears. As with other instruments, this can't be changed once the TTS-1 is inserted, so if you want multiple outs, do so when you insert the instrument.

Here's how to assign parts to outputs.

1.   Click on the System button toward the upper right.

2.   A bright red System Settings box will appear; click on its Option button, and another window will appear (see Figure 13.16).

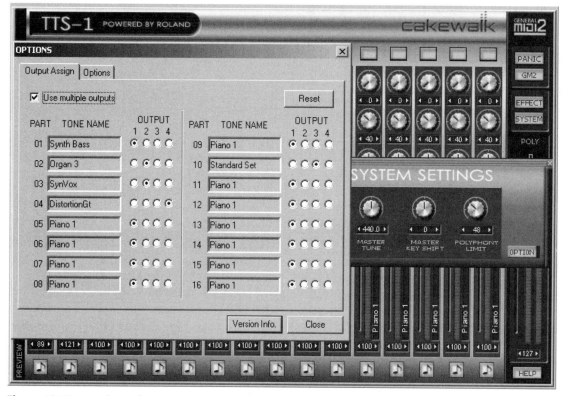

Figure 13.16   It takes a few mouse clicks to get there, but you can assign each TTS-1 part to one of four outputs.

3.   Under the Output Assign tab, assign parts to outputs by clicking the radio button to the right of each part. Note that you can assign multiple parts to the same output, but you can't assign one part to multiple outs.

4.   To reassign all the parts to Output 1, click on the Reset button. This may be important if you're using the built-in reverb and/or chorus effects. (See the section "TTS-1 Effects" in this chapter for more information on these effects.)

Other System Settings

The red System Settings window also provides three other useful adjustments:

- **Master Tune.** Variable in 0.1-Hz increments, from 415.3 Hz to 466.2 Hz.

- **Master Key Shift.** Transposes from –24 to +24 semitones.

- **Polyphony Limit.** Allows a maximum of 10 to 128 voices.

To change a parameter value, you can click on a knob and drag it, but also note the numerical field below each control. Clicking on the arrows to the side provides "fine tuning"—for example, if you click on the Master Tune's right arrow, the value increments by 0.1 Hz. Furthermore, if you double-click on the numerical field, you can type in a number and click on OK to enter it. All numericals work the same way, including the ones for the level, pan, and send controls on the main "front panel."

Editing a Part

At the top of each part's channel strip, you'll see an Edit button. Click on it, and a window will open with a variety of editable parameters (see Figure 13.17). You can still tweak any visible "mixer" parameters, even when the Edit window is on top.

Figure 13.17 The TTS-1 offers sound-shaping options for each instrument.

There are two timesaving features within the Edit window:

- You can cycle through the parts via the part left/right arrows toward the upper left, so it's not necessary to close the Edit window, open one for the next channel, close it, open another one, and so on. You can also just click on one of the main window's Edit buttons to choose a part.

- The little preview button with a note symbol plays a prerecorded note or riff in the style typically used by the selected sound. (You can choose between the two, as described later in this chapter under "Other System Options"). This duplicates the button at the bottom of each channel strip. However, you can't latch it, so it won't play while you tweak parameters.

The editable synth parameters are pretty standard fare and described in the TTS-1 documentation. (Click on Help in the lower right for more information on the TTS-1). However, there are a few fine points.

- The On/Off button in the top row enables/disables only the tone controls (bass, mid, treble). The Filter and Character controls are always live.

- In the middle row, note that even if the Vibrato depth control is at zero, you can still add vibrato with your synth's mod wheel. This requires that the Mod Depth parameter in the lower row be at a non-zero value—the main Vibrato depth control is designed to add a constant amount for each note you play.

- Delay doesn't fade in the vibrato; instead, it switches in after the elapsed delay time.

- The lower row has controls for Tuning, a Mono/Poly switch, a Portamento control with on/off switch, the aforementioned Mod Depth, and Bend Range (up to a maximum of two octaves).

  The drum set sounds have their own editable parameters (see Figure 13.18).

- A middle strip lets you step through the various drum sounds; each one has adjustable Level, Pan, Coarse Tune, Fine Tune, Reverb Level (send), and Chorus Level controls.

- The MIDI Edit button, when enabled, lets you choose the drum sound to be edited by playing its corresponding MIDI note.

- Note that the master channel Pan control weights the various drum sounds more to one side or the other of the stereo field, but the pan relationship between the various drums is maintained within those constraints.

- The lower strip of parameters (Filter, Resonance, and Tone controls) affects all drum sounds in the program, and they are not individually adjustable for each sound.

- As with other sounds, the On/Off button in the lower strip affects only the Tone controls.

Figure 13.18 The drum programs have some parameters that are individually editable for each drum sound, as well as parameters that alter all drum sounds in the program.

TTS-1 Effects

There are two effects, Chorus and Reverb (Figure 13.19). Each part's "mixer channel" has a chorus and reverb send control, which is duplicated in the Edit window. However, note that the effects sends are taken only from instruments whose outputs feed the main output (Output 1 in a multi-output setup). Furthermore, the Reverb returns only to the main output. As a result, if you're using multiple outs and you turn up the Reverb and/or Chorus send control for any parts that aren't assigned to Output 1, they won't be processed.

Figure 13.19 Choose the chorus and reverb algorithms and then adjust the parameters as desired. If you're not using the processors, turn them off to save CPU power.

The effects have primitive editing capabilities. Click on the Effect button (above the master Volume slider), and the Effects window will appear. Here you can choose one of six chorus/flanger algorithms and one of six reverb types. The only reverb parameter you can edit is reverb Time, but chorus lets you alter Rate, Depth, Feedback, and Rev Send, which sends some of the chorused sound to the reverb.

Saving Performances

A TTS-1 "performance" is the sum total of all settings—instruments assigned to parts, edits you've made to the instruments, effects settings, and so on. If you come up with a particular performance you like, there are three ways to save it for later recall.

■ The simplest is to save the project containing the performance. When you call up the project, the TTS-1 will appear as you last left it, pretty much like any other virtual instrument.

■ To save a performance independently of a project, type a name for the performance in the Presets field at the top of the instrument and then click on the floppy disk button (see Figure 13.20).

Figure 13.20   Here, a preset is being saved. The drop-down menu will let you choose from any of the presets you've stored. If you select a preset and then click on the X button, it will be deleted.

■ Another way to save a performance independently of a project is to click on the System button, click on the System Settings Option button, and then click on the Options tab (see Figure 13.21). The top line has buttons to load or save a performance file. There's no preordained folder for this; I just created a TTS-1 Performances folder inside the Cakewalk folder on the root drive. TTS-1 performances have a .GMF suffix.

Note that if you call up a performance, it's a good idea to set the patch selection parameter for any MIDI channels feeding the TTS-1 to None before you hit playback. Otherwise, if a patch is specified, it will be called up in the TTS-1, and you'll need to reload the performance.

Saving Edited Sounds

This process isn't exactly obvious, but that's what this type of book is about! The confusion arises because the part Edit window has a Write button. So you click on it, choose a program

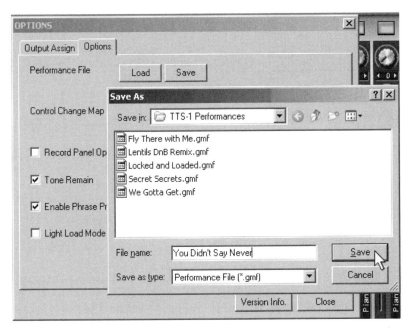

Figure 13.21   You can create a library of TTS-1 performance setups for use in any project.

location in a User Normal bank (1–4 or the User Rhythm bank if you're saving a drum set), and you're asked if you want to overwrite the existing patch. So you click on OK…. Done, right?

Well, not really. The patch will show up in a MIDI channel track if you select the correct bank and patch, but if you exit SONAR Home Studio at this point, open it again, and call up the same bank, the patch will be gone, and all the patches in the User Bank will have reverted to piano.

The reason this occurs is that although writing the edited part stores it in the bank, the bank is in RAM. So, you need to do the additional step of saving the bank. Once you have the edited patches written into the bank, click on a patch name, either in the part Edit window or in the strip to the right of the channel fader in the main Mixer view. From there, select Save Bank. Choose the bank you want to save (User Normal 1–4 or the User Rhythm bank for drums), give it the desired name, and save it in an appropriate folder.

The next time you want to access your edited sounds, click on a patch name, select Load, and choose the bank containing the sounds you want to use.

MIDI Control

Almost all parameters—knobs, sliders, and buttons—can be controlled by MIDI controllers (not notes, though).

Just right-click on the parameter you want to control, and the Control Change Assign window will appear (see Figure 13.22). You can enter a controller and channel number, or more conveniently, just check the Learn box and diddle the controller you want to use (such as a foot

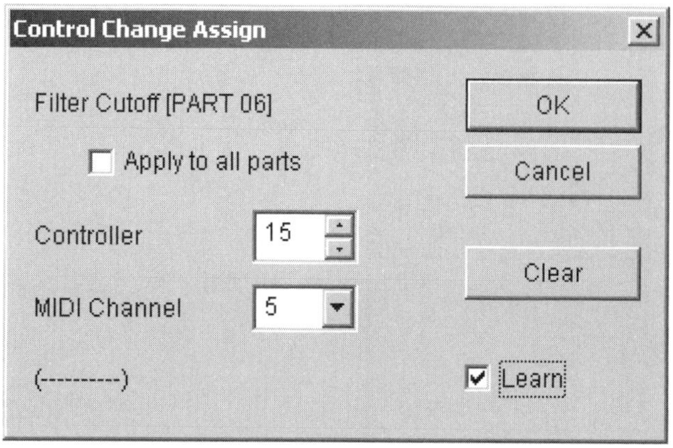

Figure 13.22 The TTS-1 offers a Learn function for MIDI controllers, which can control virtually any TTS-1 parameter.

pedal hooked up to a keyboard, mod wheel, or fader on a keyboard's control surface)...and you're done. However, there are a couple of fine points to keep in mind.

■ If you assign a controller that was previously assigned to a different parameter, the previous assignment will be shown in the window's lower-left corner. Any new assignment cancels the previous assignment. So, you can't control multiple parameters with the same controller.

■ You might think the Apply to All Parts function means that if this box is checked and you assign a controller to filter cutoff, the control will affect filter cutoffs for all parts that are sounding. But instead, it assigns the parameter in question to respond to the same continuous controller number for all parts. For example, if you assign Controller 15 to filter cutoff in Part 6, and the Apply to All Parts box is checked, then Controller 15 will also affect filter cutoff in any other selected part. Furthermore, checking Apply to All Parts forces each part to respond only on the MIDI channel whose value equals the part number. In the aforementioned example, if you wanted to control filter cutoff in, say, Part 11, Controller 15 would have to appear over Channel 11. If Apply to All Parts is not checked, then a part can be assigned to respond to a controller coming in over any MIDI channel.

Controller Maps

If you click on the System button, select Option from the System Settings window, and then select the Options tab, you'll find the option to Load and Save Control Change Maps. Under Load, you have four options: Minimum Map, Normal Map, Logic (which uses the mappings from Logic, a sequencer that was purchased by Apple and is now Mac-only, although at one point it was PC-compatible as well; I guess this is done as a favor to those who used Logic PC and switched over to SONAR Home Studio), and File, where you can load maps you created and saved.

So what are these maps? When you go to create an automation envelope in a MIDI track and select MIDI, you'll find that TTS-1 parameters will be premapped to particular controllers and labeled in the envelope drop-down menu (see Figure 13.23). Also, you can create custom maps to work with external hardware controllers.

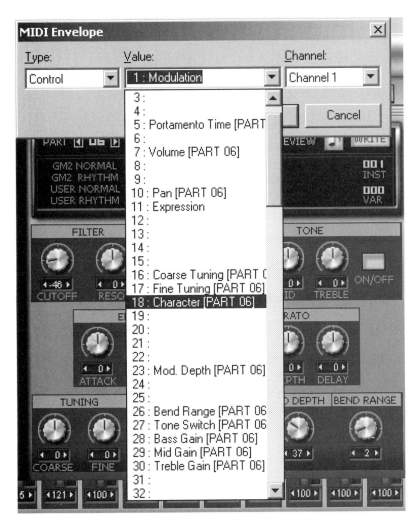

Figure 13.23 The Normal map has been loaded, which assigns the most commonly automated TTS-1 parameters to various MIDI controllers.

If you load the Minimum map, only a few parameters show up. The Normal map is what you'd, well, normally use. However, if you create a bunch of custom MIDI assignments, then you can save those assignments as a file. This is handy if you use lots of assignments or you like doing real-time control from external MIDI fader boxes.

Speaking of real-time control, note another option just below the Control Change Map buttons: Record Panel Operations. When checked, if the MIDI track driving the part is recording, then any front-panel control movements will be recorded as MIDI data. On playback, the knobs will move to reflect those controller changes.

Summing up, there are three ways to record automation with the TTS-1:

- Using track automation envelopes

- Recording knob motions from the TTS-1 panel

- Recording MIDI data from an external control surface and passing it through to the TTS-1

Other System Options

As for the three other check boxes under the system Options tab:

- Tone Remain allows notes to sustain while changing from one program to another. This uses up more voices but will not be an issue in most cases—the TTS-1 is pretty efficient. Just make sure you've set the polyphony control high enough to accommodate any transitions.

- Enable Phrase Preview determines what happens when you click on the little note symbol. If unchecked, you'll hear a single note when you click, which plays the associated sound. If checked, clicking on the note plays a phrase in a style representative of how the current instrument is played.

- Light Load Mode reduces CPU consumption even further by using less-intensive internal algorithms. Unless your CPU is *seriously* performance-challenged, though, odds are you won't need to use this option.

Overall, the TTS-1 is an effective tone module, and the editability makes it that much more useful. When you throw in the ability to add expressiveness through the use of external controllers, you can make some pretty nifty sounds.

DropZone

DropZone is a simple sample player (see Figure 13.24) that can load two *Elements*, which can be any of several formats.

- **WAV.** The standard file format for Windows computers.

- **AIF or AIFF.** The standard file format for Macintosh computers. However, these days, both computers can usually read both file types.

- **Ogg Vorbis.** A data-compressed file format similar to MP3, but which is freely available and has no associated licensing fees.

Figure 13.24   DropZone plays back samples in a variety of formats, including time-stretchable REX files.

■ **REX.** A format devised by Propellerhead Software in conjunction with Steinberg. It breaks an audio file into small "slices," which can accommodate tempo changes. A REX file also contains companion MIDI data that plays back these slices in order, although that file is often transparent to the user. If you speed up the tempo, the slices play closer together; if you slow down the tempo, they play farther apart. REX files are very well suited to drum sounds and other percussive instruments, but they don't work with as many different types of material as Groove Clips. For example, Groove Clips are much better for tempo-stretching pads than REX files are.

■ **SFZ.** These are multisampled files that are used in many other Cakewalk instruments, including Rapture and Dimension Pro.

What Is Multisampling? What Is an SFZ File?   When sampling an instrument sound, it's possible to transpose that sample, so that sampling, say, a G note on a bass can cover a wider range than just that one note—such as from E below the G to C above the G. However, transposing too far alters the timbre and produces an unrealistic sound. So, it's more common to sample several notes and assemble them into a multisample. For example, if you sample each open bass string—E, A, D, G—you could have the E string cover from E to F#, the A string from G to B, the D note from C to E, and the G note from F to A.

An SFZ file is a text file that points to the location of different samples on your hard drive and specifies the range each sample will cover. (An SFZ file can also deal with many other parameters; the SFZ spec is actually quite deep.) So in the example of the bass given a moment ago, if you load its SFZ file into DropZone, it will automatically load the individual samples and map them across the keyboard to create a playable instrument.

Waveforms, Elements, and Programs

Let's look at DropZone's hierarchy of sounds. An *Element* consists of a waveform file with an associated set of parameter values for filter, envelope generator, LFO, and so on. You can save and load Elements. Bringing one of the file types described a moment ago into DropZone is easy: Just select which Element you want it to populate (Element 1 or Element 2) and then drag the file from the desktop or other folder into the Element's waveform display. If you want to be able to play two Elements at the same time, switch over to the other Element and load another file by dragging and dropping. A DropZone *Program* saves or loads the whole thing—the two Elements, their associated waveforms, and the various parameter settings.

Note that there are separate Pan and Volume controls for the two Elements; you select an Element for editing by clicking on the Element 1 or Element 2 tab.

Program Handling (Loading and Saving)

DropZone comes with a bunch of ready-to-go programs, samples, and SFZ files. There are two ways to load a program.

- Click on the Program name at the very top. A Program Browser appears (see Figure 13.25).

- Click on the file handling icon and select Load Program (see Figure 13.26). A traditional Windows browser opens, where you can look anywhere for Programs. The file handling is pretty standard except for two options: Initialize Program returns the program to its default state, with no samples loaded, and Save Default Program saves the current Program as the Program that will be called up initially when you load DropZone.

However, the program-opening process is more flexible than it might appear at first. If you choose Multisamples from the Browser, you can select SFZ files and individual WAV files. DropZone is smart enough to know these aren't Programs, and it loads the selected file into whichever Element currently has the focus (in other words, the Element tab that's selected). This is an alternative to the drag-and-drop method mentioned a moment ago.

Being able to load two files and play them back simultaneously is very useful, but it is particularly so with REX files—for example, you can combine a drum and a percussion loop and have a mini rhythm section.

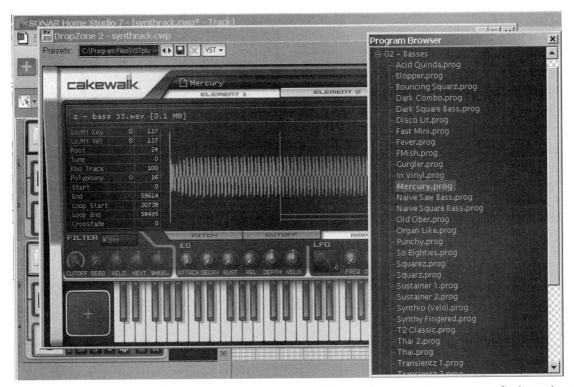

Figure 13.25   Clicking on the Program name opens up a Program Browser where you can find a variety of sounds.

Editing the Elements

There are several ways you can customize an Element via the matrix of editable parameters toward the left and the controls above the keyboard.

- **Split or layer Elements.** You can split or layer Elements via note value or velocity. As one example of a split, you could have a bass sound cover the lowest two octaves and a piano sound cover all other octaves. The split point would be based on note value. Or you could layer two sounds to cover the entire keyboard, with one Element being a soft electric piano sound and the other a loud electric piano sound. You could set the layers so that they're triggered by particular velocity values; with lower velocities, the softer sound would play, and with higher velocities, the louder sound would play. Here's how to set splits and layers.

  - To split based on notes, enter the low and high key range for each Element in the Lo/Hi Key fields.

  - To overlap within a split, set the Hi note for one Element higher than the Lo note for the other Element. This layers the range they have in common.

  - To split based on velocity, enter the desired velocity range for each Element in the Lo/Hi Vel fields.

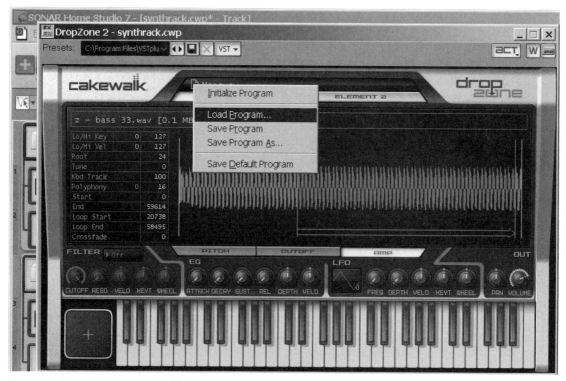

Figure 13.26 Clicking on the file handling icon to the left of the Program name lets you not only load, but save Programs as well.

- To overlap a layer based on a velocity split, set the Hi velocity value for one Element higher than the Lo velocity value for the other Element.

As one example of the latter option, one Element could respond to velocities from 0 to 127, so it would play regardless of velocity. The other Element could respond to velocities from 100 to 127 so that it plays only when you hit the keys really hard, which layers both Elements.

- **Tuning parameters.** The Root parameter transposes the waveform in half-steps. Tune does fine-tuning and changes the waveform in cents (1/100th of a semitone).

- **Keyboard Track.** This sets the difference in cents between successive keys. Normally, this is set to 100 key, so each key plays a semitone. If it is set to smaller values, then there is less of a pitch change as you go from one key to the next. For example, with a setting of 50 cents, each key would be a quarter-tone apart. With a setting of 200 cents, each key would be a whole tone apart.

- **Polyphony.** You can limit the number of notes each Element can play simultaneously. Lower values may help save on CPU power.

- **Start.** This sets where the waveform starts playing back. For example, with a snare sound, moving the Start point later would cut off some of the snare's attack.

- **End.** Similarly, this sets where sample playback ends.

Looping Controls

Looping can be a fairly complex topic. But if you're ready to dive in, let's go!

Looping plays a selected portion of the file over and over again, as long as a key is held down. With DropZone, the looped portion of the waveform is shown in orange, as opposed to the rest of the waveform, which is blue (see Figure 13.27). Typically, the file plays to the end of the loop and then jumps back to the loop's beginning. Looping is used in two main ways. One is to repeat a phrase. For example, if you load a one-measure drum part and loop it, as long as you hold down the key that triggers the drum sound, the phrase will repeat—kind of like an interesting metronome.

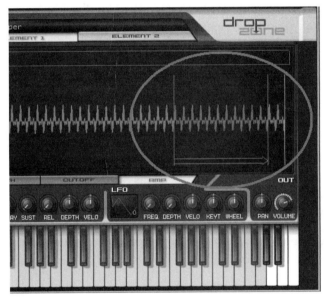

Figure 13.27   The looped portion of the DropZone Element is circled.

The other way to use looping is to make it possible to create shorter samples if a sound sustains. For example, suppose you sample a trumpet note. A trumpet note can play for as long as the trumpet player can hold it, so how long do you make the sample? In this case, you can record the note, but as soon as it reaches a steady, sustained sound, you can loop just that portion of the trumpet and give it infinite sustain. That way, you can hold the sound for as little or as long as you'd like.

Looping is tricky, because you have to set loop points very carefully or there can be clicks (due to an abrupt level difference) when playback returns from the end of the loop back to the beginning. So, DropZone gives you very fine control over the loop start and end points.

- **Turn looping on and off.** Click within an Element's waveform display and type **L**. When there's a loop, the Loop Start, Loop End, and Crossfade parameters become active.

- **Change looping mode.** Click within an Element's waveform display and type **D**. An arrow at the bottom of the loop indicates the direction.

  - If it points to the right, the file plays through to the loop end, jumps back to the loop beginning, plays through to the end, jumps back to the beginning, and so on.

  - If it points to the left, the file plays through to the loop end and then reverses direction and plays back to the beginning. It then jumps back to the loop end, plays through to the loop beginning, jumps back to the end, and so on.

  - If it points in both directions, the file plays through to the loop end, reverses direction and plays back to the beginning, reverses direction again and plays to the end, reverses direction and plays back to the beginning, and so on.

- **Changing loop points.** The Loop Start and Loop End parameters adjust where the loop starts and ends. When changing either one, you need to retrigger a key to hear the change.

- **Crossfade.** This mixes a little bit of the loop end in with the loop beginning. If you get clicks when looping, and changing the Start and End parameters can't fix it, use Start and End to minimize any clicking as much as possible and then increase the amount of crossfade. Often, this will get rid of the click.

Synth Signal Shaping

For signal shaping, there are tabs for Pitch, Filter Cutoff, and Amp. Each has an ADSR envelope with controls for Depth and Velocity response, as well as an individual LFO (low-frequency oscillator, which produces a period control change—like tremolo or vibrato) for each modifier.

The Filter. The filter is a multimode type, meaning that it has 16 different filter responses that can affect the timbre in 16 different ways (see Figure 13.28). The filter has the following controls:

- **Cutoff.** This changes the frequency that affects the timbre. For example, a low-pass (LP) filter lets through low frequencies but not high ones. Turning the Cutoff control counterclockwise removes progressively more highs. Conversely, a high-pass (HP) filter lets through high frequencies but not low ones. With this response, turning Cutoff clockwise removes progressively more lows. Other responses are BP (band-pass), BR (band-reject), AP (all-pass—creates very short delays), PK (a peaky response), Comb (a sound somewhat like phase shifting), and Pink (darkens the tone subtly). You can also bypass the filter by turning it off.

  Most responses also add a number and the letter P, such as 2P, 4P, and so on. This represents the number of poles in the filter response. Without getting too technical, suffice it to say that more poles mean a more drastic filtering response.

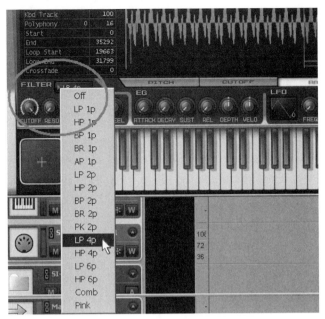

Figure 13.28 The filter itself is the usual multimode affair found in Cakewalk instruments, with 16 different filter responses. Here, the Low-Pass 4-Pole response is being selected.

■ **Resonance.** This changes the sharpness of resonance effects. Your ears will tell you what sounds best, but beware—turn this up too far, and you can get some sudden blasts of major volume. When you edit resonance, keep the volume down.

■ **Velocity, Keyboard Pitch, and Wheel.** These three can have positive or negative amounts. For example, positive values with velocity mean that hitting the keys harder raises the cutoff frequency. Negative values with keyboard tracking raise the cutoff frequency as you play lower notes on the keyboard, while positive values raise the cutoff frequency as you play higher on the keyboard. Wheel determines how the mod wheel affects the cutoff. With positive values, rotating the wheel away from you raises the filter cutoff frequency; with negative values, rotating the wheel away from you lowers the cutoff.

> **About the Envelope Generator (EG).** An envelope generator creates a control signal that varies over time. The envelope generators in DropZone include controls for Attack, Decay, Sustain, Release, Depth, and Velocity. If applied to pitch, Attack causes the pitch to rise from some initial value, over a length of time specified by the Attack control. The pitch then falls over an amount of time specified by the Decay control and ends up at a steady pitch set by the Sustain amount. The pitch stays at the sustain value as long as the key is held down. After releasing the key, the pitch falls back to its initial value over the time specified by the Release control.

Depth sets the amount of pitch change, and it offers negative and positive responses so that the Depth can either raise or lower the pitch. Velocity ties the envelope level to the dynamics of your playing. With positive values, the harder you hit the keys, the more the envelope raises pitch. With negative values, hitting the keys harder causes the envelope to lower pitch more.

Pitch Tab. The modifiers here include an envelope (see the preceding sidebar) and LFO. The LFO offers 20 possible waveforms. Although you can increment/decrement through the waveforms one at a time by clicking with the left and right mouse buttons, respectively, on the LFO waveform, you can also use the mouse scroll wheel to choose from the waveform options. Even better, you can change the LFO phase continuously—Shift-click on the LFO waveform and then drag left or right. The LFO also has controls for Frequency and Depth, and the LFO Depth can respond to Velocity, Keyboard Pitch, and Wheel. These three can have positive or negative amounts. For example, positive values with velocity mean that hitting the keys harder increases the LFO frequency. Negative values with keyboard tracking increases the LFO speed as you play lower notes on the keyboard. Wheel determines how the mod wheel affects pitch. With positive values, rotating the wheel away from you raises the pitch; with negative values, rotating the wheel away from you lowers the pitch.

Cutoff Tab. The EG and LFO work the same as for pitch, except that they affect the filter cutoff frequency.

Amp Tab. You guessed it—same as above, except this affects how the level changes. For example, you can use the LFO to create tremolo effects and the envelope to create dynamics.

Step-by-Step: Modify a DropZone Bass Sound
This assumes that DropZone is inserted in the project, is receiving MIDI, and drives some kind of audio output you can monitor.

1. Click on the File Handling icon and select Initialize Program.

2. Click on the Element 1 tab.

3. Click on the program name in the top line to call up the Program Browser.

4. Unfold the 02 – Basses folder and double-click on Fast Mini.prg. This will load into Element 1.

5. Play a note; it's a sustaining bass sound. We'll make it more percussive.

6. Click on the Amp tab.

7. Turn the EG Depth control fully clockwise.

8. Start turning the Decay control clockwise. Note how you can alter the sound's percussiveness.

9. Finally, let's check out what the filter does. Select a filter type from the drop-down menu and then vary the cutoff while playing to hear how the filter affects various frequencies.

Using REX Files with DropZone

There's more to looping than ACIDization/Groove Clips, like REX files. While some complain that SONAR Home Studio doesn't have native support for REX files, in some ways it does one step better by including DropZone—an excellent REX file playback instrument that requires very little CPU power.

When you drag a REX file into DropZone's waveform view, you can see the slices that separate different sections of the audio file.

Holding down a note in the virtual keyboard's lowest octave (C3 to B3) plays the REX loop through once (assuming you hold down the key for the loop's duration), and playing on different pitches within that octave transposes the key. Starting with C4 and going up in pitch, each key plays a slice of the REX file, with successive keys playing successive slices.

The latter is very useful with, for example, a drum loop that has kick and snare. If a slice isolates the kick and another isolates the snare, you can create your own kick/snare part by playing the corresponding keys.

When triggered from an external MIDI source, you can trigger from C2 to B2 to play the loop at lower pitches; however, you can also do this from the virtual keyboard—even though in theory you can't transpose the keyboard itself—by transposing the REX file via the Root parameter. For example, if you want the virtual keyboard's bottom two octaves to trigger loops instead of just the lower octave, enter –12 for the loop's Root parameter value.

What's especially interesting about both the envelopes and the LFO is that they're applied to each individual *slice* of the REX file, not the REX file as a whole. So, if you have (for example) a drum loop, you can tighten up the envelope decay to make it more percussive or add some attack to "mush" it. This also applies when playing slices from individual keys; each slice gets its own envelope.

However, there is a limitation compared to some other REX file players, like Cakewalk's own RXP instrument included in SONAR: RXP can export the MIDI part of the REX file that drives the slices. With DropZone, the REX file is treated simply as a stretchable audio file.

MIDI Learn Functions

One of my favorite features about DropZone is that every knob offers MIDI Learn. It's easy to use and quite powerful:

1. Right-click on the knob and select MIDI Learn.

2. Move your MIDI controller. DropZone will learn the assignment.

3. To remove the assignment, right-click on the knob and choose MIDI Forget. (Note that the context menu also shows the controller number currently assigned to MIDI Learn.)

Three other context menu options are Set Min, Set Max, and Reverse (see Figure 13.29). These are handy for giving finer control resolution.

Figure 13.29   A knob's context menu controls the MIDI Learn function. Here, Reverse is being selected for the Filter Cutoff.

For example, suppose you're using a band-pass filter setting with high resonance, and the only useful range of the filter's Cutoff control is from about halfway up to two-thirds up. Normally, your MIDI hardware controller covers the full cutoff range, but not if you use Min and Max. To restrict a knob's range:

1. Set the knob to the lowest value you want.

2. Right-click on the knob and from the context menu, select Set Min.

3. Set the knob to the highest value you want.

4. Right-click on the knob and from the context menu, select Set Max.

By doing this, the full range of the MIDI hardware controller covers only the range specified by the Min and Max settings. If you select Reverse, the "sense" of the controller reverses—in other words, if turning up the hardware controller raises a parameter's value, in Reverse mode turning up the hardware controller lowers the parameter's value.

Incidentally, having MIDI Learn available means that you have two automation options for DropZone: recording MIDI controllers and/or using VST automation.

Customizing DropZone's Look with Reskinning

Like many other recent Cakewalk plug-ins, DropZone is skinnable—look in your "VSTplugins" folder for the DropZone folder; then open its Resources folder to see the various graphic Elements.

You can modify these for any look you want (see Figure 13.30), but I'd advise saving a copy of all the original graphics in case you need to revert to them at some point. You'll also find a folder for the documentation in the DropZone folder, which answers the perennial Cakewalk instrument question, "So where's the documentation?"

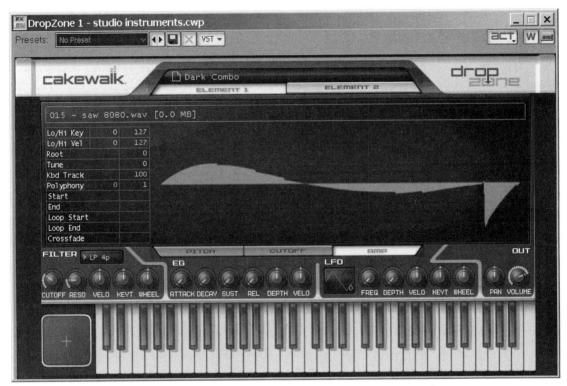

Figure 13.30   This figure shows a couple changes to DropZone's look—although you can't see that the overall color has changed, note that the field labels have a white typeface to make them more readable. The field values are the original color.

Dimension LE

Dimension LE (see Figure 13.31) plays back instruments from the library included with SONAR Home Studio. This library even includes Garritan Pocket Orchestra, a collection of orchestral sounds, as well as more traditional instruments suitable for a variety of genres. It allows for up to four Elements and has much in common with DropZone. As a result, to save space (and paper), I'll refer back to DropZone where appropriate.

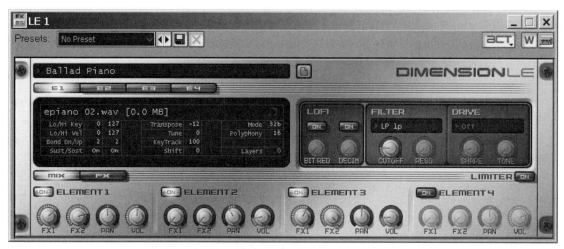

Figure 13.31   Dimension LE, after loading an electric piano sound.

Architecture

A Dimension LE Program can contain up to four Elements, which, like those in DropZone, can be split or layered. There are also two global effects processors (FX), and each Element has two send controls (one for each FX) that can send a portion of the Element sound to the effects.

As in DropZone, an Element consists of a waveform file with an associated set of parameter values (in this case, LoFi, Filter, and Drive). Loading a Program brings in the entire collection of Elements and associated settings. You can also bring a WAV, AIF, or SFZ file (but not a REX or Ogg Vorbis) into an Element by dragging it into the waveform name field, just below the four Element select buttons and above the waveform parameter matrix. You can also load it as described in the "Program Handling (Loading and Saving)" section for DropZone. However, unlike DropZone, the matrix of waveform-related parameters is *not* editable—you need the full version (Dimension Pro) for that. Dimension LE is basically a playback engine. As a result, if the waveform you bring in needs to have, for example, its tuning changed or needs to be layered in a different way, you can't change it.

Dimension LE specializes in two types of Elements. One is standard instrument playback, where you hit a key and hear a note (for example, French horn, bass, and so on). The other is loops that sync to the host tempo and play for as long as you hold down a key.

Program Handling (Loading and Saving)

This works the same way as with DropZone.

Mixing the Elements

There are buttons to select Mix or FX editing. Let's look at Mix first.

Individual Elements can be turned on and off with the On button to the left of each Element name. Furthermore, you can click on the Mix button to allow for adjusting the FX sends, pan, and volume for each Element (see Figure 13.32). For example, with a big pad sound, you might want to pan one layer right and one layer left to give a big stereo spread.

Figure 13.32 Three Elements are active and being mixed. Note how Element 1 is panned to the center, while Element 2 is panned full left and Element 3 is panned full right to create a big stereo image.

The more you turn up an Element's FX control, the more obvious the processing becomes.

Editing the FX

To add FX to the mix, click on the FX tab.

Choose a modulation effect (Chorus, Symphonic, Phaser, or Chorus/Flanger) by clicking on the drop-down menu arrow toward the left of the Modulation FX field (see Figure 13.33). You can also click within the field to cycle through the various options. Similarly, with Reverb you can select from seven different reverb types.

Figure 13.33 Here's the FX page. The Symphonic effect is being chosen for the modulation FX. Reverb is using the Large Hall algorithm.

Here's what the modulation FX controls do.

- **Freq.** Sets the modulation rate, from slow to a faster, almost vibrato-like effect.

- **Delay.** Edits the modulation's initial delay; modulation occurs around this initial delay.

- **Depth.** Determines how much the modulation affects the signal.

- **Feedback.** Feeds some of the output back to the input, giving a sharper, more resonant sound.

- **Dry/Wet.** Sets the balance of the processed and unprocessed sounds.

Next, let's look at the Reverb controls.

- **Predelay.** With a real room, there's a certain amount of time that elapses between a sound leaving a sound source and the time it hits the first wall and bounces off to create the first reflection. Predelay adjusts that time.

- **Size.** Adjusts the size of the virtual room, from smaller to bigger.

- **Damp.** With an acoustic space, sounds bounce around but lose energy over time. In the process, high frequencies are absorbed, particularly if there are soft surfaces in the room—drapes, carpet, people, and so on. Turning Damp clockwise simulates the effect of having a room with high absorption, where echoes start out bright but end up losing more and more highs.

- **Tone.** This is an overall Tone control. Turning Tone counterclockwise produces a bassier sound.

- **Dry/Wet.** Sets the balance of the processed and unprocessed sounds.

Editing the Elements

There are three processing modules for each Element (LoFi, Filter, and Drive). These edit one Element at a time, as selected by the four Element select buttons toward the upper left.

LoFi Effect. After all the years of trying to get perfect audio quality, now we have a bunch of effects designed to mess up the sound. These are used a lot in rap, dance, and other kinds of dance-oriented music. They also simulate the sound of older digital gear.

- **Bit Reduction.** Click the On button above the knob to enable the effect. Turning the knob clockwise reduces the number of bits, giving a rougher, buzzier sound. Note that the effect is most noticeable past the halfway point.

- **Decimation.** Click the On button above the knob to enable the effect, which gives the same result as lowering the sample rate—a clangorous, metallic tone.

Filter. The Filter works identically to the one in DropZone and again offers 16 different responses, but it is limited to Cutoff and Resonance controls.

Drive. This produces five different distortion effects, like a guitarist's fuzz box.

- **Shape.** This alters the distortion's character.

- **Tone.** Turning this clockwise removes high frequencies, giving a mellower tone.

Step-By-Step: Editing a Dimension LE Program

Let's take a polite church-organ sound and turn it into more of a snarling rock organ.

1. Click in the Program Name field to open the Browser, unfold the Organs category, and select Church Organ 2.

2. First, let's spread out the sound. Pan Element 1 to center, Element 2 full left (counterclockwise), and Element 3 full right (clockwise).

3. We're going to take off the churchy reverb sound and instead add chorusing to create a rotating speaker effect, so while you have the Mix settings up, turn Element 1–3 FX1 controls fully clockwise and the FX2 controls fully counterclockwise.

4. Now let's rough up the sound. Click on the E1 button to select Element 1 for editing. Set Drive to Soft, and turn up Shape all the way.

5. Repeat Step 4 for Elements 2 and 3.

6. Now we'll add our rotating speaker effect. Click on the FX button so you can edit the FX.

7. In the Modulation FX field, choose Chorus. Turn Freq up all the way, Delay up about 2/3 (25ms), Depth up about 2/3 (70%), and Dry/Wet up about 2/3 (70%).

We have a very different sound compared to the original church organ. To vary the speed of your virtual rotating speaker, play with the Modulation FX Freq control.

Square I

Square I has three oscillators, a noise generator, and one filter. We've already encountered many of its Elements—envelopes, controllers, and so on—in DropZone and Dimension LE, so I'll concentrate on what makes Square I different (see Figure 13.34).

Navigating Square I

The controls work by clicking on the control and then "turning" the knob (circular motion). However, if you hold down the Alt key while moving the control, it works linearly (like a fader). Ctrl-click returns the control to its default setting.

Several of the controls in Square I have two different functions, accessed by clicking on the control's label to toggle between the two. Following are the dual controls, listed for each main function.

■ **Oscillator.** Shape/Mode, Fine/Phase, Coarse/Pitch EG, Bend Range/Bend Mode, Main Tune/Transpose.

■ **Filter.** Aftertouch/Breath.

Figure 13.34 Square I is an interesting synthesizer—it can generate random patches and step through various oscillator waveforms while synched to the host tempo.

- **Pitch and Filter LFO.** Speed/Delay, Aftertouch/Breath.

- **Amplifier and Amp LFO.** Aftertouch/Breath.

- **Delay effect.** Cutoff/Feedback.

There are also two alternate *functions,* not just controls. To toggle between them, click on the function names. The two functions are:

- Random Wave LFO / PWM LFO

- Filter (hp) / Filter (lp)

You can also turn various sections off and on, such as the oscillators, the LFOs, and the FX—look for the little square buttons associated with these sections. This is a holdover from when computers didn't have enough power to run soft synths, so you turned off sections to save power. With today's computers, it's unlikely that you'll have to be too concerned about this.

The oscillators are the most complex part, so we'll deal with those last and cover the easy stuff first.

Program Load and Save

The lower right shows six banks (a, b, c, d, e, f). Click on a bank letter and then right-click on it to access its bank of 127 Programs. But there's a cool extra feature: Clicking on the Square I logo generates a random patch automatically. If you like it, save it; if not, keep clicking.

There are no patch management functions within Square I, so it's best to depend on the fact that any edits will be saved within a SONAR Home Studio project. It's still worth naming them, though, to be able to call them up within the Program. Here's how I do it.

1. Call up a blank Program. (If you call up an existing Program, modify it, and then save it, you will overwrite the existing Program.) You'll find these in Banks b through f.

2. Create your Program. Don't forget about the randomization feature!

3. To name your preset, go to the Presets field at the very top of Square I. Double-click on the existing name and type in a new one.

4. Click on the floppy disk icon.

The Program will be saved into the Square I bank and Program that you called up in Step 1, although it won't be named.

Note that this saving occurs only within the project; you won't be able to access different patches in a different project unless you export the patch so you can then import it later. To do this:

1. Create a folder to hold your Program, perhaps in the Cakewalk SONAR Home Studio folder.

2. Click on the VST drop-down menu (just above the Square I panel, around the middle) and then select Save Preset.

3. A standard Windows browser will open. Navigate to the folder you created to hold Square I patches.

4. Type the file name you want to use for the patch.

5. Click on Save.

To import this in the future:

1. Go to the VST drop-down menu and select Load Preset.

2. Navigate to the folder where you've stored your Square I patches.

3. Click on the patch and then click on Open.

Note that when you import a file, its name doesn't show up in the Presets name field. Nonetheless, the sound gets imported.

Filter

The filter can switch between low-pass and high-pass response when you click on the Filter label above the Cutoff and Resonance controls. In addition to these controls, the filter has its own envelope. The Envelope control sets how much the envelope modulation affects the filter cutoff, Keyb sets keyboard tracking, and we've already covered how Velocity and Mod Wheel control parameters. The Aftertouch/Breath control allows a keyboard's aftertouch (a controller whose level depends on how hard you press down on a key after it's down) or a breath controller (a controller whose level depends on how hard you're blowing into it) to introduce envelope modulation. The harder you press (with aftertouch) or blow into a breath controller, the more the envelope affects the filter cutoff frequency.

The Filter LFO, Amplifier, and Amp LFO controls are very much like what we've covered before. However, note that the Filter and Amp LFOs have "power switch" buttons (as mentioned earlier) that need to be enabled for them to work.

Amplifier

Here's how the controls work that we haven't checked out yet. All of these relate to the Amplifier and Amp LFO section.

- **Stereo Spread.** Clockwise gives more of a stereo effect; counterclockwise makes the signal mono.

- **Shape.** This changes the shape of the LFO's waveform.

- **Pan.** This applies the Amp LFO signal to panning.

Effects

There are three effects, each with an on/off button: Chorus, Delay, and EQ. Chorus works like the chorus in Dimension LE. EQ boosts or cuts at high or low frequencies. (Turn counterclockwise to cut, clockwise to boost). Delay has four controls.

- **Level.** This adjusts the level of the delayed signal.

- **Time Left.** This sets the left channel delay time.

- **Time Right.** This sets the right channel delay time.

- **Feedback.** This sends some of the output back to the input to create repeating echoes.

Oscillators

This section is one of Square I's more interesting features. There are three oscillators, each with the following four controls. There's also a Noise Source with no controls other than level.

- **Level.** This sets the oscillator's volume.

- **Shape.** This chooses from nine different waveforms.

- **Mode.** This is the alternate to Shape. (Click on the Shape label to access it.) It offers five modes that determine how notes start when you press a key. The first four affect where along the waveform a sound will start when you play a key—choose whatever sounds best to you. The fully clockwise option chooses fixed pitch, where whatever note you play on the keyboard doesn't affect pitch—it's determined solely by the Coarse and Fine frequency controls.

However, note that Oscillator 2 has two additional modes (for seven total) at the extreme clockwise settings. The next-to-last position causes Oscillator 2 to modulate Oscillator 1, creating a type of synthesis called FM (for *frequency modulation*—what Oscillator 2 is doing to Oscillator 1) synthesis. The full clockwise position causes Oscillator 2 to modulate both Oscillator 1 and Oscillator 3. FM synthesis can create interesting metallic and clangorous sounds that are particularly useful for percussive patches.

- **Fine.** This sets oscillator fine tuning.

- **Phase.** This is the alternate to the Fine knob, and it can affect the tone with some different Mode options.

- **Coarse.** This changes the oscillator pitch in semitone steps. Normally, it covers ±12 semitones, but in Fixed Pitch mode, it covers ±24 semitones, and when Oscillator 2 is in FM mode, it covers ±48 semitones.

- **Pitch EG.** This is the alternate to the Coarse knob, and it determines how much the pitch envelope modulates each oscillator.

Envelopes

The envelopes are very similar to the ones in DropZone, but the Pitch envelope has some differences. Its Start control determines the initial pitch, and unlike a traditional ADSR envelope generator, the attack needn't necessarily go to the highest possible value, as there's an Attack Level control. There's also a Release Level control that sets where the level ends up.

LFOs

The LFOs work similarly to those in the other instruments we've described, except for the Random Wave LFO—in my opinion, Square I's coolest feature. (In it, you can also see the first glimmers of the step sequencers used in Cakewalk's Rapture—an excellent virtual instrument plug-in.) Here's what its controls do.

- **Speed.** This sets the LFO frequency, and therefore how rapidly the LFO steps through the various oscillator waveforms. You can also sync to SONAR Home Studio's tempo using the Sync control.

- **Osc 1, Osc 2, and Osc 3.** These edit the number of oscillator waveforms the LFO will step through—turn clockwise for more.

- **Sync.** If the button above this is on, then the LFO speed will sync to the project tempo; the Sync knob determines the rhythmic subdivision of the sync. There's more about sync-to-tempo in Chapter 18, "SONAR Home Studio's Plug-Ins."

Roland Groove Synth

The Roland Groove Synth has a split personality: It's a preset synth with a bunch of sounds and limited editing, as well as a drum module with 27 kits that range from the classic electronic drum sounds (TR-909, -808, and -606) to dedicated drum kits for rock, ambient, house, techno, hip-hop, jungle, industrial—you name it. It's easy to use, easy to tweak, and easy on your computer, so it's a good starting point for getting involved in virtual instruments.

Preset Selection

To choose a Groove Synth sound, click in the LCD.

You'll see a menu with 30 sound categories, each of which has a side menu with a varying number of patches (see Figure 13.35). Click on the patch, and it will load pretty much instantly.

Preset Editing

Groove Synth editing is basic, but it allows for essential tweaks. Editing works separately for sounds and rhythm sets; we'll look at sounds first.

In addition to being where you select patches, the center section (see Figure 13.36) has mostly parameters that alter tone. The Filter Cutoff and Resonance controls work as with the other synths; the Tone section (which needs to be enabled to work) has standard Bass, Mid, and Treble controls; and the Character knob adds difficult-to-describe variations to a sound—tweak it until you like what you hear.

The Mono control has nothing to do with mono or stereo sound; instead, it limits you to playing one note at a time. This can add a more realistic playing feel when emulating single-note instruments, such as flute, sax, voice, and so on.

The remaining controls (see Figure 13.37) affect the patch sound as follows. Note that with many controls, 0 doesn't mean no effect, but represents a nominal setting.

- **Envelope.** This alters the Attack, Decay, and Release characteristics.

- **Vibrato.** This includes LFO control for Rate, Depth, and Delay.

- **Porta(mento).** When enabled, this adds a glide time between notes; it's most effective with mono sounds.

- **Mod Depth.** This controls the depth of an external modulation signal from a keyboard's mod wheel.

Figure 13.35   The Groove Synth has a ton of sounds that you can drop right into a project.

Figure 13.36   The Groove Synth's center section is where you select presets and adjust tone.

Figure 13.37 Groove Synth's other controls affect a variety of different parameters.

- **Bend.** This determines the amount of bend, in semitones, when you move a keyboard's pitch bend wheel all the way away from you or toward you. For example, with a setting of 2, the maximum pitch bend range is 2 semitones.

- **Tuning.** Coarse changes the pitch in semitone increments, up to ±48 semitones. Fine varies the pitch from −50 to +50 cents.

- **Level.** This adjusts the Groove Synth's master volume.

- **Pan.** This places the Groove Synth's output in the stereo field.

Rhythm Set Editing

When you call up a Rhythm Set, the interface is quite different. You can still call up presets from the blue LCD strip, but you can also call up individual drum sounds for editing.

To select a drum sound, click on the green LCD below the blue one, and you'll see a list of all available drum sounds in the current Rhythm Set (see Figure 13.38). You can also step through the drum sounds by using the < > arrows toward the right of the green LCD.

There are two different editing options for Rhythm Sets: global options that affect all drums in the Rhythm Set and parameters that affect only individual drums. We'll cover the global editing options first; these are the controls that are outside of the center black area (see Figure 13.39).

- **Tone controls.** These are global controls. As with the sound presets, there are Treble, Mid, and Bass controls. You need to activate the Tone controls with the Tone button.

- **Filter.** There are controls for filter cutoff frequency and resonance.

- **Level.** This sets the Rhythm Set's overall volume.

- **Pan.** This "master" pan control (there are also pan controls for individual drum sounds; see next) places the Rhythm Set in the stereo field.

The controls in the center black area affect only the selected drum sound.

- **Voice Level.** This sets the level of the selected drum sound.

Figure 13.38   Each drum sound in a Rhythm Set can be selected for editing.

- **Voice Pan.** This determines where the selected drum sound sits in the stereo field.

- **Coarse Tune.** This transposes the drum sound pitch over a ±48 semitone (eight octaves total) range.

- **Fine Tune.** This transposes the drum sound pitch over a ±50 cent range.

Using Global Controls for Individual Sounds

Note that if you want different settings for the global controls for different drum sounds, it's not a problem. For example, suppose you want a resonant filter sound on just the kick and snare, and you want the other drums to be unaffected. Here's what you'd do:

Figure 13.39 Rhythm Sets have a number of editable parameters.

1. Insert two instances of the Groove Synth.

2. Call up the Rhythm Set you want to use in both Groove Synths.

3. In one Groove Synth, turn the Voice Level controls all the way down on the kick and snare sounds. This takes the kick and snare out of the mix.

4. In the other Groove Synth, turn the Voice Level controls all the way down for all sounds except the kick and snare. Now you can set the Filter Cutoff and Resonance controls as desired for just the kick and snare.

Studio Instruments

Studio Instruments are the crowning touch to SONAR Home Studio 7's roster of instruments, because you can not only play them, you can also use them as inspiration-starters—each instrument has a section with patterns as well as a section with sounds. Let's start off with the Patterns section, because it's very similar for all four Studio Instruments.

Studio Instrument Sound Selection

When you want to load a Studio Instrument sound, click on the Prg button (see Figure 13.40). After selecting Load Program, you can then select the particular sound for the instrument.

Studio Instrument Pattern Selection

The middle of the pattern selection area has a browser (see Figure 13.41). You can unfold those categories that have a + sign to the left to reveal the patterns for that category.

Transport Section

Double-click on a pattern to hear it play through once. For further control, use the transport section buttons (see Figure 13.42).

From left to right, the buttons are as follows:

■ Selects the previous pattern from the Browser list.

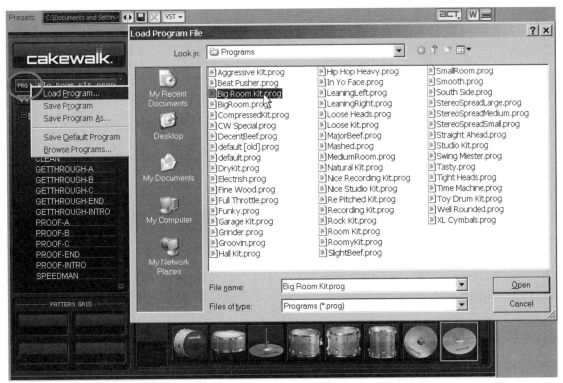

Figure 13.40   You can load any of 51 different kits into a Studio Instruments Drum Kit. Click on the Prg button, select Load Program, choose your program, and then click on Open.

- Selects the next pattern from the Browser list.

- Stops playback.

- Starts playback.

- Click on the Loop button if you want a pattern to repeat continuously once triggered. Click on Stop to stop playback.

Pattern Grid

The Pattern Grid provides a simple way to trigger up to four patterns. These will play through once unless the Loop button is enabled.

To load a pattern into the Grid, simply drag it from the Browser into one of the Grid slots (see Figure 13.43). You can click on a pattern to hear it or play it from a MIDI controller. (The notes that trigger the four patterns are G#0, A0, A#0, and B0.) If you play patterns from a MIDI controller, you can record this data into the Studio Instrument's MIDI track so that the patterns play back as part of a sequence.

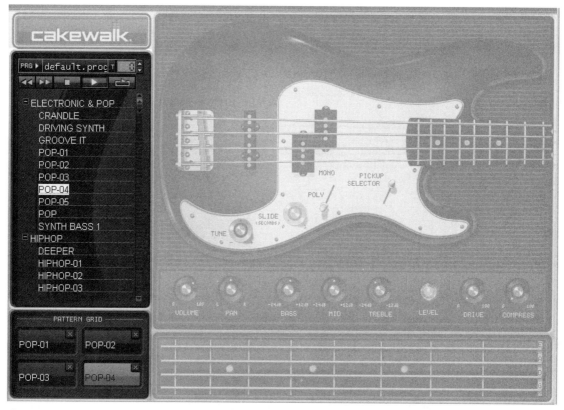

Figure 13.41 Pattern selection and playing is very similar for all Studio Instruments. This shot shows the bass's preset section.

Figure 13.42 The transport section handles playback control.

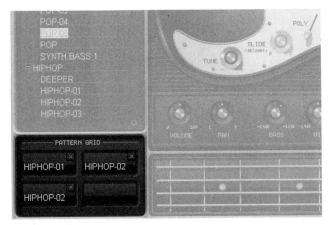

Figure 13.43   You can load different patterns into a Studio Instrument's Pattern Grid and then trigger them manually or automatically.

Studio Instruments Drum Kit

The Drum Kit has eight drum-sound slots and 51 drum kits, some built-in processing, and lots of patterns. We'll look at the sound-generating part first.

First, you'll want to load a kit. Each kit loads various drum sounds in the eight drum sound channels along the bottom (see Figure 13.44). You can then play the drums in four ways.

- Click on the graphic of the drum set. Note that clicking on different sections of the drum changes dynamics.

- Click on a drum icon along the bottom. The icons are also velocity-sensitive—click lower in the icon for lower-velocity sounds and higher for higher-velocity sounds.

- Create a MIDI part in the SI Drum's MIDI track—for example, using the Step Sequencer.

- Play notes from an external MIDI controller.

   There are three strips of controls above each drum icon (see Figure 13.45). You can think of each drum as having its own channel strip. From top to bottom, these are:

- **Tune.** This transposes the drum pitch up to ±24 semitones.

- **Pan.** This places the individual drum sound in the stereo field.

- **Vol.** This adjusts the level of the individual drum sound.

Along the right, from top to bottom, you'll find:

- **Volume.** This is the master Volume control for the mix of the drums. If the meters above this control hit the top bar, turn down the volume until the top bar lights rarely, if ever.

Figure 13.44 The Studio Instruments Drum Kit is an eight-drum drum sound expansion module.

- **Reverb amount.** This adds in room sound.

- **Compression amount.** Increase this to even out the drum dynamics.

Studio Instruments Bass

The Bass loads sounds similarly to the other Studio Instruments, via the Prg button. However, unlike the Drum Kit, the Bass has a Transpose field to the right of the selected program. This allows you to transpose up to ±12 semitones.

There are two groups of controls—the bass controls on the bass graphic itself and the amp controls below the bass (see Figure 13.46). On the bottom, there's a representation of a bass neck; you can click on its strings to trigger notes. (You'll also see a graphic with the note name.) However, if you play bass, it's strange to have the low notes toward the right of the neck and the high notes toward the left—it's as if you're watching someone play bass instead of playing it yourself.

The bass controls do the following.

- **Tune.** This changes the bass tuning by ±6 semitones.

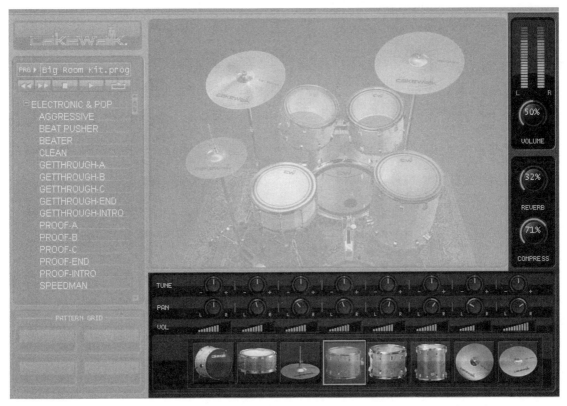

Figure 13.45   Controls for the SI Drum Kit's sounds are along the bottom and right side.

- **Slide.** The pitch glides from one note to the next note over the time set by this control. Note that this works only with the Poly/Mono switch in Mono.

- **Poly/Mono switch.** With Poly, the Bass will play as many notes as you play. With Mono, the Bass will play only one note at a time. This can clean up bass parts that tend to use single notes anyway, and it allows for using the Slide control.

- **Pickup selector.** In theory this changes the tone, but I don't hear any significant variation.

The amp controls offer these functions.

- **Volume.** This sets the instrument's overall level.

- **Pan.** This places the instrument in the stereo field.

- **Bass, Mid, and Treble.** These are standard tone controls.

- **Level light.** If this lights bright red, the instrument is distorting. Turn down the Volume control until the light is rarely, if ever, bright red.

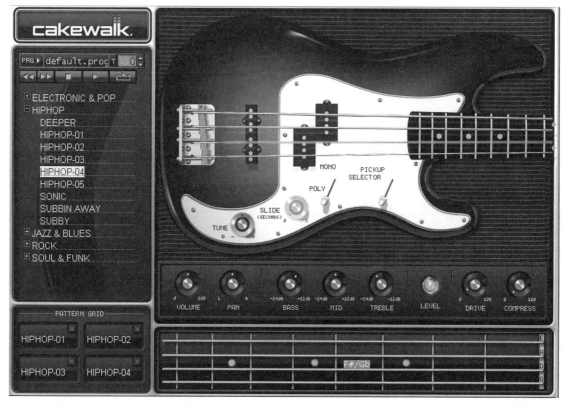

Figure 13.46 The Studio Instruments Bass includes both instrument and amplifier controls to change the sound.

- **Drive.** This adds a crunchy grit to the sound as you turn it clockwise. This can help the bass cut through a mix, although you don't want to take this *too* far—it could end up interfering with guitar or other instruments.

- **Compress.** This makes for a smoother bass sound by evening out the dynamic range.

Studio Instruments Electric Piano

The Electric Piano also loads sounds via the Prg button. Like the Bass, it has a Transpose field (±12 semitones) to the right of the selected program.

The Tune, Pan, and Volume instrument controls (and the Level light) work identically to the Bass; Tone makes a mellower sound as you turn it counterclockwise.

Here's the story on the effects (each of which has an In/Out switch; see Figure 13.47).

- **Drive Depth.** The Drive section works like the one for bass, except that it includes an In/Out switch.

- **Chorus Depth.** Turn Depth clockwise to thicken the sound.

Figure 13.47 The Studio Instruments Electric Piano includes effect and instrument controls for sound editing.

- **Tremolo Depth.** Tremolo provides a pulsing effect; Depth controls the intensity of the pulsing.

- **Tremolo Rate.** This affects the tremolo's speed. (However, note that Rate doesn't sync to SONAR Home Studio's tempo.)

Studio Instruments String Section

The String Section instrument is actually three separate instruments—bass, cello, and violin. There's a Prg button for loading a variety of presets using the three instruments and a Transpose (±12 semitones) field to the right of the selected program.

Each of the three instruments has its own Volume and Pan controls (see Figure 13.48), which work like the Volume and Pan controls we've encountered in the other Studio Instruments. There are also seven additional controls that affect the entire string section.

- **Attack.** This adds a rise time for the string note to go from soft to loud, like a fade-in.

Figure 13.48 The Studio Instruments String Section includes three instruments mapped to different ranges on the keyboard.

- **Release.** This sets how long it takes for the strings to decay to full off after you take your fingers off the keys (or MIDI notes in the track driving the String Section stop).

- **Tune.** This edits pitch, up to ±6 semitones in 0.1-semitone steps.

- **Master.** This sets the overall volume for all three instruments.

- **Tone.** This changes the String Section's timbral quality.

- **Chorus.** This adds a chorus/ensemble effect.

- **Reverb.** This adds an effect like the instruments playing in a concert hall.

Conserving CPU Power with Software Instruments

With fast computers, you may run out of musical good taste before your computer runs out of power for driving virtual instruments. But when you are using lots of soft synths, especially in older or slower computers, too many virtual instruments can bring a CPU to a crawl.

Fortunately, there are two ways to save CPU power. Freezing tracks is covered in Chapter 14, but you can also permanently convert soft synth tracks to hard disk audio tracks, which take much less power than virtual instrument tracks. This process is called *bouncing*, and here's how to do it.

1. Click on the track number for the MIDI track driving the soft synth(s) and then Ctrl-click on the track that carries the synth's audio. Both the MIDI and audio tracks must be selected, or bouncing won't work.

2. Mute all other tracks. To be certain that you bounce only the tracks you want, solo the selected tracks.

3. Show the bus being fed by the audio track(s). We'll use the master bus as an example.

4. Observe the master bus playback meters while you play the part you want to bounce. If there is any distortion, reduce the level of the audio track(s) feeding the master bus.

5. In SONAR Home Studio, select the range of measures you want to bounce.

6. Select Edit > Bounce to Track(s). A window will appear with the destination track, the format, the source bus from which the signal is derived (typically whatever connects to your master out), and the Mix Enables section (see Figure 13.49). I generally just leave all the Mix Enables options checked, because if it says, for example, to use master FX and there's no master FX, it doesn't matter. But if there is a master FX being used and I

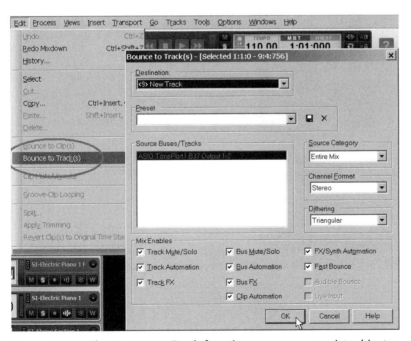

Figure 13.49   The Bounce to Track function can convert a virtual instrument track to a hard disk track, thus saving CPU power.

don't check the box, the results of adding the effect won't show up in the bounced signal.

7.   Click on OK to initiate the bounce. This new track will include any processing you may have added. If you're certain you'll use the hard disk track, you can delete the virtual instrument tracks. However, if you think you may want to edit the instrument track in the future, check out the next section on archiving tracks.

Archiving Virtual Instrument Tracks

You can also save CPU power by *archiving* unneeded virtual instrument tracks. This process mutes the track and disconnects it from the CPU, so it takes virtually no power—but you can also unarchive tracks if you want to make any changes.

To archive a track folder, click on the small A in the track's lower right (see Figure 13.50). To archive a single audio or MIDI track, select it and then choose Tracks > Archive. This is also a toggle for unarchiving.

Figure 13.50 Folder tracks let you archive by clicking the A button in the track folder's lower right.

14 Track Freezing

As you found out in the previous chapter, virtual instruments are a tremendously cool addition to the world of digital recording, but they come with a price: They hog CPU power, which means you may not be able to use as many as you'd like, SONAR Home Studio may not be able to run at a low enough latency to be satisfactory, or both. This is because the instruments calculate their sounds in real time when they play back audio.

The Freeze function gets around the CPU problem by capturing that playback and recording it as a hard disk audio track. That means SONAR Home Studio can simply play back that audio track instead of having the instrument recalculate its sound every time it plays back, thus saving a lot of CPU power. SONAR "archives" the instrument as long as the track is frozen, thus "disconnecting" it from the CPU. However, freezing isn't permanent: You can unfreeze a frozen track at any time if you need to re-edit the part or change the instrument parameters.

An added benefit is that if you freeze a virtual instrument that loads samples into RAM (for example, samplers that don't stream from hard disk), freezing reclaims the RAM as well. Nor is freezing limited to instrument tracks—you can freeze audio tracks that are loaded with effects (such as reverb) that can cause a CPU hit.

How to Freeze

Freezing is simple. In the Track view, click on the track's Freeze button, which looks like a snowflake (see Figure 14.1). Clicking on Freeze automatically premixes the track or instrument audio (with any effects); the progress bar along the bottom moves as the track is rendered to audio. The original audio clip display disappears and is replaced by a representation of the frozen clip against a blue background. Note that what's displayed may differ from the original audio because it reflects any changes to the waveform caused by processing. The FX bin is also disabled.

If the track is already frozen (as evidenced by the snowflake on the button being white), you can click on it to unfreeze the track and return it to normal operation.

You can also freeze a soft synth from the Synth Rack view, but the options here are slightly different (see Figure 14.2).

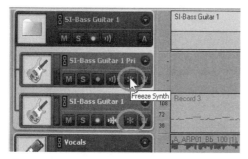

Figure 14.1 Audio and instrument tracks have Freeze buttons. With instrument tracks that have both MIDI and audio components, freezing either track causes the other one to be part of the freezing process as well.

Figure 14.2 There are two places to freeze on the Synth Rack view—on individual instruments (with one button for Freeze and one for Unfreeze/Refreeze), and the button in the top toolbar that looks like a snowflake (this option allows for additional freeze options).

Let's first look at how the Synth Rack view's upper button shown in Figure 14.2 works. Click on it, and your options are:

- **Freeze Synth.** This acts as I've already described.

- **Unfreeze Synth.** This discards the premix, returns the audio clip display to normal, and re-enables the FX bin.

- **Quick Unfreeze Synth.** This keeps the premixed audio but shows the original audio and enables the FX bin. This function is useful if you want to test a change on the unfrozen track for comparison. For example, if you're not sure you like a particular effect and you also want to perhaps change an envelope, do a Quick Unfreeze. Disable the effect, change the envelope, and then listen. To compare this to the frozen version, select Quick Freeze. You can toggle back and forth between the two until you make up your mind. Note, however, that you can Freeze or Quick Freeze only while the transport is stopped; you can Unfreeze or Quick Unfreeze at any time.

One limitation of the Quick Freeze option is that if you make a change during the quick unfrozen state and like it, you can't go directly to Freeze Track to freeze the changed version—you need to Quick Freeze, Unfreeze, and then Freeze again. (However, any changes you made to the track while in the quickly unfrozen state are retained when you Unfreeze.)

- **Freeze Options.** We'll look at this in detail in the next section.

Whichever option you choose applies to whichever instrument is selected in the Synth Rack view. Therefore, certain options may be grayed out—for example, if the track is already frozen, Freeze Synth will be unavailable.

Freeze Options
Although track freezing is basically a one-button operation, there are ways to customize how the freezing process works (see Figure 14.3). Here are your options.

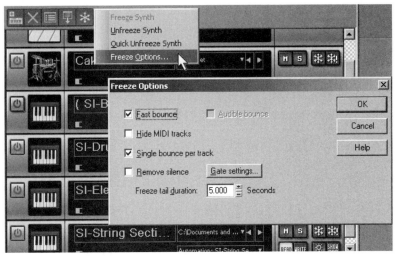

Figure 14.3   There are several parameters that customize how freezing is performed.

- **Fast Bounce.** This will freeze the track faster than real time. If a synth works only in real time, or if it's going through external hardware effects in addition to or instead of internal plug-ins, this should be unchecked.

- **Hide MIDI Tracks.** I recommend leaving this unchecked so you can see MIDI tracks even if an instrument track is frozen—that helps let you know what's going on the song. However, if you really are done fiddling with a track, hiding any associated MIDI tracks will declutter your workspace.

- **Single Bounce per Track.** This premixes the clips in a track into a single frozen clip. If the option is unchecked, SONAR Home Studio will create separate clips for each clip in the track to be frozen when you freeze, but you'll need to set the Remove Silence gate settings. (See the following point.)

- **Remove Silence and Gate Settings.** This causes SONAR Home Studio to recognize the silence between clips as the place to separate the clips. This seems unnecessarily complex for what should be a quick operation, and I've never found a situation where I needed it, so I always leave Single Bounce per Track checked.

- **Freeze Tail Duration.** This allows you to set a duration that extends beyond the last clip to accommodate decay tails from delays, reverb, and so on. The default is five seconds, which does what you need almost all the time, but there's no real limit on length.

Editing Frozen Tracks

You can do a lot with a frozen track: move it, split it, cut pieces, copy pieces, and even convert a frozen track—or a part that's been cut into its own clip—into a Groove Clip. As expected, because this all affects the premixed audio, unfreezing discards the premixed audio, and you lose any edits you've made. However, before unfreezing, you can always bounce the frozen/edited track to a new track. (Choose Edit > Bounce to Clip[s] or simply drag the audio to a standard audio track.) When you do, unfreezing the original track does not unfreeze the copy, so the copied, edited track is available if you still need it.

15 The ReWire Connection

In the pre-DAW era, studios routed their signals through *patch bays*—rack panels with enough jacks so that casual observers often confused the typical studio with an old-school telephone switching office. If you wanted an instrument to go into a recorder or an aux send to feed a reverb, or if you wanted to bring tape outs back into a mixer, the patch bay (along with its Medusa-like collection of patch cables, which, of course, were never *quite* the right length) made it all possible.

Virtual studios are making the giant patch bay obsolete—plug-ins become part of the signal path with "virtual" patch cords, while digital audio outs appear in virtual mixers. But the most ambitious example of large-scale virtual patching, the industry-standard ReWire software technology developed by Propellerhead Software, tightly integrates two (or sometimes more) complete *programs* to work together.

ReWire requires a host or mixer program such as SONAR Home Studio and a client, slave, or synthesizer program (for example, Propellerhead Reason, Steinberg Groove Agent 3, Arturia Storm, Ableton Live, and so on). Some programs, such as Storm and Live, can be either a host or a client. However, note that you can't open multiple instances of a single ReWire instrument with SONAR Home Studio.

When you ReWire a client into a host (see Figure 15.1), the client's outputs go into the host's mixer and appear as individual audio tracks. ReWired programs also share transport/sync functions (with single-sample accuracy), and if you set a loop within SONAR Home Studio, any sequencer in the ReWired application should match that loop. Furthermore, any of the client's synchable instruments or processors will respond to the host's tempo. The programs also run in parallel, so if you have sequences recorded in the client, they'll play back and augment whatever you've recorded in SONAR Home Studio. Conversely, projects recorded in SONAR Home Studio can take advantage of the client's virtual instruments and other features to augment the arrangement.

There's a misconception that ReWire uses considerable computer resources, but it's just an interconnection protocol. However, by definition, you'll be using at least two programs together, each of which is generally processor-intensive. Most modern computers can handle this if you have sufficient RAM and a relatively fast processor. To save CPU power, it's common

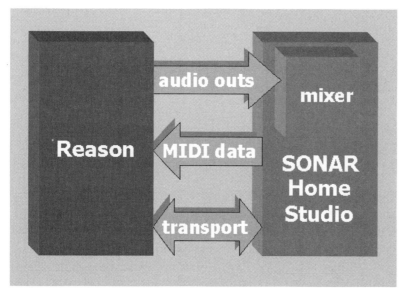

Figure 15.1   This shows what happens conceptually when you ReWire a client program, such as Reason, into SONAR Home Studio.

to convert ReWired instrument tracks to digital audio tracks in the host (as described in Chapter 13) so that the ReWired device is no longer necessary during mixdown.

Note that if you install a ReWire application while SONAR Home Studio is open (which you shouldn't do anyway—it's best to install programs with no other programs running), you'll need to reboot your computer for SONAR Home Studio to "see" the ReWire application. Finally, although you can use ReWire with MME drivers, that's sort of like owning a Porsche that can't get out of first gear—use ASIO or WDM drivers.

Opening a ReWire Application

We'll cover ReWire from a general standpoint first and then get into step-by-step specifics.

1.   Open SONAR Home Studio and open a project (new or otherwise).

2.   Choose Insert > ReWire Device and specify the device you want to ReWire into SONAR Home Studio (see Figure 15.2).

3.   Choose the settings as you would for a virtual instrument (see Figure 15.3).

- **MIDI Source Track.** Check this—it creates a MIDI track for driving the ReWire application.

- **First Synth Audio Output.** If you check this, SONAR Home Studio adds two audio tracks that carry the client's mixed stereo output. This is recommended for when you first get into using ReWire.

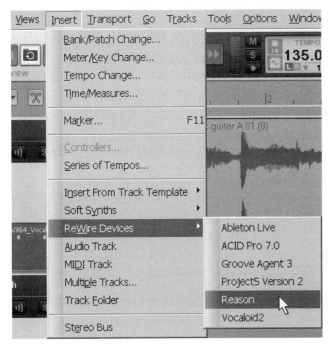

Figure 15.2   ReWire devices are inserted in a way very similar to virtual instruments.

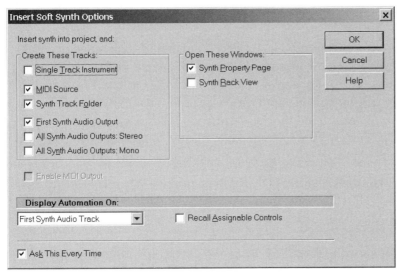

Figure 15.3   Here are suggested settings for a typical ReWire device.

- **All Synth Audio Outputs.** If you check this, you may end up with *a lot* of channels—in the case of ReWiring Reason, SONAR Home Studio's mixer would sprout 64 audio tracks, which is the maximum number of audio tracks SONAR Home Studio can handle! Although you can always delete the channels you don't use, in many cases it's easier to do any mixing and processing of the client within the client and simply send a mixed output (First Synth Audio Output) to SONAR Home Studio.

- **Synth Property Page.** This must be checked, because ReWire applications need their interfaces open in order to function.

- **Synth Rack View.** This calls up the Synth Rack window. I generally leave this unchecked to avoid window clutter; you can always choose View > Synth Rack if you want to see it.

- **Ask This Every Time.** I usually leave this checked because sometimes I want First Synth Audio Output, and sometimes I want All Synth Audio Outputs, depending on the project.

After making your selections, click on OK. It takes a few moments for SONAR Home Studio to load and insert Reason, so be patient if it seems nothing is happening for a few seconds.

4.   After a moment, the client will open, and the user interface will appear. If you see any warnings, ignore and click through them. For example, Reason will say "MIDI input problem" because your interface's MIDI inputs are assigned to SONAR Home Studio, and Reason doesn't "see" them. But this doesn't matter, because SONAR Home Studio will pass any MIDI data through to Reason.

5.   Choose Options > Audio > Advanced tab. Under Playback and Recording, uncheck Share Drivers with Other Programs. Sharing drivers is not a good idea, because switching to another program—as would happen if you're bouncing back and forth between SONAR Home Studio and the ReWire application—can mute SONAR Home Studio's outs. Although you can work around this by shifting the focus back to SONAR Home Studio or initiating playback on the ReWire slave or master, because ReWire takes care of audio and MIDI integration, it's better to let the host handle the I/O.

6.   You've now ReWired your client into SONAR Home Studio. When it's time to close your session, close the client first and then close SONAR Home Studio. You won't break anything if you do these in the wrong order, but you'll get an error message reminding you it's necessary to close the client first.

Step-by-Step: Using Reason as a Synth Rack for SONAR Home Studio

Although SONAR Home Studio ships with a fine collection of virtual instruments, it doesn't include a sampler, a semi-modular synthesizer, or some other goodies. But if you want to augment your collection of instruments, you can use Propellerhead Software's Reason as a great multi-timbral sound module for SONAR Home Studio. Here's how:

1. Follow Steps 1 through 5 in the "Opening a ReWire Application" section earlier in this chapter.

2. In SONAR Home Studio, you'll see an audio track for Reason's stereo mixer outs and a MIDI track to drive them (see Figure 15.4).

Figure 15.4 Because we checked Synth Track Folder in the Insert Soft Synth Options dialog box, Reason's stereo mixer outs and MIDI tracks are located inside a Reason folder. Note that the top of Reason's "hardware interface" shows that Reason is in ReWire Slave (Client) mode.

3. Test the setup by clicking on SONAR Home Studio's Play button or the Play button in Reason's transport. Reason's default song should start playing through its SONAR Home Studio audio track, with the Reason and SONAR Home Studio sequencers playing back in tandem.

4. To use Reason as a multi-timbral module, you'll want to delete any existing tracks (such as the ones the Demo Song loads). Better yet, create a Reason template with the instruments you want to use and save it as SONAR Instrument Rack. You can even save this so that it opens up as the default; see Reason's documentation for more information on saving templates.

5. Click on the MIDI track's Output parameter and check that Reason is selected.

6.   Click on the MIDI track's Channel parameter, and a wonderful thing will happen: You will see a list of all the available instruments in Reason. Select the desired instrument (see Figure 15.5) and then play a few keys to verify that you can hear the sound.

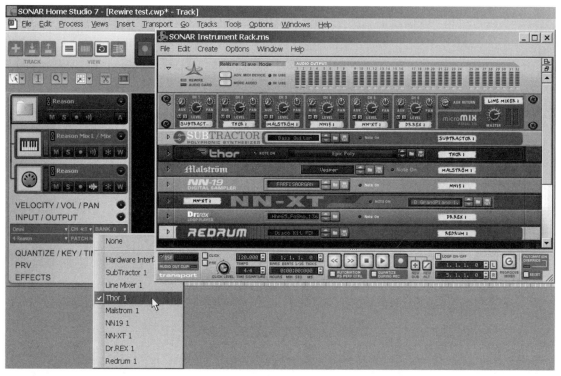

Figure 15.5   To direct the incoming MIDI data to a specific Reason instrument, choose it in the MIDI track's Channel field.

7.   Enable the Record option for the SONAR Home Studio MIDI track, click on the transport Record button, and start playing.

8.   Insert a separate MIDI track for each instrument you want to use. As before, select Reason as the out and choose the instrument you want to play with the CH(annel) field.

9.   As you keep adding tracks of Reason instruments, you can trigger notes for any of the instruments simply by clicking on the appropriate SONAR Home Studio track. This makes it very easy to do overdubs or tweak Reason's parameters.

Recording Real-Time ReWire Controller Edits

Here's an example of using MIDI control to tweak Reason parameters in real time, while recording the control signals in SONAR Home Studio. If you have a master keyboard with a few assignable controller knobs (for example, foot pedal, data slider, mod wheel, or whatever) or a MIDI control surface (see Chapter 20, "Control Surfaces"), you can do the tricks I'm about to describe. Note that this process does *not* involve using Reason's MIDI remote option.

With this technique, you can do real-time adjustments of any parameter listed in Reason's MIDI implementation chart. This is a PDF file included on the Reason CD; in the standard installation, it's accessible from Start > Programs > Propellerhead > Reason > MIDI Implementation Charts.

For example, suppose you want to automate Subtractor's Amplitude Envelope Decay parameter. According to the MIDI implementation chart, this parameter is controlled via MIDI Controller #9, so assign your physical controller (for example, the data slider) to transmit data as Controller #9 (see Figure 15.6).

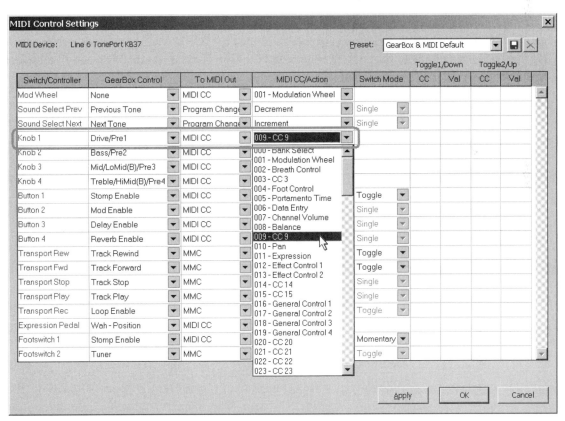

Figure 15.6   Line 6's KB37 is a combination MIDI mini-keyboard, audio interface, and control surface. It comes with software whose MIDI preferences let you assign the knobs and switches to various functions. In this example, Knob 1 is being assigned to MIDI Continuous Controller #9.

Now put the focus on Reason by clicking on it and then move the physical controller; Subtractor's Amp Env Decay slider should follow your motions. When you want to record, do so normally (arm the track in SONAR Home Studio and then click on Record in the transport) and play notes and/or tweak the control. After you stop, you'll see the note and controller data in the Clips view.

Switch back to Reason, rewind to the beginning, and then press Play (or do this in SONAR Home Studio and then put the focus on Reason). The part will play back, and you'll see Reason's Amp Env Decay slider follow the controller data.

Some Subtractor parameters you might want to automate are not listed in the MIDI implementation chart (specifically, Filter Frequency, Filter Resonance, LFO 1 Amount, Phase Difference, and FM Amount). These are all tied in with the mod wheel; each also has an Amount parameter that determines how much the mod wheel affects the parameter.

To modulate only one of these parameters, set the parameter's corresponding Amount knob (in the bend/mod wheel section) to the desired maximum amount of modulation when the mod wheel is up full, and then record mod wheel motion into the MIDI track. For example, to modulate the Filter Frequency with the mod wheel, turn up the F. Freq control as desired and then record the mod wheel motions.

Furthermore, independent modulation for these parameters is also possible because each of the Amount knobs in the bend/mod wheel section can be MIDI controlled. Therefore, if you set the mod wheel amount to the maximum, you can then modulate the Amount controls to alter a parameter. For example, assuming the mod wheel is up full, modulating the F. Freq control (which responds to MIDI Controller #33) will vary the filter cutoff, while modulating the LFO1 Mod Wheel Amount (MIDI Controller #35) will modulate that parameter independently.

Step-by-Step: Using SONAR Home Studio's Step Sequencer with Reason's ReDrum

I like the ReDrum module included with Reason, except that it's tedious to produce sequences that last longer than 16 steps. Although you can produce sequences with up to 64 steps, that requires bank switching among sets of 16 steps. And because there's no way to copy a sequence from one set of 16 steps to another, you have to program each set of 16 steps from scratch.

By rewiring ReDrum into SONAR Home Studio, you can use SONAR Home Studio's Step Sequencer interface in conjunction with ReDrum's sounds. Although you can't translate the sequence created in SONAR Home Studio to a pattern in Reason, it really doesn't matter; you can simply use ReDrum as a tone module for SONAR Home Studio and the Step Sequencer as an interface for ReDrum. Here's how to do it:

1.　Open SONAR Home Studio.

2.　Select Insert > ReWire Devices > Reason and choose the appropriate Soft Synth Options, as described previously.

3. Now do your Reason "housekeeping": Load a drum kit into ReDrum and select the ReDrum track in Reason's sequencer so that any incoming MIDI data gets routed to ReDrum.

4. Select the SONAR Home Studio MIDI track that drives ReDrum.

5. Assign this track's output to Reason and its channel to ReDrum (as selected in the drop-down menu).

6. Choose Views > Step Sequencer.

7. The Step Sequencer's note assignments should default to the notes for ReDrum (MIDI notes 36–45). If not, you can always reassign them or load an appropriate drum map. For more information on the Step Sequencer, refer to Chapter 10.

8. Click on a Step Sequencer step and then hit the Step Sequencer's Play button. SONAR Home Studio will create a loop whose start point is the Now time and that lasts for as long as you have steps in the Step Sequencer.

9. Program your drum part.

Saving a ReWired Project

When you save a SONAR Home Studio project that incorporates a ReWire device, the next time you open the project, SONAR Home Studio will automatically load the ReWire device. However, any tweaks you made to the ReWire device *are not saved* with the project. Save the ReWire program separately and call it up after you call up SONAR Home Studio.

For example, if you're using Reason with SONAR Home Studio, save a modified Reason rack with a suitable file name in the appropriate SONAR Home Studio project folder. Then close Reason and SONAR Home Studio. The next time you open the desired SONAR Home Studio project, use Reason's File > Open command to load the file containing the tweaked parameters and patches.

The ability to add a rack of virtual instruments to SONAR Home Studio allows a degree of flexibility that recalls a monster patch bay—without the wiring hassles or patch cords. Be sure to experiment with the ReWire protocol if you want to get acquainted with a very clever and useful tool.

16 Mixing with SONAR Home Studio's Console View

After you've written your song, recorded your tracks, and done whatever overdubs and edits are necessary, you're ready to *mix* all these separate elements into a cohesive musical experience. The short form on mixing is you adjust the levels, tonal balance, and stereo placement and add any needed effects until the song sounds totally wonderful.

Mixing involves a huge number of decisions. At any given moment, which instrument should be most prominent? Do you want to mute some parts that in retrospect don't need to be part of the mix? Who is your target audience—do you want a raw, punk-type sound or something more mainstream?

Mixing is a combination of art—you have to be able to judge what sounds good—and science—where you need to know which technologies and processes will produce the sounds you want. A common mistake among those getting into mixing is to want to include *everything* in the mix, but much of the mixing process is about being ruthless and cutting out anything that doesn't support the song.

One caution: Loud, extended mixing sessions are very tough on the ears. Mixing at low levels keeps your ears "fresher" and minimizes ear fatigue; you'll also be able to discriminate better between subtle level variations. Loud mixes may get you hyped up, but they'll also trip your ears' built-in "limiting." (Ears don't hear in a linear fashion.)

However, because the ears' frequency response changes depending on level, if you mix or master at *too* low a level, you might boost the bass and treble too much. Mix at a comfortable listening level—neither too loud nor too soft. Then check at both high and low levels to find a good average setting.

Feel or Perfection?

Some older recordings, created under technically primitive conditions, still conveyed a joyousness and enthusiasm—a "feel"—that made for great music. And some newer albums are so perfect, so automated and equalized, that the sound is sterile. Don't fall into the trap of being so self-critical that you never complete anything, but also don't get so loose that you think everything sounds great and you lose the ability to do critical evaluations.

Perhaps the most important part of mixing is knowing when to say enough! It's also important not to use something just because you can. Sure, SONAR Home Studio can do 64 tracks—but that doesn't mean you have to fill up every one of them to get your money's worth out of the program.

With SONAR Home Studio, you can save your mixes as you go along. It's a good idea to do this, because you may find that it was the first or second mix, not the last one, that had a certain visceral quality that got lost along the way.

Challenges Facing the Solo Artist

The ability of one person to write, play, produce, record, master, and even duplicate music is unique to modern times. But just because we *can,* does that mean we *should?* There's much to recommend human interaction, thanks to the reality check that comes from a trusted associate who can give honest, objective feedback.

The key to pulling off the difficult task of being a solo musician is *not to fall in love with your music.* Distance yourself from what you do, so you can make the kind of objective decisions normally reserved for the producer. Following are some tips on how to create "better music through detachment."

The Radio Factor

A song's intro is crucial. If a radio station or A&R person doesn't like the first 10 seconds, you're probably not going to get another chance.

Here's a test for intros. Picture a party filled with all kinds of people, with a radio playing in the background. A commercial comes on, followed by an announcer saying the station logo, and then they lead into your song. Imagine this scene as vividly as you can.

Try to put yourself in the position of one of the partygoers, then "look" around you. How do the people react? Do they stop talking and listen? Do they listen for the first few bars, then go back to conversing? Do they ignore it entirely? Is there something in the first few seconds to grab their attention and keep it? For your tune to be played on the radio, think of it in the context of radio play. It has to be able to segue from anything to anything, appeal to short attention spans, and be different. Doing this exercise can help clarify what needs to be done to make the song stand out.

Try It Live

The quickest way to find out whether a song works or not is to play it in front of an audience (preferably non-musicians). But if you can't do that, to simulate the effect of playing a piece one-on-one to an audience, go back to square one, pick up a single guitar or keyboard, and re-arrange the song for playing as a solo performer in real time. This will force you to concentrate on the essence of the music: melody and lyrics. Getting, say, a great kick drum sound is far less important.

Remember, songs were once honed on the road and then captured in the studio. Now songs are often created in the studio and re-created on the road. As you mix a tune, always imagine an audience is listening. It will make a difference in how the song develops.

Avoid the "Cleverness Factor"

For me, the paramount lesson from doing years of studio work behind songs was that *everything* supports the lead singer. Your instrumental parts are there *primarily* to make the lead vocal more effective.

Many years ago, I came up with a lyrical, melodic bass part for a verse. It was composed in isolation, while waiting for the engineer to get a good snare drum sound, and I fell in love with the part. But played behind the vocal, it was too distracting. The producer told me to simplify the part, and I ended up playing something that any moron who had just picked up a bass could play. It was hard to let my clever bass part go, but the simpler version made a far greater contribution to the tune.

When mixing, many times it's what you *mute* that makes the song work, not what you leave in. *The less there is going on, the more important the remaining parts become.* The mixing process is your last chance to be brutally honest: If something doesn't work quite right, get rid of it, regardless of how good it sounds on its own.

Consider Your Goals

Of course, all this advice assumes that you *want* to connect with an audience. But I don't necessarily advocate that. Creating music is, in the larger sense, about self-discovery, and that can be a magical process.

I feel there are only three ways to be successful. One is to be totally true to yourself and hope that the music you create strikes a chord in others as well. This usually creates the brightest stars with the longest careers, because there's nothing artificial. And if it doesn't "fit" with a mass audience, at least what you have is honest, and your friends will probably love it.

The second option is to carefully study past hits, cool chord progressions, pick lyrical subjects with wide appeal, etc., and do mixes that are designed to appeal to specific audiences. I've known songwriters who approach writing more as a business than as art, and that's fine too; it can lead to a comfortable, well-paying career without the drawbacks of fame.

However, combining the two approaches often yields the best results. Let the artist in you create, and then let the hard-headed, objective part of you produce, mix, and master. Go ahead, love your music—but don't be *in* love with it if you want to remain objective.

Enough opinions...let's get technical.

About Frequency Response, Hearing, and Monitoring

One goal of mixing is to produce a balanced, even sound. The music should have a full, satisfying bass without muddiness, a well-defined midrange, and sparkly (not screechy) highs.

To achieve this, as well as use equalization properly, you need to understand frequency response.

Frequency response defines how a system records or reproduces the spectrum of audible frequencies, which stretches from 20 Hz to 20,000 Hz. (Hz, short for *hertz*, measures the number of cycles per second in a wave; 1 kHz or kilohertz equals 1,000 Hz.)

Frequency response is usually shown on a graph (see Figure 16.1). The Y axis (vertical) shows level, and the X axis (horizontal) indicates frequency. The audible range is further divided into bands. These aren't precisely defined, but here's a rough guide.

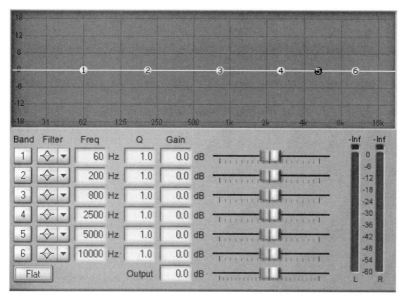

Figure 16.1   Here, the graph in SONAR Home Studio's equalizer shows a straight line from 0 to 20 kHz. This is called a *flat response,* which means that no range of frequencies is accented or diminished. Note that the gain controls are set to 0.0 dB, so they are neither boosting nor cutting their associated frequencies.

- Bass. Lowest frequencies, typically below 200 Hz.

- **Lower midrange.** 200 to 800 Hz.

- **Midrange.** 800 Hz to 2.5 kHz.

- **Upper midrange.** 2.5 kHz to 8 kHz.

- **Treble.** 8 kHz and higher.

For example, bass guitar and kick drum occupy the bass range. Vocals are in the midrange and lower midrange. Percussion instruments, such as tambourine, have lots of energy in the treble region.

Monitoring and Acoustics

All the effort you put into recording and mixing is for nothing if your monitoring system doesn't accurately reproduce the sounds you hear. The issue isn't simply the speakers; monitoring involves your ears, the acoustics of the room where you're mixing, the amp and cables that drive your monitors, and the speakers themselves. All of these elements work together to determine the accuracy of what you hear, and therefore, how you mix and master. If you've ever done a mix that sounded great on your system but fell apart when played elsewhere, you've experienced firsthand what can go wrong with the monitoring process.

The Problem with Ears

Unfortunately, your ears—the most crucial and important components of your monitoring system—aren't perfect, thanks to a phenomenon called the Fletcher-Munson curve. Simply stated, the ear has a midrange peak and does not respond as well to low and high frequencies, particularly at lower volumes. The response comes closest to flat response at relatively high levels, so the mix literally changes depending on your listening levels. For best results, don't monitor too loud or too soft, but at typical listening levels—that's how your listeners will hear it.

Another limitation is that a variety of factors can damage your ears—not just loud music, but excessive drinking, deep sea diving, and just plain aging. I've even noticed that flying temporarily affects my high frequency response, so I wait at least 24 hours after getting off a plane before doing anything that involves critical listening.

You've heard it before, but believe me: Take care of your hearing so at least your ears aren't the biggest obstacle to monitoring accuracy. I often carry the cylindrical foam ear plugs you can buy at sporting good stores and wear them while walking city streets, at clubs, when hammering or using power tools, or anywhere my ears are going to get more abuse than someone talking at a conversational level.

Room Variables

The room in which you monitor also influences how you mix. Your room can even cause some frequencies to cancel out almost completely (Figure 16.2). As sound bounces around off walls, the reflections become part of the overall sound, creating cancellations and additions.

As the walls, floors, and ceilings all interact with speakers, it's important that any speakers be placed symmetrically within a room. Otherwise, if (for example) one speaker is 3 feet from a wall and another 10 feet from a wall, any reflections will be wildly different for the two speakers and affect the response.

Another example of how acoustics affects sound is when you place a speaker against a wall, which seems to increase bass. Here's why (Figure 16.3): Any sounds emanating from the rear of the speaker or leaking from the front (bass frequencies are very nondirectional) bounce off the wall. Because a bass note's wavelength is so long, the reflection will tend to reinforce the main wave. This is a greatly simplified explanation, but it gets the principle across.

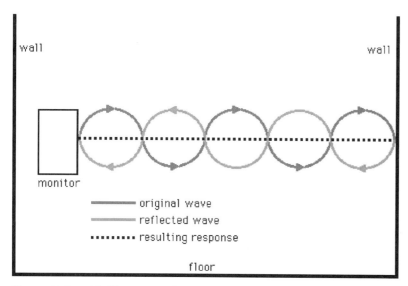

Figure 16.2 This illustration shows a *standing-wave* condition, where a wave reflects back from a wall out of phase, thus canceling the original waveform. At other frequencies, the reflection can just as easily reinforce the original waveform. These frequency response anomalies affect how you hear the music as you mix.

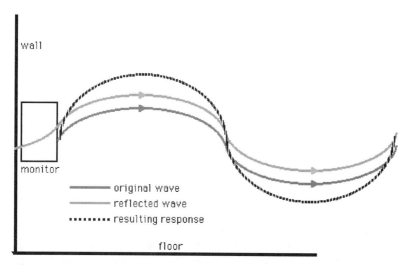

Figure 16.3 Placing a speaker with its back against the wall often gives an apparent increase in bass; placing it in a corner accentuates bass even more.

The subject of acoustically treating a room deserves a book in itself. If you have the money, hiring a professional consultant to "tune" your room with bass traps and similar mechanical devices could be the best investment you ever make in your music. But if you can't treat your room, fortunately you can get around many of the problems associated with poor room acoustics by using near-field monitors.

Near-Field Monitors

In smaller studios, near-field monitors have become the standard way to monitor. With this technique, small speakers sit around three to six feet from the mixer's ears, with the head and speakers forming a triangle.

Near-field monitors reduce (but do not eliminate) the impact of room acoustics on the overall sound, as the speakers' direct sound is far greater than the reflections coming off the room surfaces (see Figure 16.4). As a side benefit, because of their proximity to your ears, near-field monitors do not have to produce a lot of power.

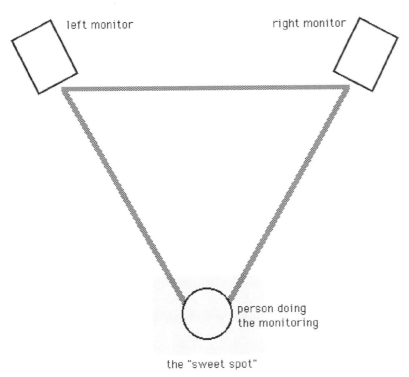

Figure 16.4 When using near-field monitors, the speakers should point toward the ears and be at ear level. If slightly above ear level, they should point downward toward the ears.

However, placement in the room is still an issue. If placed too close to the walls, there will be a bass buildup that will differ at different frequencies. High frequencies are not as affected because they are more directional. If the speakers are freestanding and placed away from the wall, back reflections from the speakers bouncing off the wall could cause cancellations and additions for the reasons mentioned earlier.

You're pretty safe if the speakers are more than six feet away from the wall in a fairly large listening space, but not everyone has that much room. One crude but effective solution is to mount the speakers a bit away from the wall on the same table holding the mixer and pad the walls behind the speakers with as much sound-deadening material as possible.

Learning Your Speaker and Room

Ultimately, because your own listening situation is imperfect, you need to "learn" your system's response. For example, suppose you mix something in your studio that sounds fine, but in a high-end studio with accurate monitoring, the sound is bass-heavy. That means your monitoring environment is shy on the bass, so you boosted the bass to compensate. (This is a common problem in project studios with small rooms.) In future mixes, you'll know to mix the bass lighter than normal in order to have it sound right.

Compare the midrange and treble as well. If vocals jump out of your system but lay back in others, then your speakers might be "midrange-y." Again, compensate by mixing midrange-heavy parts back a little bit.

Also, decide on a standardized listening level. I believe in monitoring at low levels when mixing, not just to save my ears, but also because if something sounds good at low volume, it will sound great when really cranked up. However, this also means that the bass and treble might be mixed up a bit more than they should be to compensate for the Fletcher-Munson curve. So, before signing off on a mix, check the sound at a variety of levels. If at loud levels it sounds just a hair too bright and boomy, and if at low levels it sounds just a bit bass- and treble-light, that's about right.

What about Mixing with Headphones?

A hundred dollars will buy you a great set of headphones but not much in the way of speakers. Although mixing exclusively on headphones is not a good idea, I recommend keeping a good set of headphones around as a reality check (not the open-air type that sits on your ear, but the kind that totally surrounds your ear). Sometimes you can get a more accurate bass reading using headphones than you can with near-fields. Careful, though: It's easy to blast your ears with headphones and not know it. Watch those volume levels!

As for hi-fi speakers, you can use them if you absolutely must, assuming they're relatively flat and unbiased. (Watch out: Some consumer-oriented speakers "hype" the high and low ends.)

Testing on Multiple Systems

I'm distrustful enough of speakers that before signing off on a mix, I'll run off a CD or two and listen through anything I can—car-stereo speakers, hi-fi bookshelf speakers, big-bucks studio speakers, boom boxes, headphones, and so on. This gives me an idea of how well the mix will translate over a variety of systems. If the mix works, great—mission accomplished. But if it sounds overly bright on, say, five out of eight systems, I'll pull back the brightness just a bit.

The more you monitor, the more educated your ears will become. Also, the more dependent they will become on the speakers you use. (Some producers carry their favorite monitor speakers to sessions so they can compare the studio's speakers to speakers they already know well.) But even if you can't afford the ultimate monitoring setup, with a bit of practice you can learn your system well enough to produce a good-sounding mix that translates well over a variety of systems—and that's much of what mixing is all about.

SONAR Home Studio's Console View

Although you can mix using the Track view, the Console view was optimized for mixing and is where you'll likely do most of your work.

The left side of the mixer shows the tracks in your project, while the right side shows the master output bus and any send return buses (see Figure 16.5). In the screenshot, you can see five tracks toward the left (the rightmost one is a MIDI track; all the others are audio tracks) and three buses toward the right (master and two send effect returns—reverb and tempo delay).

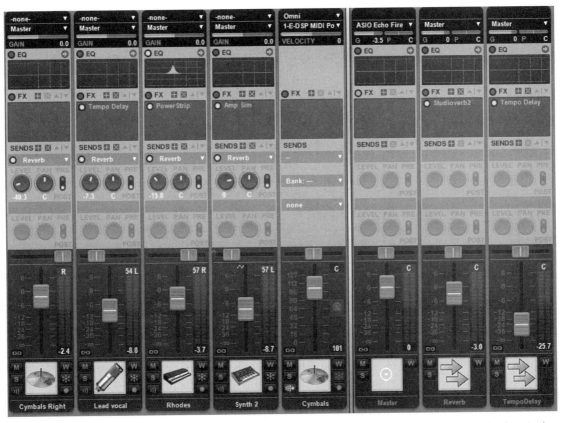

Figure 16.5 The Console view consolidates the most important mixing elements into a single window: tracks, send returns, levels, pan, input trim (gain), EQ, effects, and sends.

The Gain sliders at the top can trim channel levels independently of the faders toward the bottom. This is handy if, for example, a track was recorded at a really low level and you need to push the channel fader all the way up. By increasing the gain, you can keep the fader at a level that's more like the other channels.

Below that is the built-in EQ where you can change the tone of the channel (there's more on EQ in Chapter 18, "SONAR Home Studio's Plug-Ins"), and below that, the FX bins accommodate plug-ins designed to process the audio or MIDI tracks. Audio processing plug-ins generally don't require as much CPU power as software synths, but you can always make sure you're operating within your computer's limits by monitoring the CPU meter in the lower-right corner. For more information on the plug-ins included with SONAR Home Studio, please refer to Chapter 18.

Next, there are send control strips, and below that, pan and level sliders. At the very bottom, the track icons are surrounded by solo, mute, freeze, automation write, record enable, input echo, and other utility controls.

We'll discuss these elements of the Console view in the context of doing a mix.

The Mixing Process

Mixing is not only an art, it's the ultimate arbiter of how your music sounds. A good mix can bring out the best in your music, while a bad mix can obscure it.

An effective mix spotlights a composition's most important elements, adds a few surprises to excite the listener, and sounds good on any system—from a transistor radio to an audiophile's dream setup. Translating a collection of tracks into a cohesive song isn't easy; mixing requires the same level of creativity and experience as any part of the musical process.

Before You Mix

Preparation for the mix begins *the moment you start recording*, and part of that involves recording the cleanest possible signal. Eliminate as many active stages as possible between source and recorder; many times, devices set to bypass may not be adding any effect but are still in the signal path, which can add some slight noise or signal degradation. If possible, send sounds directly into your audio interface—bypass any mixer or preamp altogether.

Always record with the highest possible fidelity. Although you may not hear much of a difference when monitoring a single instrument, with multiple tracks the cumulative effect of stripping the signal path to its essentials can make a significant difference in the sound's clarity.

The Arrangement

Before you start turning knobs, scrutinize the arrangement. Solo projects are particularly prone to clutter because as you lay down the early tracks, there's a tendency to overplay to fill up all that empty space. As the arrangement progresses, there's not a lot of space for overdubs.

Here are a couple of suggestions when tracking that will make it much easier to create a good mix:

- Once the arrangement is fleshed out, go back and recut any overly busy tracks that you cut earlier. Try to play these tracks as sparsely as possible to leave room for the overdubs you've added.

- With vocal-based songs, experiment with building a song around the vocals instead of completing the rhythm section and then laying down the vocals. I often find it better to record simple "placemarkers" for the rhythm section and then immediately get to work cutting the best possible vocal. Then I go back and rerecord the rhythm section. When you recut the rhythm section for real, you'll be a lot more sensitive to the vocal nuances.

- Erase or mute clips or tracks that don't contribute anything to the arrangement. Usually less is more, because then each sound will have more impact.

Twelve Steps to a Great Mix

You build a mix over time by making a variety of adjustments. There are (at least!) 12 major steps involved in creating a mix, but what makes mixing so difficult is that these steps interact. Change a track's equalization (tone quality), and you also change the level because you're boosting or cutting some element of the sound. Alter a sound's stereo location, and you may need to shift the ambience or equalization. In fact, you can think of a mix as an "audio combination lock"—when all the elements hit the right combination, you end up with a good mix.

Let's look at these 12 steps, but remember, this is just one person's way of mixing—you might discover a totally different approach that works better for you.

Step 1: Mental Preparation and Organization

Mixing requires a tremendous amount of concentration and can be extremely tedious, so set up your workspace as efficiently as possible. Turn off your phone's ringer, minimize distractions, and take a break periodically (every hour or so is a good interval) to rest your ears and gain a fresher outlook on your return. Even a couple minutes of off time can restore your objectivity and, paradoxically, complete a mix much faster.

Step 2: Review the Tracks

Listen at low volume and familiarize yourself with the tracks. Make sure all tracks are named (loading an appropriate track icon can also help you parse track assignments more rapidly), note which tracks have active plug-ins that may need to be adjusted, and the like. Group sounds logically, such as having all the drum sounds on consecutive channels.

Step 3: Put on Headphones and Listen for Glitches

Fixing glitches is a left-brain activity, as opposed to the right-brain creativity involved in doing a mix. Switching back and forth between these two modes can hamper creativity, so do as much cleaning up as possible—erase glitches, bad notes, scratch tracks, and the like—before you get involved in the mix.

Use the Solo button to solo each track and listen to it from beginning to end. With MIDI tracks, check for duplicate notes that flam or create chorusing-type effects, and avoid overlapping notes on single-note lines (such as bass and horn parts).

You can also use SONAR Home Studio's Deglitch option (choose Process > Deglitch; see Figure 16.6) to clean up MIDI tracks by removing all notes with velocities below a certain level or durations shorter than a specified amount.

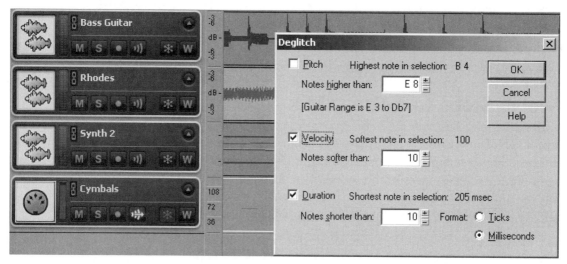

Figure 16.6 SONAR Home Studio's Deglitch process can help clean up MIDI tracks.

With audio tracks, listen for any spurious noises just before or after audio appears (for example, mic-handling sounds if the vocalist likes using a handheld mic, vibrating strings on an unplayed guitar, hum from a bass amp, kick drum pedal squeaks, and so on). It's amazing how many little noises you'll hear on vocal tracks, such as clicks from someone moving their tongue prior to singing. These low-level glitches may not seem that audible, but multiply them by a couple dozen tracks, and they can definitely muddy things up.

It's easy to edit audio with SONAR Home Studio; just zoom way in and adjust the height of the track for a comfortable view. To select a particular piece of audio, Alt-drag across it. (Enable Snap if you want the region to follow the rules set up for snapping; see Figure 16.7.) Once the audio is selected, you can cut or copy it or choose among the various audio processing options accessed by choosing Process > Audio (Gain, Normalize, Remove DC Offset, and Reverse).

Step 4: Render Soft Synths as Audio Tracks

If you're sequencing soft synth devices via MIDI, consider converting them to hard disk tracks or "freezing" them, as described in Chapter 14. This will free up DSP processing power for any effects you want to use during mixdown or perhaps will allow you to replace a not-so-great-sounding reverb with one that requires more CPU power.

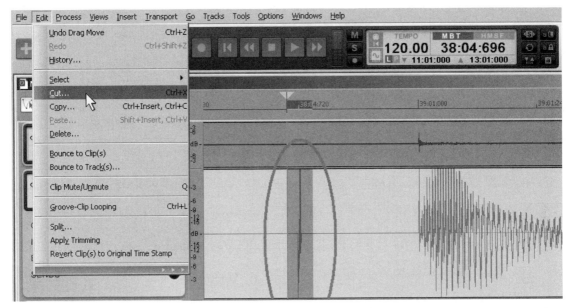

Figure 16.7   The click in the circled area has been selected by Alt-dragging across it. Selecting Cut from the Edit menu removes the click from the audio track.

Step 5: Set Up a Relative Level Balance among the Tracks

Now that our preparations are out of the way, it's time to get into mixing itself.

Do not add any processing for now (see Figure 16.8). Concentrate on the overall effect of hearing the tracks by themselves and work on the overall sound; don't get distracted by detail work. With a good mix, the tracks sound good by themselves—but they sound even better when interacting with the other tracks.

I always set levels in mono initially, because if the instruments sound distinct and separate in mono, they'll only open up more in stereo. Also, you may not notice parts fighting with each other if you start off in stereo.

Step 6: Adjust Equalization (EQ)

This can help dramatize differences between instruments and create a more balanced overall sound. Work on the most important song elements first (vocals, drums, and bass), and once these all "lock" together, deal with the more supportive parts. See Chapter 18 for more information about EQ.

Any Console view channel that passes audio (track, bus, master) has a fixed equalizer toward the top. To enable it, click on the button to the immediate left of where it says EQ (see Figure 16.9). To see the EQ settings (Properties), click on the arrow button. The EQ's display will show a thumbnail of the current EQ frequency response graph.

Figure 16.8   The Console view in the initial stages of a mix. There aren't any effects, including EQ, and no sends. The pan controls are centered, and the level faders are setting a relative balance.

If you right-click on the EQ's display, a context menu appears. You can choose whether the EQ is before or after any effects in the effects bins (EQ Pre Fx and EQ Post FX, respectively), show the Properties page, and enable/disable EQ. For the last two, I find it a lot easier just to use the two dedicated buttons that do the same thing.

For mixing, EQ is extremely important because there's only so much space in the audio spectrum, so each sound has to avoid fighting with other parts. But note that processing added to one track may affect other tracks; for example, if you boost a guitar part's midrange, it may

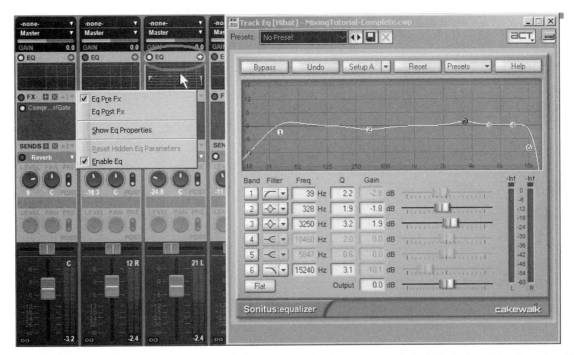

Figure 16.9 The EQ Enable button and Show Properties button are circled. Note how the thumbnail graph matches the curve in the EQ. Also, right-clicking on the EQ's thumbnail brings up a context menu with additional EQ-related options.

interfere with vocals, piano, or other midrange instruments. If you add more treble to a bass part so that it cuts better on little speakers, make sure it doesn't start fighting with the low end of a rhythm guitar part. Sometimes boosting a frequency for one instrument implies cutting the same region in another instrument to make room.

One common mistake I hear with tapes done by singer/songwriters is that they (naturally) feature themselves in the mix and worry about "details" such as the drums later. However, because drums cover so much of the audio spectrum (from the low-frequency thud of the kick to the high-frequency sheen of the cymbals), and because drums tend to be so upfront in today's mixes, it's sometimes best to mix the drums first and then find holes in which you can place the other instruments. For example, if the kick drum is very prominent, it may not leave enough room for the bass. So, boost the bass around 800 to 1,000 Hz to bring up some of the pick noise and brightness. This is mostly out of the range of the kick drum, so the two won't interfere as much.

Try to think of the song as a spectrum; decide where you want the various parts to sit and their prominence.

Step 7: Add Any Essential Signal Processing

By "essential," I mean processing that's an integral part of the sound (such as echo that falls on the beat and therefore changes the rhythmic characteristics of a part, distortion that alters the timbre in a radical way, vocoding, and so on). Because this particular type of sound will presumably be a part of the mix unless you change your mind later, you want to take it into account when mixing the other instruments.

The Console view (see Figure 16.10) has an effects bin where you can insert effects that mirror the one in the Track view.

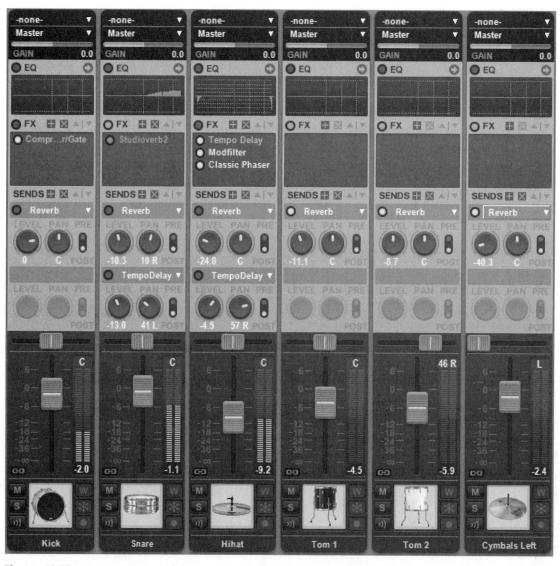

Figure 16.10 You can insert, delete, and reorder effects within the FX bin. To reorder, just drag the effect to the desired position.

There's a small toolbar above the bin, with the following controls from left to right:

- **FX enable.** If the FX button is orange/red, the effects bin is off. Otherwise, it's on.

- **+ symbol.** Click on this to call up a menu and insert an effect.

- **X symbol.** Deletes the selected effect. (Selected effects have green letters.)

- **Up/down arrow buttons.** If you have more effects inserted than the bin can display, use the arrows to scroll through the list.

Step 8: Create a Stereo Soundstage

Next, use the pan controls to place your instruments within the stereo field. Your approach might be traditional (in other words, the goal is to re-create the feel of a live performance) or something that can exist only in the virtual world. Also, remember that you can automate panning moves in SONAR Home Studio. An instrument needn't have a static location throughout a song; for example, you might want to spread background vocal parts wider in some portions of the song and narrower in others.

Because bass frequencies are less directional than highs, most engineers place the kick drum and bass toward the center (see Figure 16.11). Also consider timbral balance; for example, if you've

Figure 16.11 The pan controls are now setting a soundstage. The kick and snare are panned to the middle, while the other drums are placed elsewhere in the stereo field. Note the panning indicator toward the pan control's lower right.

panned the hi-hat (which has a lot of high frequencies) to the left, and there's another instrument with a lot of highs (tambourine, shaker, and so on), pan it somewhat to the right to provide balance. The same technique applies to instruments with lots of midrange.

Stereo placement can significantly alter how we perceive a sound. Consider a doubled vocal line, where a singer sings a part and then doubles it as closely as possible. Try putting both voices in opposite channels and then put both voices together in the center. The center position gives a somewhat smoother sound, which is good for weaker vocalists. The opposite-channel vocals give a more defined, sharp sound that can really help accent a good singer.

Step 9: Make Any Final Changes to the Arrangement

I'll say it again: Less is more, so minimize the number of competing parts to avoid clutter and keep the listener focused on the tune. Get rid of anything that doesn't serve the song. Conversely, if you find that a song needs some extra element, this is your final opportunity to add an overdub or two.

You can also use mixing creatively by selectively dropping out and adding specific tracks. This type of mixing is the foundation for a lot of dance music, where you have looped tracks that play continuously, and the mixer sculpts the arrangement by muting parts and doing radical level changes. You can do instant mutes and solos by applying SONAR Home Studio's automation capabilities to these buttons rather than using the faders. See Chapter 19, "Automation in SONAR Home Studio," for more info on automation; note that a Write Automation button is located conveniently at the bottom of each channel strip in the Console.

Step 10: The Audio Architect

Start building the acoustic space in which your song lives by adding reverberation and delay to give the normally flat soundstage some acoustic depth. This is sort of the equivalent of adding spices during the cooking process; it provides the final touch that makes the song as tasty as possible.

For example, you may want an overall reverb to create a particular type of space (club, concert hall, auditorium, and so on), but you may also want to use a tempo delay to add a rhythmic pulsing to some selected channels (see Figure 16.12).

The Console view's sends section has a small toolbar above the sends, with the following controls from left to right:

- **+ symbol.** Click on this to insert a send.

- **X symbol.** Click on this to delete the lowest send in the chain (closest to the fader). Note that you can't undo this operation, so you may prefer to click on the bus's destination field and select None.

- **Up/down arrow buttons.** If you have more sends inserted than the sends section can display, use the arrows to scroll through the list.

Figure 16.12 Using send buses allows you to send a portion of a channel's signal to a global effect, such as reverb. In this example, there's no send from the kick going to the reverb, a fair amount on the snare, and a lesser amount on the toms and cymbals. Also, note the hi-hat is sending some signal to the tempo delay processor.

Concerning reverb—probably the most common and popular send effect—in the early days of recording, the general procedure was to add just enough reverb to be noticeable and simulate the effect of playing in an acoustical environment. Nowadays, reverb devices have become so sophisticated that they can create effects in their own right that become as much a part of a tune as any instrumental line. However, don't drown a part in reverb. If a part is of questionable enough quality that it needs a lot of reverb, redo the part. A bad part is a bad part, no matter how much reverb you put on it.

Step 11: Tweak, Tweak, and Retweak

Now that the mix is on its way, it's time for fine tuning. If you're into automation, start programming your mixing moves. Remember that all of the aforementioned steps interact, so go back and forth between EQ, levels, stereo placement, and effects until you get the sound you want. Listen as critically as possible; if you don't fix something that bothers you, it will forever bother you every time you hear the mix.

Step 12: Know When It's Time to Quit!

With a home studio, you have the luxury of leaving a mix and coming back to it the next day when you're fresh and after you've had a chance to listen over several different systems and decide what tweaks you want to make. This is one reason why automation is so wonderful—if everything was perfect about a mix except one little thing that bothers you, you can edit the automation to fix the one problem.

I can't emphasize enough that you should mix until you're satisfied. There's nothing worse than hearing one of your tunes six months later and kicking yourself because of some flaw you didn't take the time to correct or didn't notice because you were in too much of a hurry to complete the mix.

However, you must be equally careful not to beat a mix to death. A mix is a performance, and if you overdo it, you'll lose the spontaneity that can add excitement. A mix that isn't perfect but conveys passion will be more fun to listen to than one that's perfect to the point of sterility. As insurance, don't always rerecord over your mixes—when you listen back to them the next day, you might find that an earlier mix was the "keeper."

In fact, you may not even be able to tell too much difference among all the mixes. A record producer once told me about mixing literally dozens of takes of the same song, because he kept hearing small changes that seemed really important at the time. A couple of weeks later he went over the mixes and couldn't tell any difference between most of the versions. Be careful not to waste time making changes that no one, not even you, will care about a couple days later.

17 Using Signal Processors and Busses

Signal processors, also called *effects*, are a key element of good mixes. They allow tweaking sounds so that they blend in better, stand out more, add interest to parts that could use a little spice, or do whatever is needed to create the ultimate mix. SONAR Home Studio uses *plug-ins*—virtual, software-based signal processors—for adding most effects. (Chapter 18, "SONAR Home Studio's Plug-Ins," contains a description of the plug-ins provided with SONAR Home Studio.)

Plug-In Basics

Plug-ins are accessory programs that "plug in" to the host. For example, a signal processing plug-in can insert into a track's FX bin, just like how you'd patch a hardware signal processor into a hardware mixing console's patch points.

There are two main types of plug-in technology: host-based (also called *native*) and hardware-based. Hardware-based plug-ins run only with certain specialized hardware computer cards or outboard FireWire boxes designed for digital signal processing, such as the UAD2 series from Universal Audio, TC Electronic's PowerCore system, and SSL's Duende Mini. Host-based plug-ins, as provided with SONAR Home Studio, use the computer's microprocessor to do any needed digital signal processing and therefore require no specialized hardware.

Native plug-ins require a certain amount of CPU power, so the more plug-ins you run (especially virtual instruments, which are also considered plug-ins), the harder the CPU has to work. As a result, there are limits to how many plug-ins you can use with a software program. If you want to run more plug-ins, the two main solutions are to use a faster CPU or to increase the system latency (the time required for the system to process signals). Increasing latency means the CPU doesn't have to work as hard, but it increases the response time when moving faders, playing soft synths, and so on.

SONAR Home Studio has a CPU meter in the lower-right corner (as well as a disk activity meter) that shows how much power is being used (see Figure 17.1).

Compare the meter's readings before and after loading a plug-in to see how much power the plug-in requires. The main advantage of hardware-based plug-ins is that they place very little load on the CPU; the hardware board does the heavy lifting.

Figure 17.1 The CPU meter indicates how much power SONAR Home Studio is drawing from the computer's CPU. Playing back hard disk audio tracks doesn't tax the CPU much; most of the power will be drawn by plug-ins—primarily virtual instruments but also signal processors.

As to plug-in formats, SONAR Home Studio accepts plug-ins that meet Steinberg's VST or Microsoft's DirectX specification. (VST stands for *Virtual Studio Technology*, a term coined by Steinberg when they first "virtualized" signal processors, mixers, and other elements into their sequencing software. In other words, these became native parts of the computer environment rather than outboard hardware devices.) Fortunately, these plug-in formats have become standards that are supported by hundreds of manufacturers. With extremely rare exceptions, any VST or DirectX plug-in made by any company can work with SONAR Home Studio. If a plug-in doesn't work, it's usually because the code doesn't follow the spec exactly.

We'll look at the effects in SONAR Home Studio in Chapter 18, but first, let's consider how you add effects to a project.

The Three Places to Insert Effects

Unlike a traditional mixer (or many software programs) that has a fixed way to insert effects, SONAR Home Studio is much more flexible. It allows using effects in three basic ways: as insert effects, bus (send) effects, and master effects. Let's get into the details for each option.

Track (Channel) Insert Effects

Insert effects are named after the insert jacks found in hardware mixers, which are found within individual mixer channels. In hardware mixers, channel inserts are located between the input preamp and the fader/pan pot circuitry. This allows for proper gain staging, as few effects are designed for mic-level signals; the preamp can bring the incoming signal up to a consistent level for feeding the effect. Also, if the effect generates any noise, pulling down the fader reduces both the signal and any generated noise.

SONAR Home Studio follows the same concept. Insert effects appear within a specific track and affect only the track into which they are inserted. Popular insert effects include dynamics control, distortion, delay, chorusing, and flanging, although almost any effect can be used as an insert effect.

Technically speaking, EQ is also an insert effect. However, because of EQ's importance, SONAR Home Studio "hardwires" EQ into each channel so it needn't be inserted—just like almost all hardware mixers. EQ can also be switched pre- or post-FX bin, so you can EQ the signal going into an effect or coming out of it.

Using Insert Effects

You can insert effects in the Console view or Track view. Both views have an effects bin (also called an *FX bin* or insert slot) into which you can insert multiple effects. However, the Track view only shows three of these effects, while the Console view shows four; if there are more FX than you can see in the bin at one time, up/down arrow buttons let you scroll through the inserted effects (see Figure 17.2).

Figure 17.2 The same track is shown in Track view and Console view. The up/down arrows for scrolling through effects in the FX bin are circled for clarity.

Here's how to manage effects.

- To work with effects in Track view, show the track controls and then unfold the Effects section. Click on Add Effect (in the Console view, click on the + sign in the FX bin header), and a menu will appear with all SONAR Home Studio–compatible effects (see Figure 17.3). Navigate to the desired effect, click on it, and then release the mouse button.

- To bypass all effects in the Track view FX bin, click on the Bypass All button. The FX bin will darken to indicate that all effects are bypassed. In Console view, if the light to the left of the FX label is orange, the bin is bypassed. Click to turn off the orange light and enable the effects.

Figure 17.3 The Studioverb2 has already been inserted in the FX bin; now the HF Exciter effect is being added. The button for adding effects is circled.

- To bypass individual effects, click on the small button to the left of the effect's name. When it's gray, the effect is bypassed; green means it's active.

- To delete an effect, click on the effect you want to delete and then click on the Track view Delete Effect button (or the X button in the Console view FX bin header).

- To change the order of effects in the FX bin, click and drag the effect to the desired position.

You can also do effects management by right-clicking in the FX bin. The context menu that appears lets you delete the currently selected effect, bypass the FX bin, choose an audio effect (similarly to the Add Effect process described above), or write-enable automation parameters for the currently selected effect.

Send Effects

Also called *bus effects* or *aux effects*, these effects are different from insert effects because they affect multiple tracks simultaneously. To understand how to use these effects, we need to discuss the concept of a bus.

Bus Basics

Let's start with the basics: A bus is basically a mini-mixer that combines a number of signals and sends them somewhere. For example, the master bus is where all your track outputs terminate. This master bus then feeds a stereo hardware output so you can monitor the results over a speaker system or headphones.

Another common bus type is called a *subgroup bus*. As an example of how this works, consider a drum set that you've miked with five mics (kick, snare, overhead, and two room mics), each of which feeds its own track. Suppose you get a perfect blend of all these signals but then decide you want the drums to be just a teeny bit louder. You now have to adjust each fader, and there's no guarantee you'll get the balance exactly right.

If you instead feed each track's output into a subgroup bus that mixes together all the tracks, then to change the level of the entire kit all you need to do is raise or lower the bus level control. With most busses, you can feed a signal into the bus either before or after the track's main fader (called pre- or post-fader, respectively), and there will be a separate send level control that's independent of the track's main fader and sets the level going to the subgroup mixer. If the drum signals are sent to the subgroup bus pre-fader, then you can turn down the main track faders so they don't influence the mix at all and create the proper balance with the send level controls.

And finally, there's the effects bus. A send level control picks off signals from each track and then sends them to the effects bus. Effects busses are typically stereo, so the effects sends section also includes a pan control so you can "weight" the effect sound toward one channel or the other.

Like any track, a bus has an FX bin. Suppose you insert a reverb in the bus FX bin. If you send a lot of signal into the bus from the vocal track and a little from the drums, the vocal will have heavy reverb, and the drums will have a little reverb. The reverb output then returns to the mixer, using (not surprisingly) an effects return that goes into the master bus. In this case, you'd probably use the post-fader send so that as you bring down the track level, the level to the bus goes down with it.

Another important point is that send bus effects are generally set for processed (wet) sound only. This is because the channel fader provides the unprocessed signal to the master bus, while the send bus effect contributes only the effect sound, adding it to the unprocessed signal. In fact, it's generally recommended that you not include any straight sound in an aux bus effect. For example, a reverb effect would be set to reverb sound only, and the bus master level for the reverb would adjust the blend of the reverb to the "dry" mix.

Because effects can work as track inserts or in a send bus, here is why you'd choose one option over the other. Every plug-in requires some amount of computing power, so the fewer plug-ins you use, the more processing "headroom" is available. Therefore, if you want to process several channels with the same effect, you're better off loading a single effect in an aux bus instead of inserting the same effect multiple times as track insert effects. For instance, when adding reverb, it makes more sense to use it as a send bus effect, synthesize the desired acoustic space, and mix in varying amounts of signal from the send bus, as determined by each channel's send level control.

One final consideration involving sends relates to trimming the overall level of all sends simultaneously. For example, suppose you start turning up more and more sends, to the point where they overload the input of the effect they're feeding. The solution is simple: Reduce the bus return channel's input Gain control (which affects the incoming signal; Volume affects the bus return channel output level), as shown in Figure 17.4.

Another example of why you'd want to use the bus input control would be if you decide that the overall reverb amount needs to be louder or softer, but you don't want to readjust every send control because the balance of the sends is already perfect. Simply use the bus input to change the overall send signal amount.

However, this is just the short-form version of trimming bus levels; see the section "Gain-Staging with Busses" for more details.

Creating a Bus

With hardware mixers, there are a limited number of busses, and they typically have specific uses. However, SONAR Home Studio treats busses as "objects" that have no dedicated purpose. Any bus you create can be an aux bus for effects, a master output bus, a bus for sending a separate mix to headphones, or whatever.

In the Console view, two busses are already "sketched in" for the audio channels, but they're grayed out until you actually assign a track to a bus. You can assign and add busses in either the Track view or the Console view. SONAR Home Studio's default project already includes a subgroup bus and effects bus, so for simple projects, that might be all you need. But remember, these are only names; you can use the subgroup bus as an effect bus if you want.

Creating a bus is very similar in the Console and Track views. The main difference is that in Track view, you need to first show the track controls and then unfold the Sends section. From here on, the procedure is pretty much the same.

In the Sends section, click on the + symbol to add a send. A menu will appear with all existing sends, as well as the option to add a new stereo bus or call up the Insert Send Assistant (see Figure 17.5).

Let's assume you just want to use the existing effect send, so there's no need to create a new bus. In the Console view, you can scroll over toward the right (if needed), to the section with busses. Figure 17.6 shows a real-world example of adding reverb to a vocal track.

Note that sends must be enabled; to do this in Track view, click on the small rectangle to the left of the send bus name. (It's green when enabled, gray when disabled.) In Console view, it's the

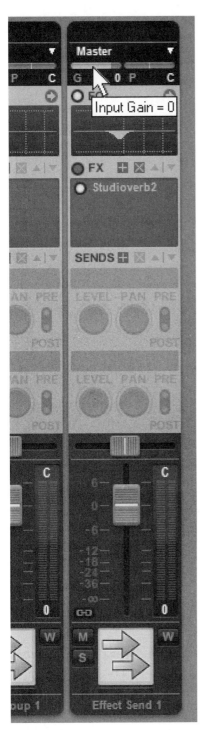

Figure 17.4 Just like any other input channel, the bus return channel has an input Gain control for trimming the incoming signal.

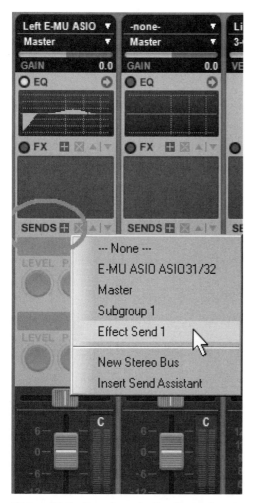

Figure 17.5 Four bus destinations already exist: The E-MU audio interface hardware outputs, SONAR Home Studio's Master bus, Subgroup bus, and Effect Send bus (currently being selected). Also note toward the bottom that you can select a new stereo bus or invoke the Insert Send Assistant.

small LED to the left of the Effect Send label. (Again, green is enabled, gray is disabled.) Disable unused sends to save CPU loading, or just delete the send altogether.

The Send Assistant

There's a certain amount of housekeeping involved in creating a new bus; you need to name it, insert the desired effect, decide whether the send should be pre- or post-fader, and the like. Invoking the Send Assistant simplifies this process by presenting a single window where you can define the bus characteristics (see Figure 17.7).

If you use the Send Assistant to create a new stereo bus, you have the option to choose a post- or pre-fader send, name the bus, choose an effect for the bus FX bin, and choose a bus output.

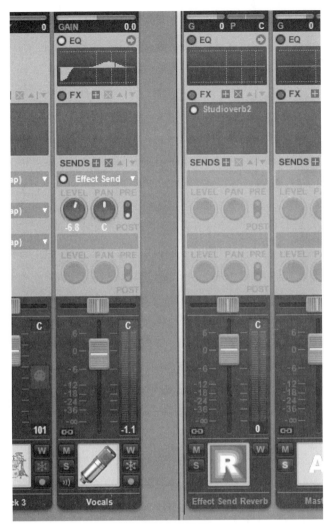

Figure 17.6 The vocals track is sending some signal, via the Sends section, to the effect send bus. The send signal is being picked off post-fader and panned to center. The Effect Send Reverb bus has the Studioverb2 inserted as the bus effect, and the reverberated signal is being mixed into the master bus.

Busses and Busses and Busses...

Note that you can create busses that feed into busses, which can in turn feed other busses. Although you'll seldom need to reach this level of complexity, here's one example of where you might need a bus feeding a bus.

Suppose you've recorded multiple drum tracks, as described earlier, and assigned them to a subgroup for easy level changes. You've also recorded backup singers into three different mics and sent those tracks to their own subgroup.

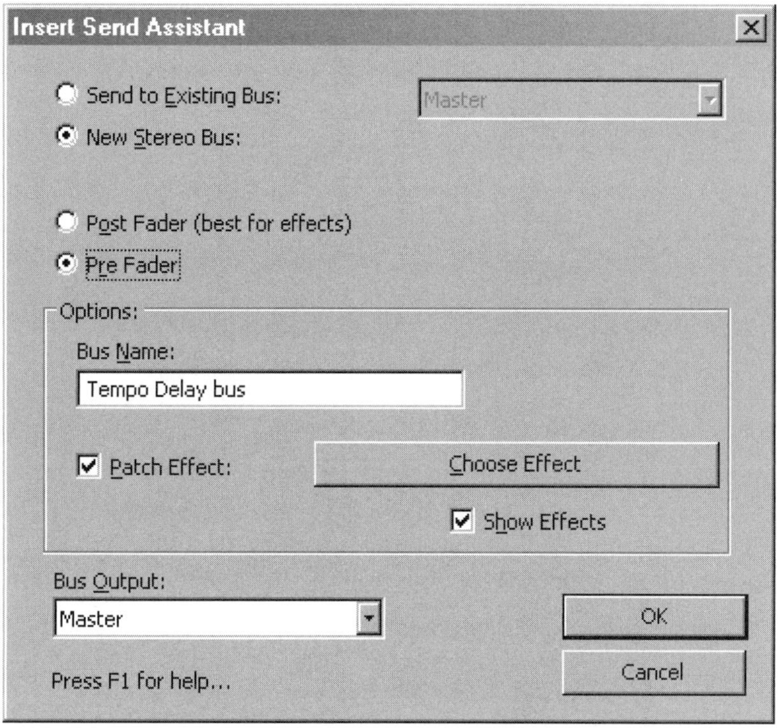

Figure 17.7   The Send Assistant simplifies the process of creating a new send bus.

Now you want to add a reverb send effect to the drums and vocals. In this case, the subgroup busses would go to a reverb bus, so we have busses feeding another bus.

Multiple busses also provide far more flexibility for effects. For example, suppose you want several instruments to go through tempo-synched delay, but you also want them to go through a reverb. Furthermore, you want other tracks to go through the reverb but not the delay. You can create a delay bus and assign that to a separate reverb bus; tracks that need reverb and no delay can have sends that go directly to the reverb bus.

Gain-Staging with Busses

When working with effects placed in aux busses, there are four places to alter levels:

- The channel's send control that feeds the bus

- The channel's main fader, if the send control is set to post-fader

- The bus input Gain control

- The bus output Volume control

Furthermore, a signal processor inserted in the bus may have input and/or output level controls, and the processor's sound may depend on the incoming level. (For example, with distortion, more input signal generally increases the amount of distortion.) If these controls aren't set correctly, overly hot levels may cause distortion, while too low a level can degrade the sound. Here's the general procedure for proper level-setting:

1. If the effect has input or output level controls, set them to unity gain. (In other words, the signal is neither amplified nor attenuated.)

2. Set the aux bus gain and output level controls to unity gain.

3. Adjust the individual send controls for the desired amount of effect. The higher you turn the individual send controls, the more that channel will contribute to the processed sound.

4. As the sends from the individual channels start to add up, they may overload the effect's input. Leave the effect input at unity gain and use the bus Gain control to reduce the level going to the effect.

5. If the signal going to the effect is too low, use the bus Gain control to bring it up. If there still isn't enough level to drive the effect, increase the processor's input control (if available) as needed.

Fine Points about Busses

When you can have busses feeding busses that feed busses, the bus solo function needs to set some rules. When you solo a bus, all busses are muted except for any busses into which the soloed bus feeds, as well as any busses that feed into the soloed bus. Were these buses muted, there would be no point in soloing a bus, as you wouldn't hear anything. Also, MIDI tracks assigned to external MIDI ports won't be muted, as the external MIDI device's audio output might return to SONAR via an audio track input.

The bus fader is always post-effect. However, you might want an effect that continues even after the master level fader has been turned down (for example, a long, repeating echo or a long reverb "tail" that fades into silence). In that case, use the bus Gain control to set level and leave the master fader set to 0.

Master Effects

This is a variation on the insert effect for individual tracks, but it involves inserting effects into the master output. These alter the entire mixed signal, not just individual tracks; for example, you might use EQ to brighten up the entire mix a bit or compression to make the mix seem a little louder overall. Master effects are handled the same way as track insert effects.

You may have heard of a process called *mastering*, where a mastering engineer adds processing to a finished stereo mix in order to sweeten the sound—think of it as a final "buffing." Although adding master effects is handy if you want to do quick mastering while mixing, if you intend to take your mix to a mastering engineer, do not insert any master effects when you export the mix as a file. A good mastering engineer will likely want to use a familiar set of high-quality mastering tools or plug-ins.

Insert Effects Tips

Now that we have an overview of the various ways effects can be added to SONAR Home Studio, let's dig into some applications and tips.

Placing Insert Effects in the Right Order

In the FX bins, plug-ins connect in series, where the output of one effect feeds the input of the next effect. It's important to place your effects in the proper order to obtain specific types of effects. Here are some observations about optimizing effects placement.

EQ Before or After Compression. There is no universal answer for this situation, because compression can serve different purposes. Fortunately, SONAR Home Studio's six-band track EQ can go before or after the effects bin (see Figure 17.8), so you're not locked into any one option.

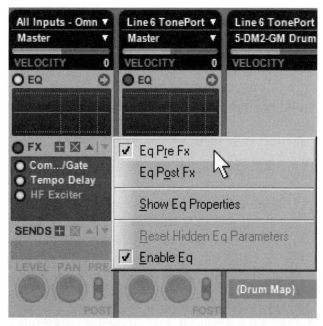

Figure 17.8 Right-click on the EQ's response graph; you can then select whether the EQ is pre-FX or post-FX. You can also enable/disable EQ from here, as well as open the Properties page that shows all EQ settings.

Consider this scenario: You've recorded a fantastic synth bass line with a highly resonant filter sweep. On some notes, the level goes way too high when a note's frequency coincides with the filter frequency. Otherwise, the signal is well behaved. But, you also want to boost the lower midrange a bit to give a beefier sound. In this case, try putting the compressor first to trap those rogue transients and then apply EQ to the more dynamically consistent sound. Because the EQ change is minor, it probably won't change the signal's overall amplitude too much.

Now suppose you don't have any problems with overly resonant filters, but you do need a massive lower midrange boost. This much boost could greatly increase the amplitude at some frequencies, so putting compression after the EQ will help even these out a bit.

But there's a complication. Because significant boosts in a certain frequency range increase level in that range, the compressor will scale those levels back down a bit. So, this reduces the effect of what the EQ is trying to do—it tries to boost, but the compressor won't let it go beyond a certain point. However, signals below the threshold do remain boosted, and this just might give the sound you want.

Another reason to place EQ before compression is to make the compression more frequency-sensitive. Suppose you have a great guitar part, and you want to emphasize the melody. By boosting EQ slightly for the range to be emphasized and then compressing, the boosted frequencies will go into compression sooner than the other frequency ranges.

Or, suppose you have a buzzy digital synth. Cut the highs a bit prior to compression, and the compressor will bring up everything else more readily than the highs. This type of technique isn't quite the same as multi-band compression, but it gives some of the same results, as there's more "punch" to the boosted frequencies.

Boost 11 Loudness Maximizer/Booster. Boost 11 (included only in the XL versions of SONAR Home Studio 7) is a specialized form of compressor that establishes a strict dynamic range ceiling. On individual instruments, Boost 11 works well to bring out a solo. Select the region containing the solo and then apply a couple dB of maximization. (Don't add too much.) This will lift it out of the mix compared to other sections of the part. For individual instruments, maximization generally goes last in the signal chain. One exception is that I prefer putting maximization before echo or reverb; processing the tails of these effects often sounds unnatural.

Also, Boost 11 can help out with the compressor/EQ order dilemma. If you place a compressor first to trap excessively high peaks and then add EQ to provide the desired timbre, you can end the signal chain with Boost 11 to give a hot sound.

Distortion. SONAR Home Studio offers three distortion plug-ins: Amp Sim, FX2 Tape Sim, and the Studio Devil VGA+ guitar amp simulator (included only in the XL versions of SONAR Home Studio 7).

I invariably place distortion before anything else, with one exception described later. Although you might think distortion should be, well, distorted, any guitarist will tell you there's clean, pleasing distortion and ugly, dirty distortion. (Which one they prefer is another issue entirely!)

If the distortion is followed by a number of clean effects, they can make the distortion sound smoother as well. The classic example is reverb. Add some really gorgeous room ambience to a distorted signal, and it takes out some of the edge, creating a sweeter distortion sound. But placing distortion after reverb will distort all the reverb tails, which sounds unrealistic as well as dirty.

The same is true for discrete echoes (delay): You want to delay a distorted sound, not distort a delayed sound, particularly if you have a fair amount of feedback to add multiple echoes. If the echo is after the distortion, then the echoes will remain clean and distinct.

The one possible exception of where to put distortion involves EQ. Most of the time, you want EQ after distortion so it can alter the distorted sound's timbre. But just as you can use EQ before compression to give a more frequency-sensitive effect, EQ before distortion allows certain frequency ranges to distort more readily than other ranges. For example, you might boost a synth's midrange to distort sooner than the bass, so that the melody gets chunky but the bass doesn't distort as much. This is an ideal situation for placing EQ before distortion. I often add EQ both before and after distortion—the first to alter what gets distorted, and the second to tweak the distorted sound itself.

Flangers and Phasers. The situation here is complicated because proper placement depends on the effects settings you chose, so you're better off experimenting and choosing whatever sounds best. Following are some general tips:

- Placing these effects in front of distortion may be ineffective, because heavy distortion can pretty much cancel out the effect. Or you might like the way the sounds cut through the distortion.

- Flangers can generate significant frequency response peaks and deep valleys. Therefore, you may want to follow the flanger with Boost 11 to restrict the dynamic range somewhat. Caution, though: With too much limiting, the flanging sound will be less intense.

- EQ placement requires experimentation. I'd usually put it before the flanger, because you can then optimize the sound to work well with the flanging effect.

Generally, flangers, phasers, delays, reverb, and other time-based effects go toward the end of the chain, just prior to any loudness maximization. (Except, as noted earlier, with individual tracks you might want reverb after the maximization.)

Creating Parallel Plug-Ins. In the FX bins, plug-ins connect in series, where the output of one effect feeds the input of the next effect. However, some really great effects can occur by placing effects in parallel. In this case, a signal splits through two effects, and their outputs are mixed together.

There are two ways to create parallel effects in SONAR Home Studio. You can use SONAR's aux send busses (see the section on sends and busses) to feed a signal into two effects, or simply clone a track and use different plug-ins on different tracks to create parallel effects. Because these cloned tracks can also have series connections of plug-ins, it's possible to do parallel chains of series effects to create what's called a *series-parallel effects chain*.

18 SONAR Home Studio's Plug-Ins

ONAR Home Studio includes several plug-ins that cover a wide variety of signal process-ing needs. Of course, one of the beauties of plug-ins is that you're not limited to what comes with the program—SONAR Home Studio can run literally thousands of plug-ins from hundreds of manufacturers. But given that third-party plug-ins can be expensive (although many free and shareware ones exist as well), it's convenient to have a wide variety of options bundled with the program.

The Common Plug-In "Header"

Most plug-ins included with SONAR Home Studio have a common header with plug-in-oriented functions.

Selecting Presets

Going from left to right across the header, you'll first see a Presets selector (see Figure 18.1). Most plug-ins include presets for common applications.

Figure 18.1 If a plug-in has presets available, you can choose one from the Presets drop-down menu.

Click on the down arrow in the Presets field, and you'll see a drop-down menu listing the presets, if any are available. Click on the one you want, and its settings will load into the effect.

The left/right arrows to the right of the Presets field select the previous and next preset in the list, respectively. This is handy for when you want to try out presets in rapid-fire succession.

Save Presets

You can also create your own presets; saving them adds them to the list. To save:

1. Double-click in the Presets name field.

2. Type in the desired preset name.

3. Click on the Save (floppy disk) button (see Figure 18.2).

Figure 18.2   After typing a name into the Presets name field, click on the Save button to add the new preset to the list.

The preset will appear in the list immediately after the preset you originally called up for the plug-in.

Delete Presets

To delete a preset, select it in the Presets name field. Then click on the X (Delete) button.

Other Header Buttons

The three buttons toward the right of the preset relate to control and automation.

ACT. Click on this to learn ACT settings for an external controller. For details on using ACT, see Chapter 21, "ACT: The Key to Hands-On Control."

W. Click to enable writing automation. As you move plug-in controls, they will write automation control signals to the track. On playback, the controls you moved will play back the automation. For more information on automation, see Chapter 19, "Automation in SONAR Home Studio." Note that this button isn't available for the older CFX effects.

Give All Keystrokes to Plug-In. A plug-in may have keyboard shortcuts that conflict with the keyboard shortcuts dedicated to SONAR Home Studio. Enabling this button directs the QWERTY keyboard exclusively to the plug-in.

Also, note that with many effects, double-clicking on a control returns it to its default value.

Equalizer Plug-Ins

SONAR Home Studio includes two equalizers: the Para-Q and Sonitus fx:Equalizer (which is also the equalizer built into each console audio channel). Equalization is such an important part of the mixing (and recording) process that we'll cover these in detail, along with information on applications. We'll start with the Sonitus fx:Equalizer.

Sonitus fx:Equalizer

In Console view, you can reveal the EQ's parameters by double-clicking on the response curve graph to bring up the full plug-in view. As usual, if the EQ is inserted in a bus FX bin or the FX bin in the Track view, then double-clicking on the FX bin field will also bring up the full view (see Figure 18.3).

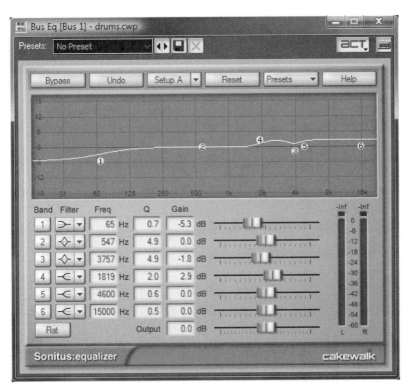

Figure 18.3 The Sonitus fx:Equalizer in SONAR Home Studio offers a sophisticated complement of controls.

A parametric equalizer is an exceptionally versatile way to adjust frequency response, as it can boost (make more prominent) or cut (make less prominent) specific parts of the frequency spectrum. The fx:Equalizer has six independent parametric stages, so you can apply equalization to six different parts of the frequency spectrum for each audio track. You'll find three main parameters in one stage of parametric equalization.

Frequency. This control determines where the boosting or cutting takes place. For example, if the high frequencies need boosting, you would dial in a high frequency. With the fx:Equalizer, this is a field where you can type in the desired frequency in hertz. Or, on the graphic view of the frequency response curve, you can simply drag the "button" associated with one of the six stages to the desired frequency (as described in more detail later).

Gain (also called Boost/Cut). Use a stage's associated slider to adjust boost or cut. Boosting increases the level in the chosen frequency range, while cutting decreases the level; the Gain field to the left of the slider displays the amount of boost or cut, with negative values indicating a cut. You can also enter a value here.

Gain is specified in decibels (dB). A change of 6 dB doubles the level (–6 dB halves it), which is a considerable amount. Changes of no more than 1 or 2 dB are common when mixing and mastering. Even changes of a few tenths of a dB can make an audible difference.

Q (also called Resonance or Bandwidth). This sets the range of frequencies affected by the boost or cut, from broad (smaller numbers) to narrow (higher numbers). Broader settings are gentler and are used for general tone shaping. Narrow settings generally help solve specific response problems. For example, suppose there is some 60-Hz hum on a recording. Setting a very narrow cut at 60 Hz will reduce the hum.

Parametric EQ Responses

Each stage also offers several different ways to affect the frequency response. You select the type of filter response by clicking on the down arrow under Filter and selecting the type (see Figure 18.4).

The most common parametric EQ response is called *Peak/Dip* or *Bandpass*, and it boosts or cuts a band of frequencies. However, there are other possible response options, such as the Shelving Response (see Figure 18.5).

A shelving response starts boosting or cutting at the selected frequency, but this boost or cut extends outward toward the extremes of the audio spectrum. Past a certain point, the response hits a "shelf" equal to the maximum amount of cut. Any fx:Equalizer stage can be set for a low shelf response; frequency is set as if this was a parametric stage, and Q determines the slope of the curve before it levels off into the shelf.

The high shelf response (see Figure 18.6) is similar to the low shelf and offers the same parameters but affects the high frequencies.

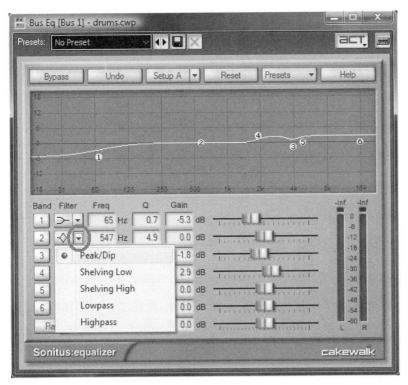

Figure 18.4 Each parametric stage offers five different ways to modify the frequency response.

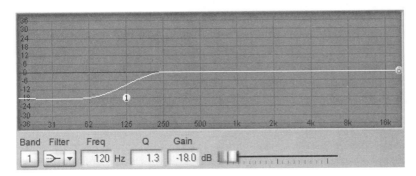

Figure 18.5 The low shelf in this screenshot is set to reduce low-frequency response.

A high-pass response (see Figure 18.7) progressively reduces response below a certain frequency (called the *cutoff* frequency)—the lower the frequency, the greater the reduction. (This is unlike a shelf, where past a certain point the amount of gain reduction stabilizes to a constant amount.) A high-pass filter is sometimes used to remove subsonic (very low-frequency) energy.

The gain (boost/cut) control is not applicable because the high-pass filter can only attenuate frequencies below a certain frequency. However, as with the low shelf, the Q parameter

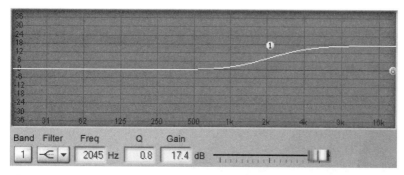

Figure 18.6 The high shelf response can boost or cut high frequencies.

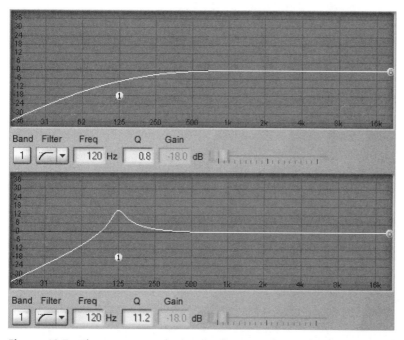

Figure 18.7 The upper graph shows a high-pass response with a low Q value, which gently rolls off low-frequency response. In the lower graph, increasing the Q creates a peak at the cutoff frequency.

determines the *slope* of the response reduction. High Q values add a resonant peak at the selected filtering frequency.

The low-pass response is the mirror image of the high-pass response, as it progressively reduces response above a certain frequency (see Figure 18.8). The reduction in response is greater toward the spectrum's higher frequencies. A typical application is removing hiss or excessive brightness.

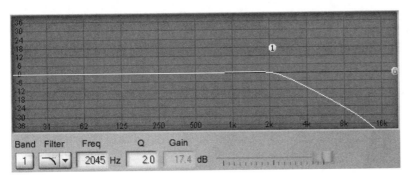

Figure 18.8 Low-pass response filter, set for a sharp high-frequency cut.

Other fx:Equalizer Controls

Each stage has its own set of parameters. If a button under Band is yellow, the stage is on. To turn it off, click on the button, and it will turn gray. To conserve DSP power, turn off any unused stages.

The Flat button resets all gain controls to 0 and disables any high- or low-pass filters but leaves the frequency and bandwidth settings intact.

You can edit most parameters directly on the EQ graph. To select a band for editing, click on its small button, which turns black. Change Frequency by dragging left or right, Gain by dragging up or down, and Q with either a mouse wheel or by holding down Shift while dragging left or right. Note that these buttons don't have to be arranged sequentially—for example, Button 2 can be to the right or left of Button 3.

To copy one band's setting to another band (or all bands), right-click on the associated band's square button under Band (not the button in the EQ graph) and choose the desired copy function. You can also reset an individual band from the same pop-up menu (see Figure 18.9).

The Undo function undoes the last parameter change. You can also create two sets of parameters, an A setup and a B setup, and choose between them or copy one to the other; we'll cover this next.

Preset Management

EQ presets can save time when mixing. You'll often find that certain instruments tend to get along well with particular EQ settings, even in different songs. When you find an EQ setting that works well, save it, because you may need it again. You can also save presets of "points of departure"—curves that have a more generic purpose (for example, brighter, more bass, and so on), which you then tweak for a specific application.

With the fx:Equalizer, click on the Presets button and add the current settings as a preset, call up one of the existing presets, or use the Preset Manager to delete, update with current settings, rename, import, or export presets. Note that this same procedure applies to the fx:Reverb plug-in, described later.

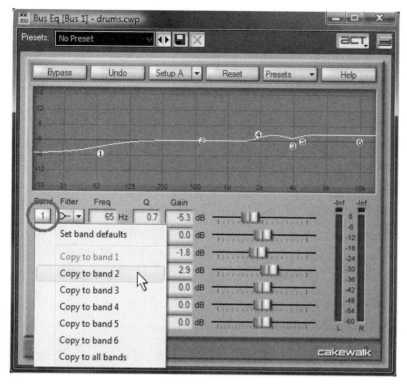

Figure 18.9 A pop-up menu lets you copy settings from one band to another or reset a band to its default (flat) setting.

The Sonitus effects also have a very useful Compare mode, accessed via the effect's toolbar. There are two independent parameter setups for each effect (three if you also count Bypass): Setup A and Setup B. You can toggle between them by clicking on the Setup A/B button, and the drop-down menu to the right of this button provides additional functionality.

Suppose you're comparing two EQ settings, have B selected, and decide you like B better than A—but think you can still do better. From the drop-down menu, select Copy to A, and the curve in B will be duplicated in Setup A. Now you can keep tweaking B, knowing that the original is safely stored in Setup B if you want to revert to it. Note that you can also copy from the other setup into the current setup (for example, copy Setup A's curve into Setup B). If you change your mind, Undo will work with this function, but remember that as always, Undo affects only the last operation.

Furthermore, the Reset function, which flattens the gain at all frequency points, works independently for the two setups so you can reset one without disturbing the other.

Para-Q

This effect is like a miniature version of the Sonitus fx:Equalizer, and it includes two parametric EQ stages that are used for tone shaping. This particular effect is very light on CPU power, so you can use lots of them in a project without bringing your computer to its knees. The Para-Q has the same basic parametric EQ controls per stage: Frequency, Gain (also called Cut/Boost), and BW (for Bandwidth, also called *Resonance* or *Q*). Figure 18.10 shows the two sets of these controls, as well as an overall Level control.

Figure 18.10   The Para-Q includes two parametric EQ stages.

Equalization Tips and Techniques

Too many people adjust equalization with their eyes, not their ears. For example, after doing a mix, I noticed the client writing down all the EQ settings I had made. When I asked why, he said it was because he liked the EQ and wanted to use the same settings on the instruments in future mixes.

But that's the wrong attitude. EQ is a part of the mixing process; just as levels, panning, and reverb are different for each mix, EQ should be tailored for each mix as well. But to do that, you need to understand how to find the magic EQ frequencies for particular types of musical material, as well as what tool to use for what application.

There are three main applications for EQ:

- Problem-solving

- Emphasizing or de-emphasizing an instrument in a mix

- Altering a sound's personality

Each application requires specialized techniques and approaches. But note that equalization is very powerful, so use it sparingly. When you make a change that sounds good, cut it in half. In other words, if boosting a signal by 2 dB at 4 kHz seems to improve the tune's sound, pull back the boost to 1 dB and live with the sound for a while. It's easy to get stuck in a spiral where if you boost the treble, the bass then lacks prominence...so you boost the bass, but now the midrange seems weak, so you boost that, and now you're back to where you started.

Problem-Solving

A common problem with instruments is a resonance or peak that interferes with other instruments or causes level-setting difficulties. Here's a real-world example that shows how to take care of this situation.

I produced several albums for the late classical guitarist Linda Cohen, who had a beautiful nylon-string guitar. It had a full, rich sound that projected very well on stage, thanks to a strong body resonance in the lower midrange that caused a major level peak. However, recording is a different matter from playing live. Setting levels so the peaky, low-frequency notes didn't distort caused the higher guitar notes to sound weak by comparison.

Although compression/limiting was one possible solution, it altered the guitar's attack. While this effect might not be noticeable in an ensemble, it stuck out with a solo instrument. A more natural-sounding answer is to use EQ to apply a frequency cut equal and opposite to the natural boost, thus leveling out the response. But there's a trick to finding problem frequencies so you can alter them; here's the procedure.

1. Turn down the monitor volume—the levels might get nasty and distorted during the following steps.

2. Set the EQ for lots of boost (10 to 12 dB) and fairly narrow bandwidth.

3. As the instrument plays, slowly sweep the frequency control. Any peaks will jump out due to the boosting and narrow bandwidth. Some peaks may even distort.

4. Find the loudest peak and then cut the amplitude until the peak falls into balance with the rest of the instrument sound. You may need to widen the bandwidth a bit if the peak is broad or use narrow bandwidth if the resonance is particularly sharp.

This technique of "boost - find the peak - cut" can help eliminate midrange "honking," reduce strident resonances in wind instruments, and much more. Of course, sometimes you want to preserve these resonances so the instrument stands out, but many times applying EQ to reduce peaks allows instruments to sit more gracefully in the track.

This type of problem-solving also underscores a key principle of EQ: It's often better to cut than boost. Boosting uses up headroom; cutting opens up headroom. With Linda's guitar, cutting the peak allowed bringing up the overall guitar level.

Emphasizing Instruments

The same technique of finding and cutting specific frequencies can also eliminate "fighting" between competing instruments. For example, when mixing a Spencer Brewer track for Narada Records, there were two woodwind parts with resonant peaks around the same frequency. When playing *en ensemble*, they would load up that part of the frequency spectrum, which also made them difficult to differentiate. Here's a way to work around this type of problem.

1. Find and then reduce the peak on one of the instruments (as described previously with the classical guitar example) to create a more even sound.

2. Note the amount of cut and bandwidth that was applied to reduce the peak.

3. Using a second stage of EQ, apply a roughly equal and opposite boost at either a slightly higher or slightly lower frequency than the natural peak.

    Both instruments will now sound more articulated, and because each peaks in a different part of the spectrum, they will tend not to step on each other.

New Sonic Personalities

EQ can also change a sound's character—for example, turn a brash rock piano sound into something more classical. This type of application requires relatively gentle EQ, possibly at several different points in the audio spectrum.

For example, to add warmth, apply a gentle boost (3 dB or so) somewhere in the 200- to 500-Hz range. However, as in the previous case, remember that if possible, cutting is preferable to boosting—for example, if you need more brightness *and* bottom, try cutting the midrange rather than boosting the high and low ends.

Miscellaneous Equalization Tips

Let's look at various tips about how best to use equalization.

- Problem-solving and character-altering EQ should be applied early on in the mixing process, because they will influence how the mix develops. But wait to apply most EQ until the process of setting levels begins; remember, EQ is all about changing levels, albeit in specific frequency ranges. Any EQ changes you make will alter the overall balance of the various instruments.

- Instruments equalized in isolation to sound great may not sound all that wonderful when combined. If every track is equalized to leap out at you, there's no room left for a song to "breathe." Also, you will probably want to alter EQ on some instruments so that they take on more supportive roles. For example, during vocals, consider cutting the midrange a bit on supporting instruments (for example, piano) to open up more space in the audio spectrum for vocals.

- One of your best reality checks is the equalizer's bypass switch. Use it often to make sure you haven't lost control of the original sound. One outstanding feature of the Sonitus fx: Equalizer processor is that you can enable or bypass each stage to determine how this changes the sound.

- Subsonic energy can't be heard, but it uses up dynamic range and should be eliminated if possible. The fx:Equalizer high-pass mode may be useful if there's subsonic energy in a track; set it to pass only frequencies above 20 to 100 Hz, depending on the instrument being equalized. Turn up the boost control as much as possible for the steepest possible slope, consistent with the sound retaining a natural quality. If you need a really steep slope, you can put two high-pass stages in a row to augment the overall effect.

- Shelving filter responses are good for a general lift in the bass and/or treble regions. They can also tame bass and/or treble regions that are too prominent.

- The ear is most sensitive in the midrange and upper midrange. Be wary of harshness when boosting in this region.

- An instrument's EQ has to be factored into the level-setting process. For example, suppose a relatively bright synth sound needs to fit into a track. It can be mixed at a lower level and still have presence, because our ears are most sensitive in the upper midrange area (around 3.5 kHz). A similar situation occurs with strummed acoustic guitars, which cover a fair amount of bandwidth. Even at relatively low levels, acoustic guitars can take over a mix (sometimes a good thing, sometimes not). So, you may want to accentuate the high end but turn the overall level way down. Thus, the guitars still add some percussive propulsion, but they don't interfere with the rest of what's going on in the midrange.

- 400 Hz is often considered the "mud" frequency because a lot of instruments have energy in that frequency range, and that energy adds together into a bit of a sonic blob. A piano may sound perfect when mixed at a certain level by itself but may sound indistinct when other instruments are mixed in. Try cutting either the piano or the other instruments a bit at 400 Hz or so, as that will open up more space for the instrument that isn't being cut. Both should come through clearly in the mix as separate entities.

Other Included Audio Plug-Ins

Let's go through the roster of plug-ins other than EQ. Note that if the plug-in has the focus (that is, you've clicked on it), in most cases you can get full documentation on how it works by typing F1. Therefore, we won't duplicate that material as much as cover applications and background.

In many respects, the best way to learn what these plug-ins do is to experiment. Edit the controls, try different effects on different instruments (even ones that don't seem logical, such as a guitar amp simulator on drums), and if you come up with a preset you like, save it.

Alias Factor

This is designed to add "low-fidelity" effects via three main functions: filtering, sample rate reduction, and bit rate reduction (see Figure 18.11).

Figure 18.11 The Alias Factor effect creates lo-fi, sci-fi type sounds. It's not for the faint of heart.

Filtering. With Cutoff mode set to Free, the Filter Cutoff and Filter Resonance controls edit low-pass filter settings. This emulates some older pieces of gear that were deficient in high-frequency response.

Sampling Frequency. With digital audio, the sampling frequency is what determines the upper frequency response limit. If the sampling frequency is lower than the frequencies being reproduced, they interfere with each other and create weird metallic-type effects. The lower the sampling frequency and the higher the frequencies in the audio material, the more pronounced the interference.

Bit Depth. CDs have a bit depth of 16 bits, which is adequate for high fidelity. Some older samplers and early digital synthesizers used 12- or even 8-bit depth; some toys use 4 bits. Lower bit depths add noise to the signal and a roughness to lower-level signals. In fact, the effect of bit reduction is most pronounced with lower-level signals and less so with high-level ones.

Mix. This lets you adjust the blend of messed-up sound with the dry, unprocessed sound.

Amp Sim

This emulates the sound of a guitar amp. Its help file can't be read in Vista, so I'll go into a bit more detail. Note that the VGA Plus amp processor is more sophisticated, but just like real guitar amps, each amp simulator plug-in has its own "personality" and therefore may be the right sound for a particular application (see Figure 18.12).

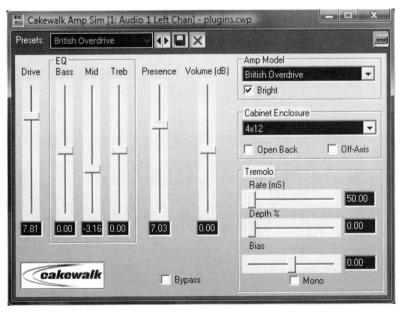

Figure 18.12 The Amp Sim provides a variety of guitar amp effects.

It's also worth noting that distortion is useful for more than guitar. For example, clone a drum track so that there are two drum tracks in parallel, process one with the Amp Sim, and mix the distorted sound in the background. This can produce a wonderfully trashy drum sound. Also, distortion can sound good on individual drums, such as kick, to add an edge.

Amp Model. This is the most basic shaper of the Amp Sim's character, so you usually decide which model you want first.

Cabinet Enclosure. The bigger the speakers and the more there are, the broader the response. Checking Open Back reduces bass and emphasizes treble because with an open-back cabinet, the waves coming from the front and back cancel somewhat, which diminishes bass response. Checking Off-Axis emulates miking the amp cabinet off to one side, which gives a thinner, less full sound.

Drive. This control dials in the desired amount of crunch or overdrive. It interacts with other controls such as tone and volume, but it is the main determinant of the amount of crunch.

EQ. These work like standard bass, middle, and treble tone controls as you'd find on a typical guitar amp. Presence adds a bit of a high-end boost.

Volume. This acts like an amp's master volume control.

Bias. This provides a subtle tonal change in the distortion characteristics.

Tremolo. Rate determines the speed of this pulsing-amplitude effect, while Depth determines the difference between the maximum and minimum levels of the pulsing. Note that the Rate *decreases* as you move the slider to the right, which is somewhat counterintuitive.

Mono. This converts stereo signals to mono, as most guitar amp setups are mono as well.

Classic Phaser

And for those who love that classic '60s swooshing sound, meet the Classic Phaser (see Figure 18.13).

Figure 18.13 Phasing provides swooshing, underwater-type sounds.

Mode. The stereo image gets progressively wider as you go from Mono, to Stereo, to Quadra.

Tempo Sync. This is an important control, as it makes the Phaser's sweep relate to the song's tempo. You can choose common rhythmic values (such as having it sweep every quarter note) as well as dotted and triplet values. If set to Off, then the LFO Rate control sets the sweep period.

LFO Depth. Regardless of whether you've chosen Tempo Sync or LFO Rate, this control determines the influence of any modulation, from subtle to a sweep that covers a wide range.

Waveform. The modulation sweep can have one of three different "shapes" that determines how long the sweep stays at the top of the sweep, how long it stays at the bottom of the sweep, and how it transitions from top to bottom. This is one of those "try it and see what sounds best" controls.

Center. This weights the phasing effect more toward the low (counterclockwise) or high (clockwise) frequencies.

Feedback. Turning this clockwise increases the effect's resonance, giving it a sharper, more whistling quality.

Compressor/Gate

The help file for this effect is pretty comprehensive, so we won't get too much into the details. However, one area that's glossed over a bit is using the Gate section, as it's mentioned principally in the context of removing noise from a compressed signal—but gating is also useful for special effects, such as creating super-percussive sounds (see Figure 18.14).

Figure 18.14 In addition to helping remove noise caused by heavy compression, gating can provide special effects.

A Gate works by muting the Gate output when the input drops below a certain level. The Threshold parameter sets this level. So, if you have a signal with a long decay, and you set the threshold fairly high, you can cut off the decay and create a more percussive sound.

To use the Gate by itself, you'll want to bypass the Compressor; but the Bypass control affects both the Compressor and the Gate. To neutralize the Compressor, set the Threshold to 0.00, Ratio to 1:1, and Input Gain to 0.00. In this case, the Attack and Release controls don't matter, and there's no compression.

For the purpose of testing out the Gate, load a drum loop into SONAR Home Studio or create a drum loop you can use. Set the Gate mode to Normal and the Threshold to 0.00. You probably won't hear anything, because the Gate threshold is higher than the incoming signal.

Now, lower the threshold. At first the Gate will let through just the peaks, but then as the threshold goes lower, more of the lower-level sounds and decays will make it through. It's even possible to alter the "mix" of some drum loops—for example, if the kick and snare are high-level and the hi-hat is considerably softer, you can set the threshold below the kick and snare level but above the hi-hat, thus effectively cutting the hi-hats out of the mix.

FX2 Tape Sim

Analog tape isn't just a recording medium; it's a signal processor, and quite a few people like the kind of warmth and saturation effects it adds. A lot of engineers prefer to record drums to tape, even if they're using a digital audio recording program such as SONAR Home Studio, because of the way tape affects the drum sound. They'll then transfer the drums over to their digital recording medium.

While the Tape Sim processor can add a bit of punch to signals, as with the Amp Sim, don't think of the Tape Sim solely as a device to emulate tape saturation—it's useful for adding certain sonic qualities to a variety of sound sources. Also like the Amp Sim, the help file can't be read in Vista, so we'll cover it in more detail. However, due to the limited number of parameters, in a lot of cases it's most convenient to try out different presets and see what you like. For example, the Medium Saturation 30 ips preset (see Figure 18.15) can sound very good on drums.

Figure 18.15 This preset adds a bit of punch to drums, but without creating any obvious distortion.

The Tape Speed and EQ Curve parameters determine the sound's character. Checking LF Boost gives the bass increase associated with a phenomenon known as *head bump*, where the physics of the tape head added a low-frequency boost. Hiss adds tape hiss (which, of course, everyone wanted to get rid of back when tape ruled the recording world).

Keep the Output Gain low as you tweak your sound. The key control is Rec Level, which sets the initial level and hardness. The Warmth control adds the crunch. For a really crunchy sound, set Rec Level and Warmth to maximum and pull back Input Gain until the degree of nastiness is just right. Finally, adjust the Output Gain to avoid clipping the track.

If you're really overloading the sound to generate mondo distortion, you might not be able to lower the Output Gain sufficiently. In this case, you'll need to use the track's output control to trim the overall level.

One of the best uses of the Tape Sim is with a kick drum track, and the LF Boost switch is Cakewalk's gift to dance music kick drums. Dial up the right amount of distortion and then add LF Boost. The end result is a kick drum that can move mountains.

Click the Bypass switch from time to time to get a dose of reality—you might be shocked at how much you can raise the overall level without hearing objectionable levels of clipping.

HF Exciter

This effect adds brightness (HF stands for *High Frequency*), but not in the same way as EQ; instead, it adds a gentle amount of high-frequency distortion that adds "sparkle" to a track. If not overused, it can restore some of the brightness associated with acoustic instruments that sometimes seems to get lost during the recording process. The control complement is very basic (see Figure 18.16).

Figure 18.16 The HF (High Frequency) Exciter is the audio equivalent of those "washday whiteners and brighteners" for laundry you see advertised on TV.

The Frequency control determines the range of frequencies that will be "excited." Usually you'll want this set fairly high unless the track you're processing is really muffled. In general, a lower

Frequency setting means you might want to pull back on the Drive control a bit to avoid an overly crispy sound. Similarly, you can use lower Mix control settings to have more of the original signal and less of the excited one.

Spread increases the apparent stereo width. Because high frequencies are more directional than low frequencies, increasing this can give a wider high-frequency stereo image.

Modfilter

You're probably familiar with the wah-wah pedal sound used with guitar, which adds a sort of vocal quality to your playing. This plug-in creates wah effects automatically in one of two ways: by sweeping a filter (similarly to how the Classic Phaser sweeps the signal phase) or by tying the filter frequency to the incoming signal level (in other words, its amplitude envelope). In the latter case, louder sounds kick the filter frequency higher, and the filter decays back to its initial frequency (as set by the Cutoff control) over a time specified by the Release control. Figure 18.17 shows a preset that creates an automatic wah effect similar to the '70s Funk Machine effect used by bassist Larry Graham and many others.

Figure 18.17 This preset causes the Modfilter to respond to the incoming signal level, thus producing an automatic wah-wah effect.

The help file is very useful for this effect, but there are a few aspects that require elaboration.

When the Filter mode is set to LFO, the controls are similar to the Classic Phaser in terms of being able to sync the LFO to tempo. One very cool application is that you can create a pulsing effect by synching to tempo and using a square wave as the LFO waveform. Use the Mod Depth to vary the depth of the pulsing, or better yet, enable automation Write and vary the depth to add variation. The Sample and Hold waveform can also be fun for creating random variations on each rhythmic interval (for example, every beat, every measure, and so on).

In EG mode, the Attack and Release controls can have a major effect on the sound. If the settings are too fast, the envelope follower will try to follow every tiny little level change, which can produce a sort of warbling or choppy effect that's not particularly smooth. Increasing the attack time to 0.03 (30ms) will pretty much get rid of this, provided the release isn't too short. For percussive material, you'll want a relatively short release; for more complex sounds, you may need a longer release time to avoid an overly choppy sound.

Note that adding a little Overdrive can help thicken the overall filter sound. As for Resonance, be careful; too high a setting can produce massive peaks. If you want to use lots of resonance, you may need to follow the Modfilter with the Compressor/Gate to reduce the dynamic range.

When used subtly, the Modfilter can add "animation" to a sound. For this application, set the filter Cutoff fairly high (around 4,000 to 5,000Hz), with low Resonance and just a little bit of Mod Depth to make the filter wiggle a bit. Try this on vocals as a subliminal type of effect.

Chorus/Flanger

The Chorus effect thickens sounds; think of a choir compared to a couple people singing together, and you have the basic idea (see Figure 18.18). Flanging produces the "jet airplane" sound effect that was big during the '60s on albums by artists such as Jimi Hendrix.

Figure 18.18 When you want to thicken a sound and make it swirl around the stereo field, the Chorus/Flanger is for you.

This plug-in benefits from an informative help file, so we don't need to get into the details too much. In fact, this is another one of those effects where playing with the presets for a while is probably the best way to learn what it does.

Pay particular attention to the help file section on the EQ mode and EQ controls, as these can make a huge difference in the sound. As with the Modfilter, high Feedback settings can produce significant peaks (especially with the Flanger presets), so be careful.

Pitch Shifter

If you want to shift pitch, the stretching options described in Chapter 3 do a better job in terms of fidelity. However, this processor can produce some really bizarre and interesting effects you can't obtain any other way. It also has a help menu that can't be read in Vista, so let's go over each parameter (see Figure 18.19).

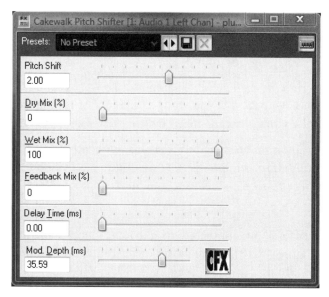

Figure 18.19 The Pitch Shifter can create some amazingly bizarre effects.

Pitch Shift. This is the main control, and it lets you shift pitch up or down up to 12 semitones. The bigger the shift, the lower the sound quality (or if you like bizarre-sounding things, the more interesting the sound quality).

Dry Mix. This sets the amount of unprocessed signal in the overall output.

Wet Mix. This determines the amount of pitch-shifted signal in the overall output.

Feedback Mix and Delay Time. These work together to produce an echo unit–type effect, but with a twist: Because the pitch-shifted output signal can be sent back to the input, each time it feeds back the pitch changes. For example, if the pitch shift is set for one semitone up, then each time it feeds back, the pitch will increase by another semitone. The Delay Time parameter sets the delay between each successive repeat.

Mod Depth. This seems to produce a more natural sound when increased, but it's the kind of control where you just mess around with it until you get the sound you want.

Although most people think of using pitch shifts for transposition, small amounts of shift can provide excellent thickening and doubling effects. Here's how to apply this to vocals.

1. Select the vocal track you want to thicken.

2. Choose Tracks > Clone. Check everything under Clone Tracks except Link to Original Clip. The clone needs to be independently editable.

3. Click on the Clone function OK button, and you now have two vocal tracks.

4. Open up the track's Effects section by clicking on the Effects button.

5. Click on Add Effect or right-click in the Effects box.

6. Choose Audio > Cakewalk > Pitch Shifter.

7. Set the Pitch Shift parameters as follows:

   - Pitch Shift = –0.24
   - Dry Mix = 0
   - Wet Mix = 100
   - Feedback Mix = 0
   - Delay Time = 2.61
   - Mod Depth = 12.16

These are just suggested settings that work well with my voice; adjust for the best effect with your vocals.

For the thickest, smoothest sound, pan the two vocal tracks to center. If you pan one vocal full right and one full left, you'll hear two individual vocals instead of a rich, composite vocal. Panning to opposites works very well for processing something like a background vocal chorus, as the individual parts should be thick enough by themselves; shifting pitch widens the stereo spread.

Also try panning lead vocals slightly left and right (for example, left channel at 10 o'clock, right channel at 2 o'clock). This gives a somewhat fuller sound and a somewhat wider stereo spread, which can also be useful under some circumstances.

PowerStrip

PowerStrip's main point of difference compared to other effects is that it can interface with a joystick, allowing you to vary two parameters at once in real time. Of course, you can also record these changes as automation moves. But you're not forced to use a joystick; the effect has a virtual X-Y control pad on the interface itself (see Figure 18.20). You can adjust this with a mouse or sweep the settings with an LFO.

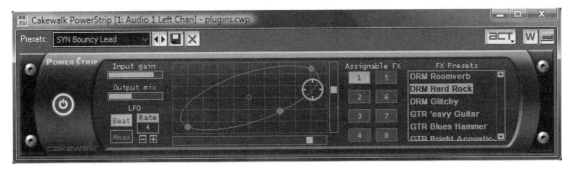

Figure 18.20 The roster of available PowerStrip effects is toward the right, and the X-Y controller is toward the middle left. In this screenshot, the X-Y controller is being linked to an LFO.

Which Parameters Get Varied

It depends on the effect, but let's give an example. If you choose the GTR Wah preset, the horizontal axis controls the wah frequency, with low frequencies on the left and high frequencies toward the right. The vertical axis controls resonance; moving up increases resonance, while moving down lowers resonance. This makes it possible not only to get a variety of wah sounds, but to have them change dynamically—use low resonance on low frequencies and high resonance on high frequencies, or vice versa (or any combination).

Preset Selection

There are two ways to choose one of the presets: Click on a preset in the window on the right (use the up/down buttons on the scroll bar to scroll through the presets), or use the standard Presets selector in the upper left. Note that the presets start with three letters that indicate the intended usage—for example, GTR indicates guitar, while AUX indicates that the effect is intended to be used as a send bus effect. Just remember that these are guidelines, not rules!

However, there is a difference between these two methods of preset selection. If you right-click on a preset in the right window, a pop-up window will appear with eight numbers. These correlate with the eight Assignable FX buttons (see Figure 18.21).

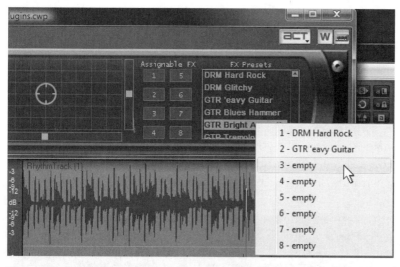

Figure 18.21   Right-clicking on a preset in the FX Presets window lets you assign it to one of the Assignable FX buttons for instant access. The highlighted preset is about to be assigned to Assignable FX button 3.

When you select a number for a preset, then clicking on the associated Assignable FX button calls up the preset you assigned. Thus, you can have eight presets available for instantaneous selection. These preset assignments are saved with a project, but note that if you select a preset using the standard Presets selector in the upper left, then all the Assignable FX buttons revert to Empty.

LFO Section

The LFO can sync to tempo, in the same way we've already seen with other effects: Select Beat or Measure and use the + and – buttons to set the number of beats or measures, as appropriate. The sweep defaults to an ellipse that sweeps equally through the two variable parameters, but note that the ellipse has three nodes. You can click and drag on these nodes to alter the shape of the ellipse, as well as reverse the sweep's direction.

All of these parameters are automatable, as well. Whatever you do to change the sweep will be automated, including the results of moving the ellipse nodes. What's more, you can click on the X-Y locus (cursor) and drag it, even if the LFO is in effect, and your movements will have priority over the LFO. The same is true if you click and drag on the horizontal or vertical scroll bars if you want to constrain the X-Y locus to a particular axis. The basic automation rule is this: As long as you're writing automation, whatever the X-Y locus does will play back. However, when playing back automation, disable the Beat and Measure buttons, or the LFO will take priority.

Incidentally, the locus follows any system cursor rules that are in effect. For example, if pointer trails are enabled in the Control Panel's Mouse function, than the locus will have trails as well.

This is an unusual and interesting effect. Fortunately, it also has a very complete help file if you'd like some more tips.

Studioverb II

When you want to add acoustic ambience to a track, the Studioverb II is an excellent choice. Considering how little CPU power it draws, the sound quality is surprisingly good, and the reverb tails are smooth and natural.

However, the large number of controls (see Figure 18.22) means it's potentially just as easy to dial in bad sounds as good ones. Although the help file gives a good definition of what the controls do, they don't necessarily tell you how to apply them—so here are some tips.

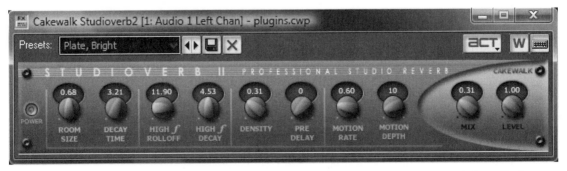

Figure 18.22   The Studioverb II doesn't just sound good; it also has numerous controls for tailoring your sound.

Room Size vs. Decay Time. When setting decay time, think of Room Size as the "master" control and Decay Time as the trim. For example, if you want a shorter decay, you'll likely get a more realistic sound by starting with a small Room Size than by starting with a big room and using the Decay Time control to shorten it.

Diffusion. This control changes the reverb's density. Higher diffusion settings create a smoother, more billowy sound, while shorter diffusion settings accentuate the individual reflections more. As a general rule of thumb, use higher diffusion settings for percussive sounds (drums, guitar, and so on) and lower diffusion settings for more sustained sounds, such as vocals, organ, and the like. With percussion, lower diffusion settings produce discrete echoes that can sound annoying, while with sustained sounds, excess diffusion can make the sound less distinct.

Motion Rate and Depth. These are "tweak until things sound right" controls. Their main use is if you notice *periodicity* (a repetitive, periodic quality) in the reverb tail. If so, increasing the Motion Depth and adjusting the Motion Rate can make any periodicity far less noticeable.

High Frequency Decay. This causes high frequencies to decay at a different rate than the rest of the reverb sound. I particularly like increasing the HF Decay with vocals, as sibilants and other expressive vocal elements are emphasized just a tiny bit.

Mix. When using the Studioverb II as a send (bus) effect, turn this to 1.00 so you hear only the reverberated sound. Assuming the send is set up to be post-fader, the track providing the send will determine the amount of unprocessed signal. When using reverb as a track insert effect, this control determines the balance of unprocessed and reverberated sounds.

Send Bus EQ Techniques. When using reverb as a send effect, sometimes placing EQ before the reverb can enhance the sound. For example, when applying EQ to drums, having too much reverb on the kick drum can make the low end overly muddy, thus obscuring the bass as well. You also might want the drums to sound a bit brighter.

Referring to Figure 18.23, note that EQ is inserted before the reverb in order to tailor which part of the drums gets reverberated.

But what happens if you want to send multiple instruments through the same reverb to give a cohesive room sound, but you need to add EQ to only one or two tracks? In this case, send a track requiring EQ to a bus with EQ inserted. Then, send that bus to the reverb bus. Tracks that don't require EQ can send directly to the reverb bus, without any intervening bus.

Stereo Delay (Tempo Delay)

This effect has an identity crisis: It's listed in the FX bin as Tempo Delay, but its front panel says Stereo Delay. No matter—it's a useful stereo delay that can sync delay times to tempo. This is another instance where the help menu will tell you most of what you need to know, but here are a few hints on getting the most out of this effect.

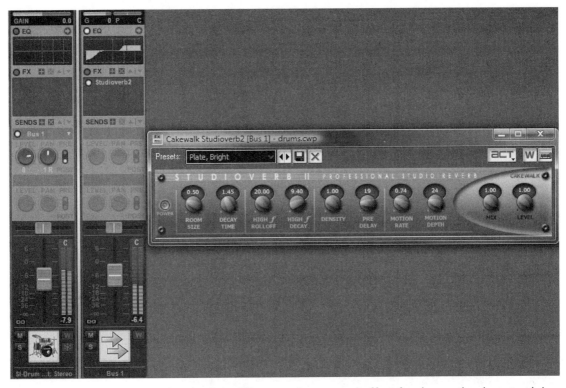

Figure 18.23 Here's a typical setup for adding reverb as a send effect for drums; the drum track is on the left, and the bus to the right. Note how the EQ is rolling off the bass, while emphasizing the highs. This gives a crispier, more distinct sound.

- For dance music where you want to add some motion to the sound, try using the 1D echo time, in Stereo mode, with a fair amount of feedback.

- To take this one level further and add stereo effects, switch to 1/2D echo time and set the mode to Ping.

- The EQ section is very powerful. Check out the effect's help menu for details on how to take best advantage of it.

- For a sound that resembles old tape echo units, turn EQ to Wide, pull the Low and High EQ controls all the way down, turn Mid all the way up, and use a fair amount of feedback.

- With percussion, try EQ in the Wide position, with the High EQ control all the way up and the Low and Mid EQ controls all the way down. This adds a bright echo that sort of "floats" above the other sounds. In fact, if you apply this to a drum part with a fairly repetitive hi-hat part, it can almost sound like there's an additional shaker or perhaps maracas part.

■ To add echo to a drum part but keep the kick solid, set EQ to STD, leave Mid and High up about halfway, and reduce the Low control.

Boost 11

Boost 11 (available only in SONAR Home Studio 7 XL) controls dynamics by reducing peak levels, which allows bringing up the overall level. For example, if the peaks are brought down by 6 dB, then that opens up 6 dB of headroom. Thus, the entire file can be brought up by 6 dB, making it sound considerably louder but without destroying the dynamics.

You don't access the documentation by typing F1, but instead, you find it within the Boost11 folder, which is located within the "VSTplugins" folder. If you don't want to hunt for it, just search for Boost11.chm. Once you locate the file, double-click on it.

The help file is good for understanding the principle of operation, but it's easy to go through the basic operation—check out Figure 18.24.

Figure 18.24 If used properly, Boost11 can increase a signal's apparent loudness without impacting dynamics too much.

Look at the Waveform In meter. Note that some peaks of the incoming signal exceed a horizontal line; this line represents the maximum available headroom, as set by the Output control. (In the screenshot, the peaks are colored white instead of red and made a little wider so they'd be easier to see in the book.) Compare this to the Waveform Out meter, where the peaks are no longer present; Boost11 has reduced the gain of only those peaks so they would not exceed the available headroom.

Adjusting Boost11 is easy: Just turn up the Boost control for the desired amount of boost. Be careful, though, because a little bit goes a long way. If you turn this up too far, the sound will become distorted—you can increase levels only so much without having undesirable artifacts.

Typically, a few dB will be all you need. If the Waveform In has a ton of red peaks, you've probably gone too far.

The Reduction meter shows how much the peaks are being reduced downward. When no peaks are present, the meter doesn't show anything. As more reduction is applied, the bar moves downward; a longer bar represents more reduction. The numeric readout under the bar indicates the maximum amount of reduction that's been applied; reset this by double-clicking on the number.

The Output control simply adjusts the output level, which is why it affects the output headroom.

Sonitus fx:Reverb

fx:Reverb accomplishes a similar result to the Studioverb II but uses a more sophisticated algorithm that offers more parameters for control, with the tradeoff being more CPU usage. Access help by typing F1 while the fx:Reverb window has the focus. For Sonitus effects, the help doesn't just describe what the controls do, but also gives suggestions on how best to set them for specific applications.

As mentioned earlier with the fx:Equalizer, the Sonitus effects handle presets differently compared to any other effects. If you're in a hurry to dial up some presets, just click on the Presets button, and you'll see two default banks of presets: Aux bus (containing presets optimized for use as a send effect) and Sonitus:fx, which has presets that are more suitable as insert effects.

VGA Plus Virtual Guitar Amp

Now you can get the sound of cranking a maxed-out guitar amp without disturbing the neighbors or blowing out speakers, courtesy of the VGA Plus Virtual Guitar Amp (available only in SONAR Home Studio 7 XL). However, because this is something you'll want to hear in real time, as you play, you'll need to do three important things.

- Minimize latency as much as possible. You want to hear what you're playing as you play it, not several milliseconds later. If you have an older computer or use high-latency audio drivers such as MME or DirectX, you may not be able to achieve acceptable latency. For best results, use ASIO drivers and an ASIO-compatible soundcard or cards that support WDM/KS (not just standard WDM; SONAR Home Studio supports Kernel Streaming WDM). Computer-wise, if at all possible, use at least a dual- or quad-core CPU (or better!).

- Use an audio interface with an instrument input designed specifically to accommodate electric guitars. These inputs are also called *Hi-Z* or *guitar* inputs. They don't affect latency, but this type of input will preserve your guitar tone rather than loading down your pickups.

- Monitor the input signal in real time. To do this, make sure that Input Echo is enabled (see Figure 18.25).

An important point is that when you record your guitar with an amp simulator such as the VGA Plus, you are not recording the processed sound—the dry guitar sound is being recorded to the

Figure 18.25   To hear the input of an audio track through a plug-in, you'll need to turn on the Input Echo function.

track, which is then being processed by the plug-in. This gives the advantage that you can change the guitar sound at any time, even when mixing down, just by changing the VGA Plus settings. And of course, you're not limited to using just the VGA Plus; you can create a virtual rack with the VGA Plus, and additional plug-ins such as delay, reverb, and the like.

For more information on using the VGA Plus, refer to Chapter 23, "Recording Guitar with SONAR Home Studio."

Managing Effects and Plug-Ins with the Plug-In Manager

As your collection of plug-ins grows, you may want to sort them according to particular functions or by manufacturer or exclude plug-ins that don't work with SONAR (such as some that accomplish specific functions in other programs, like video filtering that has nothing to do with audio). For these tasks, there's the Plug-In Manager.

Consider Figure 18.26, which shows all plug-ins that SONAR Home Studio found. Clearly, some of these have nothing to do with audio processing. It doesn't hurt anything if they show up, but we can prevent SONAR Home Studio from listing them, thus making for a neater listing.

To do this, choose Tools > Cakewalk Plug-In Manager. You'll see a window with three main columns (see Figure 18.27).

The left column contains categories of plug-ins. When you click on a category, the middle column shows all plug-ins registered under that category. The right column is where you can build up a custom menu layout for plug-ins.

Looking at the middle column, you can see all the registered DirectX-compatible effects. The Cakewalk ones are clearly labeled, but you can see unrelated plug-ins from CyberLink,

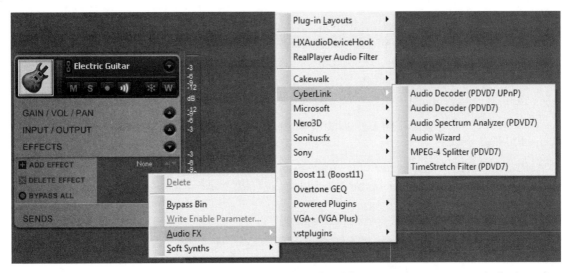

Figure 18.26 These CyberLink plug-ins have nothing to do with SONAR, but we can exclude them from showing up by using the Plug-In Manager.

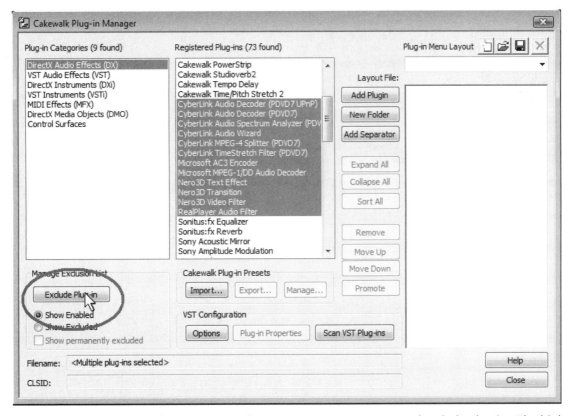

Figure 18.27 Cakewalk's Plug-In Manager lets you rearrange, rename, and exclude plug-ins. The high-lighted plug-ins are about to be excluded.

Microsoft, Nero, and RealPlayer. The Sonitus plug-ins are also listed, along with several Sony audio plug-ins that became available when Sony's excellent video editing program, Vegas, was installed on the same computer. We definitely want to keep the Sonitus effects, and as a bonus, we can use the Sony plug-ins within SONAR Home Studio, so we'll keep those.

We can highlight the ones that aren't compatible with Cakewalk and then click on Exclude Plug-In, and they will no longer show up in the plug-in menu that gets called up when you right-click on the FX bin.

HXAudioDeviceHook is another plug-in we don't need to see. If it's on your system too, click on the categories until it shows up and exclude it as well. Now when we look at the FX listing, it's much neater (see Figure 18.28).

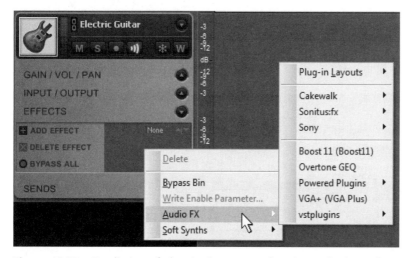

Figure 18.28   Our listing of plug-ins is now restricted to only those that actually matter to SONAR Home Studio.

Although this book isn't intended to be a manual but more about applications, we'll still take a quick look at how you would create a custom layout for plug-ins.

You build the custom layout in the right column. For example, suppose you want to organize plug-ins by function, such as Dynamics, Guitar Amps, Modulation Effects, Equalizers, and the like. You create folders by clicking on the New Folder button and then add plug-ins to the folder by clicking on the desired plug-in in the middle column and clicking on Add Plugin (see Figure 18.29).

There are other options for organizing your plug-ins. For example, you can click on a plug-in or folder in the right column and move it up or down by clicking on the Move Up or Move Down button, respectively. Once you've organized the plug-ins as desired, you can save the layout—or even save multiple layouts and choose the one you want (see Figure 18.30).

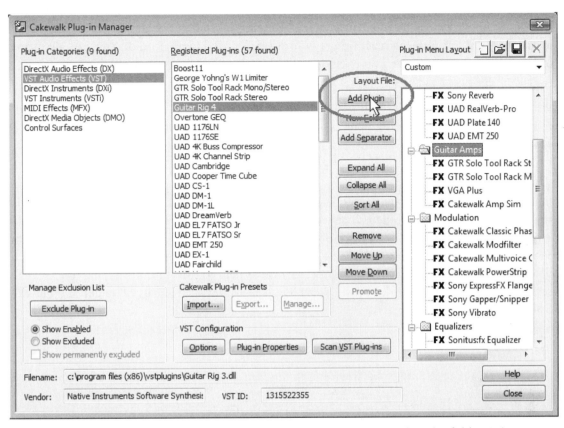

Figure 18.29 Guitar Rig 4 from Native Instruments is about to be added to the folder Guitar Amps.

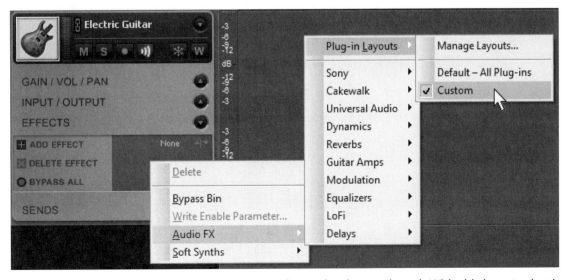

Figure 18.30 Under Plug-In Layouts, the Custom layout has been selected. With this layout, plug-ins have been mostly organized by function, with some remaining plug-ins sorted by manufacturer.

The Plug-In Manager can do more, such as scan for plug-ins and import or export presets—great for collaborating on projects with others who use SONAR Home Studio. You can also show excluded plug-ins just in case you excluded one that shouldn't have been.

If you're new to SONAR Home Studio, then you can probably manage the plug-ins you have. But as you add more plug-ins to your setup, you'll find the Plug-In Manager to be very helpful in terms of organizing your collection—look at the associated help file for more information.

Speed Up Startup

When you open SONAR Home Studio, it scans for VST plug-ins to check whether new, unregistered plug-ins have been installed since you last launched the program. However, if you have a fairly stable setup and don't add a lot of plug-ins, you can save a few seconds each time you open SONAR Home Studio by choosing Options > Global, clicking on the VST Plug-Ins tab, and unchecking Scan for VST Plug-Ins on Startup. When you do add a plug-in, run the VST Configuration Wizard manually by choosing Tools > Cakewalk Plug-In Manager and clicking on Scan VST Plug-Ins.

19 Automation in SONAR Home Studio

The mixing process used to involve turning knobs, sliding faders, and pushing switches on a physical mixing console (or what the British call a *mixing desk*). We can still work that way thanks to control surfaces (Chapter 20, "Control Surfaces"), but we can also edit virtual knobs, faders, and switches onscreen.

During the mixing process, lots of "moves" are necessary—bringing instruments in and out, bypassing effects, altering pan position in the stereo field, and, of course, changing levels. *Automation* is a technique that causes SONAR Home Studio to "remember" your various moves. For example, if a track's level (or bus level) needs to vary throughout a piece, you can concentrate on getting those changes perfect while the automation records your moves. On playback, the level will vary exactly as you specified. (The virtual fader will even move to reflect the changes.) You can then work with other tracks, or if your moves weren't perfect, you can edit the automation or redo portions of it.

Also, many effects and soft synth plug-ins can be automated, although the specifics depend on the way the plug-in was designed. We'll discuss this later on. What makes synth automation so wonderful while mixing is that it allows adding nuanced expressiveness to otherwise potentially "static" electronic sounds.

MIDI tracks implement automation similarly, but of course they have a different repertoire of parameters they can control. Volume, pan, mute, reverb, and chorus are the "stock" automatable parameters, but you can basically automate anything through the use of MIDI controllers and create *automation envelopes* for these controllers.

Automation is one of the keys to a pro-sounding mix. If on playback you decide that a track should have been softer or louder, no problem: Just redo the automation. Eventually, you'll get all the levels exactly the way you want.

The Four Ways to Automate in SONAR Home Studio

There are four ways to automate parameters in SHS.

Method One: Move Onscreen Controls in Real Time While Recording the Moves as Automation

This is the easiest option for many people, and it's very intuitive. It's also the primary way of doing automation with the mixer. To find out whether you can automate a mixer parameter by moving its associated control, right-click on the control. If you can select Automation Write Enable, then the parameter can be automated. After being selected, a red outline will appear around the control. You can select multiple parameters for automation or even select *all* eligible parameters in a track (Level, Pan, Mute, Send Level, and Send Pan) by clicking a track's W button (as in Write) in Track or Console view.

When you select all parameters, the W glows orange. If only a few parameters in a track are enabled for automation, then the W glows yellow (see Figure 19.1). Click Play, and any moves will be remembered as automation data. Note that you don't have to go into Record mode to record automation—as long as the W is glowing, automation will be recorded.

Figure 19.1 Note the outlines around some of the controls. Cymbals Left has only its Level fader enabled for automation, whereas the Bass Guitar track has all automatable channel parameters enabled.

With soft synths, if the W button appears toward the upper right of the instrument's window and is enabled, then any controls that respond to automation will have their moves recorded when you move them. If no W button is present, no automatable parameters will be available (see Figure 19.2).

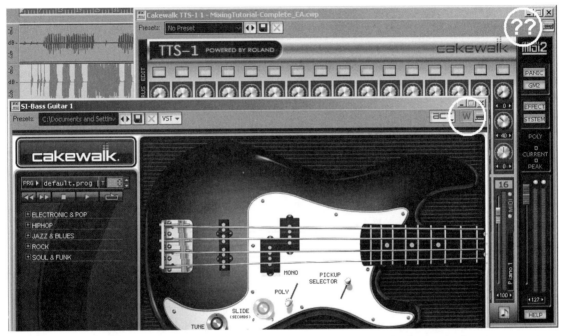

Figure 19.2 Each Studio Instrument soft synth has a W button, which means its parameters are automatable by simply moving the onscreen controls. However, the TTS-1 does not have a W button, and its parameters can't be automated by moving controls.

Note that automating some parameters, particularly with signal processors and soft synths, may produce small clicks or other glitches as they're changed. This is a technical limitation of the plug-in design, so there's little SONAR Home Studio can do about it.

To record automation by moving controls:

1. Make sure that the desired controls are write-enabled for automation, as described previously.

2. Click on the transport Play button. You do not need to click on Record or anything else; recording automation is independent of recording MIDI notes or audio. As long as parameters are write-enabled for automation, automation data will be recorded when you move the control during playback or recording.

3. To start recording automation data, click on the control and move it.

4. To stop recording automation data, release the mouse button.

5. To resume writing automation moves, click on the control again and move it.

When you're recording automation, a reddish overlay starts on the track where automation begins and ends when you stop recording automation. SONAR Home Studio draws the automation envelopes in real time, but if you're overwriting existing automation data, the previous data isn't removed until you stop recording automation moves and also stop the transport.

SONAR Home Studio is "smart" about how it handles automation overdubs. If playback occurs over an area that has automation data and the mouse button is released, then the existing automation data remains unchanged. As soon as you push down on the mouse button, any moves overwrite existing automation data.

When you're finished recording automation, it's a good idea to turn off Automation Write Enable. (Click on the glowing W to toggle it off.) That way, you won't accidentally overwrite any automation you've recorded.

Method Two: Draw Envelopes or Modify Existing Ones

Moving an onscreen control while recording automation creates a corresponding automation envelope that shows up in the track. You can edit an existing envelope or draw a new one from scratch, as well as show, hide, copy, and paste envelopes.

As moving onscreen controls creates envelopes and drawing envelopes moves the onscreen controls they affect, these methods are somewhat interchangeable. The method to use depends on the application. For adding an expressive wa-wa effect, I'd go for recording control motion; but if I wanted to have a fade-in that lasted exactly one measure (or edit an existing envelope), the envelope drawing approach would likely be easier.

Here's how to create a mixer envelope (see Figure 19.3).

1. In Track view, right-click on the clip (or on a blank space in the track) to which you want to add the envelope.

2. Choose Envelopes > Create Track Envelope.

3. Select the mixer envelope you want to create.

Also, here's how to create an envelope for an effect or soft synth parameter (see Figure 19.4).

1. In Track view, right-click on the clip (or on a blank space in the track) to which you want to add the envelope.

2. Choose Envelopes > Create Track Envelope.

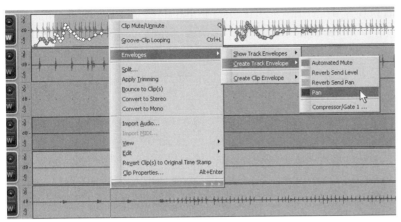

Figure 19.3 Right-clicking on a track makes it easy to create a mixer envelope. In this example, we're about to create a pan envelope. With a couple more steps, you can also draw envelopes for plug-in effects and soft synths.

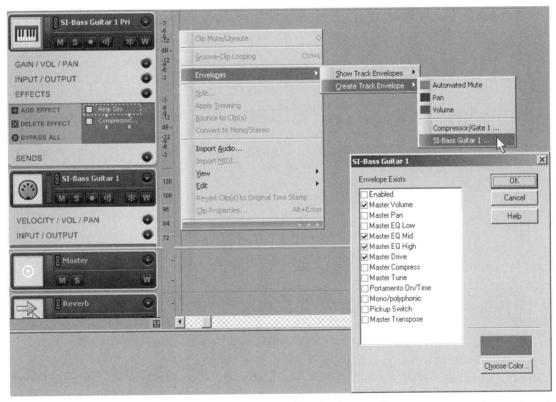

Figure 19.4 In this example, the Studio Instrument bass is about to have some parameters automated (Master Volume, Master EQ Mid, Master EQ High, and Master Drive). Creating envelopes for effects and soft synths is similar to creating envelopes for mixer parameters.

3. Any automatable effects or soft synths will be listed below the automatable mixer parameters. Choose the desired effect or soft synth for which you want to create an envelope.

4. After choosing the effect or synth, a window will appear that lists the automatable parameters with a check box next to each one.

5. Check the parameters that should have envelopes. Note that when you click on a parameter or check box, you can choose an envelope color (although I usually just stick with the defaults).

6. Click on OK, and the envelopes will appear in the track, initially as straight lines. Now you can modify them (as described next) to create particular envelope shapes.

Editing Envelope Shapes

After creating the envelope, you can use a variety of tools to modify it.

- Double-click anywhere on the envelope with the standard arrow cursor to add a breakpoint (node) or right-click on the envelope and select Add Node from the pop-up menu.

- Click on the node and drag to move.

- Right-click on the envelope between two nodes and specify a particular shape (see Figure 19.5).

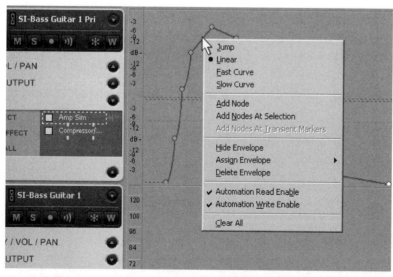

Figure 19.5 Right-click on a segment between nodes to specify the shape of the curve. Jump means that the envelope continues at the same level as the first node on the envelope line; then when it reaches the second node, it jumps immediately to that value.

- Nodes can snap to grid, or you can turn off the grid to move nodes around freely.

- Click on the line or curve between two nodes; then drag up or down to move the entire curve or line up or down. If you Ctrl-click or Shift-click on multiple nodes to select multiple lines or curves, then clicking on the line or curve between *any* two nodes of the group moves all the lines or curves up or down (see Figure 19.6). Note that these nodes do not have to be contiguous; any line where the beginning and ending nodes are selected will move together.

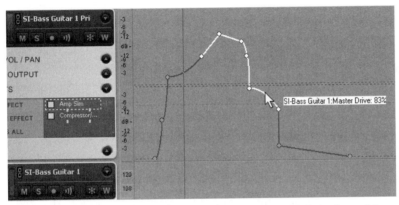

Figure 19.6   Multiple nodes have been selected, so all the selected lines (as highlighted in white) move together when you click and move any one line.

- To delete a single node, click on it to select it and then hit your keyboard's Del key or right-click on the node and select Delete Node from the pop-up menu.

- To delete multiple nodes, Shift-click or Ctrl-click on the nodes to be deleted. Then hit the Del key or right-click on any of the selected nodes and choose Delete Node from the pop-up menu.

- To select a range of nodes, first make sure the track is active (for example, click on the track icon); then drag across the Timeline for the desired range.

- To copy a track or bus envelope, select the range of nodes to be copied (see the previous bullet point), and then right-click within the track and choose Edit > Copy (or press Ctrl+C). In the dialog box that appears, uncheck all boxes except Track/Bus Automation and then click on OK (see Figure 19.7). The envelope data will go to the clipboard.

- When pasting an envelope, select the track where you want to paste the data and then choose Edit > Paste (or press Ctrl+V). You can do this from the Edit menu or from the context menu obtained by right-clicking in the track. In the dialog box that appears, click on Advanced to reveal the options for what you want to paste. Check Track/Bus

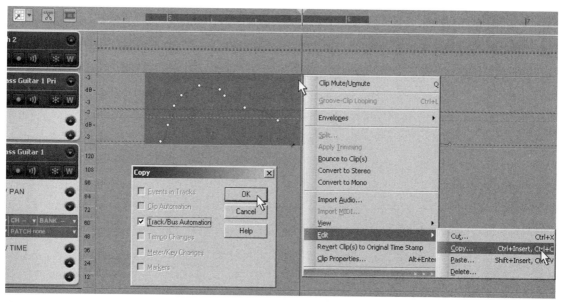

Figure 19.7   Selecting an envelope range to copy, choosing Edit > Copy, and then checking the Track/Bus Automation box copies the selected envelope range.

Automation (or Clip Automation if appropriate, as described later). Also note that you can paste a particular number of repetitions, place the data in a different track or bus, choose how the new data affects old data, and more (see Figure 19.8).

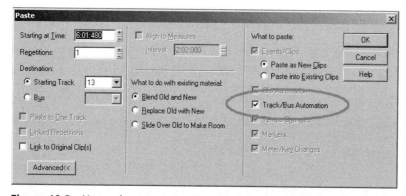

Figure 19.8   Not only can you paste a track/bus automation envelope, you also can set the time where you want to paste it (defaults to the Now time), whether you want multiple/repeated pastes, whether you want to blend the pasted data with existing data, and so on.

- You can select a clip's envelope(s) while selecting a clip or select the clip without any envelope(s), depending on which cursor you choose. Go to the leftmost button in the Track view toolbar, click on the down arrow next to the cursor button, and either check or uncheck Select Track Envelopes with Selected Clips (see Figure 19.9).

Figure 19.9 When selecting a clip, you can choose whether any track envelopes are selected along with the clip.

■ If there are so many envelopes that the track starts to get cluttered, right-click on the envelope and choose Hide Envelope from the pop-up menu (or delete the envelope if you want it to go away permanently). Or, right-click on the track and choose Envelopes > Show Track Envelopes (see Figure 19.10). Click on the envelopes you want to hide or show. (Each envelope box is a toggle; the box next to the envelope name looks "pushed in" when visible and flat when hidden.) To show the envelopes again, follow the same path, but this time click on the names or boxes of envelopes that are hidden.

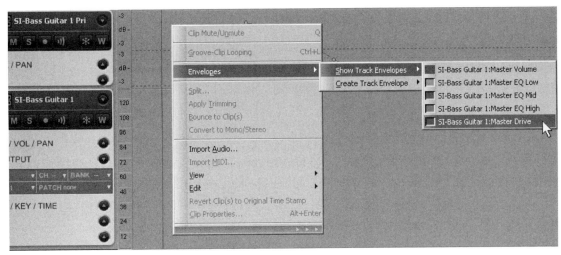

Figure 19.10 You can choose to hide envelopes if the track gets too cluttered with envelopes.

■ SONAR Home Studio has an option to assign an envelope to a different parameter. Right-click on the envelope or envelope node, select Assign Envelope, and then select the appropriate destination. The Reassign Envelope window will appear; the top line shows the current assignment, and below that, there's a list of alternate assignments. Choose the new parameter you want the envelope to control (see Figure 19.11) and then click on OK.

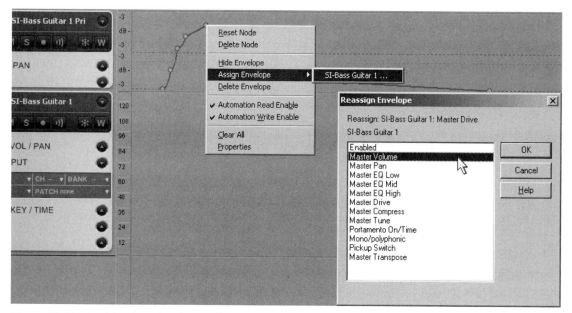

Figure 19.11   In this example, the Studio Instruments bass master drive envelope is being reassigned to the master volume envelope.

Do we actually *need* this kind of flexibility? As one example of how you'd use the copy envelope function, after recording a lead vocal and using envelopes to get rid of noise between phrases and such, I decided to double the vocal by singing it again. After singing the part, I copied the level envelope to the new vocal, and it did a great job of getting rid of the noise and trimming the levels—I needed to make only a few small tweaks.

Another example of envelope copying involved two rhythm guitar parts playing power chords in opposite channels. I wanted to add some rhythmic "chopping" effects, so I did that for four measures on one of the tracks and then copied the envelope to other parts in the track where it would sound good. Then I copied the same pattern, but offset by an eighth note, into the other channel so there was a cool panning/chopping effect.

Clip Envelopes

Envelopes last for the entire duration of a track. However, SONAR Home Studio also offers clip envelopes for gain and pan that affect only individual clips. In most other respects, they are like track or bus envelopes in that you can add nodes, delete nodes, show or hide envelopes, and so on. (One difference is that you cannot copy a clip envelope independently of the events within a clip.) Also note that these envelopes are independent of whatever is happening with the track envelopes. For example, you might want to add a radical stuttering effect to a clip through clip automation but have it fade out over a time specified by a track envelope. Audio clips have automatable pan and gain (see Figure 19.12), while MIDI clips have only automatable velocity.

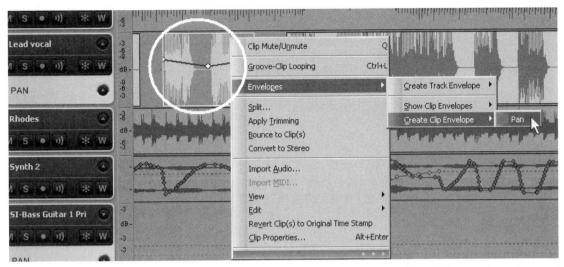

Figure 19.12   The circled clip already has a clip envelope for gain; an additional clip envelope for pan is about to be added.

Method Three: Recording Automation Data from an External MIDI Control Box

Most SONAR Home Studio parameters accept MIDI data sent from an external hardware controller (see Chapter 20 on control surfaces) or via the ACT protocol (Chapter 21, "ACT: The Key to Hands-On Control"). Using an external MIDI controller for automation follows the same basic procedure as recording a control's onscreen motion, because the onscreen control mirrors the external controller. After setting up a parameter to respond to an external control signal and enabling Automation Write, the data generated by your controller will appear as an automation envelope—just as if you'd moved an onscreen fader.

To control a parameter via a MIDI controller (usually a MIDI continuous controller, but you can also use note on, note on/off, mod wheel, RPN, or NRPN data):

1. Right-click on the parameter you want to control and select Remote Control. The Remote Control window will appear.

2. Click the radio button for the MIDI message you want to use (typically a controller, although you might want to use a MIDI note for a function such as Mute). You can enter the controller number in the associated field, but if you don't know what the number is, just move your hardware controller and then click on Learn. For example, if you want to control a parameter with a synth's data slider, but you're not sure what controller number it generates, move the slider and then click on Learn (see Figure 19.13).

3. Arm the onscreen control for automation by right-clicking on it and selecting Automation Write Enable.

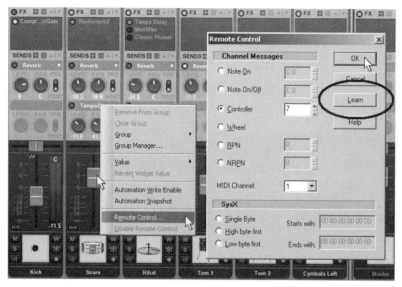

Figure 19.13   The snare track's Volume slider is being set up for control by a hardware controller that's generating Controller 7 messages over MIDI Channel 1.

4.   Click Play on the transport and move your hardware controller as desired.

5.   Click on Stop when you've finished your automation moves and uncheck Automation Write Enable so you don't record additional automation moves accidentally.

A related method also works with soft synths. For example, suppose a soft synth's filter cutoff responds to Controller 74. Set your hardware controller to generate Controller 74 and then record the controller into the MIDI track that drives the soft synth. On playback, the MIDI controller messages will drive the synthesizer and appear as standard controller data within the MIDI track.

Method Four: Snapshot Automation

Snapshot automation isn't a dynamic process, but instead it captures the automation setting at a particular Now time. This automation value remains until the next snapshot. A typical application would be if you want the levels on multiple tracks to change at the same time when a song goes into, say, the chorus. Set up all the parameters exactly how you want them at the beginning of the chorus and then take an automation snapshot of each parameter.

Here's how to take an automation snapshot for a parameter.

1.   Place the Now time where you want to enter the automation event for a parameter.

2.   Adjust the parameter (for example, fader, pan, and so on) to the desired value.

3.   Right-click on the parameter and select Automation Snapshot (see Figure 19.14). Note that you don't have to write-enable the track or bus.

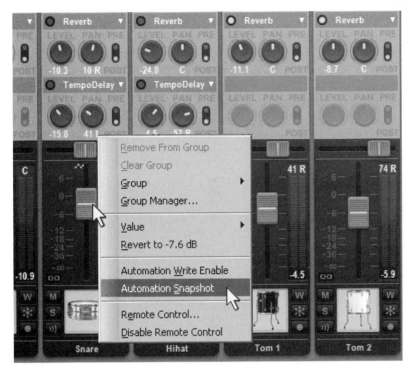

Figure 19.14   The snare track's Volume slider has been set to a position that will become an automation snapshot.

4.   If an automation envelope for the parameter already exists, a node will be added at the value you specified. If no envelope exists, one will be created with a node at the specified value.

When you play back your project, whenever the Now time goes past a snapshot, the parameter automated by the snapshot will jump to the snapshot value.

20 Control Surfaces

Computers have helped the recording process in many ways—but in some cases, they have also taken away some of the fun of recording. Processors are great, the ability to archive and sort material is wonderful, and digital audio has made tape hiss part of history. Yet many of us control this technology with a mouse, along with a keyboard that was designed well over a century ago. Compare this to a hardware mixer/recorder combination. The act of mixing used to be a physically satisfying experience—almost a performance in its own right—that was more fun than drawing envelopes with a mouse. While being able to edit with a great degree of detail is a real plus of digital systems, people often miss the all-important physical component. Fortunately, there's a simple solution.

Hardware Controller Basics

We'll define a hardware controller as a device that provides physical controls for software-based functions. This is a broad definition, but there are many types of controllers. Cakewalk was actually one of the pioneers in hardware controllers, when they partnered with Peavey Electronics on the StudioMix. This provided hands-on control for mixing, transport functions, and more by incorporating several faders for level control and knobs for panning and other functions.

A hardware controller may seem like a luxury, but there's a sound physiological reason why a controller can help the music-making process. Our brain is a dual-processing system; the two hemispheres process different material. The right brain deals with more abstract, creativity-oriented issues, while the left brain is more analytical—it follows directions and does the math.

The need for controllers becomes apparent if you do your own engineering. While playing/recording, you don't want to have to think; you want to dedicate all your brainpower to the right hemisphere, so it can get creative. Having to pause and do troubleshooting, name tracks, select channels, and so forth can kill creativity.

Also, having to do everything serially because the mouse is a monophonic device is a drag. Suppose you want to bring three channel levels up a little bit. You have to group the three together, move them, and then upgroup. It's a lot faster just to move three physical channel faders up a bit.

Computers are great for offline activity, such as editing. After you've done your audio recording, you'll be in a more analytical, left-brain mode that fits what computers do best. Even then, hardware controllers can speed up operations.

Types of Hardware Controllers

There are several types of hardware controllers (Figure 20.1).

Figure 20.1 Controllers come in all shapes, sizes, prices, and capabilities. Clockwise from upper left: Radikal Technologies SAC-2.2, Evolution UC-33, Behringer BCF2000, Native Instruments Kore, M-Audio Trigger Finger, and PreSonus FaderPort.

- **The "fits like a glove" model.** These are designed for specific programs; a good example is the VS-700C controller, which was designed for SONAR (but also works with SONAR Home Studio). The legends are program-specific, the knobs and switches have been programmed in an ergonomic manner, and there's tight integration between hardware and software. If a control surface was made for a certain piece of software, it's likely that will be the optimum hardware/software combination.

- **General-purpose DAW controllers.** While designed to be as general-purpose as possible, these often include templates for specific programs. They typically include hardware functions that are assumed to be "givens," such as tape transport-style navigation controls, channel level faders, channel pan pots, solo and mute, and so on. A controller with tons of knobs/ switches and good templates can sometimes give more fluid operation than "approved" controllers. A good example is the Mackie Control, which has become an industry standard; many non-Mackie controllers can emulate the Mackie Control protocol.

■ **Synthesizers/master keyboards.** Some synthesizers, such as the Yamaha Motif series, the Korg M3, and Roland Fantom-G have sliders and controls with templates that provide a control surface for various programs. But even those without explicit control functions can sometimes serve as useful controllers, thanks to the modulation wheel, data slider(s), footswitch, sustain switch, note number, and so on. As many programs allow controlling functions via MIDI notes, the keyboard can provide those while the knobs control parameters such as level, EQ, and so on.

■ **Really cheap controllers.** Hey, remember that old drum machine sitting in the corner that hasn't been used in three years? Dust it off, find out what MIDI notes the pads generate, and use those notes to control transport functions (maybe even arm record or mute particular tracks). A drum machine can make a compact little remote if, for example, you like recording guitar far away from the computer monitor.

And don't forget that SONAR Home Studio offers a way ("key bindings") to customize QWERTY keyboard commands. Even though these options aren't as elegant as using real hardware controllers, tying common functions to key commands is a great way to save time and improve workflow. You'll find more about key bindings in Chapter 1.

Although standard faders are useful, especially for signal processing and soft synth parameters, for mixing you really want *motorized* faders. These follow the automation moves and are touch-sensitive; you can leave the automation enabled, and the faders will follow along with whatever automation is already recorded on the track. Watching the faders move up and down as if controlled by phantom hands is also kind of magical! As soon as you grab the fader and move it, new moves overwrite old ones.

Adding a Controller to SONAR Home Studio

SONAR Home Studio has specific, "fits like a glove" support for the following controllers:

■ TASCAM US-428

■ Joystick panner

■ Red Rover

■ C.M. Labs MotorMix

■ Mackie Control C4

■ Edirol PCR-M30

■ Cakewalk VS-700

- Cakewalk VS-100

- Peavey StudioMix

- Radikal Technologies SAC-2.2 and SAC-2K

- Edirol PCR-300

- MMC (MIDI Machine Control) devices

- Mackie Control XT

- Mackie Control

Another option, Cakewalk Generic Surface, allows adapting unsupported controllers to SONAR Home Studio—so the program can basically handle anything.

Step-By-Step: Adding Mackie Control to SONAR Home Studio

Here's how you would add a Mackie Control—or a device that emulates a Mackie Control—to SONAR Home Studio.

1. The Mackie Control needs to connect via MIDI ins and outs. These can be physical 5-pin DIN connectors or USB over MIDI (Figure 20.2). So, patch the Mackie Control's MIDI out to your MIDI interface's MIDI in and the Mackie Control's MIDI in to your MIDI interface's MIDI out.

2. Boot up SONAR Home Studio.

3. Choose Options > MIDI Devices. Check the ports to which your controller connects and then click on OK.

4. Choose Options > Controllers/Surfaces.

5. Click on the Add New Controller/Surface button (the one that looks like a yellow star).

6. From the pop-up menu, select your supported control surface in the Control Surface field (in this case, Mackie Control).

7. With the In Port and Out Port pop-up menus, choose the appropriate MIDI ports from what you selected in Step 3.[

8. Click on Close to exit the Controllers/Surfaces dialog box.

While the Controllers/Surfaces dialog box is up, you can hit the F1 key to bring up more information.

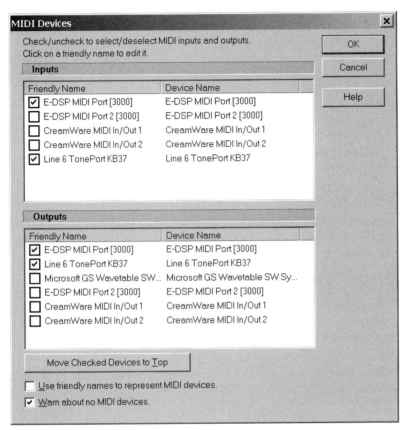

Figure 20.2 MIDI ports from an E-MU 1820 interface (using a physical MIDI connector) and a Line 6 KB37 interface (using USB over MIDI) have been enabled.

Step-By-Step: Using the Behringer BCF2000 with SONAR

The Behringer BCF2000 is an inexpensive hardware controller with eight moving faders and eight knobs; it's well suited to control volume, pan, and other parameters with SONAR Home Studio. It connects via USB and carries MIDI data over USB. Note that before doing any of the following, it's best to download and install the latest BCF2000 MIDI-USB drivers (available from the support section of the Behringer website at www.behringer.com).

1. Turn on the BCF2000 while holding down the fourth button from the left in the upper row. Keep holding this down at least until the software version (currently 1.10) shows in the display. If the version isn't at least 1.10, go to the Behringer site and follow the instructions to update your unit.

2. If the display then shows EG, turn the BCF2000 off and turn it back on *without* holding down any buttons. The display should now show MCSo, which means it's in Mackie Control emulation mode for SONAR.

3.   Check to make sure that in the row of LEDs below the four switches below the display, USB mode is illuminated. If the USB mode light is on and the display says MCSo, you're ready to open SONAR Home Studio. (Note: If the USB mode light is not on, unplug and then replug the BCF2000's USB cable, wait a bit, and open SONAR Home Studio anyway; sometimes that "wakes up" the USB connection.)

4.   Open SONAR Home Studio.

5.   Choose Options > MIDI Devices.

6.   If you've downloaded the latest drivers, the BCF2000's MIDI ports will show up as BCF2000. Check BCF2000 for both the input and output device; then click on OK.

7.   Go to Options > Controllers/Surfaces.

8.   Click on the Add New Controller/Surface button.

9.   Under Controller/Surface, select Mackie Control—*not* Mackie Control XT or Mackie Control C4. Also select BCF2000 for the Input and Output Port parameters.

10. Verify that in the Controllers/Surfaces window, the Controller Surface field shows Mackie Control, and the In Port and Out Port show BCF2000. Check WAI as well, so the Where Am I function (which, in Track view, places a colored strip to the left of the channels being controlled) is enabled. If all is well, click on Close.

11. Choose a track that has some audio in it and click on the W (Write Automation) button.

12. Click on Play and move the BCF2000 fader associated with that track.

13. On playback, the fader should move to reflect your automation moves. (You might want to click on the W button again to turn off writing, just so you don't hit anything accidentally and change the automation.)

Also note that you can set up the BCF2000 and several other hardware controllers as an ACT controller. This is a whole other type of control, so refer to Chapter 21, "ACT: The Key to Hands-On Control," for more information on ACT.

MIDI Remote Options

The most complete control option is using a supported control surface, as described earlier. But what if you just want some hands-on control over some crucial parameters while mixing?

In the Track or Console view, you can control gain, volume, pan, aux send levels and pans, the aux send Pre/Post switch, phase invert, and the Interleave (stereo/mono) switch. Controls can respond to a wide variety of MIDI messages, including SysEx. The Learn function is particularly handy if you're not sure what controller number a particular piece of hardware generates. To set up a parameter for remote control:

1.   Right-click on the parameter you want to control (Figure 20.3).

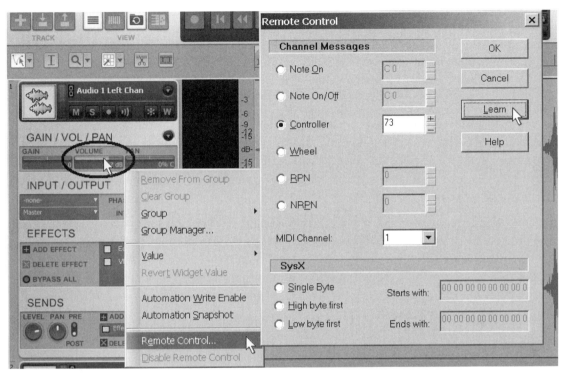

Figure 20.3   Right-clicking on the Volume control (circled) brings up a context menu; choosing Remote Control brings up the Remote Control window. In this example, MIDI Controller 73 was moved and then the Learn button was clicked. So, MIDI Controller 73 will now control Channel 1's Volume control.

2.   If it can be remote-controlled, Remote Control will be available; select it, and the Remote Control window will appear. (If the parameter is already assigned, there will also be a Disable Remote option in the context menu.)

3.   This window is where you assign a controller to the parameter. Choose Note On, Note On/Off, Controller, Wheel, RPN, or NRPN. When using a controller, you can just move the controller from one extreme to another and back again and then click on Learn. The Remote Control box will indicate the controller number.

As you vary the hardware controller's physical knob, the associated parameter should change in tandem. You can also create automation this way by proceeding with standard automation techniques (right-click on the parameter and select Automation Write Enable), as described in Chapter 19. If you initiate Play, moving the control generates a standard automation envelope.

Also note that you can vary several parameters with one controller. Simply assign each parameter to the same controller.

Using Control Surfaces

To me, the main advantage of using hardware faders is the ability to add real-time, spontaneous dynamics. I love pumping that single snare drum that hits on the offbeat just before the chorus kicks in, but there's more to dynamics than that.

Adding small rhythmic "pushes" to the level creates a more animated, lively mix. Unlike pitch discrimination, the ear isn't all that sensitive to small level changes. Thus, these small variations are felt rather than heard. Although many musicians are satisfied to draw in level changes with a mouse, they'll never convince me that the mix will have the same degree of animation as one where you make on-the-fly, spontaneous decisions about which tracks should dominate or lay back further in the track.

Once you've set up a hardware controller, try to stick to a particular setup and program. Spend some time optimizing the control arrangements, but past a certain point, leave things alone and learn the functions so they become second nature. Soon you'll find yourself flying around the controls instead of moving a mouse around and pointing to things on a screen. The more fluid you can make the recording process, the happier your right brain will be...and when your right brain's happy, everything flows better.

21 ACT: The Key to Hands-On Control

Ever wished that you could use your favorite control surface to change not just mixer controls, but also effects plug-in parameters and virtual instrument settings? Apparently someone at Cakewalk wished that too, because ACT (*Active Controller Technology*) is SONAR Home Studio's way of mapping parameters—effect settings, virtual instrument controls, mixer faders, pan pots, and the like—to a particular hardware controller. Whatever has the focus is what gets controlled at that moment. For example, if the Modfilter effect has the focus, then your hardware controls that. On the other hand, if the Console view has the focus, then the controller affects the mixer controls.

How ACT Works: Under the Hood

A plug-in will show up under ACT if the plug-in has automatable parameters and ACT can access the automation. So far, ACT works with every automatable VST plug-in I've used; DirectX plug-ins have to expose true DirectX 8 automation parameters (as opposed to MIDI control parameters). But you needn't concern yourself with that, because a plug-in will be accessible by ACT or not—in either case, the reason doesn't matter.

When you give focus to a plug-in, SONAR Home Studio looks at the ACT data to see whether there's a specific mapping of your surface to that particular plug-in. If there is no learned mapping, SONAR Home Studio looks at a second set of data that has generic data (including preferred parameters and preferred control type—rotary, slider, or switch) for various plug-ins. If the plug-in has an entry in this file, SONAR Home Studio does its best to match the parameters to your control surface.

If you use ACT's Learn function (as described later in this chapter) to set up your own mappings, SONAR Home Studio remembers those mappings and modifies a generic data file to take the learned preferences into account. This is really considerate, because if you add a new control surface at some point, the generic mapping will try to map the parameters to the control types you've chosen.

If there's no generic data or learned data available, SONAR Home Studio tries to match particular parameters to appropriate control types. For example, even a plug-in that has no

ACT data will typically have its Enable parameter assigned to a switch. I was pleasantly surprised that almost anything I called up had its parameters show up in ACT.

To use ACT in a way that truly helps your workflow, it helps to customize it for your own needs. I don't think the main reason ACT exists is to assign *every* single parameter to a control, even though it pretty much can. For me, the best use of ACT is to set up a consistent set of controls for the options I use the most. For example, with almost all synths, I'm into tweaking filter cutoff and envelope attack, decay, and release times. Therefore, I've used ACT's Learn function to assign these to the *same knobs* for all the soft synths I use.

Getting Your ACT Together

In the following examples of how to use ACT, we'll use the Behringer BCF2000 control surface with motorized faders. However, the same basic principles apply to using any control surface with ACT. (With the BCF2000, I first installed the various BCF2000 drivers, which showed up under Options > MIDI Devices as BCF2000 for MIDI in and MIDI out.)

Important: In Chapter 20 on control surfaces, we also used the BCF2000 as an example of how to use a control surface when mixing. *However, this is not the same as ACT.* For example, when used strictly as a control surface, a controller's motorized faders can respond to fader movements you make onscreen because communication with SONAR Home Studio is bidirectional. This isn't the case with ACT, where the control surface simply sends commands to SONAR Home Studio. As a result, I'll use the BCF2000's native Control mode rather than the Mackie Emulation mode used in the control surfaces chapter and describe how to start up the BCF2000 in native Control mode. Although I'm describing how to use a specific controller, remember that other controllers follow a similar procedure.

1. Turn on the BCF2000 while holding down the first button from the left in the upper row. Keep holding this down at least until the software version (currently 1.10) shows in the display. If the version isn't at least 1.10, go to the Behringer site at www.behringer.com and follow the instructions to update your unit.

2. If the display then shows EG, turn the BCF2000 off and turn it back on *without* holding down any buttons. The display should now show bC, which means it's in standard Behringer Control mode.

3. Make sure that in the row of LEDs under the four switches below the display, USB Mode is illuminated. If the USB Mode light is on, you're ready to open SONAR Home Studio. (Note: If the USB Mode light is not on, unplug and then plug the BCF2000's USB cable, wait a bit, and open SONAR Home Studio anyway; sometimes that "wakes up" the USB connection.)

4. Open SONAR Home Studio.

5. Select Options > MIDI Devices and check BCF2000 under the Inputs and Outputs field. You can check multiple inputs and outputs if needed (for example, if you have a keyboard hooked up to a different MIDI input). After making your assignments, click on OK.

6. You now need to designate your controller as an ACT controller surface. Choose Options > Controllers/Surfaces and then click on the Add New Controller/Surface button. (It looks like a little gold star.) A dialog box shows up that lets you choose the desired controller/surface; select ACT MIDI Controller, not the name of your particular hardware controller. Also, choose the device's MIDI Input and Output Ports in this dialog box (see Figure 21.1), which in this case should say BCF2000. Click on OK in the Controller/Surface Settings box; then after making your assignments, click on Close in the Controllers/Surfaces box.

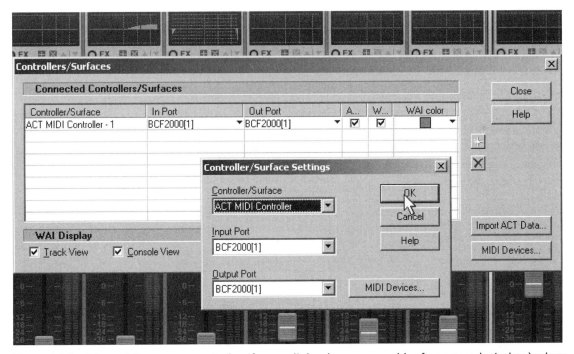

Figure 21.1   After adding a new control surface, a dialog box appears (the foreground window) where you can specify that your controller/surface should serve as an ACT MIDI controller, as well as specify the input and output MIDI ports. After doing this, you'll see the ACT MIDI controller listed under Connected Controllers/Surfaces (in the background window). Both ACT and WAI are checked, for reasons explained in the text.

Now your control surface is connected. ACT has templates for several commercially available control surfaces (if not, you can use a generic template), but it's important to use the controller preset around which ACT based its template. Fortunately, SONAR Home Studio makes the process pretty painless.

1. Call up the ACT MIDI Controller window by choosing Tools > ACT MIDI Controller. A dialog box will appear.

2. From the Presets drop-down menu, choose the controller you want to use (see Figure 21.2). There are sometimes notes next to the controller name, such as the preset ACT wants to see. The BCF2000 preset has a custom designation, which means that SONAR Home Studio can send MIDI data to the BCF2000 and create a preset in the BCF2000 that's ideal for ACT.

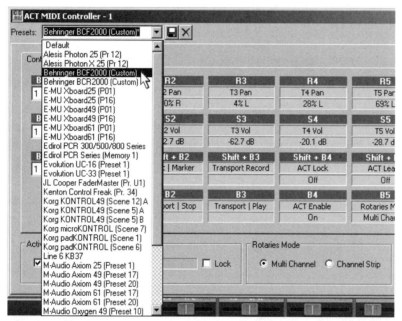

Figure 21.2 One of SONAR Home Studio ACT's features is preset templates for many popular controllers.

3. To send the data for the custom preset, click on the Options tab. The Comments field shows notes about the BCF2000. (Always check out these comments, regardless of the controller!) Click on the Send button under MIDI Initialization Messages, and SONAR Home Studio will send SysEx to the BCF2000 (see Figure 21.3). I sent it into Preset 9, as recommended by the comments, and then saved the preset at the BCF2000. It takes a while to send the preset data; be patient. When the BCF2000 display returns to the preset number, the transfer is complete.

When you choose a controller, SONAR Home Studio makes certain assumptions about it. For the BCF2000, it assumes (correctly, of course) that there are eight rotary controls, eight sliders,

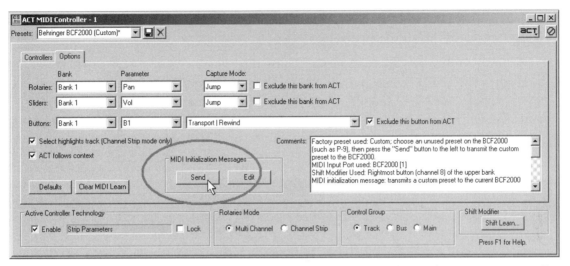

Figure 21.3 The Options tab has a lot going on. You can use it to send MIDI data to some controllers, choose a particular control surface, and select a capture mode. With the BCF2000, clicking on Send transmits preset data that's designed specifically for controlling SONAR Home Studio. Also note the Enable button in the lower-left corner—make sure it's checked before you attempt to use ACT.

eight buttons, and a "Shift" key so you can get eight more options by using Shift in conjunction with a button. This is a pretty typical configuration. Because you'll likely want more parameters available for control, there are multiple banks for the various hardware controls (for example, four banks for the sliders).

Also under the Options tab, there's a Capture Mode field with a choice of Match or Jump.

- With Match selected, the hardware controller needs to match the existing programmed value before it will change. In other words, suppose your fader in SONAR Home Studio is set to 0.0, and the fader on your controller is at –20. If you move the fader, there will be no change in SONAR Home Studio's fader until the hardware controller hits 0.0, at which point the two values "match," so now when you move the fader, SONAR Home Studio will follow along.

- With Jump selected, as soon as you move the fader, SONAR Home Studio jumps immediately to that value (in this example, from 0.0 to –20).

You can choose a different capture mode for the bank of eight rotary controls and the bank of eight sliders. This is particularly appropriate for the BCF2000, as the rotary controls are "endless encoders" and suitable for controlling synth parameters. Thus, if these are set to Match and you want to do something like tweak filter cutoff frequency, you won't experience any jumps from the existing value to the new value; there will be a smooth transition.

If you move controls and the ACT parameters don't change, there are two main reasons (other than improper setup) why this may be the case.

■ The Capture Mode option under the Options tab may be in Match mode, and the controls haven't matched their associated values yet.

■ Sometimes, ACT forgets its assignments. To fix this, choose Tools > ACT MIDI Controller so that the ACT MIDI Controller window appears (see Figure 21.4). Click on the unresponsive parameter's cell (for example, T1 Pan). The parameter name will change to MIDI Learn, and all other cells will go blank. Turn the control you want to associate with this parameter, and SONAR will "learn" (or relearn) the assignment. Repeat as necessary.

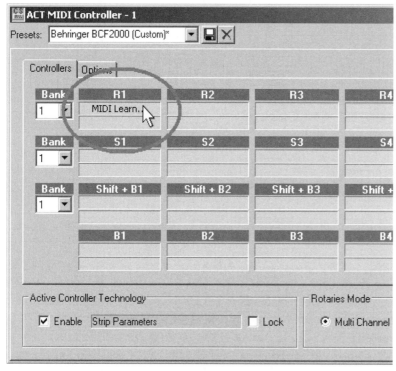

Figure 21.4 The parameter controlled by rotary control R1 is about to be reassigned to whatever control is moved next. Note that if you click on the label above the cell, you can rename it.

Using the MIDI Learn function also lets you control multiple parameters with one hardware control. Click on one parameter's cell, and when it goes into MIDI Learn mode, move your hardware controller. Then click on another parameter's cell, and when it shows MIDI Learn, move the same hardware controller. Now the hardware controller will control both parameters.

The Options tab offers some other important options.

■ ACT Follows Context means that even if a plug-in is in front, clicking on a track will allow ACT to control track parameters. I'd recommend keeping this checked.

■ Note the Exclude This Bank from ACT check boxes. Checking a box means that a particular bank will not follow the focus. For example, if you want to use the rotaries to control plug-in parameters but reserve the sliders exclusively for Console view mixing, you'd exclude the Sliders bank that controls volume from ACT.

The Fun Part: Making the Controllers Wiggle

We'll talk about controlling Track and Console view parameters before we get into plug-ins.

There's some intelligence built into the way SONAR Home Studio handles ACT, although it can be a little confusing at first because sometimes ACT makes decisions for you. For example, the first time I fired up the ACT MIDI controller plug-in and checked out the Controllers tab, the pan and volume parameters were available for only four tracks, even though there were eight slots in the ACT MIDI Controller window. Eventually it dawned on me that was because *the project had only four tracks.* As soon as I inserted more tracks, additional pan and volume assignments showed up until all eight slots were filled.

If there are more than eight tracks, SONAR Home Studio's WAI (Where Am I?) feature comes into play. This places a colored band alongside the tracks that are being controlled (to the left of tracks in Track view; see Figure 21.5), which in most cases is a contiguous group of eight tracks.

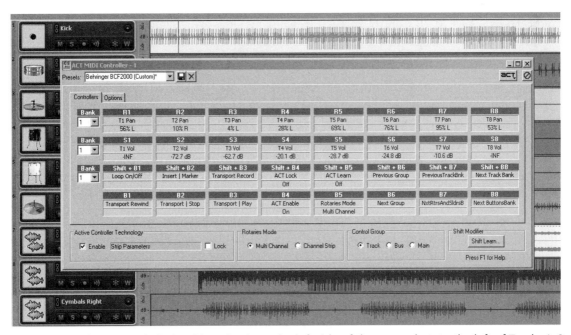

Figure 21.5   The WAI strip is the thin strip along the left side of the screenshot, to the left of Tracks 1–8. Correspondingly, the ACT Controller window shows that rotary controls R1–R8 control pan for T1–T8 (Tracks 1–8) and sliders S1–S8 control volume for T1–T8.

In the Controllers/Surfaces dialog box under Options, you can choose whether the WAI display shows up in the Track view, Console view, neither, or both by checking the appropriate boxes; however, I've never been able to get this to work properly in Console view.

If you want to control a different group of tracks, just drag the WAI strip. Assuming an eight-channel controller, you could drag the WAI so that the controller affects Tracks 7–14, 9–16, or any other contiguous combination of eight tracks. However, you're not limited to eight tracks: If you hook up two eight-channel controllers, one could control Channels 1–8, and the second could control 9–16.

Another useful feature is that you can shift the controller among fader groups: Track (which we've already looked at), Bus (where the faders and pans affect buses), and Main (as expected, controllers affect the main outs). In the Tools > ACT MIDI Controller window, Options tab, there's a section called Control Group where you can select among these. In the BCF2000, they're mapped to button B6, so you can step through the different groups just by clicking on this button.

Using ACT with Effects

Suppose you want to control the Modfilter plug-in parameters with a hardware controller. Once the effect has the focus, it will already be premapped to your controller. When you move knobs, panel knobs on the Modfilter should move, too. If not, with the Modfilter still having the focus, choose Tools > ACT MIDI Controller to see which parameters are assigned to which controllers. If a controller doesn't change the parameter, you may need to reassign the controller to the parameter cell using the Learn function, as described previously.

However, we're going to get a little controversial here, as I'm going to break away from the conventional wisdom on how to use ACT. Many SONAR Home Studio users are into learning the various existing ACT assignments, and they try to keep all those assignments in mind as they move from plug-in to plug-in. However, the parameters aren't always mapped to controls the way you'd like. For example, if you call up the Compressor/Gate and move the BCF2000's eight rotary controls, going from left to right on the controls doesn't go through the parameters from left to right on the Compressor/Gate.

If you choose Tools > ACT MIDI Controller, the Controllers window will show which controls affect which parameters for whatever has the focus. But what if you want different control assignments? This kind of task involves using another aspect of ACT's Learn function to alter the standard "generic" data.

1. Click on the ACT button toward the upper right of the effect or the ACT MIDI Controller window. (It doesn't matter which one; they're duplicates.)

2. Move the parameters you want to control *in the order you want to assign them to hardware controllers*. For example, with the Compressor/Gate, I moved Attack,

Release, the three Compressor controls, the three Gate controls, and Level. You can't just click on these; you actually have to change their existing values.

3.   Move the hardware controllers you want to assign to these parameters, again in order. For example, to control the first eight parameters going from left to right with the rotary knobs and the level with the master slider, you'd move rotary knobs 1–8 and the master slider, in that order.

4.   After you've chosen your parameters to assign and your controllers, disable ACT Learn by clicking on the ACT button again.

5.   A dialog box will come up that says "[X] parameters and [X] controls were touched. Do you want to keep these assignments?" (see Figure 21.6). If X represents the number of parameters and controls you moved, click on Yes. Otherwise, click on No and start over.

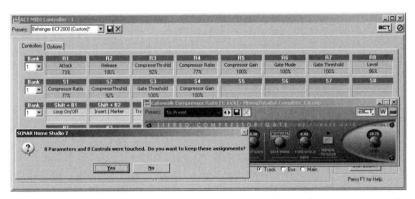

Figure 21.6 The Compressor/Gate parameters have been remapped from the default settings to something that seemed more logical, at least to me. Note how they're mapped to the rotary controls and, for convenience, to the sliders as well.

Because the sliders weren't doing anything when the Compressor/Gate had the focus, I also mapped them to the Compressor/Gate parameters so I could reach for either a fader or a slider and get the same results.

So what's controversial about this approach? I take it one step further and do a sort of "ACT on demand." If I'm tweaking a particular group of controls, I'll assign them to the physical controls, do my tweaks, and move on. With a few exceptions, I don't worry too much about consistency from plug-in to plug-in, and I regard most ACT mappings as temporary, to be used as needed.

It may be a little difficult to wrap your head around ACT at first. But once you have your controller set up and your assignments made as desired, and maybe you've adopted my easy "ACT on demand" approach, you'll find it can be a great way to get hands-on control over the various functions in SONAR Home Studio.

Trading ACTs This is pretty advanced stuff, but if you come up with some really great mapping for a plug-in or whatever that you want to share with someone else, there's no way to simply export that mapping and import it elsewhere. However, there are a couple of options that come close. In the Controllers/Surfaces dialog box, there's an Import ACT Data button at the lower right. Clicking on this and navigating to an XML ACT data file will merge it into your main ACT database, so if Cakewalk develops mappings in the future, you'll be able to import them.

You can also share your entire genericpluginparams.xml file with another user. (It's found under Documents and Settings > [Administrator or All Users] > Application Data > Cakewalk > ACT Data.) If you know how to edit XML, you could also edit this file down to create a smaller set of plug-ins to export.

22 Groove Clips

Suppose you have a great drum loop that was recorded at a tempo of 110 BPM, but you want to use it in a dance tune that chugs along at 125 BPM. Normally this would be a problem, but SONAR Home Studio can "compress" the time so that the 110 BPM loop plays back at 125 BPM. This could also work in the reverse manner: A faster loop could be "stretched" longer so that it plays back at a slower tempo.

Time stretching/compression lets your digital audio loops run at different tempos or follow along with tempo changes; one of SONAR Home Studio's strongest features is not just the ability to do time stretching/compression, but to do it on the fly, in real time. You can even transpose pitch in real time, so that if there's a key change in a project, the file will change pitch in tandem.

How Time Stretching Works

SONAR Home Studio's time stretching uses the principle of cutting an audio loop into "slices," each of which represents a discrete sound, sound group (for example, kick drum and snare hitting at the same time), or specific rhythmic interval, such as a sixteenth note. When you change a loop's tempo, each slice's start point shifts to accommodate the change. For example, if the original loop is at 130 BPM and there are slices every sixteenth note, if you change tempo to 140 BPM, the slice start points will move closer together to retain a sixteenth-note relationship.

SONAR Home Studio calls a file that has been sliced to allow for time stretching/compression a *Groove Clip*. (Note that there are actually two types of Groove Clips: audio and MIDI. We'll cover audio Groove Clips first and then the MIDI version.)

During the process of changing where the slice points occur, SONAR Home Studio adds or removes samples to lengthen or shorten the loop, respectively, and then cross-fades these segments to smooth any transitions within the loop. Speeding up generally truncates or time compresses the decay, because the ear is most interested in the sound of an attack. When slowing down, the decays are extended to lengthen the slice accordingly. The key to successful time stretching with rhythmic loops is making sure the slices fall exactly at attack transients, which tend to define the rhythm, and nowhere else. There must also be enough slices to define the beat, but not so many that the loop gets cut up excessively, which may create sonic artifacts or other glitches during the stretching process.

SONAR Home Studio can read "ACIDized" files (in other words, ones that have pitch and tempo information embedded in them according to Sony ACID's file format; Sony ACID was the first program to allow this kind of on-the-fly stretching). These should already have been optimally sliced and will follow tempo (and pitch) changes without requiring any type of preparation. However, a non-ACIDized file will not have these time-stretching properties until you convert it into a Groove Clip (Figure 22.1). This automatically adds slicing markers, which you can edit later to optimize the stretching process. (Note that you can not only load ACIDized files into SONAR Home Studio, you can load SONAR Home Studio Groove Clips into ACID.)

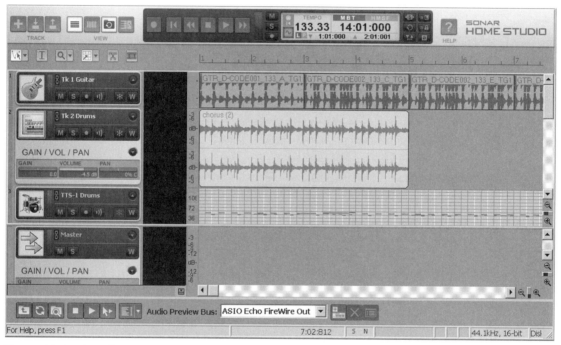

Figure 22.1 The Clips in Track 1 were recorded at 133.33 BPM, so they work perfectly with the song, whose tempo is also 133.33 BPM. The Clip in Track 2 was originally slower and lasted 4 measures and 2 beats. But note the Clip's rounded corners, indicating this is a Groove Clip instead of a standard audio file. It has been time compressed so that it takes up exactly four measures and fits the song tempo.

Bringing Loops into SONAR Home Studio

There are several ways to bring a file or loop into SONAR Home Studio:

- Drag and drop from the desktop into an audio track. The file starts at the point where you release the mouse button, consistent with any snap you've set.

- Drag and drop from the desktop into a blank space in the Track view. This automatically creates a track, and the file starts where you release the mouse button, consistent with any snap you've set.

■ Click on the Import a Digital Audio File button in the main toolbar (Figure 22.2).

Figure 22.2 A button on the main toolbar is dedicated to importing digital audio files.

■ Choose File > Import > Audio and then navigate to where the file resides. Double-click on the file (or click on it once and click on Open), and the file will end up in the active track, starting at the Now time.

■ Right-click in the Clips pane track and select Import Audio from the context menu.

■ Use the Loop Explorer, as described next.

The Loop Explorer

The Loop Explorer (View > Loop Explorer, type Alt+1, or click on the main toolbar's Loop Explorer button; see Figure 22.3) provides a way to locate and audition loops (as well as standard audio files) and see their properties.

Figure 22.3 There's a dedicated button on the main toolbar to call up the Loop Explorer view.

If the loop is a Groove Clip or ACIDized file, it will play back at the project tempo as you audition it.

If you don't see the Loop Explorer, you may need to click on the splitter bar (Figure 22.4) and drag upward.

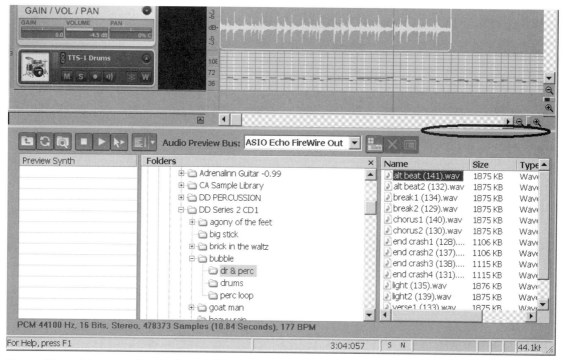

Figure 22.4 A loop has been selected for auditioning. Double-clicking on the loop inserts it in the Clips pane. Part of the splitter bar has been circled for clarity; click on this and drag up if you don't see the Loop Explorer.

The Loop Explorer is laid out like Windows Explorer, with a tree structure in the middle for navigation; files show up in the right pane. (The left pane is for auditioning MIDI files.) When you click on an audio file, its properties (sample rate, bit resolution, mono/stereo, number of samples, duration in seconds, original tempo, and, if applicable, the original key) appear in a line of text at the bottom of the window.

The Loop Explorer toolbar has five main sections (Figure 22.5).

The three buttons to the left relate to navigation. From left to right, these are:

- Go up one level in the tree

- Refresh (for example, if you've changed a sample library CD-ROM or DVD-ROM)

- Call up Windows Explorer

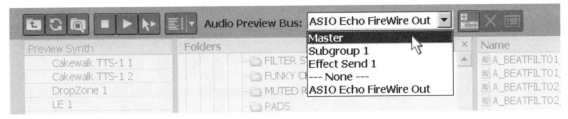

Figure 22.5 The Loop Explorer has a toolbar in the upper left with 10 buttons. There's also a drop-down menu for choosing the audio bus over which you can preview loops and audio files. In this example, audio is being assigned to the master bus.

The next three buttons to the right control auditioning. Again from left to right:

- **Play.** Click this to play the selected file.

- **Stop.** Click this to stop the selected file from playing.

- **Auto.** When this option is enabled, clicking on a file causes it to play automatically.

Once playing starts, unless Auto is enabled, a file will continue to loop until you select another file or click on Stop. Either of these actions stops the file from playing. If Auto is enabled, the only way to get the Loop Explorer to shut up is to click on Stop.

If you double-click on a file in the Loop Explorer, the file will insert in the active track, starting at the Now time. You can also drag it into a track. What's more, you can Ctrl-click on discontiguous tracks in the Loop Explorer or Shift-click to select contiguous clips and drag all of them into the Track view at once. There's more about this in the next section, "Loop Explorer: Multitrack Mode."

The next toolbar button to the right has a drop-down menu that chooses the display mode for the right pane: Icons, List, or Details. Another item, Folders, shows/hides the middle pane. To the right of this button, the Preview Bus drop-down menu provides a list of available outputs over which you can monitor the loops.

The three buttons to the right of the Preview Bus field relate to exploring MIDI files.

Finally, note that there's a splitter bar between the left and middle panes and the middle and right panes, so you can change the proportion of the window taken up by each pane.

Loop Explorer: Multitrack Mode

The Loop Explorer window's main function is to audition loops, which you can then import into the program and, if needed, convert into Groove Clips. But you can also audition multiple loops simultaneously in this window (Figure 22.6). This is particularly good with "construction kit" sample CDs that might have several loops for snare, hi-hat, percussion, and so on; you can test the parts together to see how well they work. Similarly, you could check out how a bass loop sounds with a particular drum loop.

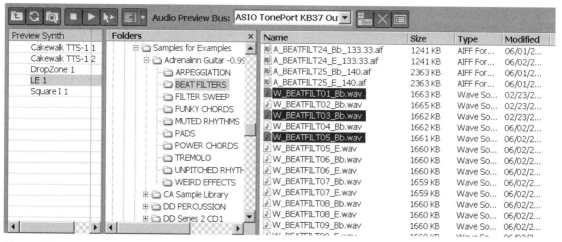

Figure 22.6 Several loops have been selected in the Loop Explorer window. Clicking on the Play button plays them all at once; if you enable Auto-Preview, additional loops play as soon as they're selected.

Unless the loops are ACIDized Groove Clip loops, you're limited to loops of the same tempo if you want them to all play together. Also, you can't include loops from more than one folder. Nonetheless, multitrack loop exploration is still a very useful technique. Here's how to do it.

1. Click on the first loop to select it.

2. Click on the Loop Explorer's Play button.

3. To add a loop, Ctrl-click on another loop in the Loop Explorer's list of files.

4. To de-select an already selected loop, Ctrl-click on it again.

I prefer to enable the Loop Explorer's Auto-Preview button, because whenever you select a loop, you'll hear it play with the others. If Auto-Preview is off, you need to hit the Play button every time you select a new loop if you want to hear it.

Multitrack loop exploration works best for loops stored on your hard drive. Loops auditioned from CD/DVD-ROMs are okay too, but because CDs and DVDs are slower than hard drives, the audio engine may stop when you add another loop, necessitating a quick click on the Play button.

Finally, after selecting all the loops you want to use, you can drag them over as a single group to the Track View pane. If there aren't enough tracks, SONAR Home Studio will create them.

Converting a Standard Clip to a Groove Clip

After importing an audio file into the Clips pane, if it's not already a Groove Clip, click on the Clip to select it and type Ctrl+L (L for *loop*). In the Track view, a Groove Clip acquires rounded corners instead of the square ones associated with regular audio clips.

When you play back a Groove Clip, if it's standard, percussive-oriented material without swing, odds are SONAR Home Studio will make a decent guess about where the slices need to go, and you'll be able to change its tempo without having to tweak. But not all Clips are so accommodating, especially when slowing down tempo. For example, suppose the Clip has a lot of swing applied to a sixteenth-note hi-hat pattern. SONAR Home Studio can place slices every sixteenth note, but the "swung" notes don't fall on that particular rhythmic grid (Figure 22.7).

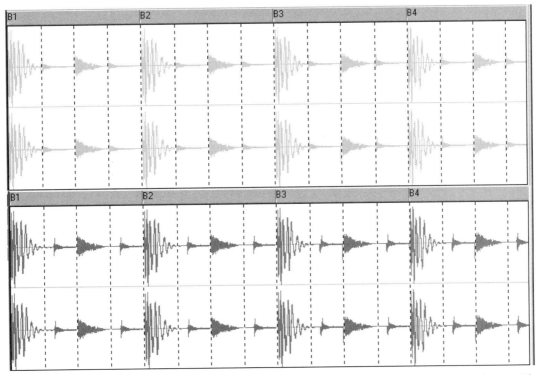

Figure 22.7   These two clips in the Loop Construction window have slices every sixteenth note. The top one has no swing, and all the drum sounds line up with the sixteenth-note grid. The lower clip has significant swing, and while the kick (the big blob of audio located at B1, B2, B3, and B4) and the open hi-hat (halfway between each kick) line up perfectly, the swung, closed hi-hat sounds do not.

Slowing down a loop where slices don't line up with attacks produces *flamming*, a sort of slapback echo sound, due to the difference between when the program thinks the hi-hat *should* hit, as opposed to when it actually *does* hit. Speeding up the loop may not sound as bad, because the flamming gets closer together—but tweaking will almost always make it sound better.

Tweaking Audio Groove Clips

The place to edit slices is the Loop Construction view (Figure 22.8), which you reach by clicking on a Groove Clip to select it and choosing Views > Loop Construction (or typing Alt+2). You can also right-click on the Groove Clip and choose View > Loop Construction.

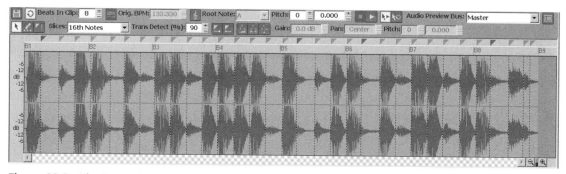

Figure 22.8 The Loop Construction window has a main view with the waveform toward the bottom, where you can see and edit slice markers. The upper section contains all the parameters available for loop construction.

The two main slice editing fields are called Slices (determines the rhythmic interval between slices), and Trans(ient) Detect (%). Higher Transient Detect percentages means SONAR Home Studio will be more sensitive to percussive attacks and therefore will add a slice at relatively low-level transients. In general, use the longest rhythmic values and lowest transient detection possible, consistent with the loop stretching properly. For most dance-oriented drum loops, eighth- or sixteenth-note slices with a transient setting of 0% to 20% works well. However, if there are significant variations (for example, the part was played by a human drummer instead of a drum machine), higher transient settings—including 100%—usually give better stretching.

Loops that don't stretch properly require editing the slice markers. Each marker has a small, triangular-shaped handle. Editing involves lining up markers with attacks to teach SONAR Home Studio the loop's precise rhythm.

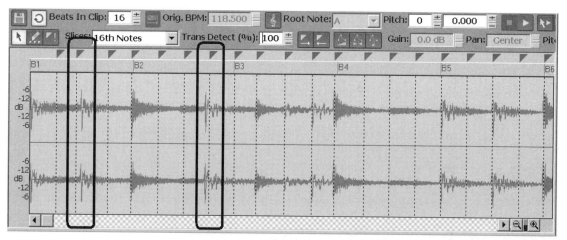

Figure 22.9 This loop was played by a human drummer, so the hits weren't always exactly on the beat. With SONAR Home Studio slicing on sixteenth notes with 100% transient detection, most of the slices fall right on transients. However, the second slice from the left and the one just before B3 (both are outlined for clarity) are not right on the beat.

Optimally, you want the marker to line up at the *precise* beginning of the transient; it's advisable to zoom in (using the + symbol toward the window's lower right) to get this as close as possible.

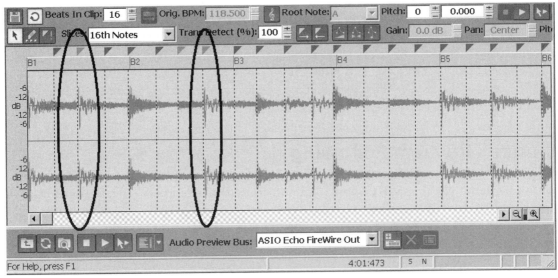

Figure 22.10   The circled markers have been moved to the precise start of a transient.

Once you move a marker, its triangle turns violet to show that it has been edited. You can also insert markers anywhere by double-clicking where you want the marker, on the same horizontal line as the other triangles. Because inserted markers are not generated automatically, they, too, will have violet handles.

High Slices and Transient Detect values may add unneeded slices during a sustained section, where no attacks exist. These may degrade the sound by splitting sounds that should be continuous, so you should remove extra slice markers. Click on the Eraser tool (Figure 22.11) and then click on a marker's handle to delete the slice.

Figure 22.11   The Eraser tool lets you delete unneeded transient markers.

All this editing may sound like a lot of work, but it's more complex to explain than it is to actually jump in and move markers around to match up with attacks. Your reward for doing so will be clips without flamming or artifacts, assuming a reasonable amount of stretching—because Groove Clips have limits to their stretching abilities. If you slow down the loop too much, you'll hear artifacts as the algorithms struggle to insert samples that extend the material. Speeding up is less problematic, because it's easier to remove existing material than to create new material that never existed. This is why pro loop-library designers often record their loops at slower tempos if possible. With good editing, you can usually increase tempos by at least 150 percent and slow down by around 15 to 20 percent.

Groove Clip Pitch Following

In addition to following tempo changes, a Groove Clip can follow pitch transposition information (in the form of a special type of marker, the project pitch marker) embedded in a project. However, to make full use of this feature, it helps to understand the relationship between the Project Pitch, Groove Clip root note, and Pitch Offset parameters. The following subsections provide an overview of how the process works.

Establishing the Project Pitch

This provides a baseline reference of the song's key against which transpositions are referenced. For example, if the project pitch is D, and you tell a Groove Clip to transpose up two semitones, the Groove Clip will play back in E.

To do this:

1. Select Insert > Meter/Key Change.
2. Under Key Signature, enter the project's key (Figure 22.12).

Defining a Groove Clip's Pitch Parameters

You can access the four parameters that relate to following pitch from the Clip Properties window (Figure 22.13). To call this up, press C while in the Loop Construction window or click on the Clip Properties button in the Loop Construction window's upper right. You can also access the pitch parameters from the Track view: Right-click on the Groove Clip, select Clip Properties, and then click on the Audio Stretching tab.

Incidentally, if you expect to cut up a loop into multiple segments, set the Follow Pitch parameters *before* you cut, so that all the segments retain the data you programmed. If you cut up the loop before setting these parameters, you'll have to enter them for every loop segment.

The four parameters are:

■ **Follow Project Pitch.** Check this box if you want the Groove Clip to follow pitch changes embedded in the project via project pitch markers that provide pitch information. Note that

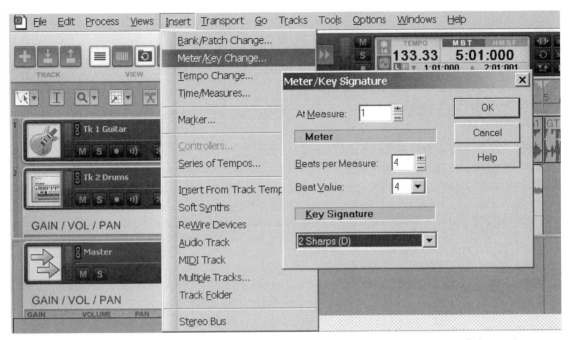

Figure 22.12 You can establish a reference pitch in SONAR Home Studio so that if the project transposes to a different key, any Groove Clips will transpose as well. In this example, the project pitch is set at D, starting at Measure 1.

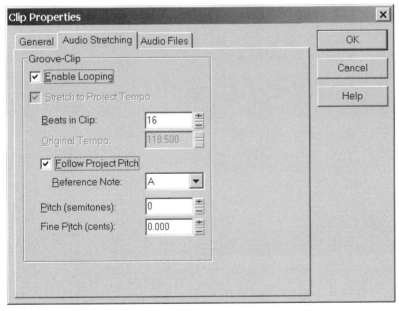

Figure 22.13 Parameters that determine whether (and how) a Groove Clip follows pitch are accessible from the Clip Properties window. Note that Enable Looping must be checked in order to have the Clip follow project pitch.

for drum parts, you will likely want to leave this unchecked, unless you want the drums' timbre to change when the project pitch changes (which can be cool sometimes as a special effect).

- **Reference Note.** Set this to the Groove Clip's original recorded key. (For example, if it was originally recorded in the key of E, select E from the drop-down menu.) Better-documented sample CDs usually include the key information for samples. Note that you can also do this from the Loop Construction window, which I'll describe shortly.

- **Pitch (Semitones).** This offsets the Groove Clip's pitch in semitones (up to +/– two octaves), regardless of whether Follow Project Pitch is enabled. For example, suppose the Groove Clip was recorded in G, the project pitch is G, Follow Project Pitch is enabled, and you set the Pitch parameter to +1. The Groove Clip will now play back at G#. If the project pitch changes to C, the Groove Clip will now play back at C#. If Follow Project Pitch is not enabled, the Groove Clip will always play back at G# (an offset of +1 compared to the original Groove Clip pitch).

- **Fine Pitch (Cents).** This offsets the Groove Clip's pitch in cents (up to +/–50.000 cents) and works exactly like Pitch Offset. This is an *invaluable* feature for loops that are slightly out of tune.

Insert Pitch Changes into the Tune

Now that we have Clips that can respond to pitch changes, let's insert some pitch change markers (Figure 22.14).

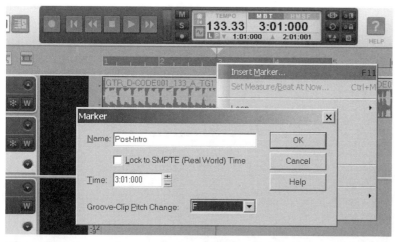

Figure 22.14 A marker is being inserted that will cause a Groove Clip to transpose to F.

Right-click on the Time Ruler at the top of the Track view's Clips pane where you want the pitch change to occur and then hit F11 (or right-click where you want the change and choose Insert Marker from the pop-up menu).

When the Marker window appears, go to the Groove Clip Pitch drop-down list and select the new pitch reference. Name the marker if desired. Click on OK, and you're finished.

Establishing the Root Pitch within the Loop Construction Window

In addition to specifying the root pitch using the Clip Properties window, you can also do this within the Loop Construction window. Note that changing the root pitch in one place automatically changes it in the other.

For melodic loops, enter the original key (the one the loop was recorded at) as follows:

1. Click on the G-clef symbol to the left of the Root Note field.

2. Specify the original key using the drop-down menu in the Root Note field (Figure 22.15).

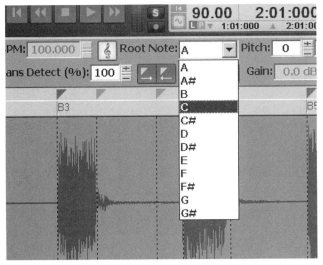

Figure 22.15 Here's the "key" to having a loop follow any key changes in the project, as set by the project pitch value.

Step-by-Step: Creating a Loop

Go to the web page for this book at www.courseptr.com/downloads and download the file W_FUNK04_Bb.WAV. Bring it into SONAR Home Studio, and let's turn it into a Groove Clip.

1. Click on the Clip and press Alt+2. The Loop Construction window will open.

2. We need to tell SONAR Home Studio how long the Clip is. Type L (or click on the Enable Looping button to the immediate left of the Beats in Clip field), and two main things happen: The number of beats appears in the Beats in Clip field (eight, in this case), and a bunch of markers appear that represent SONAR Home Studio's

guess as to where the transients should fall (Figure 22.16). Usually SONAR Home Studio gets the number of beats right, but you can enter a number in the Beats in Clip field if you need to change the default.

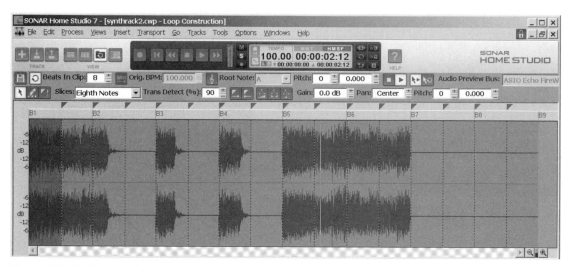

Figure 22.16   Here's what we have so far: An eight-beat loop with slices set every eighth note.

3.   Set the project tempo in the main program to 100 BPM (the same as the original loop tempo) and press Ctrl+Shift+spacebar or click on the Preview Loop button to hear what we have so far. As with the Loop Explorer, there's a drop-down menu for choosing the Audio Preview bus. Caution: Don't hit the main transport Play button when you're auditioning the loop; use only the Play button in the Loop Construction window. You won't break anything, but the loop may play at different times or play from the project and the Loop Construction window simultaneously, which may produce distortion or a sudden jump in volume.

4.   While you're at it, click on the button to the immediate right of the Preview Loop button (or type **A**) to enable Slice Auto-Preview. This lets you hear a slice if you click on it in the main Loop Construction window view. The next button to the right, if enabled, causes the selected slice to loop; leave it off for now. (Note: You can also move through the slices consecutively by using your computer's Page Up and Page Down buttons or by clicking on the Move to Previous Slice and Move to Next Slice buttons in the Loop Construction view toolbar, just to the right of the Trans Detect % field. If the Slice Auto-Preview function is enabled, you'll hear each slice as you move to it.)

5.   When you play the Clip, you'll hear that there are several guitar chords. What we want to do is put a slice at the precise beginning of each chord's attack, so that each chord lives in its own slice.

6. The Slices drop-down menu puts slice markers at specific intervals. This can save you a lot of time if you're slicing something like a drum machine pattern with a regular sixteenth-note hi-hat pattern; just set the slices to sixteenth notes, and you're probably done. In fact, if you set the Trans Detect % value to 0, slices will show up only at the interval you specified. But I'm not going to make things that simple for you, because this is a guitar part played by a human! So, we're going to add slices manually.

7. Select No Slicing from the drop-down menu. Note that SONAR Home Studio has detected three transients—the most obvious transients in the file. These are at Beats B3, B4, and B5.

8. Set the Trans Detect (%) parameter to 100 and then hit Return. This makes SONAR Home Studio more sensitive to transients, and several more slice markers will show up at these transients.

9. Now click in each slice in the waveform. You'll note that SONAR Home Studio has done a pretty good job of isolating the chords, except for the two chords that fall around Beat 6. We need to add more markers for these chords.

10. Use the horizontal zoom-in button (+) so that this slice fills most of the Loop Construction window and then add a slice at B6. To do this, double-click in the row that has the other marker triangles, right above where you want the slice. A violet triangle will appear. (Violet indicates a slice marker that's created manually, as opposed to the red, automatically generated markers.)

11. Click on the slice that ends with the marker at B6. You'll hear a chord. Now, grab the slice marker at B6 and move it a bit to the right. Click on the slice again. If you hear the next chord's attack, move the slice marker to the left—*you want the slice marker just before the start of the next chord.* Conversely, if you don't hear the start of the next chord, move the slice marker to the right until you do and then back it up just a bit.

12. Play the slice to the right of the marker you just added. We still need two more markers to mark the two chords that occur in this slice. Follow the same procedure in the previous step to place these two slice markers just before the start of the chord.

13. Now you should have something that looks like Figure 22.17. Change the project tempo to 150 BPM and preview the loop. It should have the same rhythm as the original, only faster.

14. Change the project tempo to 70 BPM and then preview the loop. This makes the digital signal processing (DSP) algorithms work a lot harder and reveals a problem: The little decays at the ends of the chords that start at B2, B3, and B4 end up getting stretched so they last longer, and therefore they sound unnatural. It's also clear that we need another slice marker at B2.

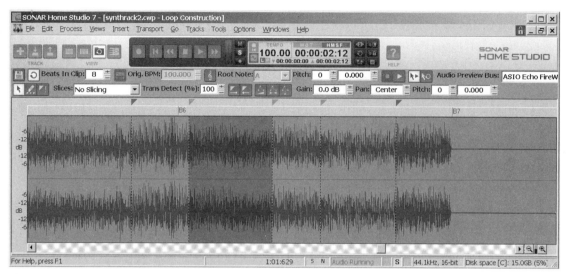

Figure 22.17 The file now has slice markers in all the right places—at the beginning of each attack transient.

15. To solve this, add another slice marker just before each of the little decays. Now play the file at 70 BPM; it sounds much better.

16. Another problem with slowing down is that sustained sections can sound uneven, because a fairly long section is being stretched. We can fix this by adding another slice marker in the middle of long sections. For example, when previewing the file at

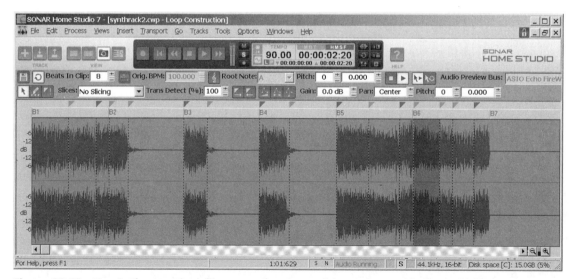

Figure 22.18 Here's the tweaked file; note the three slice markers added just before each chord's final decay. These help create a more realistic sound when slowing down the tempo. Additional slice markers have been added to prevent wavering, as described next.

70 BPM, note how the first slice has some wavering. Add a slice marker in the middle of this slice, and the wavering goes away. Try the same technique with the slice that begins at B5 as well.

You can tweak Groove Clips forever, but this one works pretty well from about 80 to 180 BPM—better than a 2:1 tempo ratio. More tweaking won't improve it by that much.

Saving Groove Clips

Although these Groove Clip settings will be saved with the project, you may want to save the file so you can call it up into a different project and have all the slice markers already sitting in the right places. Either of the following options will save the Groove Clip as an ACIDized WAV file.

- Drag the loop from the Clips pane to your desktop (or a folder on your desktop). Keep your finger on the mouse button until the file has finished copying.

- In the Loop Construction window, click on the Save Loop to WAV File (floppy disk) button.

MIDI Groove Clips

Cakewalk was the first to apply ACID-style thinking to MIDI clips, creating what they call *MIDI Groove Clips*. You can convert any ordinary MIDI clip into a MIDI Groove Clip by selecting the clip and choosing Edit > Groove Clip Looping or typing Ctrl+L. You can recognize a MIDI Groove Clip from its beveled edges, just like an audio Groove Clip.

MIDI Groove Clips have a couple really useful features. If you roll them out to create multiple iterations, you can modify any iteration without affecting the others. This is great for drum grooves, where you need a basic pattern but also want to add variations. But if you *want* variations in one pattern to affect subsequent ones:

1. Split the rolled-out Clip at the beginning of the iteration you want to use. (Place the Now time at the Split point and then type **S.**)

2. Click on the end of the Groove Clip to the right of this split point and roll it back in, until the Clip is the length of the part you want to loop.

3. Make your changes to that part, and when you roll it back out, all subsequent iterations will reflect the changes you made.

However, note that this technique can also have unintended consequences: If you make a bunch of edits in a series of Groove Clip iterations and then roll back into the original clip, you'll lose all your edits. To keep all the edits, turn the Groove Clip back into a regular clip by selecting the entire Groove Clip and choosing Edit > Bounce to Clip(s).

Advanced Looping Techniques

Now that we've covered the basics of looping, let's cover some advanced techniques that can turn looping into a highly creative tool.

Gain, Pan, and Pitch Envelopes

SONAR Home Studio adds a "processing" element to loops, thanks to gain, pan, and pitch envelopes (Figure 22.19). These aren't envelopes in the sense of having attack and decay; you set the value on a per-slice basis. For example, a slice can be panned in the stereo field, but you can't change the pan position within the slice. (Of course, you can still use track envelopes in the track containing the loop to add continuous variable changes.)

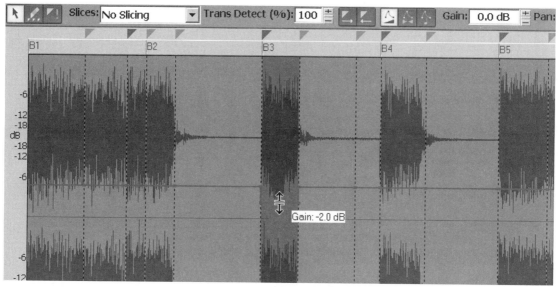

Figure 22.19   A slice's gain is being reduced by −2.0 dB.

The edits can be done graphically or by entering numbers in fields. For graphic editing, there are three toolbar buttons below the Root Note field, each of which corresponds to show/hide for an envelope. (Each envelope is a different color.) Click on the envelope within the slice and then drag up or down to edit.

The numeric fields to the right of the toolbar buttons for gain, pan, and pitch also apply to the selected slice. The only significant difference is that when working graphically, you can change pitch only in semitone steps. When doing so numerically, there is a field for semitones and another field for fine tuning.

There are some limitations—gain changes might produce pops if there are significant level shifts—but being able to change these parameters allows for very creative options. For example, the gain envelope is useful for applications such as bringing up particular kick or snare hits. Changing pitch can add really interesting effects to individual slices; using extreme amounts of loop transposition can make very electronic, "buzzy" sounds even with ordinary drum sounds (such as congas).

However, note that if you save a loop with this kind of processing, the processing parameter values aren't saved with the file. (They are, however, saved with the project, so when you call up the project, any processing within the loop remains intact.) So if you bring the loop back into SONAR Home Studio or any other program that reads ACIDized files, you'll hear the raw, looped file without gain, pitch, or pan changes. The only way to save these changes as part of the loop is to bounce it to a track (choose Edit > Bounce to Track(s); this creates a standard WAV file) and then re-edit the copy into a Groove Clip.

Creating Truly Bizarre Loops

The Groove Clip function isn't just a way to loop; it's also a way to process rhythmic tracks in totally bizarre ways. Try out these effects; you won't believe your ears!

1. Call up the Loop Construction window.

2. Set the main Pitch parameter (to the left of the Root Note field) to +24.

3. Set Trans Detect to 100%.

4. Press Play or Preview to start the loop playing.

5. Experiment with the Slicing slider. Start with 64th notes for the most robotic/metallic effect, then try 32nd, sixteenth, eighth, and so on. Each slice setting produces a different type of unusual effect.

Although a +24 pitch shift is a somewhat "magic" pitch parameter, +12 also produces useful effects. On the other hand, −12 and −24 give weirdly pitched, slowed-down effects that also sound fabulous layered with the original loop. Often, you can simplify the loop beats by setting the Trans Detect slider to a low value, such as 10%.

These bizarro loops seem most effective when layered with the original loop, which should be set to normal loop settings. They also make great breakbeats when you drop out the original loop.

When Loops Show Up in the Wrong Place

Sometimes I've dragged a loop into the project, but instead of going where I wanted it to go, it would start one hour into the song or at some other seemingly arbitrary time.

This drove me crazy, because I had to keep moving them back to the beginning. The solution is to choose Options > Global, and in the Audio Data tab, uncheck Always Import Broadcast Waves at Their Timestamp (Figure 22.20). It turns out the samples were Broadcast WAV files with a timestamp that specified starting at 1:00:00.

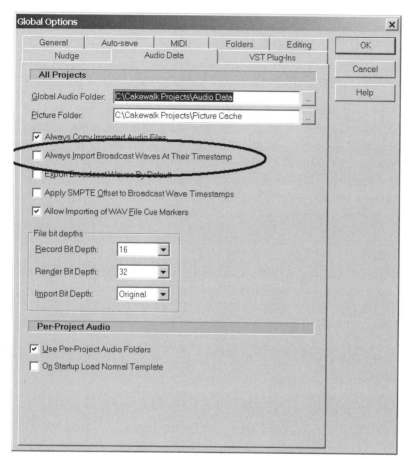

Figure 22.20 Unchecking Always Import Broadcast Waves at Their Timestamp prevents loops from going to some arbitrary start point.

Retrograde Groove Clips

The object here is to reverse the order of the slices within a Groove Clip, thus creating a new variation on the loop. This works best with loops that are staccato and have sharp attacks. Otherwise, when continuous sounds are broken up, clicks can occur at the splice points.

1. Click on a Groove Clip to select it and then choose Process > Audio > Reverse.

2. Disable Groove Clip looping for the file. (Click on it and type Ctrl+L.)

3. Once the file has been converted into a standard audio clip, again choose Process > Audio > Reverse.

4. Re-enable Groove Clip looping. Press Play and enjoy the retrograde fruits of your labors.

ACIDization versus REX There are two main time-stretch protocols used in SONAR Home Studio: ACIDization, as covered in this chapter, and the REX file protocol (developed by Propellerhead Software in conjunction with Steinberg). Do we really need two time-stretch protocols? Yes, because they're quite different—which is why SONAR Home Studio supports both. ACIDization uses DSP-based stretching, sample removal, and cross-fading. REX files cut a piece of digital into slices and then use MIDI data to vary when those slices are triggered. The REX process's main use of DSP is to synthesize a decay when gaps appear between slices, which happens when playing back a file at a slower tempo.

With percussive sounds, REX files have the potential for higher fidelity, as the sound is essentially unaltered except for the decay effect mentioned above. However, sustained sounds don't lend themselves to the REX process, because they can't be sliced without causing discontinuities in the sound. ACIDization's ability to cross-fade covers up discontinuities with sustained sounds and delivers far better-sounding results.

When altering pitch, both are somewhat iffy—they work best for time stretching. With either one, fidelity is better when speeding up compared to slowing down. As a general rule of thumb, REX is best for percussive loops that need to be tempo shifted over a wide range. ACIDization is best for sustained sounds but does an excellent job (with proper ACIDization) with percussive loops as long as they don't have to be slowed down too much.

Bottom line: ACIDization is more versatile overall, but REX is superior in a lesser number of scenarios. For more about REX, see the section on DropZone in Chapter 13 on virtual instruments.

Even More Groove Tips!

Before signing off of this chapter, let's look at a collection of groove-oriented tips.

- To preview a selected loop in the Loop Construction window, hit Shift+spacebar. You can also use this to stop the preview if it's already playing.

- If you bring a non–Groove Clip file into SONAR Home Studio, convert it to a Groove Clip, and then try to save it over the original file, the Groove Clip parameters will not be saved. Use Save As to save it under a different name. This is a safety measure to prevent you from overwriting source files.

- MP3 files can be ACIDized in the Loop Construction window. But if you try to save them externally to the program, they will be converted to WAV format in the process.

- While in the Loop Construction window, choose the Select tool by hitting the S key and the Erase Marker tool with the E key.

■ Before getting too much into editing, try adjusting the Basic Slices and Transient Detection sliders first. Often, choosing different values will solve flamming and other problems without the need for editing.

■ Use the lowest Slice Rhythmic Value possible (for example, eighth note instead of sixteenth note), consistent with good sound. Extraneous slices can cut off drum decays. This is particularly annoying with kicks, because you lose some of the fullness and ring.

■ SONAR Home Studio will endeavor to keep any markers that you've moved manually in their assigned positions, so you can experiment at any time with the Slicing and Transient Detect controls without losing the positions of your carefully placed markers.

■ When you save a SONAR Home Studio song or bundle, it retains all the Groove Clip parameters.

23 Recording Guitar with SONAR Home Studio

In the early days of sequencing and DAWs, guitarists were pretty much left out in the cold. But that's changed over the years, as guitarist-specific hardware and plug-ins have appeared to make sequencing simpler for those who favor six strings over 88 keys. Let's cover general guitar recording topics that relate to SONAR Home Studio, as well as several SONAR Home Studio–specific techniques.

Old School/Nu Skool Recording

There are three basic ways to record guitar with SONAR Home Studio:

- Mike an amp, use a DI (*direct injection*) box, or use both, and record the guitar as you would any other miked or direct signal. (A DI box accepts a guitar signal at its input and outputs a line-level signal suitable for feeding an audio interface's line-level input.)

- Record directly into the computer, using amp modeling and similar plug-ins to get your sound in the "virtual world."

- Combine the two, where you record from an amp but also do *re-amping* (covered at the end of this chapter) or other types of virtual processing.

If you're into using a mic to record an amp, then it's likely that you already have a suitable interface/preamp combination that can also accept a DI box's output. Because this is pretty standard recording practice (unlike feeding a guitar directly into your computer), there are no particularly special issues to consider.

However, those who favor recording both an amp *and* direct signal (a technique often done with bass, too) can take advantage of SONAR Home Studio's Nudge feature to "tune out" time or phase differences between the two signals. These differences occur because the direct signal hits SONAR Home Studio instantly, whereas the miked signal will hit sometime later, depending on the distance from the sound source. (The delay is approximately 1ms per foot.)

To do this, first zoom way in on both the direct and the miked signal, as you'll be dealing with very small timing increments. You want to line them up, which will require moving the miked signal earlier (see Figure 23.1). There are three ways to do this.

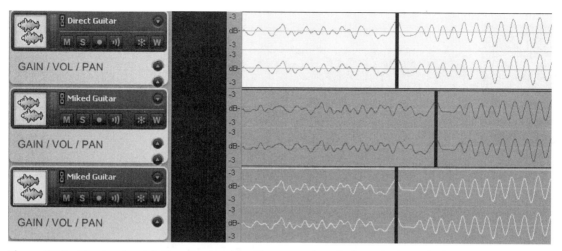

Figure 23.1   The top track is the direct guitar. The second track down is the miked guitar signal, which is delayed by 3ms because the mic was about three feet away from the speaker. The lower track shows the second track moved forward in time, so that it lines up with the direct track. The thick black lines indicate a readily identifiable peak that serves as a reference for lining up the tracks.

- Click on the miked clip, and with Snap to Grid turned off, drag it forward until the waveforms line up.

- Use the Nudge feature. Choose Process > Nudge > Settings, and for the three nudge groups, select the desired amount of nudge (see Figure 23.2). For example, if you choose 4 milliseconds with Nudge Group 1, you can then move the clip forward or backward in 4-millisecond increments using (for Group 1) the 1 and 3 numeric keypad keys.

- Invoke Process > Slide (see Figure 23.3). This has two disadvantages: You can't enter amounts in samples or milliseconds, and unlike Nudge, there are no "native" keyboard shortcuts. The advantage is that because you can enter values in ticks (which gives sufficient resolution), if you record with a consistent mic position, once you figure out the right amount of slide, you can just enter the amount in ticks, and you're done.

Recording Directly into the Computer

If you record through a guitar preamp or a hardware modeling device, you get your sound in the box and then send it to whatever convenient line input your computer may have. Feeding your guitar's output *directly* into your computer is another matter entirely, because conventional line inputs will load down the guitar (reducing highs and level), while a mic input will likely have too much gain and contribute noise.

One solution is a standard audio interface with a high-impedance input designed specifically for guitar. Most modern interfaces (for example, Edirol, MOTU, PreSonus, and so on) provide this

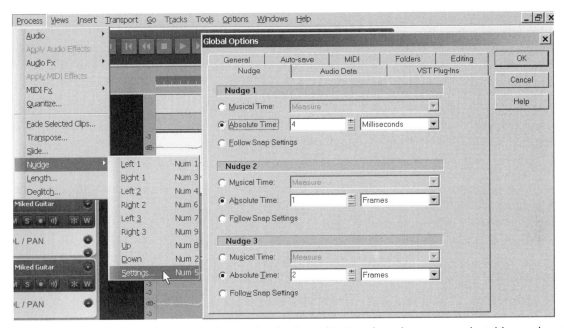

Figure 23.2 You can "nudge" tracks forward or backward in time based on a user-selectable number of seconds, milliseconds, frames, samples, or ticks.

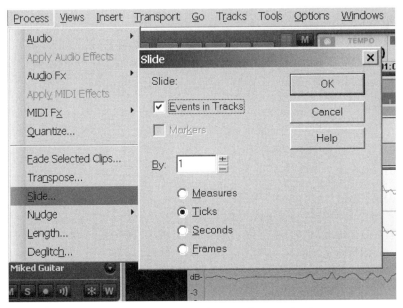

Figure 23.3 The Slide function is designed to make it easy to move a track by a fixed, consistent amount.

option, but there are also more guitar-centric interfaces. For example, Waves offers a hardware interface that buffers your guitar signal and then feeds into a standard line-level audio interface input. Native Instruments and IK Multimedia go one step further, offering hardware interfaces that plug directly into your computer via USB.

If you take this approach of feeding your guitar directly into a computer, then you can use plugins inserted into SONAR Home Studio to shape the guitar's sound. This means you'll need to monitor through SONAR Home Studio itself, which brings up the issue of *latency*—the time it takes between hitting a string and hearing it come out of your interface.

You make adjustments that affect latency by choosing Options > Audio. Because SONAR Home Studio has two low-latency driver options (ASIO and WDM), you have a bit more flexibility compared to some other programs because you can try both (if available) to determine which gives the least amount of delay. With today's fast computers, it should be possible to obtain low enough latencies that any delays aren't objectionable (see Figure 23.4).

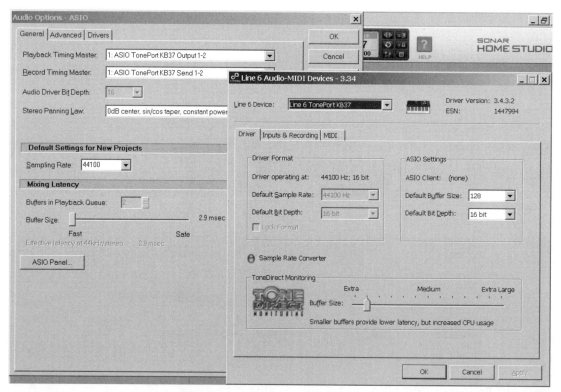

Figure 23.4   The Line 6 KB37 combines a two-octave keyboard with guitar and mic/audio interfacing. It's using ASIO drivers (probably your best bet for Windows) and has a latency of 128 samples, which translates to about 3ms. Although the system introduces additional latencies, this is fast enough to give a natural feel while playing guitar.

If you decide to try WDM drivers, SONAR Home Studio profiles your interface and chooses a relatively conservative latency setting. From there, you can choose Options > Audio > General tab and experiment with the Buffer Size slider until you find the best compromise between minimum delay and best audio performance. With ASIO, there will be an ASIO control panel for your interface that sets the basic latency (expressed in either samples or milliseconds). You can call up this panel by clicking on the ASIO Panel button in the Audio Options' lower left. SONAR Home Studio locks to this value; you can't change the buffer size using the Options > Audio dialog box.

Overall latency depends on the interface, drivers, computer speed, and how much you're asking the computer to do at any given moment. (Hint: If you're overdubbing guitar after several soft synths have been added, freeze their tracks as described in Chapter 14 before recording guitar— you'll be able to lower the latency as a result, because the CPU won't have to work as hard.) But one thing's for sure: If the audio starts crackling, popping, or breaking up as you play, then the latency is too low. Increase it until the audio performance improves.

There's yet another option for getting your guitar signal into SONAR Home Studio: Several hardware guitar processors, such as the Line 6 POD X3, Korg Pandora PX5D, DigiTech RP and GNX series, M-Audio Black Box, and the like include USB outputs for feeding into a computer. With all of these options, you get the sound you want *before* the signal hits the computer. As a result, you can monitor the device output and hear the sound that will be recorded; there's no need to listen through SONAR Home Studio (unless you're adding more plug-ins within the program), which means that latency isn't an issue. If you're the kind of guitarist to whom any latency whatsoever is annoying, this type of approach is probably best.

SONAR Home Studio's Bundled Guitar Goodies

SONAR Home Studio comes with two plug-ins designed specifically for guitar: Gallo Engineering's Studio Devil Virtual Guitar Amp Plus (VGA+) and Cakewalk's Amp Sim. VGA+ is a complete guitar amp and effects simulator, whereas the Amp Sim is designed for a more *à la carte* approach where you add other modules, such as compression, EQ, reverb, and the like.

On a more utilitarian level, there's also a Chromatic Tuner. To tune your guitar:

1.   Select the appropriate input for the track recording your guitar.

2.   Make sure the track's Input Echo button is on, or the Tuner won't work.

3.   Right-click in the track's effects bin and choose Audio FX > Cakewalk > Tuner.

4.   The tuner is always active. The button above the Cakewalk logo mutes the audio when gray and enables audio when orange (see Figure 23.5).

5.   Pluck a string on your guitar. As you play, the display will show the note being played, with both a meter display and dual-LED (sharp or flat) display.

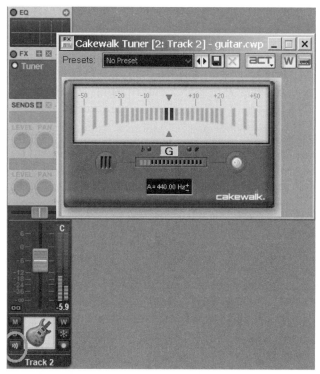

Figure 23.5   Insert the Tuner as a plug-in or click on the Add FX button, and make sure the track's Input Echo (circled) is on.

Monitoring through SONAR Home Studio

Remember that to hear your guitar through plug-ins:

- The track has to select the input being fed by your guitar.

- The Input Echo button must be enabled.

As for getting a good guitar sound, we'll start with the VGA+ and then get into a more customized amp approach based on using the Amp Sim module.

VGA+ (Virtual Guitar Amp Plus)

You can divide the VGA+'s interface into an upper and a lower half, and each of these has two halves as well. The upper half has two strips with controls that provide the basic amp emulation, while the lower half has two more strips that add a variety of effects.

The upper strip's upper left has a drop-down menu where you can choose from 18 preamp models, while below it, another drop-down menu offers 14 speaker cabinet models (see Figure 23.6). You can mix and match among these, so there are plenty of tonal options—it'll take you hours to

Figure 23.6 The upper strip lets you choose different preamps and speaker cabinets, as well as alter the overall tonal characteristics.

explore them all. The two toggle switches to the left of the drop-down menus bypass the preamp and speaker cabinet modules.

To the right of these drop-down menus, the Gain control sets the overall amount of "crunch" and distortion. The Boost switch increases distortion dramatically, while Bass, Mids, Treb(le), and Pres(ence) are tone controls. Note that adding Boost ups the noise level considerably, and in many cases, you don't really need it.

The power amp parameters (see Figure 23.7) don't affect the sound as much as the preamp and speaker cabinet parameters, but they can fine-tune the overall sound. MOSFET gives a brighter sound, Tube-A is somewhat darker, and Tube-AB is between those two. Sparkle—well, actually, that's a pretty good description! Turn fully clockwise for maximum sparkle. The on/off switch bypasses the power amp section.

The top FX strip has two different effects: compressor and modulation (see Figure 23.8).

Figure 23.7   The next strip down determines the power amp characteristics.

A compressor evens out your guitar's dynamic range by reducing loud peaks and bringing up soft passages, thus giving more sustain. There's an on/off switch, while the Amount control sets the degree of compression—turn clockwise for more sustain.

The modulation effect is more complex. It also has an on/off switch and a selector for four different types of effects:

- **Tremolo.** A periodic, cyclic variation in volume.

- **Chorus.** Duplicates the guitar signal, delays it, and then subtly varies the delay time of the delayed signal. This makes one instrument sound like two instruments of the same type playing in ensemble.

- **Flanger.** Flanging is the process of sweeping the delay time of a delay line over a short range, typically from 0 to 10 or so milliseconds, and combining the delayed signal equally with the signal present at the input of the delay line. This produces an animated, swirling effect that resembles a jet plane flying overhead, as well as metallic effects and, at longer delays, robot voices.

Figure 23.8 The top FX strip offers a compressor and a modulation effect.

- **Phaser.** This audio effect varies the phase of a signal and mixes it with the original signal. The phase differences between the two waveforms create a subjectively pleasing alteration of the waveform that resembles the sound created by a rotating speaker system.

Here's how the remaining five controls work.

- **Type switch.** Chooses between two different "characters" for the selected effect. With Tremolo, Flanger, and Phaser, Type 1 is mono, and Type 2 is stereo.

- **Style.** Also changes the sound's character. With Tremolo, counterclockwise gives a smoother tremolo effect, while clockwise gives a more "pulsing" sound. With Phaser and Flanger, turning Style clockwise gives a sharper, more resonant sound.

- **Speed.** All of these effects have a periodic character that modulates the effect over time. Speed sets the period.

- **Depth.** Determines how much modulation is applied; except for Tremolo, where this control has no effect, more modulation results in a more intense effect.

- **Mix.** Sets the blend of the dry, unprocessed signal and the processed signal. When fully counterclockwise, there's no processed signal; fully clockwise is all processed signal. For the Chorus, you'll get the most intense effect with Mix set halfway.

Each of the effects in the lower strip (see Figure 23.9) has an on/off switch. The Delay/Echo has five additional controls:

Figure 23.9 The lower FX strip provides three effects: Delay/Echo, Ambience, and Noise Gate.

- **Pong/Norm switch.** In Norm position, the echoes are panned to center. With Pong, echoes bounce sequentially back and forth between the left and right channels.

- **Delay.** Sets the amount of time between echoes.

- **Feedback.** Mixes some of the output back to the input, thus creating repeating echoes. More feedback means the echoes "sustain" longer.

- **Style.** Fully clockwise gives the sound of a modern digital delay, while turning more counterclockwise inserts filtering into the feedback path, giving the sound of older analog and tape echo devices.

- **Mix.** Sets the blend of the dry, unprocessed signal and the delayed signal. When fully counterclockwise, there's no processed signal; fully clockwise is all delayed signal. In most cases, you don't want the delays to overwhelm the dry signal, so you'd set Mix to around the 9 o'clock setting.

Ambience imparts some "air" to the guitar amp, as if it was being recorded in a room. The Level control adds in reflected sounds to create the ambience effect.

The Noise Gate removes noise when you're not playing guitar. While not playing your guitar, turn the Noise Gate on/off switch to On and turn the Threshold control fully clockwise. Turn the Threshold counterclockwise until you hear noise and then turn it slightly clockwise so the noise disappears.

Step-by-Step: Creating a "Guitar Rack" Track Template

One of SONAR Home Studio's highly useful features is the ability to create a track template. This lets you put together a "rack" of effects in a track and then save it for later recall (including the cute little track icon, of course!). Let's go through the process of creating an effects rack for overdrive rhythm guitar, using the included SONAR Home Studio effects, and then save it as a track template. As a bonus, you can download the track template (with the stunningly original name of CraigOverdrive.cwx) from www.courseptr.com/downloads.

1. Because SONAR Home Studio includes a Chromatic Tuner, we might as well take advantage of it to keep everything in tune. After creating an audio track, click on the Add Effect button and choose Audio > Cakewalk > Tuner. (If you don't hear anything after inserting it, remember to click the button above the Cakewalk logo so it turns orange.) I just leave it on all the time so I can tune a string whenever needed.

2. Compression is a good effect to place right after the Tuner, because you can smooth out the dynamics and increase sustain prior to feeding the distortion. So, add another effect—this time, the Cakewalk Compressor/Gate (see Figure 23.10). The Acoustic Guitar preset is a good place to start. But I drop the threshold much lower (around –20) for more sustain and bump up the output level a bit.

Figure 23.10 Compression tames out the dynamics a bit, which can give the distortion a smoother quality.

3. Next up: Insert the Sonitus:fx Equalizer. The purpose of this effect is to shave off just the highest part of the spectrum, because distorting this region can create a harsh sound (see Figure 23.11). Set the parameters as shown in Figure 23.11, making sure

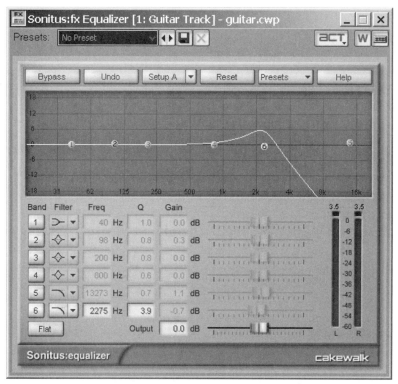

Figure 23.11 In this particular patch, the EQ is set up as a high-cut filter to reduce potential harshness caused by distorting high frequencies.

that Stage 6's Filter parameter is set to Lowpass. The Sonitus EQ has the useful ability to change the Q for the high-frequency shelf, thus making the shelf steeper but also adding a slight response bump at the cutoff frequency. This can work very well with guitar to give a little more definition in the upper midrange if you've pulled back the highs a bit. Note that in this particular patch, the EQ doesn't have much effect on the sound. However, the track template is designed to be somewhat general-purpose, and there are times when I use this EQ to boost the midrange a bit (thus making those frequencies more touch-sensitive when they hit the distortion stage), roll off more highs for a mellower sound, or trim the bass when I want a thinner rhythm guitar part.

4. Next, insert Cakewalk's Amp Sim to add distortion. It's neither the most versatile nor best-sounding amp simulator on the planet, but like all of these devices, it has its own sound that can be a useful addition to your sonic toolkit. I like to push the Drive control up a bit (see Figure 23.12), because Amp Sim is best on light or over-the-top

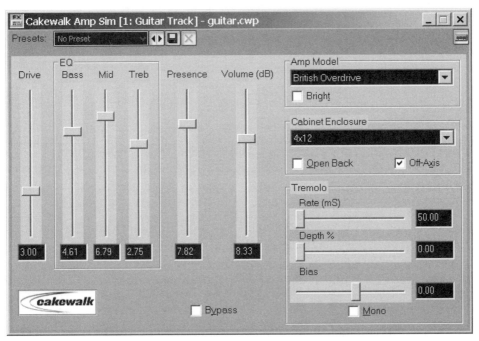

Figure 23.12   These settings give a pretty nice overdrive sound.

distortion; like many distortion modelers, its hardest task is trying to get that "just on the edge" sort of bluesy distortion. Boosting the mid control a bit and cutting the treble gives a rounder tone, and of course, all this is greatly influenced by the amp model and cabinet enclosure you choose.

5. The Cakewalk Compressor/Gate follows the distortion, but we're not using the Compressor—only the Gate section (see Figure 23.13). This mutes any hiss while you're not playing your guitar. To adjust the gate, set Gate mode to Normal and then turn the Gate Threshold fully counterclockwise. Without playing your guitar, start turning the Threshold clockwise until the hiss just goes away. When you play, the gate should sense there's a signal, thus opening up and letting through the guitar sound.

Figure 23.13   The Compressor/Gate is a useful module for keeping noise under control. This is especially important because the use of heavy compression early in the signal chain tends to bring up any low-level noise. Note that the compression ratio is set to 1:1; this disables the compression part of the effect.

6. To wrap a little ambience around the lead, next would come delay, reverb, or both. For now, let's insert the Studioverb 2, set for a medium-sized room (see Figure 23.14).

Figure 23.14 Reverb can add some room or hall ambience to give the sound more space.

7. Now let's use some track EQ to shave the hits just a little bit more, to round the tone. Right-click in the EQ plot and select Eq Post Fx (see Figure 23.15). This means the EQ will do its thing *after* (post) all the guitar effects, not before. Note that only Band 6 is active; it's rolling off highs above about 5 kHz, with a Q setting of 3.2 to add a little resonance.

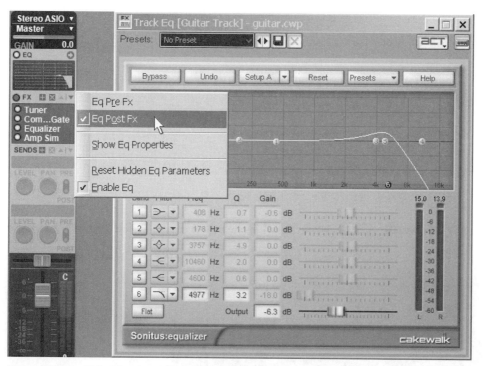

Figure 23.15 This EQ takes a little high end off of the guitar processing to give a warmer, rounder tone.

8. Once you have your effects set up as desired, it's worth saving the whole rack as a track template. This is easy: In Console view, right-click in the blank space to the left of

the fader (or in Track view, move the cursor until it becomes a double arrow), right-click, and select Save as Track Template (see Figure 23.16). (Note that there are other places where you can right-click in Console view to bring up the context menu that lets you choose Save as Track Template, but the space to the left of the fader is probably the easiest to use.) Navigate to where you want to save the template.

Figure 23.16   Once you save a track template, you can recall it at any time into a track.

9.   Loading a track template into a track is equally simple. Right-click in a track space as described in the previous step and select Insert from Track Template. Follow the path to the desired track template (see Figure 23.17; in this case, I saved my CraigOverdrive track template in the Audio > Guitar folder).

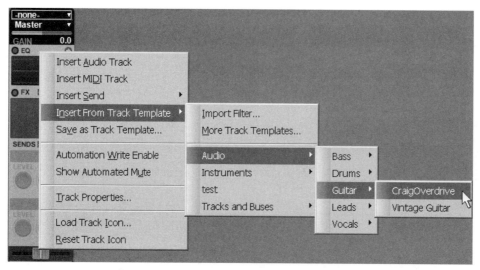

Figure 23.17 The previously saved track template is now being inserted into a different audio track.

Re-Amping with SONAR Home Studio

Wouldn't it be great if you could choose a guitar's amp tone *while mixing down* instead of being locked into the tone you used while recording? Thanks to plug-in technology and fast computers, you can.

For years, engineers and guitarists have used a technique called *re-amping*. With this, a guitarist splits the guitar signal in two: One feed goes direct to an amp, and the other goes straight into the recorder via a direct box. As the guitarist plays, the amp signal is recorded—but so is the straight signal, on a separate track.

During mixdown, if the amp track sounds fine, that's great. But if not, the engineer can mute the amp track, feed the straight track's output into a different amp, and then record the output of the other amp. Or, another option is to keep the original amp track but add a new amp track to provide stereo or layered effects.

SONAR Home Studio allows a new twist on the traditional re-amping concept. The key to what makes virtual re-amping possible is that the program records the dry, unprocessed guitar signal to the track, not the version through the plug-in. So, any processing that occurs depends entirely on the plug-in(s) you've selected; you can process the guitar in any way you'd like during the mixdown process, including changing virtual amps, patching in high-quality reverb, or whatever.

Although I've presented input monitoring in a guitar re-amping context, this has other uses as well—for example, vocalists often like to hear themselves with compression, reverb, EQ, and so on while singing. By monitoring through SONAR Home Studio, they can hear what their voice will sound like through particular plug-ins, but these can always be changed on mixdown.

24 Songwriting with SONAR Home Studio

Approaches to songwriting vary considerably, from those who strum some chords on a guitar for ideas, to those who start with beats, to those who seem to draw inspiration out of nowhere and want to record what they hear quickly—before the inspiration fades. As a result, this chapter isn't about what you should do to write songs, but rather, it describes some particular SONAR Home Studio tools that can be very helpful if you're into songwriting.

Although songwriting styles are very personal, I think we can nonetheless agree on a few general points: While songwriting, you want your tools to stay out of the way and be transparent. You want a smooth-flowing, efficient, simple process; songwriting isn't about endlessly tweaking a synth bass *patch,* but about coming up with a great bass *part.* Thanks to the fluid nature of digital recording, almost anything can be replaced or refined at a later date. You want an environment that can simplify turning your abstract ideas into something tangible, while losing as little as possible in the translation. So, let's look at some SONAR Home Studio techniques that can help you accomplish that goal.

The MIDI Quick Start

Normally you need to arm a MIDI track before you can record on it, but it's possible to defeat this so that recording starts on *any* selected MIDI track as soon as you click on the transport's Record button. I realize the default setting is there to prevent accidental overwriting of MIDI tracks, but personally, I find not having to arm a track liberating—it saves time and makes the recording process flow faster.

To do this:

1. Choose Options > Global.

2. Check the box for Allow MIDI Recording without an Armed Track (the tenth box down from the top; see Figure 24.1).

3. Click on OK to close the Global Options menu.

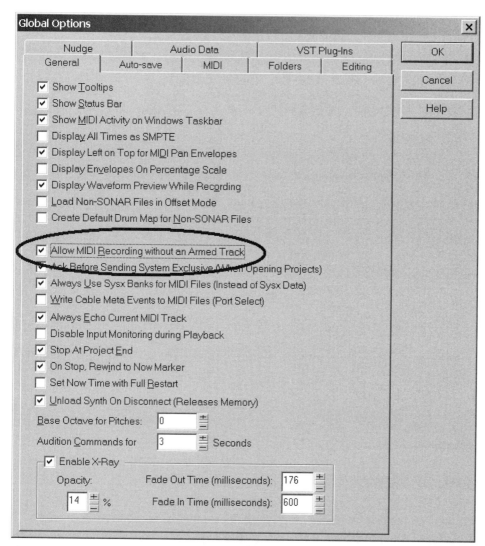

Figure 24.1 It's possible to record MIDI tracks without having to arm them first, which can be a real timesaver over the course of a song.

Template Files

It's much easier to write when you have a friendly environment ready to go as soon as you boot up. Cakewalk allows saving files with a special extension, .CWT, which indicates that the file is a template. When you open SONAR Home Studio and click on the Create a New Project button, you'll see a list of available templates, including Normal. This is a special template because it's the default template that will load when you create a new project (assuming you don't select a different template).

SONAR Home Studio includes nine templates. While they're useful, you'll likely want to create some custom templates for the way you like to work. For example, if you always use the Studio

Instruments Drums to do drum parts, it makes sense to include that in your template, assigned to a track and ready to go.

When creating custom template files, analyze the type of tasks you do and what would be your ideal starting point for composition. Template files aren't just about storing and recalling a particular number of tracks; you can set up particular configurations of virtual instruments, metronome settings, MIDI and audio data, and more.

After creating the template, you need to save it a little differently compared to the way you'd save a standard file.

1. Select File > Save As.

2. Navigate to your Templates folder. (If you don't know where it is, choose Options > Global and click on the Folders tab. The Templates entry will show the file path.)

3. Enter the file name.

4. Under Save as Type, choose Template or simply type in the suffix .CWT (Cakewalk Template).

The next time you create a new project, your template will show up as one of the options.

So, what do you want a songwriting template to include? Following are some recommendations.

Workstation Synth

If you use MIDI, then having a virtual synth with a large number of sounds available is a good place to start. That way, whether you want to lay down a bass line, play some drums, or work on chords with a piano, you're covered. And if you don't use MIDI, then consider changing your habits: If you start writing a song with MIDI tracks and later decide you need to change tempo or key, you can do so far more easily than changing tempo or key with digital audio. And of course, another advantage to MIDI is that if you end up with a "keeper" part, but you want to change instruments or edit a few notes you didn't like, you can edit MIDI data easily…or replace a MIDI track with a "live" instrument.

As to which workstation to use, of course there are the TTS-1 and Dimension LE synths included with SONAR Home Studio. If you want to go beyond those, there are plenty of alternatives on the market: Native Instruments Kontakt, IK Multimedia SampleTank, MOTU MachFive, SONiVOX Muse, Ultimate Sound Bank PlugSound Pro, EastWest Colossus, and others.

But even though I have several very cool workstation programs, my choice for a songwriting template is still the TTS-1. While it doesn't have the breadth or sound quality of the other products mentioned earlier, it takes virtually no CPU power. This makes it easy to maintain low system latency, which can be important if you plan to play acoustic or electric instruments in real time through SONAR Home Studio.

Although there's much more on the TTS-1 in Chapter 13 on virtual instruments, I want to high-light the features that are most important for songwriting (see Figure 24.2). For starters, the GM2 set has more presets than a standard GM set. For example, there are seven acoustic pianos instead of the standard GM Grand Piano, Bright Piano, and Electric Grand. The TTS-1 also has four outputs, just in case processing, such as a tempo-synced rhythmic delay, is vital to a

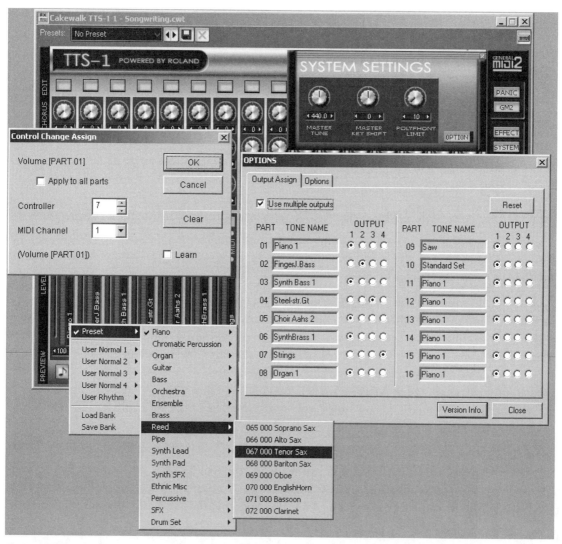

Figure 24.2 The TTS-1 has several useful options, pasted into place here from multiple screenshots. Clockwise from upper right: The System settings screen is where you can transpose the instrument and limit polyphony; an output assign screen (with an additional Options tab) takes advantage of the four outputs; there's access to a full GM2 soundset; and it's easy to assign controllers to the level faders for the 16 channels.

particular sound (although generally, I'd advise you not to concern yourself with effects too much while songwriting—you can always deal with the effects later).

Furthermore, you can set up control changes for the various volume faders. If you have a control surface, it's easy to throw together a quick mix without having to spend too much effort. There are other goodies: You can specify a polyphony limit to guarantee minimal CPU consumption, and a Master Key Shift control allows you to transpose the entire instrument (except for the drum channel, of course) if you decide to change key to accommodate a particular vocal range. And because the TTS-1 is GM-compatible, you can do an "instant sonic upgrade" just by loading a GM set from a more full-featured workstation.

Also note that the TTS-1 is quite editable; just click on the Edit button above each mixer "channel." I realize that mentioning editability may go against the premise that you want things to move rapidly while writing songs, but in this case, the editing options are quite simple: filter, tone, envelope, vibrato, and so on. Therefore, if you like an instrument but need, for example, a more percussive sound, it's easy to do. And remember, you're staying within one instrument, so everything you might want to adjust is only a few clicks away.

And I can't resist mentioning a couple other favorite features. If you click on the System button, select Option, and then click on the Options tab, you can check Light Load Mode (see Figure 24.3), which saves even more processing power. If, while you're there, you also check Enable Phrase Preview, then clicking on the note symbol at the bottom of each mixer channel plays a little riff so you

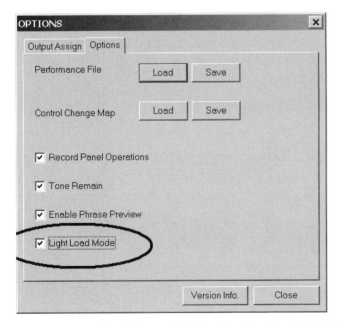

Figure 24.3 With Light Load mode, the already-efficient TTS-1 becomes even more so—you can play back lots of instruments, even with slower, older computers.

can hear the sound's intended usage. For more details about these features and others, click on the Help button in the TTS-1 screen's lower-right corner.

While the TTS-1 may not get the same amount of respect as its more expensive and capable competitors, don't overlook its talents as a hardworking songwriting companion that asks for little in return.

To MIDI File or Not to MIDI File?

If you have a workstation in your template, it might make sense to have some tracks with MIDI files for drums, bass lines, or whatever to get you started. But be careful, because you don't want to box yourself in. I suggest having only a few MIDI drum tracks—for example, a four-on-the-floor kick with snare for dance music and a typical rock pattern for rock music. Treat these more as a glorified metronome than a "real" drum part, or you might influence yourself to do what you've done before—and you don't want to fall into a rut.

Track Templates

Track templates save huge amounts of time. For example, you may like particular EQ and compression settings on your vocals, but you may also like variations on these for different mics you use. Although you can include tracks with these settings in your songwriting template, if you add too many tracks you don't use to the template, the template will end up being cluttered and confusing—the opposite of what you want.

A better strategy is to save track templates for your favorite sounds and load one at a time, as needed, into your songwriting template. For example, you might want to start off with a lead vocal track template as you start getting lyric ideas together and then call up a different track template for harmony vocals. Or, if you use an amp simulator, create a track template with it sitting in the effects bin, along with SONAR Home Studio's chromatic tuner plug-in and a compressor to give sustain (see Figure 24.4). A track template memorizes not just levels, but bus settings, hardware settings (input and output), track parameters and icons, names, and so on.

The best way to build up a collection of track templates is to simply create one when you come up with a track setup you like. To do this, in Track view, right-click on a blank spot within a track and select Save as Track Template.

Best of all, you aren't limited to saving a single track as a template; you can save a *collection* of tracks, which can optionally be contained in a track folder. To save multiple tracks as a template:

1. Ctrl-click on the track icons to select the tracks you want to save in the template.

2. Right-click on a blank space in any of the selected tracks and choose Save as Track Template.

Figure 24.4 This shows a track that's optimized for rhythm guitar (with tuner, VGA Plus amp simulator plug-in, and compressor set up as a pseudo-limiter) being saved as a template.

All selected tracks will be saved as a single template and recalled as a group when you call up that template.

To save a track folder of tracks as a template:

1. Ctrl-click on the track icons within the folder that you want to save as a template track folder. You don't have to select all tracks, but only selected tracks will become part of the template.

2. Right-click on a blank space in any of the selected tracks and choose Save as Track Template. Note that you can't right-click on the folder track itself; you have to click on one of the tracks within the folder.

You can load a track template from either Track view or Console view. Right-click on a blank space in either view where a track would normally sit and select Insert from Track Template. Here you can choose from one of the presets included with SONAR Home Studio or a track template you've created yourself.

If you import a track template and it seems to be missing certain elements, see whether any of the elements are being filtered in the Track Template Import Options dialog box.

The Track Template Import "filter" allows you to recall only specific aspects of the template (see Figure 24.5). For example, if you check Track Folders and select a track template with a collection of tracks that were contained in a folder, the entire collection—including the folder— will be recalled. But if you don't check Track Folders and recall the same track template, the collection of tracks within the folder will be recalled as standard tracks, without a parent folder. Other filter options let you decide whether you want to import bus assignments, mute/solo/arm status, effects, sends, and so on.

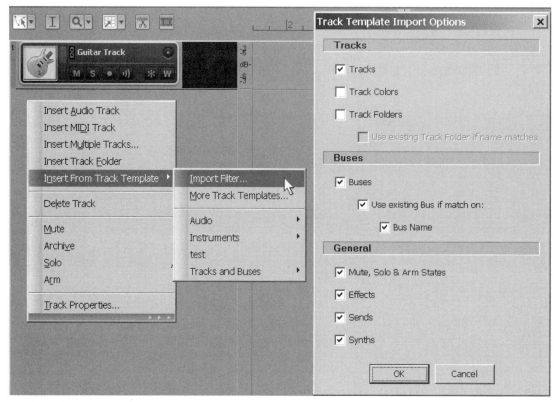

Figure 24.5 You can import entire track templates or, by using the Import filter, just particular aspects of the track template.

Final Considerations

Be careful to strike a balance between having enough templates to make your life easier and not so many as to confuse the issue. I tend to use templates as points of departure that can be modified with a few mouse clicks. For example, rather than save track templates with different amp sim settings, I'll create one template with an amp sim and recall a preset from within the amp sim itself.

It's also important to create fairly general templates that don't force you into a particular sound. One of the joys of making music is the occurrence of happy accidents where you might, for example, pull up the wrong synth preset and find it works perfectly in a song. Be careful that you create *templates*, not *formats*; there's a big difference. To leave plenty of space for your creativity to flourish, let templates take *some* of the work out of getting a song off the ground—but not *all* of it.

25 Creating Beats

Beats are the essence of hip-hop, rap, dance, urban, and other electronically oriented forms of music. Let's take a look at how to create beats in SONAR Home Studio and then use those beats as the foundation for a rhythm track designed to power an electro/dance-style piece of music.

We Got the Beat

Many beats use analog/drum machine–sounding drums. For those types of sounds, you needn't look any further than the TTS-1 soft synth, which has some excellent analog/Roland TR-type drums titled Analog Set. So, after opening a new project, let's get started on the drums.

1. Choose Insert > Soft Synths > Cakewalk TTS-1.

2. Choose your desired soft synth options in the window that appears. I make sure that Synth Track Folder is checked so that the MIDI and instrument tracks end up in a folder, and I also check Synth Property Page so the instrument's GUI opens upon insertion.

3. We'll put the drums in MIDI channel 10 (Track 10 on the TTS-1) just to be in step with the General MIDI spec. At the TTS-1, click on the track name for channel 10 and then choose Preset > Drum Set > 026 Analog Set.

4. Now let's create a drum pattern. Turn your attention to the TTS-1 instrument MIDI track. Unfold the Input/Output section and set the MIDI channel output (CH) to 10.

5. You can use any method of note entry you like for recording, but let's use the Step Sequencer. With the MIDI track still selected, choose Views > Step Sequencer.

6. Set the number of beats and steps for the Step Sequencer; 8 and 4 are good starting points, respectively.

Now we're ready to create a drum pattern. If you click on the note names to the Step Sequencer's left, you can audition the various drum sounds. (Double-clicking on them opens up the Drum Map Manager.) Let's start with C3, the kick. Click on the Step Sequencer Play button and then click on the steps (the squares) in the C3 row where you want a kick drum sound. If you click in the wrong step, right-click on it to clear it.

You'll find suitable backbeat/snare-type sounds on D3, Eb3 (claps), and E3. You can always click all three of these on the same beat if you want a really big sound. Furthermore, there's a closed hi-hat on G#3 and an open hi-hat on Bb3. These are good for adding an off-beat effect. Db3 has a "low clave" type of sound suitable for accents.

Don't forget that you can add as many rows as you like to accommodate more sounds—just right-click to the right of any row and select Insert Row. You can drag a row into any position. For example, in Figure 25.1, I added another row and dragged it to the top to add the tambourine sound at F#4. This is also how you cut, copy, and paste row steps, as well as shift steps left or right if you want to try out some variations.

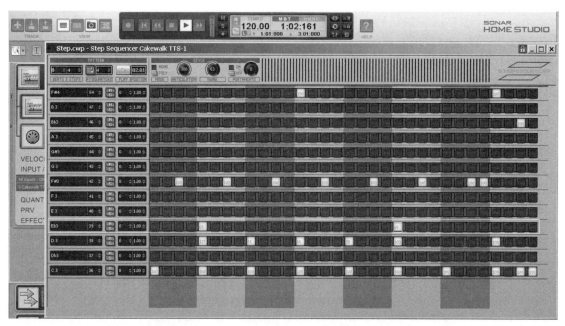

Figure 25.1 The completed drum pattern in SONAR Home Studio's Step Sequencer. The gold steps indicate ones that are playing back.

When creating the beat that kicks off the creative process for a tune (this is, of course, a matter of personal preference), I try to create one that's relatively complete—in other words, the beat that will be used at the peak of the song. For some reason I find it more natural to simplify the beat for other sections by stripping out parts than to start with a simple beat and embellish it later.

Create a beat using whatever sounds you like, and then we'll move on to tweaking. But first, hit save! Remember the primary rule of using anything that involves a microprocessor: *Whenever you've created something you don't want to lose, save.* Or, choose Options > Global > Auto-Save and set SONAR Home Studio to auto-save every few minutes or after a particular number of changes.

Tweak the Seq

Once you've created the beat, it's time for fine-tuning.

- In the Step Sequencer (included only in the XL version of SONAR Home Studio 7), you can fine-tune velocity values on a step in three ways: Double-click on a step and enter a new velocity value in the numerical field that appears, click and edit using the mouse scroll wheel, or click on a step while holding Shift and then drag up or down to increase or decrease velocity, respectively.

- For individual rows, you can add a velocity offset (for example, add 27 so that the default values of 100 turn into 127) or a multiplier (for example, multiply all velocity values by 1.2) in the two fields to the immediate left of each note grid.

- A little bit of swing can make a pattern more humanized. In the group of Style controls toward the top of the Step Sequencer, set Swing to a value higher than 50, and whatever beat you create will groove a whole lot more.

Don't overlook that you can edit the TTS-1 drum sounds themselves. Click on the small square in the TTS-1 virtual mixer at the top of channel 10 (or wherever you placed the drums). This opens up an Edit window for that channel (see Figure 25.2). Toward the center of the window, you can select the sound to be edited and then adjust the Level, Pan, Coarse and Fine Tune, Reverb Level, and Chorus Level values.

Figure 25.2 Each TTS-1 sound can be edited to some degree. With drums, you can edit each drum sound individually.

Select the sound to edit with the big right/left arrows, or if you click on the MIDI Edit button, the sound will follow any incoming MIDI note. (Curiously, notes are indicated as an octave lower than on the Step Sequencer—for example, C3 in the Step Sequencer shows as C2 in the Edit window.)

Toward the bottom of the window, you'll find Bass, Mid, and Treble controls, along with a Filter that can add resonant effects. Remember to click the On/Off button to the right of the Tone controls to make these effects active.

Finally, above the window's Level fader (any Level changes are reflected on the TTS-1's main Mixer view), there's a master pan control, as well as master send controls for the chorus and reverb.

And where do you edit the chorus and reverb? Glad you asked. In the TTS-1 main Mixer view, in the upper right, click on Effect. This brings up a window with Chorus and Reverb options (see Figure 25.3), including chorus and reverb types, reverb decay time, and several chorus-related parameters.

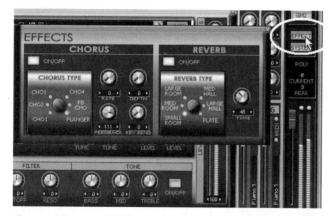

Figure 25.3 Using the TTS-1's chorus and reverb can add more character to sounds, particularly because these effects sound different compared to the other ones bundled with SONAR Home Studio. The settings shown work well with electro-style drum loops.

For electro-type drum patterns, try selecting Small Room for the reverb type, and set the Time parameter to around 45–60. Turn up the master send control, either in the instrument Edit window or on the main Mixer view, and the sound will blossom into a bigger, deeper sound with more character.

Although chorus may not seem all that useful for beats, you can get a very electronic, resonant-sounding effect by selecting Flanger as the chorus type, turning Rate and Depth to 0, and turning Feedback above 100. This is where the individual send controls for the different drums really come in handy, because you likely wouldn't want to add this resonant effect to the entire drum beat. I use it most often on the kick and on "natural" sounds (such as tambourine) to make them sound more electronic. Note that it's also possible to send the chorus through the reverb via the Rev Send control, and this can add yet another twist to the sound.

From Beat to Rhythm Track

So far, we've used the Step Sequencer to layer various sounds and create a two-bar pattern, tweaked the drum parameters for the best possible sound, and maybe even added some effects within the TTS-1. Now it's time to take that beat and expand upon it.

Close the Step Sequencer and focus on the Track view. If the track isn't in PRV view (if it is, disable it; see Figure 25.4), you'll see that the Step Sequencer has created a MIDI Groove Clip, as identified by the four rounded corners. This means you can "roll it out" by clicking on the right edge and dragging it to the right to create multiple iterations of the clip.

Figure 25.4 To see the Step Sequencer as a Groove Clip, make sure the PRV button is dark (disabled).

For example, suppose you want to work on the first 16 measures of the piece. Figure 25.5 shows the original two-bar clip rolled out eight times so that it lasts 16 measures.

At this point, if you double-click on this clip, it will simply reopen the Step Sequencer, and any change you make to the sequence will be reflected in each iteration of the clip. But what we want is to be able to work on this clip to build the song, by simplifying it toward the beginning and letting it build over time. To do this, right-click on the clip and select Bounce to Clip from the context menu or click on the clip to select it and choose Edit > Bounce to Clip.

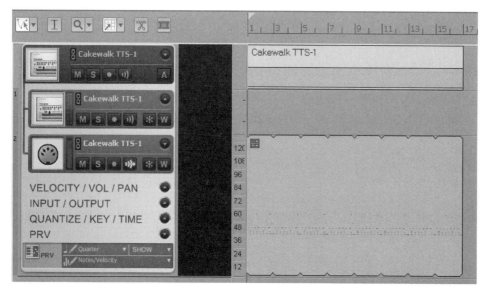

Figure 25.5 The original step sequence filled only the first two measures. Here, the Groove Clip it generated has been rolled out to fill 16 measures.

The clip now turns into a standard MIDI clip (see Figure 25.6), and if you double-click on it, the Piano Roll view will appear for editing the clip (assuming you haven't customized this particular shortcut).

As a side note, suppose that after creating this clip you decide that you'd really rather work with it as a 16-measure step sequence in the Step Sequencer. No problem: Right-click on the clip and select Convert MIDI Clip(s) to Step Sequencer. If you don't see this in the context menu, click on the row of arrows along the bottom to open up a side menu with other options. You'll be asked what step resolution you want to use, which will probably be sixteenth notes if that was your original Step Sequencer resolution.

But we'll assume you want to treat it as a MIDI clip, so let's make it easy to edit. First off, it's convenient to shorten the note durations a bit. Why? Suppose the Step Sequencer generates four consecutive sixteenth notes, and you're working in the Piano Roll view. They'll each be exactly one sixteenth note in length, so you won't really be able to see the note start and end if you're zoomed out.

So, select all the notes in the track, choose Process > Length, check only Duration out of the various check boxes, enter 70 in the Percent field, and then click on OK (see Figure 25.7). This will put a little space between consecutive notes, making it easier to see where they begin and end.

Now start carving. Take out some of the percussion so that when it comes back in, there's some real drama. Add a sixteenth-note lead-in on the kick, just before—for example—Measure 9. The object is to strike a balance between hypnotic groove and variations to add interest.

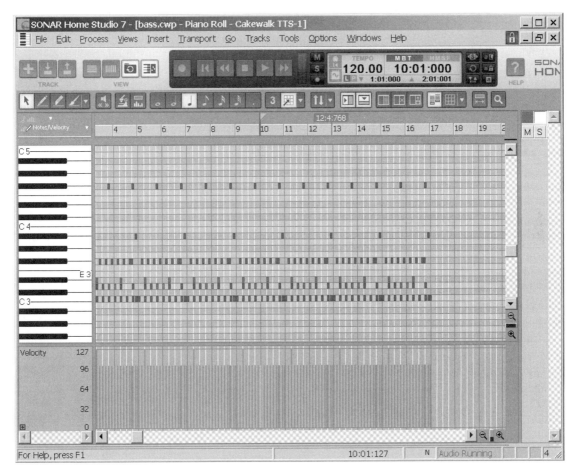

Figure 25.6 Once a Step Sequencer–generated Groove Clip is converted to a standard MIDI clip, double-clicking on it opens the Piano Roll view.

Send in the Audio

Now we're getting somewhere, having taken our simple beat and built it into a much longer part, with some editing to add more interest. However, remember that in SONAR Home Studio, a virtual instrument feeds the equivalent of an audio track. As a result, we can put effects in the audio track's effects bin and further alter the sound. What's more, thanks to automation, we can create variations in the sound of the effects.

For example, one of my favorite effects is synchronized delay, which the Tempo Delay effect does very well. The 1/2D Tempo Sync setting works well for dance tracks; Figure 25.8 shows typical parameter settings to add a rhythmic delay.

However, having this delay on constantly can get irritating, so let's automate the delay mix to bring it in and out at strategic times. For more details on Automation, see Chapter 19; the

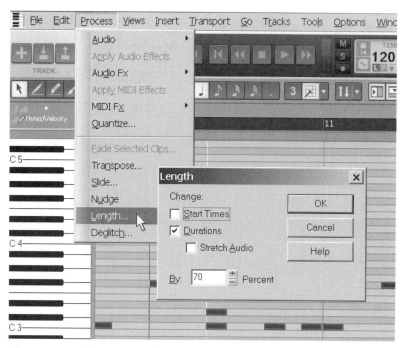

Figure 25.7 Shortening the durations of the notes makes it easier to see where they start and end when you're editing in the Piano Roll view.

following section demonstrates a basic way to add interest to beats, but there's a lot more to the subject of automation.

Step-By-Step: Adding Automation to an Effect

1.   Right-click in the audio track containing the Delay plug-in.

2.   From the context menu, choose Envelopes > Create Track Envelope > Tempo Delay 1.

3.   A window will appear with all available delay parameters for automation. Check Mix (see Figure 25.9). Note that if desired, you can choose a color for the automation curve that will be displayed in the track.

Figure 25.8 Typical settings for a tempo delay effect. Note how the highs and extreme lows are rolled off a bit to avoid having the echoes "step on" the main notes.

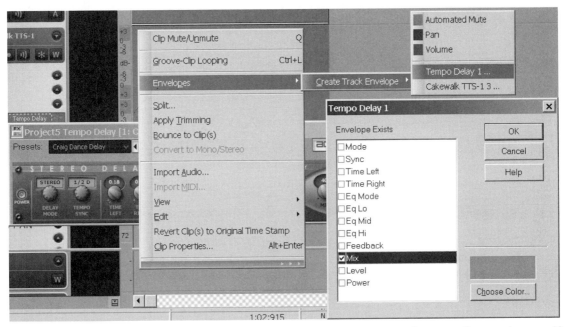

Figure 25.9   Before you can add automation to change a parameter over time, you first need to specify the parameter(s) you want to automate.

4.   Click on OK.

5.   A line will now appear in the track that represents the Mix control setting. Double-click on the line to create a node that can be dragged anywhere you want. Drag up to increase the level of delay in the mix; drag down to reduce it.

At this point, we've gone from a simple two-measure drum pattern to the start of a drum track. We can copy what we have and use it elsewhere in the song, or we can come up with variations on a theme.

26 Recording Bass with SONAR Home Studio

Although much of the material in Chapter 23 on recording guitar applies to bass, there are a few other considerations that apply to bass. However, note that some of these techniques apply to guitar and other instruments as well.

Using the Chromatic Tuner with Bass

SONAR Home Studio's Chromatic Tuner plug-in works with bass as well as guitar, although it seems to have a hard time with the low E and A strings—I tune by hitting the harmonic (twelfth fret) on these two strings, which works fine.

Parallel Effects

You don't want to lose the bass's low end, but effects (especially ones designed for guitar) can thin out the sound. One solution is to mix both unprocessed and processed bass tracks so that you blend both the thinner processed sound and the fuller dry bass sound.

A good example is using wah with bass; the Modfilter can provide wah effects. But first, you need a parallel processing setup. The easiest way is to clone the bass track and use the cloned track for effects. (Alternatively, you can feed the bass track to a send—with an inserted effect— that terminates in the master bus.) Here's how to create a parallel processing setup for bass by using the Clone Track function.

1. Select the track you want to clone (for example, click on the track icon).

2. Right-click on a blank space in the track, and from the context menu, select Clone Track(s) as shown in Figure 26.1.

3. Check Clone Events and Clone Properties. Uncheck Clone Effects. Check Clone Sends only if the cloned track should feed the same send effect as the original track; in most cases, you probably won't check this. You can also choose a specific track to hold the cloned audio, but you'll likely just choose the next higher-numbered track compared to the original.

4. When you've specified how you want the track cloned, click on OK.

Figure 26.1 Cloning a bass track lets you put effects on one track, while the other track gives a consistent bass sound. Note how Clone Effects is not checked, because we want to clone only the audio—but we do want to clone events and properties.

Now let's add some processing.

1. In the cloned track, click on Add Effect and choose Audio > Cakewalk > Modfilter.

2. Mute the original track so you hear only the cloned track (Figure 26.2).

Figure 26.2 The settings shown here add an automatic wah effect to the bass. Note that the original track is muted so that for now, you hear only the processed sound.

3. Listen to the cloned track and adjust the Modfilter for the desired wah sound. From left to right, I suggest the following Modfilter settings as a good starting point: LFO – 4 – 202 – 9.8 – 23 – SIN – 1.50 – 0,05 – 0.24 – 0 – 0.0.

4. Unmute the original track so you can hear both the processed and the unprocessed tracks together.

5. Adjust the balance of the two tracks (Figure 26.3). The usual procedure is to set a good level with the dry track and then adjust the level of the processed track to create the proper balance.

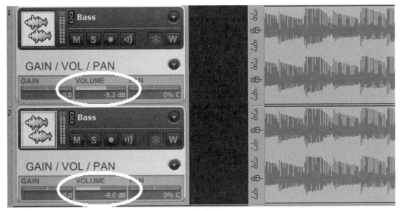

Figure 26.3 Use each track's Volume slider to adjust the balance of dry and processed sounds.

Once you've set the balance perfectly, you may need to raise or lower the entire bass sound. Rather than tediously adjust each level all over again to get the right balance, it's simpler to just Quick Group the two tracks so that adjusting one level adjusts the other one in tandem. Here's how to use the Quick Group function.

1. Click on the original track's Quick Group button.

2. Shift-click or Ctrl-click on the cloned track's Quick Group button, as shown in Figure 26.4. (Note that you could also click on the cloned track first and then the original track—the order doesn't really matter.)

3. Click on one of the faders and adjust it. The other track's fader will follow along.

4. To ungroup the two faders, click on any Quick Group buttons. The one you clicked on will continue to be enabled; click on it again to disable it.

Crunching the Bass

Distortion can be a cool effect when you want to add some grit, but be aware that SONAR Home Studio's Amp Sim is not intended for bass. So, this is another situation where parallel

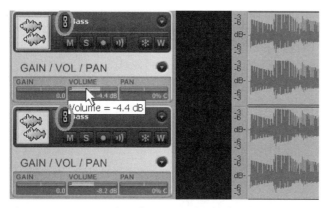

Figure 26.4 Grouping the original and the cloned track allows you to adjust the level on one track and have the other one follow along. Each Quick Group button is circled for clarity.

effects work well: You can create just the distortion component in the Amp Sim and mix it in support of the dry signal.

The conventional approach to "crunching" bass is to distort the bass and reduce the highs to prevent it from sounding too buzzy. But at least to my ears, when processed that way, the sound seems somewhat disconnected and layered—not like the crunch you get from a good amp.

The following approach is a bit unconventional, but I feel it creates a more integrated distortion effect that sits better in a track.

1. Clone the audio track containing the bass part and add the Sonitus equalizer effect to the cloned track by choosing Audio > Sonitus:fx > Equalizer. This will become the distortion track.

2. Use the Add Effect function to insert the Cakewalk Amp Sim after the Sonitus EQ. If needed, click on the Amp Sim effect and drag it before the EQ to make sure the two effects are in the right order (EQ before Amp Sim).

3. For the Equalizer (Figure 26.5), choose Highpass response for Band 1 and Lowpass for Band 6. Set Band 1's Frequency to 225Hz and Q to 1.4. Set Band 6's Frequency to 944Hz and Q to 1.4.

4. For the Amp Sim, select British Overdrive with the 4 × 12 Cabinet. (These are the biggest amp sim speakers offered—maybe in the next version of SONAR Home Studio, we can get an Ampeg 15-inch speaker emulator!) Set Drive, Bass, and Treble to minimum. Set the Mid control up about two-thirds of the way and add a touch of Presence (Figure 26.6).

5. If you want to tweak this further, enable another of the Equalizer bands and set it to the Peak/Dip response. Experiment with boosting and cutting at various frequencies to dial in a distortion sound from subtle to buzzy. Also, try different settings for the Amp Sim Drive and EQ controls.

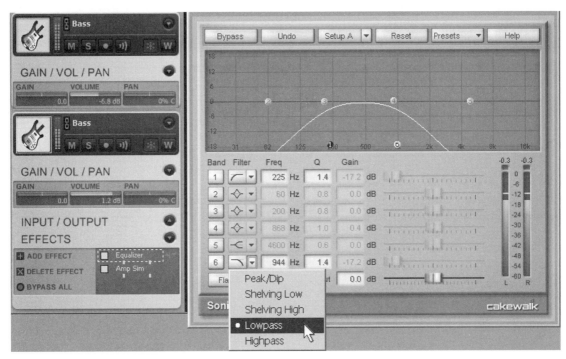

Figure 26.5   Adjust the Sonitus EQ to cut off the highs and lows prior to feeding the Amp Sim.

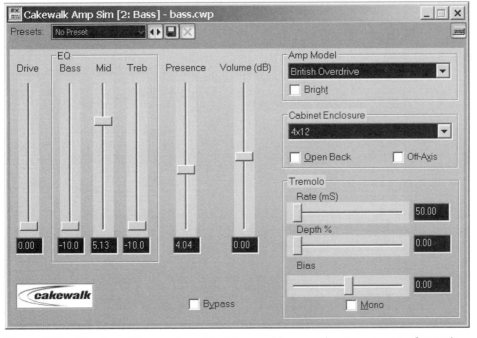

Figure 26.6   The Amp Sim can be edited to provide a moderate amount of crunch.

What's interesting about this approach is how much it sounds like an overdriven bass amp. For contrast, disable the EQ's lowest band: The sound is now more like a fuzz bass (not that there's anything wrong with that!) as opposed to amp overdrive.

Compression also works well in parallel, because you can squash the bass signal as an effect and then bring up that squashed track a bit to reinforce the main bass track. This seems to be most effective when used subtly, because it brings up the lower levels without negating the higher-level dynamics.

Track Template for Bass

As with guitar, it's convenient to have a point of departure, and SONAR Home Studio's track template function can provide that for bass as well. This example shows how you can create a track template with multiple tracks (Figure 26.7).

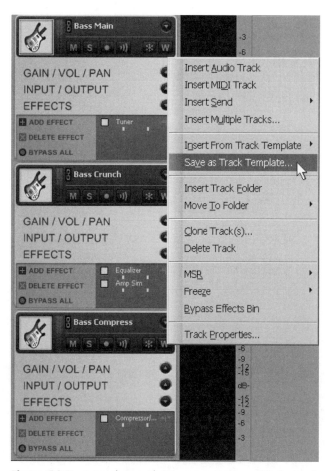

Figure 26.7   A track template can contain multiple tracks.

Track 1 is the main bass track into which you record your track, which is why it has a tuner. Track 2, the Bass Crunch track, includes the Equalizer/Amp Sim combination mentioned previously. Track 3 includes the Compressor/Gate, set for heavy compression, should you want to add a compressed sound in with the main sound.

To save the group of tracks as a track template:

1. Click on the main track's track icon to select the track.

2. Ctrl-click on the other tracks' track icons so all pertinent tracks are selected.

3. Right-click on an empty space within any of these tracks' track header and then select Save as Track Template.

4. Navigate to where you want to save the track template, name it, and then click on Save.

When you load the track template, you can now record your bass part into the main track. You'll then want to duplicate that audio in the other tracks. In this case, the Clone Track(s) function isn't appropriate because we already have our tracks; we just want to copy the audio into them. There are two ways to do this.

Drag and Drop

Ctrl-click on the main audio clip and drag it into the other tracks. Make sure that these copied versions start at the same time as the main audio. This creates *linked* clips (as indicated by the clip's dotted border), which have the same name and track color; if you change the name or color of one track, it will affect all other linked tracks.

If you want to unlink a clip, right-click on it and click on the row of right-facing buttons on the bottom of the menu. From the menu that appears, select Unlink. When the Unlink Clips dialog box appears, select Independent Not Linked At All and then click on OK.

Cut and Paste

1. Click on the main audio clip and then choose Edit > Copy (or right-click on the clip and from the context menu, choose Edit > Copy).

2. In the Copy dialog box, check only Events in Tracks and then click on OK.

3. Place the Now time at the beginning of the main clip you copied and then select one of the tracks with processing.

4. Choose Edit > Paste (or right-click in a blank area of the track clips pane associated with that track and, from the context menu, choose Edit > Paste), verify that the Starting at Time field shows the start time of the main clip and that the Starting Track field shows the desired track, and then click on OK. These copied clips are not linked.

With track templates containing multiple tracks, you might want to create a track folder and put all the tracks in there. That allows you to "fold up" the track folder and have only a single track in the Track view (but not Console view, which doesn't support track folders), thus neatening up your workspace. There's more information on track folders in SONAR Home Studio's help files—click on the Index tab, and type in Track Folder.

27 Creating Loop-Based Music with SONAR Home Studio

While some still dismiss loop-based compositions, they are the lifeblood of groove music—and many musicians use at least the occasional loop, if for no other reason than to provide a solid background when songwriting. Also, when doing audio-for-video work, sometimes the music is not *supposed* to be prominent—a loop library allows you to create original, interesting background scores in minutes (not hours) that add a lot to videos.

SONAR Home Studio handles loops extremely well: As described in Chapter 22, it can edit the transient markers in Groove Clip and ACIDized loops to optimize time stretching and play back REX file-based loops. So, let's cover how to create a typical loop-based music project. I'll be describing a way to put together projects that works well for me, but feel free to come up with your own variations, tailored for the way you work and the kind of music you make.

Collect and Audition the Loops

First, collect "candidate" loops for the composition. The bigger your collection of loop libraries, the better. (Choice is good!) However "construction kit" loop CDs, which consist of a piece of music and its constituent elements, may be all you need for quick projects. And don't forget that SONAR Home Studio already includes quite a bit of content.

Note that even if a loop library claims to have ACIDized loops, few companies take the time to optimize transient markers for stretching over a wide range (ditto REX files). Sony does the best job of editing ACIDized loops for optimum stretching. Early M-Audio libraries are very good, and Nine Volt Audio's offerings are also better than average. As a result, unless you're comfortable editing transient markers yourself, you're probably best off choosing loops in the same general tempo range. Regarding key, the greater the amount of transposition, the more you'll notice a deterioration in sound quality.

The easiest way to audition candidate loops is with SONAR Home Studio's Loop Explorer window (covered in Chapter 22), but I recommend bouncing CD- or DVD-based loop libraries over to a hard drive or USB memory stick and auditioning from the drive. Auditioning directly from optical media is much slower.

Going Native

Hopefully, any loops you use will include information on the original tempo and key; this may be part of the file name or included in a separate piece of documentation. If this information isn't available, though, finding out a Groove Clip's native tempo and key is not difficult. It's a good idea to check both to make sure you're not straying too far from the loop's original characteristics, which helps preserve the best fidelity.

To determine the key, click on the loop to select it and then choose Views > Loop Construction or type Alt+2. The Root Note field should indicate the original loop pitch. To confirm, turn off the Follow Project Pitch button by clicking on the G-clef symbol so it goes "dark" (see Figure 27.1). Click the Loop Construction window's Play button, and the loop will play back at its native pitch.

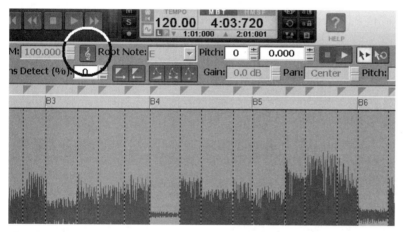

Figure 27.1 If you disable Follow Project Pitch (the corresponding button is circled), the Root Note field will become grayed out, and the loop will play back at its native pitch.

Determining the native tempo is a little more complex.

1. Make a copy of the loop and then click on it and type Ctrl+L to turn off looping. I like to put this loop at the beginning, in an empty track, because that makes the process of detecting tempo easier.

2. Let's assume that when looped, the loop is two bars long. Unless the loop was recorded at the project tempo, it will land either before or after the two-measure boundary (see Figure 27.2).

3. Adjust the tempo until the loop end lines up exactly with the start of Measure 3. Once these two match (see Figure 27.3), then the project tempo is the tempo at which the loop was recorded.

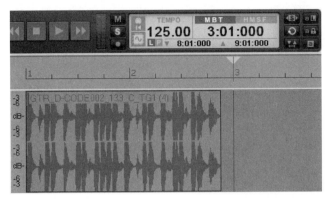

Figure 27.2 Note how the loop end is shorter than two measures by about half a beat. This means it was recorded at a faster tempo than the project tempo, which is 125 BPM.

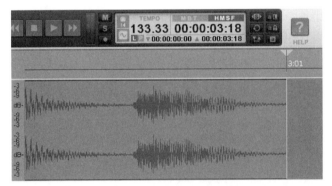

Figure 27.3 Increasing the tempo to 133.33 BPM causes the loop end to fall exactly at the start of Measure 3. Therefore, the loop was recorded at 133.33 BPM.

Auditioning REX Files

If you want to audition REX files for potential use in a project, the easiest way is to insert the DropZone soft synth and use it to audition files. There's more on using DropZone with REX files in Chapter 13 on virtual instruments.

Preventing Loop Boredom

One complaint about loop-based music is that loops get boring after a while. And, in fact, they do—but not if you add some editing magic to make them more vibrant.

Tempo Changes

Groove Clip/ACIDized and REX files can both follow tempo changes, which is an exceptional advantage—having a "flat line" tempo that goes on and on and on and on and on and on (and on!) at the same tempo can be pretty boring. You can make a song come alive with some judicious tempo tweaks, such as speeding up to add tension or slowing down to add release.

If you haven't worked with tempo changes, you're in for a treat, because these changes can add a huge amount of interest to your music. One of my favorite techniques is to pull back just a little on the tempo before a "big chorus." (And if the chorus isn't big, the slight tempo shift will make it seem bigger because it builds anticipation.) For information on how to create tempo changes within SONAR Home Studio, see Chapter 6.

Pitch Changes

Changing keys (modulation) was a technique used in many pop songs of days gone by to make something that repeated sound "different," and maybe it's time for a revival. With SONAR Home Studio, it's easy to experiment with key changes by adding pitch markers, as described in Chapter 22.

Loop Chopping

Because repeating loops can get boring, why not chop them up into pieces to add variety? Figure 27.4 shows several techniques designed to make a loop-based tune more interesting.

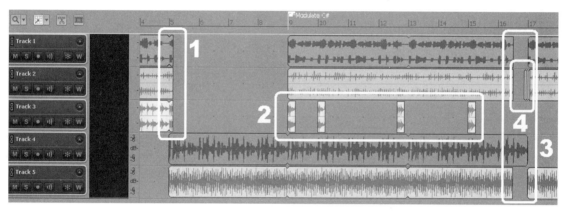

Figure 27.4 This screenshot illustrates several arrangement tricks that add interest to a loop-based composition.

Referring to Figure 27.4, circled section 1 shows how three loops in Tracks 1, 2, and 3 have been extended an eighth note to add an extra downbeat to start off the next section. In circled section 2, a drum loop has been chopped into individual hits, almost like one-shots, to add accents.

Circled section 3 shows that the loops in Tracks 1, 2, and 5 have been pulled back for two beats, giving a "breakbeat" that's carried by the loop in Track 4. Circled section 4 (the small one) highlights the beginning of the loop in Track 2. The loop has its first sixteenth note cut, copied twice, and then placed as two successive sixteenth notes leading into Measure 17.

Also note the pitch transposition that occurs toward the top of the timeline. (The original project pitch is C.) At Measure 9, the project modulates up a half-step, from C to C#. (What you *don't* see are the subtle tempo changes occurring to the track.)

Arranging

Loop-based music is all about arranging. Some assume this must be easy, but it takes practice to really "build" a song through loops. You want to strike a balance between having a hypnotic groove and introducing enough surprises to keep your listeners interested but not distracted.

For example, you can start with a fairly basic percussion loop, add a simple bass part, and then just before the two loops wear out their welcome, bring in a "big" drum loop along with some kind of step-sequenced, electronic-sounding bass line. Simultaneously, take out the percussion loop (the drums should be enough), but bring it back in later when you need to increase the excitement level somewhat.

There's also no need to limit yourself to just cutting and pasting loops. Using faders (preferably a hardware controller, but you can use the mixer's virtual faders in a pinch) to add crescendos and dynamics can augment the drama. Inserting signal processors into tracks can also add variations, such as using automation (Chapters 19 and 25) on a delay processor to increase the delay level when you want to build the song into something more intense.

Final Thoughts

But isn't that a lot of editing, given that loops are supposed to make our lives easier? Maybe. However, loops aren't designed to be *music*; they're designed to be *components* of music. How you put those components together is what creates the actual music—and in that respect, what you get out of it depends on what you put into it.

28 Combining Audio and Video with SONAR Home Studio

Video is becoming an ever-larger part of today's music scene. It's a great promotional tool for your band—think video business cards—as well as a way to dress up your website with performance clips and music videos. But video is also becoming part of daily life, whether it's documenting a family event or shooting video souvenirs.

All you really need to get started in video is a video camera, computer, and video editing software. There are two main consumer camera types: Those that record to MiniDV tapes and those that record to solid-state memory (for example, an SD card). MiniDV cameras typically have a FireWire port (what Sony calls iLink), so your computer will need a FireWire port in order to transfer video footage to a hard drive for editing. If your computer doesn't have FireWire, you can get a FireWire port card that plugs into your motherboard or, for laptops, FireWire interfaces that fit into card slots. (Note: Avoid combination FireWire/USB cards, as some users report decreased performance.) If your camera records to SD cards, most newer computers have memory card readers built in, or you can buy an inexpensive USB card reader peripheral.

As for video editing software, you have quite a few choices. For Windows, Sony Creative Software's Vegas Movie Studio family of software is a great balance of functionality and low cost. You also may need a high-capacity external USB 2.0 or FireWire drive, because video data takes up much more space than audio data. (If you have a FireWire-based camera, I'd suggest a USB 2.0 drive—it's certainly fast enough, and it won't interfere with the FireWire bus.)

And of course, after you've edited your video, you'll want to add music to it—that's where SONAR Home Studio comes in. Just remember that it can't edit video or have more than one video track open; SONAR Home Studio assumes the video component of your project is complete, and you're going to be dealing primarily with the audio aspects.

Why use SONAR Home Studio? Aside from the obvious reasons—you can overdub narration or create a soundtrack—the ability to deal with Groove Clip loops is very helpful when creating scores and background music, because you can stretch tempo so that the music lines up appropriately with the video.

Let's take a step-by-step approach to dealing with video in SONAR Home Studio.

Step 1: Import Video

SONAR Home Studio can import videos in several formats: Video for Windows (.avi), Quick-Time (.mov), MPEG (.mpg), and Windows Media Video (.wmv). Choose File > Import > Video and navigate to the file you want to import. Select it and then click on Open (see Figure 28.1).

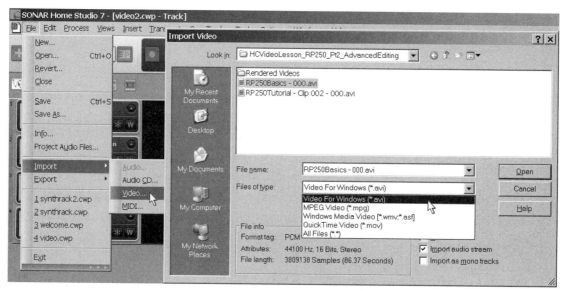

Figure 28.1   A video clip is being imported into SONAR Home Studio. Note how Import Audio Stream is checked in the lower-right corner so that both video and audio tracks will be imported into their own tracks.

You can filter which formats you'll see by using the Files of Type field; choose All Files if you want to rummage around and see everything that's available.

As to the boxes in the lower right, I suggest checking Show File Info. It doesn't show much about AVI files (the Windows mouseover function will, though, if you place your mouse over the file name), but it does display data on size and attributes for most file formats.

Also, check Import Audio Stream if you want the video file's associated audio, such as audio from a camcorder, to be loaded into its own track. Be aware that with long files, it can take a while to import the audio and video.

Import as Mono Tracks splits stereo audio and brings each channel into two separate mono tracks. There's no real reason to check this unless you specifically need to separate the left and right channels.

There are a couple cautions:

- The audio stream is copied to your project folder, but the video stream is not—SONAR Home Studio points to its location on disk. As a result, I strongly suggest copying the video file to the project folder (even though it will take up a lot of space), so you don't end up in a situation where if you've moved the original video file, you open up the SONAR Home Studio project and see a blank screen because it can't find the video.

■ Some video editing programs will divide the video and audio into separate files upon saving or archiving the project data. If you import a video file and the audio stream isn't imported, check to see whether it's saved separately as a .wav or other file type. Then, choose File > Import > Audio and browse to the audio file you want to bring into the project.

Step 2: Recompress the Video

Video files can be huge, particularly the .avi types generated by typical MiniDV cameras. Requiring SONAR Home Studio to handle that, as well as virtual instruments, multiple tracks, and processors, is asking quite a lot, but there are ways to make the process less taxing on SONAR Home Studio and your computer.

In terms of handling track playback, the concept of keyframes is important. These are like markers in the video file, sort of the video equivalent of MIDI's song position pointer messages, and are used to locate sections when rewinding through the sequence or repositioning the Now time. Without keyframes, SONAR Home Studio has to work much harder to calculate the current position, so it's best to use files that have keyframes every few frames or so.

Raw footage imported from a MiniDV camera will not have enough keyframes, and SONAR Home Studio's overall performance will suffer as a result. When you click on Play, you may think SONAR Home Studio has frozen for a few seconds until it finally kicks into gear. If you're getting clips from someone else, you can request that the video be provided to you with keyframes every few frames or so.

However, odds are you're not going to be using SONAR Home Studio as a replacement for high-end video editing; you just want to create audio against a reference video or, at most, render an audio/video compressed format file for the web. So, I recommend taking whatever video you have and recompressing it as a Windows Media Video file that not only takes up less space, but also has a keyframe every frame for easy navigation. SONAR Home Studio makes this easy for you:

1. Once your video and audio stream are loaded into SONAR Home Studio, choose File > Export > Video.

2. Give it a file name (such as RecompressedVideo.wmv).

3. Under Save as Type, choose Windows Media Video.

4. Click on Encoding Options.

5. Enter the title, author, rating, and other info if desired, and check the Frame Indexing box. (There's no need to check Multipass.)

6.   As shown in Figure 28.2, from the Profile drop-down menu, choose Windows Media Video 8 for Broadband (NTSC, 1400 Kbps) or choose PAL instead of NTSC if that's the standard where you live.

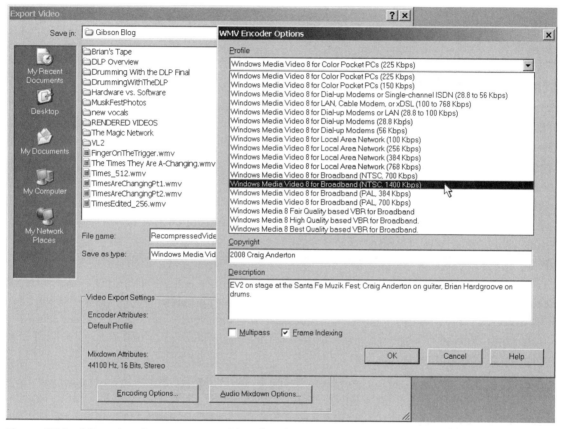

Figure 28.2   After choosing to export video for the purposes of recompressing, click on Encoding Options and then choose the desired export option from the Profile drop-down menu.

7.   Click on OK and be patient (with long AVI files, be *very* patient!) while the video is tagged with keyframes and exported as a Windows Media Video file.

8.   Remove the existing video track from SONAR Home Studio (but not the original track you imported, of course) and its associated audio component.

9.   Import the RecompressedVideo.wmv file as the video track and use that instead.

Playback and handling of the video track will now be much more responsive. As a typical example, recompressing can transform a 4-GB file into a svelte 200-MB file—1/20 the size.

Step 3: Display the Video

SONAR Home Studio has two ways of displaying video.

- As a series of thumbnail images in a separate video track, which is always at the top of the Track view. We'll cover this in Step 4.

- In a separate Video window (which can be in addition to the thumbnails).

Let's deal with the Video window first, because it's probably what you'll use the most. You can open it by choosing Views > Video, typing Alt+6, or double-clicking on the thumbnails in the video track. This is where having a second monitor is great, because you can stick the Video window there. However, if you don't have dual monitors, you can make sure the Video window is always visible by floating it.

To float the Video window, click in its upper-left corner and select Enable Floating (see Figure 28.3). This ensures that the window will always stay on top of non-floating windows.

Figure 28.3 Floating a window means that it can be placed outside the usual window boundaries of SONAR Home Studio—even to a separate monitor. What's more, you'll always see the video, even if you're clicking on background windows. Note the thumbnail images on the top track.

Right-clicking on the video image brings up multiple display options.

- Check Animate; otherwise, the window will just show a static of frame of where you began playback.

- Insert can insert a piece of video, but don't think this has anything to do with video editing—it just replaces the existing video. Delete removes the video track.

Stretch Options determine the window size and proportions.

- Original Size shows the video at its native size, which for DV is typically 720×480 pixels. You can resize the video by clicking and dragging any of the four window corners. With video set to original size, resizing to dimensions smaller than the video will cut off some of the video, while resizing to a larger size will cause a border to surround the video—the picture size always remains constant.

- Stretch to Window means that no matter how you resize the window, even to being a little sliver, the picture will stretch to fit the window. Aside from the humor value of seeing a terribly distorted picture, this does have a practical use because sometimes you don't need to see everything in perfect proportion, and you can resize the video to fit in some convenient blank portion of your workspace.

- Preserve Aspect Ratio is useful because you can resize the Video window at will, and the picture will always be the right proportion.

- Integral Stretch is even better, because it resizes in increments. For example, suppose the window is sized to show a 720×480 picture. As you resize smaller, as soon as the window size is smaller than 720×480, the picture shrinks to 360×240. This prevents the picture distortion that can occur by using nonintegral picture sizes.

- Full Screen causes the window to fill the screen. (With a second monitor, it will fill the second monitor.) You won't see the time readout or anything else; this is a reality check that makes it look like you're watching TV. As soon as you click elsewhere, the video returns to the previous size.

The Time Display Format determines whether the time display in the window is set to Measures: Beats:Ticks, SMPTE, Frames, or None. But one cool feature is that you can choose the font and color, so you can make the numbers VERY BIG if you want to be able to see them from across the room (see Figure 28.4). Also, note that you can select a black or white background color. If you set the background to black and choose a font such as 36 pt. Arial Bold in yellow for the typeface, the time display will be very readable.

Finally, if you're coping with a funky, slower computer, you can throttle back the video display a bit to place even less stress on your CPU. Right-click on the video display or thumbnails, select Video Properties, and then click on the Render Quality tab.

Selecting Preview mode reduces the CPU load, and you can reduce the load even further by reducing the frame rate (for example, to 10 FPS) and video size (see Figure 28.5). This is something you can do at any time, so you can work with the full frame rate and video size as you start, and then as your efforts evolve more toward tweaking the audio than synching it to the video, you can reduce the render quality as you insert more soft synths and such. Incidentally, note that render quality has no effect when exporting files—it affects *only* the video playback within SONAR Home Studio.

Figure 28.4 By editing the time display's font, color, and background, you can end up with a highly visible display.

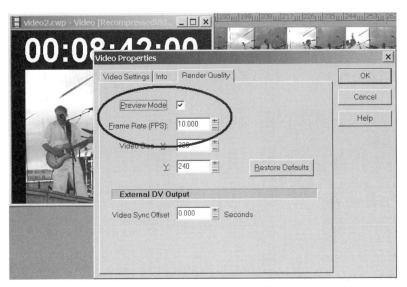

Figure 28.5 If your computer has a hard time keeping up with the video, don't despair: Go into Preview mode and, if needed, also lower the frame rate and/or reduce the image size.

Step 4: Work with the Video Track

The video track provides some controls for thumbnails, but it also lets you manipulate the video to a very limited degree.

If you can't see the thumbnails, click at the top of the first track (audio or MIDI) and pull down on the splitter bar to reveal the video track thumbnails (see Figure 28.6; alternatively, you can

Figure 28.6 There's a splitter bar between the video thumbnails track, which is always at the top of the track list, and the remaining tracks below.

show/hide the video track by clicking on the Show/Hide Video Track button to the immediate right of the Track View timeline). Conversely, if you don't need to see the thumbnails, click on the splitter bar and drag up. Note that pulling the splitter bar up or down changes the height of the thumbnails, and that when you do this, the thumbnails retain the correct aspect ratio. Zoom in far enough, and you can see individual frames—which is great for when you need to line up a hit at the *exact* moment the intergalactic cosmic explosion begins.

The topmost field in the title bar (see Figure 28.7) includes the track name. Below that, Duration (a read-only parameter) shows the total length of the video in bars:beats:ticks. Frame Loc shows

Figure 28.7 The video track offers several parameters for control over the video clip, as well as how thumbnails are displayed.

the location of the Now time with respect to the number of frames. The round button to the right of these shows or hides the video frame numbers toward the lower left of each thumbnail, while the square, rightmost button shows or hides the video thumbnails.

Here's the meaning behind the three numeric parameters toward the bottom of the track.

- Start (right arrow symbol) specifies where in the sequence the video will begin playing back. For example, you may want to have the music begin against a black screen before the image part of the video actually starts, so you would edit the Start time so the video comes in later. Because this is SMPTE, you can communicate to anyone else involved in the project how much to offset the video compared to the audio.

- Trim-In (down arrow symbol) cuts time nondestructively from the beginning of the video, specified in H:M:S:F. Use this if, for example, you're given a five-minute video and you're just composing a closing theme for the last two minutes.

- Trim-Out (up arrow symbol) works similarly to Trim-In for trimming the end of the clip.

One fine point about thumbnails is that not all Windows Media videos report their frame rate to SONAR Home Studio. If they don't, SONAR Home Studio won't display thumbnails even though the file will still play back.

Step 5: Create the Soundtrack

Well, if you're reading this book, you probably already figured out how to play and engineer music, so there's not much to say other than...make a really good soundtrack!

Step 6: Export the Finished Project

You can export the finished project, including video and audio, to one of SONAR Home Studio's supported video file formats: AVI (video for Windows), WMV (Windows Media Video), or MOV (QuickTime). For the highest possible quality, you might want to delete the recompressed video file and reimport the original one. But be aware that this will likely increase the time required to export the video by a substantial amount, and the final quality might not be all that much better compared to using the recompressed file.

We already covered the export process under Step 2, but if you're exporting to the WMV format, you may want to choose a different profile than the Broadband NTSC option we chose earlier—this uses a lot of bandwidth. Unfortunately, unlike many dedicated video-editing programs, you can't choose a specific set of video- and audio-rendering parameters. But there are enough choices that you should be able to find a suitable compromise between quality and size, depending on the target medium.

For example, if you expect to stream a WMV video over a dial-up modem, under Encoding Options you have four different choices. You also have four options each for local area network or broadband settings. With so many people having high-speed web access, a good choice is Windows Media Video 8 for LAN, Cable Modem, or xDSL (100 to 768 kbps). This results in a larger file size because it can downshift if needed for lower bandwidths or upshift for high bandwidths, so all that data needs to be included.

If you want a smaller file size that works well in most situations, try Windows Media Video 8 for Local Area Network (256 kbps). This should stream decently on less-than-wonderful broadband connections, such as cable modem when everyone's on at the same time. Higher kbps values will give better quality, but there may be interruptions if the online connection is slow, because the receiver has to buffer incoming data (in other words, collect enough data to stream) before playback can continue.

If you're handing off a soundtrack to someone else, you want a high-quality audio mixdown, so you can just export the audio. If you need to include the video for reference, choose Video for Windows under Save as Type, and under the encoding options, choose a video codec option that's compatible with the target system. Cinepak is usually a good choice, or you can try exporting as an uncompressed AVI file, which almost anything should be able to handle—but this results in a huge file size.

There are also separate export options for QuickTime…and at this point, matters are probably getting pretty bewildering. To explain all the encoding options for QuickTime, Windows Media Video, and Video for Windows—as well as what types of codecs you can expect to find on your computer—would take multiple chapters, and it's doubtful there's that much interest among those reading this book in the fine points of video exporting.

So do yourself a favor and keep it simple: Stick with Windows Media Video exports, try the profiles I recommended earlier, and if you have the time, experiment with the various encoder profiles until you find a good combination of size and resolution. Frankly, the way I learned what all the various export parameters did for different file formats was by experimenting; I've never found a reference, including the SONAR Home Studio help files and the documentation for various pro video applications, that truly explained the real-world implications of choosing specific options.

In any event, now you know how to import video, so add a soundtrack—or process the camcorder audio, if it was a live gig—and congratulate yourself on joining the audio-for-video generation.

What about Sound Effects? One SONAR Home Studio limitation is that you can't tie sounds to specific SMPTE times. This is important because of the difference between *absolute* time and *musical* time. If a door slams at 00:12:30:12, then it's always going to slam at that time. If you put an effect in a sequence and it hits at this time, but then you change the sequence tempo, the sound's location will change to stay consistent with musical time—ahead of absolute time if you increase the tempo and behind if you decrease the tempo.

However, there is a workaround, because markers can be tied to specific SMPTE times; when you insert the marker, check the Lock to SMPTE (Real World) Time box. Place the sound effect at the marker and name the marker after the sound effect. If the tempo changes, select the Clips tab under Snap to Grid, check Markers, and close the Snap to Grid dialog box. Finally, move the sound effect so that it snaps to the marker. Yes, it's inelegant…but it works, especially if you don't have too many sound effects you have to tie to absolute time.

Index